Quiz Kids

ALSO BY MARTIN A. GARDNER

*The Marx Brothers as Social Critics:
Satire and Comic Nihilism in Their Films*
(McFarland, 2009)

QUIZ KIDS

*The Radio Program
with the Smartest Children
in America, 1940–1953*

Martin A. Gardner

McFarland & Company, Inc., Publishers
Jefferson, North Carolina, and London

LIBRARY OF CONGRESS CATALOGUING-IN-PUBLICATION DATA

Gardner, Martin A.
　　Quiz Kids : the radio program with the smartest children in America, 1940–1953 / Martin A. Gardner.
　　　　p.　　cm.
　　Includes bibliographical references and index.

　　ISBN 978-0-7864-3976-8
　　softcover : acid free paper ∞

　　1. Quiz kids (Radio program)　 2. Radio quiz shows — United States.　I. Title.
PN1991.77.Q85G37 2013
791.44'72 — dc23　　　　　　　　　　　　　　　2013027019

BRITISH LIBRARY CATALOGUING DATA ARE AVAILABLE

© 2013 Martin A. Gardner. All rights reserved

No part of this book may be reproduced or transmitted in any form or by any means, electronic or mechanical, including photocopying or recording, or by any information storage and retrieval system, without permission in writing from the publisher.

On the cover: *left to right* Joe Kelly, Jack Lucal, Joan Bishop, Gerard Darrow, Cynthia Cline, Richard Williams (Billy Rose Theatre Division, The New York Public Library for the Performing Arts, Astor, Lenox and Tilden Foundations); *background image* iStockphoto/Thinkstock

Manufactured in the United States of America

McFarland & Company, Inc., Publishers
　Box 611, Jefferson, North Carolina 28640
　　www.mcfarlandpub.com

Table of Contents

Preface   1

1. Children on My Mind   7
2. The Brains Behind the Brains   30
3. How to Become a Quiz Kid   49
4. The Whirlwind Begins   55
5. The Quiz Kids — Selected Short Subjects   77
6. Rising Stars   96
7. Hooray for Hollywood   115
8. Soldiering On   143
9. Box 1100   165
10. Quiz Kids, Too?   170
11. Any Bonds Today?   177
12. Don't You Know There's a War On?   197
13. Peace   212
14. Kids Will Be Kids   234
15. Goodbye, Mr. Kelly   240

Appendix A: Questions and Answers   255
Appendix B: The Quiz Kids, Programs and Guests   260
Appendix C: Quiz Kids Program Chronology   286
Chapter Notes   287
Bibliography   301
Index   309

Preface

If you grew up in the 1940s you probably tuned in to any number of serialized radio adventure programs. They were broadcast every weeknight during the two hours late in the afternoon, just before dinner. (You may have listened on Saturday mornings, too.) Listening to those programs was a nice way to ease into the rhythm of family life after a day in school. If you didn't have any family responsibilities to complete you could spread out and lie on the floor to listen until it was time to eat, when the radio programs shifted to the more serious reportage of the news of the day, followed by the evening's usual programs that appealed to grownups, too.

Radio programs offered household entertainment and information. Just as on television now, there were programs for every member of the family and they were all free: comedy, drama, adventure, news, political analysis, sports, religious programs, popular and classical music, children's programs, and quiz shows.

This book is a history of a unique weekly quiz show that burst into public consciousness and zoomed to popularity practically from its first broadcast. Named *Quiz Kids*, it aired on national network radio weekly for 13 years and featured five gifted children who exhibited their intelligence and knowledge. The Kids answered challenging questions that had been submitted by listeners throughout America. Parallel to the history of the program, the book offers a view of radio during its golden age, set within the backdrop of World War II and the dramatic changes in America — social, cultural, and political — during those years. *Quiz Kids* began at a period of time when it was still possible if you lived in Chicago to get home delivery of milk by horse and wagon and ended in the early years of the nuclear age.

The program aired from 1940 to 1953. Its longevity was outstanding in broadcasting where programs would live or die in a 13-week cycle (and still do). Quiz shows on radio first caught the attention of Americans during the 1930s; most of them didn't last, either on air or in memory. *Quiz Kids* was different. Within a few weeks of its debut, this program featuring precocious youngsters was making radio history. Its popularity continued to grow week after week.

The show captured the imagination of its listeners beyond the wildest expectations of its producers. *Quiz Kids* became a phenomenon. This was live broadcasting. Listeners marveled at the Kids' abilities and the speed with which they answered the most difficult of questions. Unlike current quiz programs on television where the contestants usually just have to know facts, the Kids had to solve problems, too. They had no pencils or paper, even to solve the most intricate math and algebra problems.

The view of the program and its place in American history and popular culture is the focus of this book. *Quiz Kids* was not a children's program, even though it featured five gifted young people who ranged in age from 5 to 15. It was a family program, challenging and serious, entertaining and humorous. Placed within the events of its day, the book sheds light on the domestic side of America during the war, the "home front." It is more than a book about a radio program. It shows how the program was surrounded by and fit into the events and other social changes that resulted in a profound shift in American society before, during, and following the war: the Great Depression, Lend Lease, military conscription, labor relations, juvenile delinquency, and the atom bomb. We see how the war's restrictions on gasoline, food, tire rationing, and the difficulty of taking trips by public transportation affected *Quiz Kids* because of the program's frequent travel schedule.

The program is one element in the general history of radio and its impact on life in America. Radio was a powerful, believable, and trusted medium at a time when Americans were facing an uncertain future and needed stability and entertainment as a relief.

Before the 1940s, when gifted children performed on radio their precocity was usually defined by how well they could sing, play a musical instrument, or tap dance. With some exceptions, the pendulum has swung again. In our present society, we usually associate precocious children with excellence in sports, music, and the performing arts. The importance of *Quiz Kids* is that through the medium of radio, this radio program helped make exceptional knowledge and education acceptable to vast audiences. We should remember it for that.

I became fascinated by the program after hearing a broadcast of one of the shows preserved on a CD. I wanted to know about the program. I wanted to read about it. There are two books about the show. Eliza Merrill Hickok, its chief researcher and assistant program director, published *The Quiz Kids* in 1947 shortly before she left the production office. Hickok, a professional journalist who wrote all the publicity for the program, presents an anecdotal account of the Kids during her seven years working as a member of the production staff. It is well-written and filled with her recollections, frequently taken from the letters she wrote to her family during the years she worked for the program. In addition to her responsibilities for writing press releases about the Kids, she was their "den mother" when the show traveled.

Ruth Duskin Feldman, a former Quiz Kid, and one of the few children who were on the program continually for several years, published *Whatever Happened to the Quiz Kids?* in 1982. She interviewed 13 of the Kids when they were adults, and wrote thorough and incisive profiles of each. She also surveyed dozens of other former Kids with a questionnaire to discover their reflections on being on the program, even if it was only one time, and how being gifted had an impact on their lives.

During the course of its history, the program was eventually televised. By the end of the 1940s when it began to become a popular medium for family viewing, television quickly dominated the broadcast media. I have written only about *Quiz Kids* on radio, where the program originated and achieved a greater awareness. We think of *Quiz Kids* as a radio show.

To explore the history of the show was a challenge. When the production office closed after the show went off the air, all of the files were discarded. There was no correspondence. There were no memos, no contracts or photographs. Miles Laboratories, the sponsor of the radio program, apparently has not kept any files about the program. There are recordings of the broadcasts; these are the crux of primary source material. Relatively speaking, there are few recordings available. Of the 598 broadcasts there are approximately 135 extant from a variety of sources on CDs or in digitized format for listening on a computer. There are a few large-format electrical transcriptions that I have heard. There may be more transcriptions owned by individuals, but these are unknown.

During the show's first seven years, making a recording, a transcription as it was called at that time, was a more difficult and expensive process than it is now. Each show had to be recorded. The transcriptions were sent to stations in other time zones for broadcast at times that coincided with the on-air schedule of the show in the Central Time Zone (the show originated in Chicago). Local network stations were instructed to destroy these transcriptions once they were played. Generally, archival storage was unimportant to broadcasters. It wasn't until magnetic tape became the standard method after World War II that recording the shows was effortless, less expensive, and easier to store. Thus, reruns were born. Fortunately for the purposes of this book, or any other research about this program or other aspects of broadcasting, the Library of Congress has a collection of 120 of the 30-minute broadcasts that they received from NBC. The library staff digitized them so that I was able to listen to them through a computer. There is also one 15-minute recording of Glenn Seaborg's guest appearance on the last half of a *Quiz Kids* broadcast in November 1945.

Several other libraries have small collections of other material: scripts, oral histories, articles in local newspapers, recordings, and collections of trade journals. I drew from sources at the New York Public Library and its Library for Performing Arts at Lincoln Center, the Paley Center for Media, Boston Public Library, the Miami-Dade Public Library, the National Archives, Columbia University Library, Chicago Public Library, the Museum of Broadcast Communications, the Sarah Lawrence College Library, and the Library of American Broadcasting at the University of Maryland. I was able to glean valuable information from the letters and memos pertaining to *Quiz Kids* in the NBC collection at the Wisconsin Historical Society.

I explored newspaper and magazine articles about the program and the Kids. There are hundreds of newspaper articles from papers throughout the nation, many of them publicity stories, but some yielding information that shed light on the progress of the show. Some of the Kids kept scrapbooks, letters, memos, and other material from their time on the program that they allowed me to see. I was able to find material that I could not have found elsewhere. One ex–Quiz Kid had the original contract between the producer and his parents, spelling out the terms of his participation in the program.

I investigated general and social histories of the 1940s and 1950s, even delving into the politics and social history in the United States prior to when the show was on the air. I looked at general trends in social and cultural history during that period and their bearing on human conduct. I sifted through newspapers from around the country for those 13 years, scraps of undocumented or partially documented clippings torn from newspapers and magazines, leaflets, advertisements, and brochures.

I did not intend this book to be only about the precocity and charm of the Kids; both Hickok and Feldman have written abundantly about them in rich and engrossing detail. In writing the story of *Quiz Kids*, and its place in radio history and American popular culture, I took a different tack. I have written about the program; how it was conceived and created in 1940, and the efforts and steps the producers and their staff took during the broadcast years following the program's debut to bring it to its irrefutable fame.

I set out to include the creative side and the contributions of the production staff to the program's history. The producers, the staff, and other people, even those who were peripheral, had an immeasurable influence on the program's history. The history of *Quiz Kids* would be incomplete without the contributions of the people behind the scenes. Instead, it would be a bland recitation of dates and technical details, a portrait in desperate need of a fully-appointed palette.

Surprisingly, the personalities of the Kids still shone through when I listened to the broadcasts, and read about them even in the briefest of articles in local newspapers from the 1940s. I learned that the Kids were "normal" children; they were not stuffy. They giggled. They cried. They fell down and scraped their knees. They played pranks. They told jokes. They acted naturally, behind the microphone and in front of audiences. They had poise, personality, and a microphone presence. They never came across as arrogant. Their charm captivated audiences everywhere. They were, in fact, America's children. They were the smartest, most verbal kids in America.

Readers' Guide

At the beginning of each chapter, except for the first and twelfth, is a question that the emcee asked the Kids during a *Quiz Kids* broadcast. As well, I have used these questions instead of the standard graphic devices used as ornaments between distinct sections in a chapter. Answers to the questions are at the end of each chapter.

I have included an appendix that lists the details of the show: the dates of broadcasts, the program number, the Quiz Kids who appeared on the broadcast, the notable guests who appeared on the program, and some of the descriptive notes. I relied on several sources for the names of the Kids: from listening to the broadcasts, from radio schedules listed in newspapers, and from the NBC program notes. The list of Kids on some of the shows is incomplete for several reasons. At the beginning of each broadcast was a roll call when the Kids would state their full names. They were not professional radio entertainers; they were not familiar with the fine points of diction and enunciation and would often mumble their last names and the names of the schools they attended. Newspapers at the time did not always list the names of the Kids on each broadcast. The NBC program notes did not always list them. Therefore, some of the information is unknown or not available.

I have only included some of the more prominent or well-known guests. It is not my intention to present a complete listing along with completely detailed notes; that would be a radio log. A listing of the prominent people in education who were guests on the program is for the purpose of understanding how they helped satisfy listeners who were curious about the legitimacy of the program and its educational value. To be a guest on the program was attractive to famous people, too. Their interest in appearing on the program was frequently to further their own careers and is indicative of the depth of respect they had for *Quiz Kids* as a pillar of American popular culture appealing to the vast radio audience of the day. The names of famous guests who were household names at that time, and may still be, are shown in boldface type.

Throughout the book I have included finite detail of a few of the more notable trips that the Kids took in connection with the program. They traveled to the White House to meet with Eleanor Roosevelt, to Hollywood to appear on Jack Benny's radio program, to the Library of Congress where they broadcast to a gathering sponsored by the Pan American Union (now the Organization of American States), to the Orange Bowl to entertain an audience of several thousand spectators at a benefit for the March of Dimes, and to several scheduled performances at war bond rallies around the country to promote the sale of bonds. The details of these, and many other trips, offer insight into the cultural climate of the time, the interaction with news events of the day, how the press reported stories about these famous kids, and a myriad of other elements that help us form a better picture of the radio program.

1
Children on My Mind

Chicago. Friday, June 28, 1940. By 8 P.M. most families had finished dinner. Those who tuned in to radio station WLS for the evening's entertainment waited expectantly until 9:30, when they normally would listen to *Alec Templeton Time*. Templeton was a 31-year-old, blind, Welsh-born pianist and composer whose customary one-man broadcast of pop standards, show tunes, humorous songs, and serious classical music had wide family appeal. Instead, listeners that evening heard Fort Pearson, a Blue Network announcer, reveal the name of a new and different program called *Quiz Kids*. This new program consisted of a panel of five bright children, ages 5 to 15, answering difficult questions that some adults might find challenging. *Quiz Kids* was Templeton's summer replacement. Setting the tone for the broadcast to follow, Joe Kelly, the master of ceremonies (his title was Chief Quizzer) asked the first question of the evening immediately without further explanation, followed by Irma Glen playing a musical introduction on the pipe organ: six bars of the familiar eight-bar refrain of "School Days," aptly establishing the theme for the broadcast.

It was the modest beginning of a radio program that became one of the most popular in America, hurling *Quiz Kids*, the program, and the Quiz Kids, the children, into national prominence for the next 13 years, while appealing to the collective subconscious of Americans everywhere. With subtle perception that approached the clairvoyant, Louis G. Cowan, the creator of the program, thought that he could produce a radio show that could rise above the usual and common distaste for scholarly subjects and be successful, even broadcasting erudite material to a mass radio audience. True, other radio quiz programs, notably *Information Please*, emphasized knowledge and scholarly excellence, but this was the first time that children were performing on a radio program by displaying their intelligence rather than singing or tap dancing as evidence of their precocity.

What made Cowan's idea for a radio program unusual was that he created it in an era when many people considered gifted, precocious children "freaks."[1] He tried to dispel that notion about the Quiz Kids, because with all their knowledge, they had the same extra-curricular interests as children who were not as intelligent or as well read. Lou thought that well educated, inquisitive, and bright children could be "normal." They didn't have to be social and intellectual misfits. "He particularly hated the disdain for learned people that centered on ... and was contained in the word 'egghead.'"[2] Gerald Nachman, a radio historian, agreed. He concluded that these precocious children were popular with adults and youngsters because they "sounded like actual children."[3]

Cowan believed that he could present education and the quest for knowledge on radio in an entertaining way. There were two motivating factors that were behind his thinking.

One was that he wanted to create a successful radio show. Having worked as a public relations agent for several years, he had to live with the endemic insecurity of that profession. Years later he described that uncertainty succinctly: "You're always subject to somebody else's whim." He wanted to be independent, to be an entrepreneur, to "create something else for radio that might become a successful "property." (In show business jargon, "property" does not mean real estate, but rather, intellectual property; such as a film or a radio show."[4])

The other factor was his idealistic attitude toward knowledge and education. He wanted to foster the idea that children could achieve success from a public school education in a democratic society. In Cowan's mind, you didn't have to go to an Ivy League university to be well educated and successful as an adult. What's more, he believed that you didn't need wealth and an elevated social status in order to obtain a good education. As Cowan's son, Paul, wrote more than 40 years later, his father always believed that "learning — that most laudable of passions — wasn't determined by class or by formal academic degrees."[5] In an interview for the *New York Herald Tribune*, Louis Cowan observed that a family's intellectual background was important in the intellectual development of those children who became Quiz Kids: "None of the Kids come from really wealthy families. But most have good intellectual backgrounds. One thing that I've noticed is that between each of these children and one or both of their parents there is an unusually close tie."[6] After the program was established, one journalist concluded that the Kids were from a normal cross-section of families and most of them came from families whose economic status was moderate or even poor.[7] *Spotlite Magazine* was more specific when it reported that at least one came from a WPA-supported family.[8]

When he was an adult, Paul Cowan remembered that his parents actually had prodded him and his siblings to excel intellectually: "At dinner both my parents would engage my brother and sisters and me in games — Twenty Questions, Geography, Botticelli, or simple marathon contests of fact — and they'd send us scurrying off to the dictionary or the encyclopedia when there was something we didn't know."[9]

Lou Cowan's idea for *Quiz Kids* did not streak forth like a lightning bolt from a darkened sky. Just as in originating successful ideas in a variety of disciplines, creating radio programs was an evolutionary process.

One of the most successful radio programs at that time was *Information Please*, first aired May 17, 1938, with a 34-year-old former teacher and book editor, Clifton Fadiman, as its moderator. The program featured a panel of well-known, unusually intelligent adults who answered difficult questions submitted by its audience. It was the most scholarly and popular program of its day, airing live from 1938 to 1948, and broadcasting reruns until 1952. Cultured and witty, the panel consisted of a famous guest and a permanent team of three eminent intellectuals. One was John Kieran, newspaper sports columnist and amateur naturalist, expert in several cerebral disciplines. Another was Franklin P. Adams, urbane newspaper columnist and member of the famous Algonquin Round Table, a group of wits who met for lunch and ripostes at the Algonquin Hotel in New York. Adams wrote witty observations on literature, society, and current events in his newspaper column, "The Conning Tower." The third panelist was the gifted composer, solo pianist, gershwinophile, and increasingly acerbic Oscar Levant, who could offer an ad lib disquisition, seriously or ironically, on practically any popular subject.

Surprisingly, notwithstanding its highbrow nature, *Information Please* became the most listened-to program on radio. This fact did not escape Lou. He thought about the success and the format of *Information Please*. Because of his own background and his family's respect for education and knowledge, he identified closely with this display of popular intelligence on a successful radio program. He was particularly delighted with it; the show was one of his favorites.

Years later when an interviewer asked him about how he thought of the idea for *Quiz Kids*, he said, perhaps tongue-in-cheek, that he had children on his mind. "I was thinking about children more ... it was the very key to the fact that this idea came into being at all."[10] There was a good reason why Lou was thinking more about children. He married Pauline Spiegel in August 1939, and Pauline, who everyone called Polly, became pregnant with their first child toward the end of that year. Their baby was due in September 1940.

Cowan actually credited his analysis of *Information Please* as the basis for his thinking about creating *Quiz Kids*. There's no exact date when he started planning the show — it could have been at the very end of 1939 — but certainly he was thinking about it shortly after the beginning of the new year. A perturbing political and social mood had been building for more than ten years, from 1929 to 1940, starting with the stock market crash at the end of the Twenties, throughout the Depression, and the beginnings of a European war in September 1939. This new war promised to escalate to another world war. Even with that decade of somber news always present in most people's minds, Lou continued to think intently and with unflagging optimism of new ideas for a radio program that would be his property. By 1940, he increased the pace.

The juxtaposition of Polly's pregnancy and his focus on creating a new radio program, with his subsequent professional dissection of *Information Please*, made it only natural that those two thoughts would meld. As Lou thought about it more, he sensed that there was something more appealing for a radio program than one that featured smart, intellectual adults. Bright children could be the twist to the format established by *Information Please*. He believed that there were many such children who were very bright and that "nobody ever pays attention to them."[11] The idea began to gel. He thought that these children, if they had the right personalities — outgoing, charming, verbally adept — could be entertaining as well, and that a radio audience would welcome this program.[12]

As the full idea for a quiz show with bright children struck him and he began to have more thoughts about it, he asked John Lewellen for his opinion. Lewellen was a former writer for *Life* magazine who worked for Lou as a full-time staff member on the firm's public relations accounts. "What do you think of it?" he asked John.[13] John protested mildly, but quickly acquiesced.[14] A few years later Lewellen admitted that he thought that the idea was "just another one on a Tuesday afternoon." To try out the nascent idea further, reported Eliza Hickok, "Mr. Cowan called in the rest of his staff. 'Sounds good,' they said, and hurried back to work on his charity accounts."[15] Sensing the irony of his employees' outwardly favorable reaction, Ann Marsters wrote in the *Chicago Herald American*, "He was delighted by the staff's reaction — forgetting, no doubt, that most people have a habit of agreeing with the boss."[16]

Coincidentally, John Lewellen was thinking about his own wife's pregnancy at the same time as Lou. His firstborn, LuAnn, said that her mother, citing Lewellen family lore, had told her that her pregnancy was the inspiration for *Quiz Kids*. LuAnn was born in November 1940. Reminded that her birth five months after the debut broadcast meant that her mother in giving birth was not the only inspiration for *Quiz Kids*, she understood that during the previous nine months there had been frequent rounds of anticipatory conversation in a small office where two of the executives had children on their minds. Lou and John, as many expectant fathers would, speculated about what brilliant kids they were going to have. Business interrupted: Why not produce a radio show about brilliant kids?

LuAnn came to the conclusion that her father and Lou had the upcoming births of their children so prominent in their thoughts that they didn't separate their personal lives — their wives' pregnancies — from their jobs. But as imminent and important as the births of their children were, *Quiz Kids* came first: "When my mother went into labor with me, my father drove her to the hospital. Lou joined John in the waiting room while she was giving birth. Both men remained in the waiting room because in those days, husbands generally did not participate in the delivery. Of course, while waiting, they began talking about business. When I was born, a nurse came to them and reported to my father that he was the father of a bouncing baby girl. John said. 'Tell my wife I'll be up as soon as we finish this question.'"[17]

Lou was encouraged by the early reaction to his idea for a quiz program featuring children. He began listing ideas. It was the first thing he did, even before he established a format or worked out any other details. Cowan was always a fountain of ideas, spewing them forth in a seemingly endless stream. "Nearly all the ideas about the program originated with Lou. We could never keep up with him; ideas came pouring out. We could never guess what was coming next. Lou Cowan was a dynamo. When he set out to promote something, he created a whirlwind," said Eliza Hickok, assistant producer and researcher, whose original duties were to help select, research, and edit questions for the Quiz Kids to answer on air.[18]

Lou Cowan clearly defined the characteristics of the children who he wanted for the program. He maintained that smart, normal youngsters could be lovable, modest, sweet, and unspoiled. They could show the results of American public school education and they could do it in a dignified, unpretentious way. Most important, he thought that this would be "good radio."[19]

Lou knew that he had to make a demonstration record quickly with a few precocious children who were gifted enough to be prospective Quiz Kids once he sold the program to a corporate sponsor. But where and how would he find these children? In fact, this was the easiest part of the search. He called Pence James, a feature writer for the *Chicago Daily News*, and "got to talking over 'smart kids.'"[20] James had written about Gerard Darrow, a 4-year-old boy with a vast and sophisticated knowledge of ornithology.[21] When he was two years old he had listened intently as his guardian aunt read and reread to him descriptive texts about birds. Then he became interested in butterflies, insects and marine life, geology, geography, and mythology. "At the age of four he could name 365 birds at sight and outline their habits without a hitch."[22]

Pence James thought that Darrow was eminently suitable for the show. After meeting Gerard, Lou concurred. The youngster's thirst for knowledge was impressive. By the time he was nine, Gerard "could not only answer any question about hundreds of birds — their habits, appearance, habitats, and mating calls, down to the last detail — but also ... was amazingly well informed on history, mythology, and the natural sciences."[23]

Imbued with more confidence, Lou invited John Lewellen and Sidney James and their wives to his house, where he and Polly hosted a "couple of parties" to interview more prospective kids. Sidney James, an old friend of Lou's, was an editor at *Life* magazine.[24]

Toward the end of January, Cowan, Sidney James, and Pence James began interviewing other potential children.[25] When Pence showed Lou his newspaper article about an 11-year-old girl, Joan Bishop, who had performed brilliantly with the Chicago Symphony in November 1938 playing solo piano, Cowan called the Metropolitan School of Music in the Kimball building on South Wabash Avenue where she took piano lessons. Lou spoke with Franklin Stead, the owner of the music school, about coming to hear her and interview her for the new radio program. Stead was delighted, and agreed to Lou's visit.

Stead's music school was in a neighborhood, almost an insular world, geographically defined by the buildings and the type of businesses that usually occupied them. The Kimball building was an imposing 16-story edifice erected in 1917 next to the building at the southwest corner of South Wabash Avenue and East Jackson Street and built by the W.W. Kimball Company, a manufacturer of pianos and organs.[26] This building, along with the building on the northeast corner occupied by the Lyon and Healy Company, manufacturer of harps, were the northern anchors in Chicago's Music Row, the Tin Pan Alley of Chicago, in the heart of the Loop. Music Row extended from the intersection of East Jackson and South Wabash on the north to the elegant Civic Auditorium Building, two blocks south at Congress Street and South Wabash, where the Republican national convention was held in 1888.[27]

The windows of the music school looked onto South Wabash, where Chicago's noisy elevated train, the El, clacked and squealed as it lumbered by frequently, its jarring mechanical cacophony acting as a dark and dissonant obbligato to the light, airy music wafting from Joan Bishop's piano playing. On that raw and dim winter day, not quite spring in Chicago, what little natural light there was on the street below was crazed and filtered through the elevated train tracks one story above South Wabash and 15 stories below through the windows in the practice room where Joan was playing the second impromptu in Schubert's Four Impromptus, Op. 90 D 899, a buoyant and cheerful allegro. She described that first interview:

I remember that it was sometime in March, and I took my lesson at 11 A.M. on Tuesdays and Thursdays. I was playing Schubert's Impromptu in E Flat when Dr. Stead, smiling, briskly walked in and told me that "the men from the radio station are here."

Then Lou Cowan, John Lewellen, Pence James, and Sidney James walked in. They sat down and quietly and politely listened to me play. When I finished, Lou introduced himself and the others, and they began asking me questions about my family and me, what I was interested in, and my musical interests. Finally, there was a question about poetry, and I answered it, adding that the author was William Shakespeare. As an afterthought, I made a pun about something in the poem and said that perhaps Omar Khayyam should have written that poem. Lou emitted a hearty laugh, slapped his knee, and said, "That's what I want to hear. That's the kind of spirit I want."[28]

Joan's spirited answer was not unusual for her. She had been performing in public from the age of three and exhibited this independence, sometimes complemented with a deflating sense of humor. When she was five she performed in a recital in which she sang Brahms' *Lullaby*, softly and sweetly, appropriate to the composer's intent. As she sang, someone in the audience demanded that she sing louder. She stopped, and then took the wind out of the heckler by saying, "You can't put a baby to sleep hollering at him." She returned to her singing, using the same dulcet tones.[29]

Cowan and his staff interviewed more prospects for the demonstration record. At first, he worked on all the details of creating his new program, including finding and interviewing prospective children. Later, once the program was established, Cowan was not involved in the day-to-day details of running the program, but he always took an active part in long-range planning and in developing creative ideas to promote *Quiz Kids*. This was a modus operandi that remained with him throughout his career. He was a gifted strategist.

Within a couple of weeks Lou and his staff selected two more prospects, a girl of 14 who had been a child prodigy and a 10-year-old boy who played the violin exceptionally well. The four children, Joan Bishop, Gerard Darrow, and the other two, met for a first audition session at Cowan's home. Lou was not going to record this session, but he asked Sidney James to be the master of ceremonies when they eventually made the demonstration record. "The first get-together was held at my house — and I must say it was a miserable failure," Cowan reported in 1941. "The children, for the most part were unresponsive, and the questions just didn't seem to hit them right." Lou was disappointed.[30]

Joan and Gerard were acceptable, but the other two were not; their general knowledge was insufficient. Lou almost jettisoned the program. "There were times," he said, "when I was on the verge of giving up the whole thing. Our first attempts in working up a children's quiz show were dreary failures."[31]

Yet he continued to search for two new children. Pence James suggested Van Dyke Tiers, about whom he had written. Van Dyke, whose actual first name is George, at that time used his middle name in place of his first at the urging of his father. Sidney James also suggested Cynthia Cline as a candidate. Still not assured that Cowan could find suitable children, the search was beginning to become stressful.

At the same time, other pressures rapidly began to mount. Unlike his usual demeanor, Lou started to become anxious. He worried that they didn't have a suitable name for the program even though in a short while they had to make their final choices of children because they were trying to produce the demonstration record as quickly as possible, with or without a program name. Ideally, he thought, the name should be memorable. So there was a standing order for everyone at the Louis G. Cowan Company to think of a name. The staff offered at least six: *Our Children, Young America Speaks, School Kids Questionnaire, Out of the Mouths of Babes, The Kids Know* and *Examination Time*.[32] None of them was infinitely memorable with the emotional lure, the immediacy, and the sparkle that Lou wanted.

An unusual source of an idea provided that sparkle. Lou and Polly invited her brother and his wife, John and Babette Spiegel, to dinner one evening. Originally planned as a simple family get-together of siblings and their spouses, this dinner party was not for any special event. Once the usual gossip about family matters was exhausted, the conversation around the dinner table probably turned to the events of the day with its inevitable focus on the war in Europe that had begun in earnest at the beginning of September 1939, when Hitler's army crossed the border into Poland to begin a blitzkrieg, subduing and occupying that country within a few weeks in its march toward Russia, the ultimate target in the east.

The war in Europe was uppermost in people's minds. The Cowans and the Spiegels were no exception. The European conflict inexorably was growing globally. Armies were brandishing more sophisticated weapons with a new, faster, more deadly style of combat than any other war had ever seen. The debate about if and when the United States would be engaged formally in the war was at the forefront of conversation among individuals and in the press nationally. The war created another uncertainty for the future, adding to the continuing bleak economic forecast. The Depression lingered; the national unemployment rate was 14.6 percent in 1940. It was little wonder that Americans had the need for entertainment as a surcease to their worries.

Movies provided an inexpensive escape, as did miniature golf and dance marathons featuring the jitterbug, a swing dance variation usually performed by limber young people at increased tempos. Radio offered free entertainment. By 1940 approximately 83 percent of all American households owned a radio.

Ultimately, the conversation at Lou and Polly's home that evening turned to Lou's idea for this new quiz program. Dinner became an informal, at-home work session, and actually an unforgettable occasion (except for the actual date) for more than 40 years. Almost as unforgettable were the Oscars and the part they played in the dinner conversation that night.

The Academy of Motion Picture Arts and Sciences broadcast its annual Academy Awards ceremony on national radio honoring the best films, performances, and behind-the-scenes production efforts of 1939. That year Bob Hope made the first of his 18 appearances as the host of the awards ceremony. This was not the first time the awards ceremony was a radio broadcast; enthusiasm for movies had reached a new high during the protracted Depression. As well, by 1940 the movies offered a simple digression from thinking about the increasing prospect of another devastating world war.

For most people who did not work in the film industry, the awards gala was an interesting but fleeting diversion often reported in newspapers the next day as front-page news. It still is. For a day or two the winners and the films are ready-made topics of social conversation around office water coolers, in beauty shops, at diners, at bus stops, and at the thousands of places throughout America where people usually gather. Today, film historians and critics consider Hollywood's output in 1939 outstanding. Of the many exceptional movies of 1939, *The Wizard of Oz* won two Oscars: for best song ("Over the Rainbow") and best original music score.

There is no document that establishes the date of the Cowans' little dinner party with the Spiegels, but it was likely Sunday, March 3. The Academy Awards ceremony was Thursday, February 29, just three days earlier.[33] Outside Hollywood, interest in the gala award ceremony generally cools after three days, so if it was not at the forefront of the Cowan-Spiegel conversation, the awards ceremony played an unexpected, but significant, supporting role that evening. If their dinner conversation even touched on *The Wizard of Oz*, it shifted quickly to a more pressing issue, exploring names for Lou's new radio program. Enter *The Wizard* as an unwitting player in the evolution of naming *Quiz Kids*. With news of the Oscars still near the surface of her thoughts, Polly offered as a name something about the Quizzer of Oz, making a pun on *The Wizard of Oz*, and Babette, who began free-associating, gingerly suggested, with a sharper pun, "Quizzard of Oz?" She then proposed cautiously, "Quizzard of Kids?" And finally, editing her own pun, she offered, confident at last, "Quiz Kids."[34] They all looked at each other. The name clicked. That was it!

Within a few weeks the Cowan Company made a demonstration record at the World Broadcasting System studios with Joan, Gerard, Van Dyke, and Cynthia. Once again the attempt was a failure. "The experience was horrible," remarked Lou. He was dejected even though he recognized that the poor performance resulted from slapdash preparation. "It was the first time all the children had been together, questions had been hurriedly composed, a script was thrown together the day before, and Mr. James was facing a microphone for only the second time in his life." Lou was distraught. He described the "horrible" recording session:

> We used 24 questions — twice as many as we now use during the same period of time — ended up with no questions left and with everyone except the kids in a state of hysteria.
>
> For sound effects we used a whistle every time the kids missed and clinked silver dollars [when they answered correctly]. During the recording the dollars spilled on the floor and the whistle was so close to the microphone that it nearly blew the engineer out of his booth.
>
> From every technical standpoint the record was abominable.
>
> And yet — through all this was shown the fact that we had four children capable of amazing an adult audience. They surprised even us with the extent of their knowledge and their brilliant answers.[35]

"It was pretty bad," noted Eliza Hickok, writing about the demonstration record, "but to Mr. Cowan's staff it proved three things — that Mr. Cowan had a good idea, that it was feasible, and that smart children can be nice and entertaining."[36]

What Lou learned from making the record was that no matter what technical difficulties might occur, these effervescent children with their superabundant knowledge would shine through and carry the show. He decided to use Gerard, Joan, Van Dyke, and Cynthia for the demo, the one he would use to sell the show. Presumably these same four panelists would be on the first broadcast once they went on air.

Notwithstanding technical or other difficulties, they still had to make a professional recording suitable to present the program to prospective sponsors. Today, it is common to send demonstration recordings to several prospects at the same time. Cowan didn't. In fact, in those days there was no tape as we know it now. Radio producers created all demonstration presentations on 78-rpm records. It was normal for them to spend thousands of dollars making those records and then circulate them to network buyers, advertising agencies, and their clients.

Lou made only one record that he would shop around. He and his staff worked assiduously on the record, making a variety of improvements after the World Broadcasting session. He knew what he wanted to achieve, but he wasn't getting it because neither Sidney James nor anyone else on the staff was a professional master of ceremonies. So, there were two formidable obstacles to overcome. Lou had to find additional youngsters who qualified, and he had to sell the show to a sponsor.

Where and how would they find more bright children, suitable for the program? They began a "huge" search. Many years later, Lou told Erik Barnouw, professor of mass communications at Columbia University in New York, "It was terribly hard to do so — trying to find kids who were bright enough to do this." He began inquiring about precocious children at Chicago-area public schools, and asking friends and business associates. Joe Bailey, an old college friend and lawyer who had come to work for Cowan, was instrumental in finding and interviewing prospective children. Cowan claimed that the "word kind of got around, and eventually we had 10 or 12 [children]."[37]

Within a few weeks, around the beginning of April, the demo was ready, and Lou began trying to sell the idea. Gerald Nachman wrote that when Cowan shopped the record to ad agencies, all of them said, "Nobody would listen to a bunch of wise-ass kids and those who did would figure the show was rigged."[38] When he tried the idea on potential advertisers, Lou heard what appeared to be a negative reaction: "Everyone said it isn't possible — you can't get the kids."

He was not a professional salesman, but Lou understood the basic truth that good salesmen know: when the prospect starts to ask questions or begins to talk about the problems in the product or service, he is involved; he's beginning to determine how to make the offer acceptable. If the prospect simply says no, or delays in making a decision ("we'll call you") then there is no interest. Lou knew that the prospective buyers were interested. He concluded that he was close to making a sale. Their extended comments and even their negative thoughts "made me realize that it would work — that we had a good show."[39] Encouraged, he continued to move forward.

Still, no one was buying. As brilliant an idea man and promoter as Lou Cowan was, he was unsuccessful as a salesman. Lou was uncomfortable in that role. He never overcame this discomfort, even years later in the corporate board rooms where he was chronically ill at ease.[40]

None of the prospects he approached expressed enough interest to discuss the terms of the sale. In desperation, Lou hired Jimmy Parks, a well-known radio program sales agent who worked for the General Amusement Corporation, one of the leading big swing band booking agents at that time, to help sell the program. Lou had been the publicity agent for Kay Kaiser's famous swing band shortly after he began his business in the early 1930s, so he was familiar with GAC and perhaps knew Jimmy Parks. If he didn't know Jimmy already, it was easy to connect with him within GAC's staff. Jimmy's job was to sell the sponsorship of radio programs to advertisers.

When Lou and Jimmy began working together, they called on advertising agencies. In the 1940s advertising agencies directed radio programs for the networks on behalf of their clients, who were the shows' sponsors. Normally one company would sponsor an entire show, and the announcers for radio programs would present the commercials live, script in hand. Gradually that changed. After World War II independent packagers, such as Lou's company, would produce and direct all sponsored radio and television shows. These independents produced and directed the pilot show, recorded it, and saw to it that it was ready for presentation to broadcasting networks and advertising agencies. Eventually it became rare for one advertiser to sponsor an entire program. Representatives sold 60-second or 30-second "spots," brief segments of time for advertising agencies to buy and then to produce commercials to fill that time on audio tape for radio and videotape or film for televised programs. Spot advertising became the standard, allowed multiple sponsors to buy time on a specific program for their advertising.

Even with the joint effort by Lou and Jimmy, 12 advertisers turned them away.[41] It wasn't until the beginning of May that they had some success. Once, without Lou, Jimmy called on Jeff Wade at the Wade Advertising Agency, and "coincidentally that day they had decided that they were going to put something else in [for Alec Templeton] and they wanted something not expensive." Wade suggested that they present the demo to one of their clients, Miles Laboratories, for their product, Alka-Seltzer. Miles Labs sponsored the Alec Templeton show for Wade. "They liked the idea of a program that kind of related to what they felt they were selling ... something with education in it and some other kind of quality." Templeton's radio performance exuded intelligence and showmanship. It was a good fit for Lou's Kids. They presented the demo to Charles S. Beardsley, vice president for marketing at Miles Labs, and he was interested.[42]

Beardsley had been instrumental to the success of Alka-Seltzer because it was his decision to use radio for their advertising a few years earlier during the low point of the Great Depression. It was radio that pushed the product and the company to success. By 1944 Beardsley was president of Miles Labs; in 1947 he was chairman.[43] He was impressed with the demo and the Kids, but he absolutely refused to believe that Lou and his staff hadn't coached the children. Lou believed that producing more demos would assure him that the program was honest and that they could find more bright children.[44] He concluded that the only thing that would convince Beardsley was to have him hear more demos with more children.

Lou learned that he was competing with three other shows for the contract with Miles Labs. Beardsley continued to exhibit high interest in the show; he was fascinated with the idea. Lou asked him to the next session. He accepted Lou's invitation and "came up to see the audition."[45]

NBC was enthusiastic about *Quiz Kids*, too. Still, their interest was qualified with a critical request. They wanted to hear more demos with some modifications that they suggested. So Lou couldn't stay with his original plan of just producing one demo; he had to make more to satisfy the network and Miles. It was an unplanned expense with no guarantee of return on his investment, but Lou risked it.

As much as he liked the content of the program, Beardsley liked the price, too. Lou described the final deal: "We [eventually] sold the show [to Miles Labs] for 13 weeks for $1,000 a show, which was, even by 1940 standards, pretty low." Lou offered it at this low price because he had faith in the show and wanted to get it on the air.[46]

Thirty-eight years later in Lou's oral history he remembered that the show's first contract was for 13 weeks, the standard minimum broadcasting contract at that time. His memory was faulty. According to John Lewellen, in a letter to Joan Bishop in June 1940, the first contract was for 10 weeks, from June 28 to August 28, while Templeton was on vacation. It was an abbreviated contract, a remnant of the usual 13-week contract, with little chance of success. Nonetheless, Lou jumped at the opportunity. Lewellen was not as euphoric. He knew that their time was limited. "If we don't have a good Crossley rating within 6 weeks, there goes the option for the future," he wrote.[47]

Sponsors of Chicago radio shows at that time preferred not to back "name" shows — programs with well-known performers — because they wanted to maintain close contact with the production staffs. More often than not, networks did not produce radio programs with name talent in Chicago; they produced them in New York or Los Angeles, requiring advertisers from outside those two production centers to fly continually to either coast to oversee the programs. Alternatively they could transfer the supervision of these shows to their branch offices, but when they made that transfer of authority there was a loss of the control that they wanted.

The so-called "idea shows" that had "taken the country by storm" in the 1930s and '40s were not considered big-budget programs. Idea shows worked on the assumption that in the long term a greater number of listeners could be attracted per dollar spent than through big talent "splashes." *Quiz Kids* was an idea show.[48] Not all idea shows were quiz programs.[49] Two years earlier, in 1938, quiz programs had become a fad, accelerated by the trend away from inflated radio program production budgets (this was, after all, the Depression) and the increasing number of advertisers (sponsors) whose allocations for advertising were too low to support those big radio budgets. Quiz programs became the answer to the problem of limited funds available from sponsors. For some producers, quiz programs were not about smaller allocations. They belittled them as a lack of a good idea for a radio program.[50]

Quiz programs were "easy to listen to." They were fun for the audience and perhaps for the contestants. The questions and the answers could be enlightening. If they were a frivolous distraction, a novelty, without the gravity of a news program, they were popular because of the entertainment they offered. Ralph Edwards, the creator of *Truth or Consequences*, when trying to determine what his audience thought about his program, discovered that they thought that *Truth or Consequences* offered a welcome relief from the unhappy news of world affairs.

Edwards believed that producing a successful quiz program was a business, as serious as any other could be. Quiz programs were important to individual radio stations and networks; they could be highly profitable. By the end of 1940 it was possible to tune in to a different major quiz on radio every night of the week — there were at least 20 different quiz programs available nationally.[51]

Now that there was real interest in *Quiz Kids*, the pressure on Lou and his staff intensified. The production team wanted the show to air on NBC's Red Network. As an indicator of the real interest in the show, *Quiz Kids*, NBC was considering it. The Red Network had the largest stations, as John Lewellen described them.[52] A more accurate definition of the difference between the Red and Blue networks was more specific than Lewellen's casual explanation. The Red Network featured programs that were sponsored — dramatic entertainment and music programs — while the Blue usually carried non-sponsored broadcasts, news, and cultural programs. Of course there were exceptions on either network. *Quiz Kids* actually debuted on the Blue Network, contrary to preliminary plans touted by Lou and John. From here on, most often I will abbreviate the name of the program as *QK*. Newspaper articles and sometimes the announcers for the program erroneously called it *The Quiz Kids*. This refers to the children (the Quiz Kids); the actual name of the program is *Quiz Kids*. However, several years later the incorrect name was so pervasive that there appeared to be no strict attempt to correct it.

With interest in the show rising, in early May Lou increased the tempo of the drumbeat; he had less than two months to refine the program and have it ready for its debut because Templeton's last show before his summer break was to be June 21. *QK* had to be ready for airing June 28. Nonetheless, before making a final commitment, NBC wanted to hear more demonstration records. Lou made two more with the Kids by the middle of May. But NBC wanted more. So, they booked studio time for Sunday, May 26, only a month before the debut. John Lewellen described this as the final demo before they went on air. Typically, they booked the studio for two hours. This time, it was for 7 to 9 P.M., but the children didn't have to arrive until 7:30 because they didn't start cutting the record until 8:00, and a half hour before recording was a sufficient warm up for the Kids.[53] The next day, Monday, they presented the demo, their third, to NBC.

A lot of work remained for Lou and his staff. To make their task more manageable, the Cowan Company and Wade Advertising formed a joint production team, consisting of Lou, John Lewellen, Joe Bailey, Walter Wade, the agency's owner, and his son, Jeff, and finally Ed Simmons, the agency's producer for the show. They had several tasks to complete before writing a new script and recording the 30-minute program. They had to devise the questions that the emcee would ask the Kids. As well, they had to decide on the program format and create the rules of the game. They had to write a new script, including continuity, for each demo record. For each demo they had to create new questions for the Kids because they couldn't use those that they had used previously: the Kids would remember those previous questions and, of course, the answers.

Then a new complication emerged. To format the show, the production team had to follow a list of special rules. NBC imposed strict guidelines about the format of the program because of its strong resemblance to *Information Please*. They didn't want to offend its sponsors, Canada Dry. As a result, the network's restrictions forbade Lou to have a permanent board of experts, banned the use of the word "unrehearsed" in connection with the show, and tried to induce the directors of *QK* (the Louis G. Cowan Company) to aim the scripts at children rather than adults.[54]

To comply with NBC's requirements, the team decided that unlike *Information Please* the panel of *QK* would be different each week. *Information Please* used a permanent three-member panel and a guest personality. *QK* was to be a panel of five children, never completely the same each week, with a guest personality appearing frequently. This decision was not just a way of constructing a difference from the more established show; it was a way to keep the program fresh. The *QK* production team went one step further. Just as children get a report card at school, during each program a team consisting of Cowan staff members, the "judges," would be present at each show to evaluate the children's replies to the questions and assign a score to the children's answers.

The production team decided that they wanted the show's format to be similar to an actual elementary school classroom, with a roll call near the beginning of each show. But rather than faithfully mimicking a classroom where the teacher reads the names of the students and they reply, indicating that they are present, *QK* would be different. The emcee would say the children's first names, and instead saying "present," or "here," the Kids would respond with their full names, ages, and the names of their schools.

At the end of each show the emcee would invite the three Kids with the highest scores that day to return the following week. Two new children would appear each week, to replace the low scorers. That way, *QK* would be changing continuously and would be entirely new at each broadcast, each week.

This little element would go a long way toward maintaining an audience of repeat listeners. It would help to build a new audience for the same reason. Listening to the same panel of children each week could easily lead to listener boredom and indifference. As exciting as this concept was for building and maintaining an audience, this always predictable element in formatting — constant change — created a major task for the staff in their weekly pre-production work. It also meant that the production office always would be busy. The *QK* staff would have to search for and interview new prospects without pause.

By May 27 Lou had presented three different audition tapes to NBC, and the reaction from the network was more promising. Network officials said that the show could go on the air after John made two or three minor changes. Two days later they recorded a fourth demo. After they showed it to NBC and Miles Labs, they had a deal.[55] It looked as if the program was nearly ready. But not quite. There was one more problem, and it was devastating. They had no quizmaster.[56] It was May 29, and the countdown had begun. Only one month to air time.

As quickly as possible they began to audition candidates for the job. In total, they auditioned 15 with the requisite intelligence and education that appeared to be fitting for such a program. Some were well-established emcees and announcers. Among them was a prominent Chicago news commentator, professors from the University of Chicago, a noted lecturer, and a writer, some of them whose names and familiar voices eventually became famous on national radio and subsequently, television: Durwood Kirby, Ed Simmons, and others.

None of these candidates was acceptable. None had the ability to relate to the Kids and make them feel comfortable when they were on air. Because of their own intellectual abilities, they tried to compete with the Quiz Kids in offering answers to questions, or to minimize their intellectual abilities.

Eliza Hickok thought that college professors should have been a "natural" for the job. Instead, they were complete failures. They displayed their own knowledge and the Kids couldn't get a word in. The lecturer, even though he was comfortable in front of a microphone, gave away the answers, and the writer was so slow that "the children could have played a game of badminton between questions."[57]

Lou concluded that the candidates for quizmaster so far "were absolutely unable to keep up with the rapidity of the children's answers. Some became obviously confused, some sounded dull, some too professional, and some sounded as if they were the whole show. It seemed almost impossible to find one person with an easy manner who could get along with the children. All those who auditioned were open-mouthed at the Kids' intelligence."[58]

Now the countdown to the show was even more daunting. After these 14 auditions, they still didn't have a suitable quizmaster. These seemingly endless tryouts were Lou's version of a Hollywood screen test. Even though a successful demo had already been made and the program sold to Alka-Seltzer two weeks earlier, this test for a quizmaster was just as essential as the hard work by the production team that had gone into making the sales demo. The production team structured the test as a typical, complete show would be, but with a panel of only four children: Cynthia Cline, Gerard Darrow, Joan Bishop, and Van Dyke Tiers, just as the previous sales demos had been.

On Wednesday, June 12, it was back to the studio for another session to try out a new prospective quizmaster, the last candidate of the 15. This time hopes were high because the well-known broadcaster, Clifford Utley, was the contender. He was an experienced announcer and on-air political commentator with an undergraduate degree from the University of Chicago, followed by graduate studies at several European universities. He was an authority on foreign relations and was in great demand because of his experience and insights.

When we listen to his June 12 audition, we hear him speak in a deep tone, well-modulated, apparently at ease, and conveying the authority that established his reputation. Not at all stentorian, he used ordinary language in his transitional remarks. Clifford Utley was a highly respected broadcaster. His sterling performance met all the anticipated qualities usually associated with his vocal presentation.

The script for his test was a simulated show, as it was for the candidates who preceded him. Although these tests were just auditions they were written to sound like authentic on-air programs with all the production values included: an announcer, commercials for Alka-Seltzer, and music. Utley presented the Kids and explained, "Our star pupils who topped the class last week, and are back with us again tonight, are Joan Bishop, Van Dyke Tiers, and Cynthia Cline."[59] The reference to the pupils who had returned from the previous week's program was a brilliant touch. It could easily convince someone listening that it was a real program in the series. If the goal was to make this demo sound real, it succeeded. It also succeeded in establishing that the first real show—the program's debut—was June 28.

But Utley did not meet Lou's standards. The Kids didn't connect with him. Years later, after the show was established, Lewellen used him as an occasional quizmaster.[60] Sixteen days to air time. The lack of success in finding a quizmaster was frustrating to everyone on the staff. With each passing day the pressure to succeed increased, so that with Utley's failure the search appeared to be at a standstill. Then, Walter Wade suggested that they should invite Joe Kelly to audition.

Kelly was master of ceremonies on the WLS program *National Barn Dance*, the inspiration for *Grand Ole Opry*. But it was more than an inspiration; *Opry* was an unabashed copy of *National Barn Dance*. Originally called the *WSM Barn Dance*, using the call letters of the local radio station in Nashville as part of the title, it made only a thinly disguised attempt to differentiate itself from the more successful Chicago-based show.[61]

Even though Joe was so likable on *Barn Dance* and was well-respected by his peers, Lou balked at Walter Wade's suggestion of testing him: "All of us were unalterably opposed to the idea of having Joe Kelly. Walter Wade ... supported Kelly because he was 'precisely the kind of person [for the job] because he would embody the adult—the idea of the adult who's absolutely baffled by these Kids.'"[62] When Walter asked Joe to audition as the quizmaster, Joe panicked. He was in shock, especially when he looked at the questions he would ask the children at the audition:

> "I wonder whether you can tell me who was famous for having solved the problem of finding the hypotenuse from the sum of the square of the other two sides [of a triangle]."
>
> The answer beneath read: Pythagoras, a Greek philosopher, sixth century B.C.
>
> "I can't even read it," Joe moaned, "what do you think I am—a college professor or something?"

With a great deal of trepidation, Joe completed the audition. "The same Quiz Kids—Gerard, Joan, Cynthia, and Van Dyke—'who had frozen' for the professors, were relaxed, happy, and eager.... They were anxious to tell Joe all about Pythagoras ... because ... he didn't know. They wanted him to know," wrote Eliza Hickok.[63] The Kids felt comfortable with Joe from the beginning. They loved him. He was so easy-going and cheery that he put them completely at ease from the minute they entered the studio. He handled it just beautifully. After he auditioned he went on vacation and didn't think anything more about it.[64]

Lou's original objection to using Joe was starting to recede. Joe wisecracked throughout the audition to hide his embarrassment about not understanding the questions or the answers.[65] After hearing him, Lou thought that of all the other prospective quizmasters, the Kids liked Joe most. He also thought that Joe was able to draw more extra comments from the Kids once they answered the questions. Joe did this better than any of the previous candidates for the job.[66] It wasn't enough just to get the answer to a difficult question, even those with a subjective answer, or a complicated math problem. Joe wanted the Kids to tell him how they knew the answer, or what their reasoning was in arriving at their conclusions or solutions. Simply, he was able to get them to expand on their answers because perhaps he didn't understand their answers (or often, the questions). But Joe, with his limited formal education, was creating a smoother, more believable program than the other prospective quizmasters had.

After the audition, Joe wasn't so sure about his performance. He thought it was a nightmare, and he was glad to go to Canada for his vacation directly following the test. His vacation was short lived. Within a few days, Wade sent him a telegram: "COME HOME AT ONCE YOU ARE THE QUIZ KIDS CHIEF QUIZZER."[67]

When he found that he had won the job, he nearly fainted, observed Rachel Stevenson. At his return to Chicago, Joe learned that the show was going on that Friday night. "'What about the questions that I'll ask the kids,' Joe asked weakly. 'Oh, you'll get those Friday night,' someone told him."[68]

Finally, it seemed that they were ready. Nine days before the debut, it was time to breathe easily. Lewellen told Joan Bishop that 33 stations, all broadcasting with 50,000 watts or higher, would carry the first program.[69] He was proud of that.

But the roller-coaster ride wasn't over. After all the hard work and the pitfalls they had overcome, another disaster loomed. This time, it really looked like the show couldn't go on. According to Lou, it was another last-minute panic. Just a few hours before the network debut of the show, during the afternoon of June 28, the lawyers at Miles Labs were worried. There was a possible impasse over Babette's coined name: *Quiz Kids*. The legal team at the pharmaceutical company discovered that a Minneapolis radio station had a local program called *Kiddie Quiz*. The lawyers for Miles thought that the station might sue the pharmaceutical company because the names of the shows were similar. The lawyers advised Lou that he should change the name of his show. Lou and his staff were frantic as they tried to think of another name. In the middle of all the chaos, someone asked calmly if anyone had called the owners of the other show to see if they would sue.[70]

Lou called WCCO, the radio station in Minneapolis. He wanted to speak with Earl H. Gammons, its chief executive.[71] Lou didn't focus on the negative — the possibility of a lawsuit. Rather than trying to find out if they would sue over the conflict caused by the possible confusion from the use of a similar name, Lou wanted to see if he could get permission to use the name they had worked so hard to create. He learned that Gammons was playing golf that day. He called the golf course and managed to get the radio executive back into the clubhouse right in the middle of his game.

Speaking with him on the phone, Lou thought that Gammons sounded annoyed: "He said that he is having a great game that day, and they got him in to answer the phone."[72] Lou spoke with him and calmly explained what was happening. He managed to get Gammons's verbal permission to use the name. It sounds incredible that Lou would get permission on the phone; he was a total stranger to Gammons. "Lou Cowan was a very engaging man. He knew how to speak and to present his case," observed Cynthia Cline Newgarden.[73] Of course Lou knew that formally they had to go through copyright lawyers to settle the matter.[74] He couldn't wait for that. He obtained permission verbally on the phone that afternoon. To put the icing on the cake, he reported that no one in Minneapolis had "the slightest objection" to the name *Quiz Kids* and "wouldn't dream of sueing [sic] the sponsors."[75] Most likely the appropriate correspondence between the copyright lawyers for Miles Labs and WCCO's lawyers quickly followed Lou's successful phone call so that these two radio executives could sign a more formal agreement.

That night, at the show's debut, everyone was nervous, except the Kids. They had arrived 30 minutes before airtime and "acted like brothers and sisters at a family picnic, romped about the studio and thought everything was simply wonderful."[76]

NBC broadcast *Quiz Kids* from Studio E in the Merchandise Mart on the Chicago River across from Upper West Wacker Drive. Marshall Field and Company had built the Merchandise Mart in 1930. It was the largest office building in the world (soon to be eclipsed by the Pentagon). NBC had constructed several broadcast studios in the building, each with the most sophisticated technology available. The studios became a favorite and exciting destination for tourists. Just as at Radio City in New York, there were tours conducted by uniformed guides. The guides offered free tickets to attend live radio shows as members of the studio audience.

Lou Cowan, master promoter and showman, remembered what he had learned nine years earlier, when he was still a student, about the power of dramatics in publicity. With a flair for theatrics, Lou had the children wear costumes — navy blue academic caps and gowns — when they appeared on the program, or later, when they did a broadcast or show at another location. Each gown featured, in white lettering, the words "Quiz Kid." Joe Kelly wore a baccalaureate robe and mortarboard, too, with "Chief Quizzer" embroidered on his robe. Critics asked about the need to have such costumes because this was radio, and the radio audience couldn't see the performers. There was usually a studio audience of about 200 for a *QK* broadcast, so the costumes were part of the marketing of the show.[77]

The first broadcast produced more than the usual quota of opening night jitters. Joe Kelly was nervous because he didn't understand some of the questions, or their answers, and didn't know how to pronounce some of the words in the questions or answers. Even usually-calm Lou Cowan was anxious: "If you hear a long pause when one of the kids fails to answer — then a dull thud — that'll be my hundred and ninety-five pounds falling out of a chair in a dead faint."[78]

The five Quiz Kids on that first program were 7-year-old Gerard Darrow; Joan Bishop, 13; Van Dyke Tiers, 13; Mary Ann Anderson, 14; and Charles Schwartz, 13. Lou and the production staff selected three Kids from the June 12 session. Cynthia Cline was not one of them even though she was one of the Kids on that session and presumably one of the four scheduled for the first broadcast, with an additional Kid to be determined. But Lou assured her that she would be on a subsequent show, soon. Lewellen explained the reasoning behind the decision. He said, "To avoid charter members (i.e., the first Quiz Kids) kicking each other off, we are going to start only three original Kids: Joan, Van, and Gerard."[79] Cynthia would be on later. In fact, she appeared for the first time two weeks after the debut, on the third broadcast, July 12.[80] At her audition for her first appearance, she amazed the sponsor when Joe gave her a subject at the beginning of the audition and asked her to write a poem about it. She completed it extemporaneously within the allotted time.[81]

The remaining two Kids for the debut were chosen from the entire pool of children who had been available to them, including those who had participated in the "horrible" recordings leading up to the actual demo. Those Kids who weren't chosen for the first broadcast were still being considered for future shows.

In addition to the excitement and creative joy felt by Lou and his staff at finding children suitable as Kids, there was the business side of the equation. Joe Bailey wrote a comprehensive agreement in just over two pages between "'Quiz Kids, Inc.,' a Chicago corporation" and the parents and natural guardians of each of the children, to be signed prior to the first broadcast. The agreement with H.W. and Ruth Tiers, Van Dyke's parents, specified the responsibilities of both Van Dyke and the producer ("Quiz Kids, Inc.") including the remuneration to Van Dyke for appearances on the program: a $100 United States Government bond if he was one of the three successful candidates to remain on the show and a $50 bond if he was eliminated. The contract also specified that if Van Dyke were to receive offers of professional employment on other radio programs or to appear in motion pictures, at concert engagements, or any other medium as a direct result of his appearance on the *QK* radio program, the producer had the option to act as his agent with commission current at that time paid to him. The agreement was signed by Joe Bailey as agent for Quiz Kids, Inc.[82]

Showtime.

The first question Joe Kelly asked on that first broadcast was: "I want you to tell me what I would be carrying home if I brought an antimacassar, a dinghy, a sarong, and an apteryx?"

Gerard quickly identified an *apteryx* as an extinct bird, native to Australia.

Van Dyke defined *antimacassar* correctly, even volunteering how it got its name from Macassar oil, which men used as a hair dressing. Mary Ann defined *sarong*, and humorously appended that it was Dorothy Lamour's mainstay, and that it was especially popular in the South Sea Islands.[83] The manner in which the Kids answered this first question set the tone for the program for that night, and for the 13 years to follow.

The Kids were extremely competitive. Each tried to be first to answer a question. At the same time, when one of them answered part of a multi-answer question, the entire group was collegial: others would complete the answer. Even if it was a single-answer question, some of the other children would volunteer amplification of the answer to proclaim their own knowledge. "One beautiful thing about this program," marveled Rachel Stevenson, "was that sometimes it took two or three children to answer the question because they'd work it out together. That's what was so much fun about [the program]. One Kid would say, 'well that was in a book called so-and-so,' and another would say, 'well, so-and-so wrote the book,' another would tell some [more], and all together they'd get graded for contributing toward the answer."[84]

Joe was nervous and sweating during that first program. He giggled frequently like a nervous schoolgirl to hide his humiliation.[85] At one point he declared, "Sakes alive, am I ever dumb." A few minutes later, completely rattled, he asked the question, "Whom might you expect to find on the master's end of the leash if you saw each of the following dogs?" But he forgot to name the dogs.[86] The rest of the production team were equally anxious during that first airing. By the end of the show Joe Kelly looked like "a sheet sprinkled down for ironing," wrote Eliza Hickok. "Lou Cowan and John were limp. The sponsor and Mr. Wade didn't look as young as they had a half-hour before."[87]

Based on his shaky performance, Lou wanted to fire Joe immediately, but Beardsley said no. He agreed with Lou's earlier conclusion that Joe was at least more human with the Kids than any of the others who had auditioned for the job, he could encourage the Kids to expand on their answers, and most important, that the Kids liked him. Beardsley reasoned that it was true that Joe needed more education. He concluded that the staff could supply it.[88] In effect, all Joe needed was a tutor.

With all of its faults, everyone agreed that it was a good show. It was friendly. The Kids had been amazing, and despite his anxiety, Joe had contributed the right combination of warmth and humor, ending with a sign-off that remained with the show for its entire life. Before going off the air, Joe concluded by saying to the Quiz Kids, "Goodnight, kids." As a group, but not quite in unison, the Kids replied, "Goodnight, Mr. Kelly." The rag-tag nature of their response to Joe made it sound as if it were spontaneous.

But it was most likely that John Lewellen wrote this warm and friendly sign-off that appeared in the scripts.[89] Probably the response by the Kids sounded uneven because the director did not rehearse or cue the Kids. Or, knowing Lou's passion for image making, he might have planned it to sound unrehearsed and natural.

Ultimately, Lou was correct. The Kids would carry the show no matter what went wrong. And the production staff behind them would help make the show work. Now, Lou could move the program forward with confidence. At last, he had his property.

2

The Brains Behind the Brains

☞ *If all our presidents up to the year 1896 stood side by side in a line, from what city to what city would the line extend?*

He was young and ambitious. He aggressively pursued his goals using every tactic that he could. He tried ideas and learned as much as he could about his profession, even the concepts that his teachers didn't touch upon when he was in college. He always absorbed new ideas that he learned from professionals in the field; he was superb at networking, as a young man and for the rest of his life.[1] Lou Cowan was more than a producer or a packager of broadcasting properties. He was a creative visionary who decided to blaze a new trail when he created *QK*. He had been involved in radio shows before, even quiz shows, but none with such an exquisitely focused intellectual viewpoint. His strong beliefs about education and the need to foster it were prominent in his thinking and challenged the generally accepted, anti-intellectual attitudes in America, as did the popular radio show at the time, *Information Please*, one of Lou's favorites.

We can trace Cowan's interest in education and intelligence and his facility with creating ideas to his family background. Louis George Cohen (his friends and business associates called him Lou) was born in Chicago on December 16, 1910. His paternal grandfather, Moses Cohen, was a scrap-iron salesman who spoke seven languages and in his spare time read secular writers such as Goethe and Tolstoy. Lou was delighted that Moses was always willing to answer his questions about books. Moses showed affection for Lou, who had the intelligence and interest in learning to carry on the family tradition of scholarship. Lou's father, Jacob, was a ne'er-do-well businessman whose raffish behavior and interest in sports seemed to be the mainstays of his unsuccessful life.

As he was growing up, Lou became interested in radio before he reached adolescence; as early as 1921 he listened to radio on a crystal set that required that he wear headphones to hear broadcasts. (Crystal sets were often home-made, constructed inexpensively using a cylindrical oatmeal box and small parts.) By 1924, the teenage Cowan had a radio with a loudspeaker. He recalled first listening to WLS shortly after its inception in that year. "WLS was owned by Sears, Roebuck, and the call letters stood for World's Largest Store," Lou explained years later.[2] When he was an undergraduate at the University of Chicago, he took courses with Harold Laswell, a professor of communications, well known for his talent in the use of propaganda. Lou chose Laswell's classes because he was fascinated with the ways in which mass communication could shape opinion.

In his student days he worked on publicity for the student musical revue and comedy organization Black Friars, similar to the Princeton Triangle Club. He was circulation manager of the university's student newspaper as well. He tripled their subscriptions. Before he graduated in March 1931, he tried to get a job in advertising and publicity and applied for jobs at various agencies in Chicago. "I was terribly anxious to get to work in advertising," he recalled, "and of course 1931 was the worst possible time to get into that field."[3] Cowan was introduced to Andrew Karzas, who owned the famous Aragon and Trianon ballrooms.

Lou also met Edward Bernays, the renowned public relations expert whose initial talent was in creating publicity, and whose first major success was in helping to devise a triumph for the American tour of Diaghilev's Ballet Russes in 1915, even though he knew nothing about dance and claimed that he was "positively uninterested in the dance."[4] His achievement with promoting the ballet tour was instrumental in helping him to build one of the most outstanding public relations firms in America. Bernays, Sigmund Freud's nephew, followed Freud's ideas on the subconscious and on psychological motivation for years and applied those precepts to his public relations projects.[5]

Lou recalled that when he met Bernays in 1931, the famous public relations man gave him some sound advice. Cowan said that Bernays "claimed that you should stress showmanship — dramatics — as the most important thing in propaganda and publicity. Publicity is your tool."

After graduation, Cowan went to see Karzas, who said "he didn't need anybody." But Lou "began to point out to him a lot of things that he needed: young men with new ideas, etc." Cowan persisted. Finally, Bruce Godshaw, head of Karzas's publicity department, created a job for Lou. He paid him $20 a week, and Lou was happy to have the job. Of course, Lou knew nothing about the work, so he went to night school to learn about advertising. Within a year Godshaw left to start his own firm, and Karzas promoted Lou to take over Godshaw's job.

Lou was restless, driven by ambition and a quest to gain more knowledge about his chosen profession. He made every effort to get the experience to go with it. While working for Karzas, he talked his way into writing a column of radio criticism for *Radio Guide*, a new magazine, and eventually had a small radio show on WCFL, called *The Man with His Ear to the Ground*, an on-air gossip column. Cowan was trying as many things as he could. "At that time I wasn't concerned about making money so much as learning.... Mr. Karzas and I had an agreement. As long as I did his things, he didn't care if I did other things as well." Lou began doing publicity for nonprofit organizations. Eventually he rented office space from Karzas in the same building, the Willoughby Tower at 8 South Michigan Avenue, because he didn't want Karzas "to feel that I was using his office as a focal point for my purpose."[6]

One of Lou's successful accounts was Kay Kyser's dance band. His responsibility was to create publicity for his client's radio show called *Kay Kyser's Kollege of Musical Knowledge*, a quiz program set to music. When the show surged to success, NBC network radio offered Kyser the opportunity to put the program on their national network. He jumped at the chance and invited Cowan to join him. Lou declined. Instead, he decided to form his own public relations company, and he began attracting business from nonprofit and Christian organizations such as the Methodist Church, the Christmas Seal drive of Chicago, and the Moody Bible Institute. He had changed his name to Cowan in 1931 when he graduated from the University of Chicago, not because he was trying to conceal or deny his religious background, but "so that he would seem more American, less obviously Jewish." (In the 1930s it was difficult for Jews to break into the communications industry.)

He produced three other radio shows for his clients during the next few years after his work with Kyser. Lou was fascinated with quiz shows, so when someone approached him with a workable idea for another quiz program he worked out the details of the program with him and helped induce a company to sponsor it. Called *Musico*, the program amounted to a "watered down" Bingo on the air. Next came a program Lou called *Play Broadcast*. Listeners were to identify famous personalities, musical compositions, and quotations from literature. They put their answers on blank cards and returned them by mail. Next there was his quiz program called *Who Said It?* The program used famous sayings and advertising slogans to test listeners' memories. Lou described it as "the first radio show to put a good advertising copywriter on a par with Shakespeare."[7] After producing those four radio programs, he decided that he liked producing radio programs better than creating public relations campaigns, so he began to think about how to develop his own radio property. Eventually, he formed a radio production company. Still, he continued working on his publicity accounts even after he was fully immersed in producing radio shows.

As he began thinking seriously about creating a new radio show, he turned to John Lewellen to get his opinion about some ideas he had. Once Lou started thinking creatively, ideas flowed from him in a gush. John knew what to expect when he went into Lou's office. No matter how excited Lou was about a new project, his demeanor and appearance were reassuring. Always bespectacled, he hid nothing. One could easily peer into his eyes. They were bright and inquisitive, shadowing great curiosity. His physical appearance was commanding. He stood six feet three inches and was solid. He was always fashionably well dressed, exuding an air of dependability and at the same time a sense of tranquility. Beneath that calm exterior, he was usually percolating ideas. Still, he was a man who was described as being unruffled and self-assured years later by people who knew him.[8] No one who worked for him ever saw him lose his temper or make impossible demands.[9]

There was a good reason that Lou frequently asked for John's thoughts. Lewellen was a writer and a key member of Cowan's staff. Before he started working for Lou, he was a writer on the editorial staff in the Chicago office of *Time-Life-Fortune* magazines. Born in Gaston, Indiana, in the same year as Cowan, his father was a farmer and his maternal forebears were small-town merchants. After attending Ball State College in Muncie, he began his career as a reporter on the staff of the *Muncie Evening Press*. Just as Lou was, John was determined to learn as much as he could about his chosen profession and the techniques of being a newspaper reporter. He continued working in Muncie for eight years, and in 1937 he went to work for *Time* in Chicago. One year later he joined the staff at Cowan Productions, where his background as a newspaper reporter was a valuable asset, not only in writing press releases, but eventually in recasting questions submitted by the radio audience for *QK*, to make the questions more concise and interesting. Eliza Hickok was effusive about John's talent: "When we were stuck, trying to solve the problem of how to present a particularly difficult question submitted, John always had the best solution. He was intelligent, practical, and easy to work with."[10]

Once John, Eliza, and Rachel Stevenson had created the questions, John and Eliza would enhance the questions, turning them into intriguing and imaginative problems for the Kids. To make the questions interesting, often John and Eliza would rewrite them with an attention-getting introduction, which they called a "lead-in." For example, a listener's simple (but difficult) question might be: "What is Arachnida?" John and Eliza would change it to suggest that the listener had read a book called *Arachnida* that followed the fortunes of 30 American families. What was this listener reading about? The answer is that the book was about the 30 families of American spiders. Arachnida is a class of arthropoda that includes spiders.[11]

The questions for the Kids were frequently relevant to a current event that was the theme of a program. John's contribution to a listener's question often gave it a new perspective, and if the Kids couldn't answer it, the listener received the Zenith radio reward for stumping them. An example of this modification might be how John and his staff could temper a question to fit a common theme on a program. When a listener had submitted a difficult question — *What was George Washington's password at the battle of Trenton?* — it was challenging enough. After adding the creative twist, Joe asked the Kids on an Easter Sunday broadcast the recast question: *The words St. Patrick are associated with the date March 17 every year. Then why were the words St. Patrick important on December 25 in the year 1776?* Clearly this was a question that required an answer that came from broad knowledge about American history. Within a few seconds one of the Kids answered, correctly: *Well, that was the battle of Trenton and George Washington used St. Patrick as his password.*

Sometimes there would be some humor, even outrageous puns, that John and Eliza injected into questions. On the same Easter Sunday program, Joe asked the Kids: *If you overheard a man say the following things it would remind you of the name of what Irish city: 2, 4, 8, and 16?* The Kids had the answer. *The city is Dublin, because he's doublin' his numbers.*[12]

When Lou moved to New York to work for Armed Forces Radio during the war, John remained in Chicago and ran the *Quiz Kids* office and the program. Lou promoted him to executive producer of *QK*. Eventually, he served in the same role on other programs produced by Cowan's Chicago production company. As well as his executive and script writing roles for Lou, Lewellen had the freedom to create his own ideas. He produced educational recordings and branched out to begin writing books that primarily explained science to children in an entertaining way. After *QK* went off the air he continued working for Cowan. He ultimately began working as a freelance writer and producer.

As sophisticated as Lewellen was, Joe Kelly, the Chief Quizzer, seemed to be just the opposite. Joe claimed that he didn't understand the questions, and certainly not the answers. He may not have exhibited the outer patina of formal education, but he did understand children and how to relate to them, and that talent was more important than being an intellectual. This quality was apparent when Lou and his team compared Joe's audition with those who preceded him.

Indeed, Joe was different. He was 39 years old in June 1940 and had been in show business ever since he was eight. He had worked extensively with children in his career, sometimes as a master of ceremonies at a children's party or on radio as host of a children's program. Joe had a gentle disposition; children liked him, and he liked them. Even before he began working on *QK*, his rise to prominence and fame in radio was not because of any qualifications as a result of his formal education, in fact, to the contrary. His cheerful nature and tact in handling the Quiz Kids brought about his national fame in radio. For most people in the general audience, both at home and in the studio, he was the only identifiable member of the production staff.

Joe was born in Crawfordsville, Indiana (about 50 miles from Indianapolis). When he was a boy he was a gifted, but untrained, soprano. When he was six years old, his mother entered him in an amateur contest at a theatre in Indianapolis. Joe sang "The Holy City" in a tear-jerking soprano voice and won the $5.00 first prize.[13] His father, a brewery truck driver, died when Joe was about to enter fourth grade in elementary school. His mother did not have enough money, or a job, to support the family. She decided that Joe's singing talent might produce some financial support.[14] Fortunately, George White, the manager of the Crawfordsville Music Hall, agreed. He hired Joe to sing "Down by the Old Mill Stream" to accompany lantern slides showing the old mill and the stream, a young man wearing a celluloid collar, and a beautiful starry-eyed girl in a fluffy white dress. White paid Joe three dollars a night. Shortly after, Edward Doyle, the manager of a touring theatrical stock company, offered to hire him as a featured member of his show. Doyle planned to feature him and call him "Master Joe Kelly, the Irish Nightingale."[15] When Joe heard that, he accepted the offer. With that, he ended his formal education, having completed third grade.

Doyle paid him $50 a week. This was a large salary in 1909. In comparison, the average weekly salary for bank employees in America in 1909 was approximately $14.80.[16] Kelly's salary was certainly another tempting reason to entice him to leave school, given his family's economic distress. Always on tour, Joe lived in small-town, shabby hotels. He furthered his education in practical ways: paying his hotel charges taught him basic math, writing letters home to his mother helped him with fundamental communication skills, reading "dime novels" (with the help of a dictionary) offered additional help in building his vocabulary and learning how to write in a more sophisticated manner.

He was so successful in his role with Doyle's company that three years later, by the time he was 11, he left the show for a new job with Neil O'Brien's minstrels. His new job came with a new salary: $75 weekly, a 50 percent increase (whereas the average for banking industry employees had risen to $17.06, only a 15 percent increase. In Joe's mind, being a song "seller" was more lucrative than being a bank teller). Doyle billed him as the "youngest minstrel in America." There was a 16-piece orchestra accompanying him when he performed.

Of course, the inevitable happened. Joe became a teenager, with the predictable cracking and changing of his voice. His career as a boy soprano was over. Moving back to Indiana, he got a job as an office boy for the Singer Sewing Machine Company.[17] He was no longer a star, but he remained optimistic as he would be throughout his life when given encouragement. During his lunch hour at Singer, he learned how to play the piano by going to the sheet music department of "five-and-ten" stores to listen to one of the music department staff playing them on the piano with the lyrics sung aloud by either the pianist or a singer to promote the sale of the sheet music.[18]

Somehow, Joe learned how to play the saxophone, too. He learned songs note by note, phrase by phrase, and played them from memory. His rote saxophone playing was born from necessity; he couldn't read music. His motivation for learning music, coupled with his ability to memorize and retain information, was a clue to the fact that Kelly was not as "dumb" as he proclaimed, or as newspaper articles portrayed him when he was the Chief Quizzer. He continued to have a prodigious memory as an adult. Upon reflection, Cynthia Cline Newgarden thinks that Joe was a canny and intelligent man. "His so-called dumb character was a role he defined for himself or perhaps Lou Cowan designed for him," she speculated.[19]

Joe's ability to remember information was an astonishing parallel to the same ability that characterized the Kids. What made the Quiz Kids so unusual was their ability to memorize general facts casually, without any prescribed goals. They would retain and remember information that they had read for long periods of time, and thus they would be able to answer those difficult questions with amplification based on things they had read and stored in their memories. Yet they were low-key about their ability to remember information and equally as understated about how they learned.

On one of the first programs, Van Dyke nonchalantly recited the chemical formula for TNT and a few minutes later described accurately the origin of the phrase "Fifth Column." Eliza and the staff were amazed. Later, they asked him where he got this information. "Oh, I read it in a Chicago newspaper a couple of days ago," was his blasé reply.[20]

Cynthia was equally as understated nearly 70 years after her time as one of the Quiz Kids, while doing a particularly difficult crossword puzzle in the *New York Times*— it was a Thursday, so the puzzle had arrived at the upper levels of difficulty. The *Times* crossword puzzle editor designs them to be more intricate and difficult each day, culminating in the most complicated of all each Saturday. That Thursday, she quickly answered the clue that simply asked for the "world's largest particle physics lab." She knew it immediately and entered the word "CERN," with a pen, of course. When asked how she knew it, she replied, unceremoniously, "Oh, I read it somewhere."[21]

Joe put his abilities with memory to good use, too, when he was a young man. Enthusiastic about the possibilities of a new career in show business, after a brief and cursory musical education and while continuing his "matriculation" at his self-created five-and-dime store music school, Joe couldn't wait to get started. He formed his own dance band, while still in his teens, called Kelly's Klowns. Surprisingly, he was somewhat successful. Then, when he was 17, he returned to the stage as an actor playing juveniles. He toured with acting companies and with a permanent stock company in Canada.

Years later he kept his music talent alive even while working full time as a broadcaster. In 1942 he wrote, and had published, a song about the Quiz Kids: "Just Ask the Quiz Kids." He wrote several other popular songs, which appear to be mostly lachrymose, and apparently reflective of his years as a youthful Irish tenor: "Kelly Blues," "Lonesome and Grieving," "Dear Little Girl," and "Gold Star Mother of Mine," as well as one that tied in to his emcee duties on a children's show, "Jolly Joe's Official Birthday Song," and the patriotic "Hats Off to Old Glory." Among his other creative accomplishments he drew a cartoon strip, *Jolly Joe's Pet Pals*, and was a radio script writer.

He married Mary James when he was 23, promising her that he would leave show business. After a series of unsuccessful ordinary jobs, he augmented his income by playing in a dance band in the evening. He and a friend formed a comedy singing act that was on local radio in Battle Creek, Michigan. Five years later, in 1930, he moved to Chicago for a job at WLS as an announcer. He was on an early morning program telling corny jokes to an audience of farmers. Subsequently, he became the popular master of ceremonies on *National Barn Dance* on WLS, which was handled by the Wade Agency, too.

Before Joe auditioned for the Chief Quizzer's job, Lou presumed that he wouldn't be suitable. He wanted someone who had the intellectual capacity to match the erudition of the Kids. Walter Wade disagreed. He pointed out that Joe had the common touch that audiences could relate to when faced with juvenile intellects that were mentally threatening to the majority of the audience in the studio and at home. When Lou acquiesced and observed Joe's performance on the first few broadcasts, he was surprised and delighted. Joe's low-key personality and gentle demeanor were perfect for the youngsters. The Kids felt completely comfortable with him.

However, Beardsley, agreeing that Joe's manner with the Kids was right, still wasn't as sure about his intellectual abilities. He kept Joe on a trial arrangement with his "contract" apparently renewable for just two weeks, but only if Beardsley was convinced that he was right for the job. This Damoclean environment lasted for at least six weeks after the show debuted, even when it was apparent to everyone — executives at Miles, Walter Wade, John Lewellen, and Lou Cowan — that Joe and the show were a hit.[22]

As understanding and gentle-mannered as Joe was, he would rein in the Kids when their answers became too long-winded. And as warm, kindhearted,

Joe Kelly (courtesy Eliza Hickok Kesler).

and easy going as he was, he was decisive when necessary. Broadcasts were live, not on tape, as is the common practice now; there was no playback during the scheduled air time, so they couldn't edit them before airing. But Joe knew how to edit material while the show was on air. It was as if he had an internal stopwatch always ticking.

If the Kids became involved in a difficult question, with all of them trying to figure out the answer, the conversation was sometimes a boisterous jockeying, each of them eager to make a significant contribution, if not the right answer completely. If they weren't sure of the answer to a difficult question, their enthusiasm was not abated, but often more vigorous. When they knew the answer, each might contribute detailed information breathlessly with amplification of the correct answer. Joe would have to tell them that they spent too much time with that one solution, and that day's program might reach a point when it looked as if it would run over its allotted time. Joe would gently chide the youngsters, but he was not a strict disciplinarian, stifling them and repressing their natural exuberance.

Then he would move the program forward, gracefully. If necessary he would cut the Kids short, acquiescing to the need to end that broadcast with the scheduled commercial for Alka-Seltzer, rather than having the show run late without a closing commercial, and the subsequent possibility of being cut off automatically by NBC to keep on schedule. Joe made those decisions firmly and calmly. He was a well-liked schoolmaster who knew how to discipline the Kids without causing any resentment from them.

He was decisive in his personal life, too — a man quick to act. On the night of April 21, 1947, two men broke into his Chicago apartment. Joe was sitting in the darkened living room of his first-floor apartment with his wife and son, discussing plans for his son's upcoming wedding. Joe said that he and his wife often sat in their living room without lights, with a night light on in the central hallway. When they heard glass breaking in the kitchen, they sat quietly for a moment. Then Joe asked his son, Joseph Jr., to get their two revolvers from a bedroom while he started for the kitchen. Joe Jr. returned with the guns and handed his father a .38 caliber revolver containing four cartridges just as Kelly Sr. opened the door of a pantry leading into the kitchen. He saw one man, who had jimmied open a window to enter, standing in the kitchen. The burglar had knocked two tumblers off a shelf onto the floor, breaking them. That was the noise that the Kellys had heard from their living room. When Joe entered the kitchen, the other burglar was still on the back porch, about to walk in through the kitchen door that his partner had opened from the inside. Joe fired all four bullets in his gun at the two men. The burglars fled before Joe Jr. could fire his fully loaded gun. They found one of the burglars dead in the yard of an adjoining building. The other got away. There was a trail of blood in the areaway alongside Kelly's apartment building. The police concluded that it was Joe's shots that wounded the fleeing intruder.[23] A coroner's jury absolved Kelly of blame in the shooting, calling it justifiable homicide.[24]

Joe's eventual dominance as the quizmaster did not come easily. His difficulty with understanding the questions and the answers was an ongoing pitfall for him. Eight months after the debut broadcast, Joe was still a negative in some circles. Lucy Milligan, the president of the National Council of Women of the United States, wrote a brief letter to Margaret Cuthbert, the director of women's and children's programs for NBC. Milligan praised the idea of *QK*, writing, "The children are marvelous and I think the idea of having such exceptional young people on the air is excellent." She was not so enthusiastic about Joe. She and her organization's radio chairman thought that Joe "is decidedly not the person to conduct the program. It is obvious that the children are mentally superior to him." She concluded that the council "cannot endorse the program as we would gladly do if it had a different master of ceremonies." She wanted Joe fired and threatened that if he continued, "our standards would not permit us to publicize it among our groups."[25]

Margaret Cuthbert sent Milligan's letter to Sidney N. Strotz, NBC's vice president in charge of programs. Strotz replied with a memo to Cuthbert saying that he had had a conversation with Lucy Mulligan about Joe before, and concurred with Milligan. He informed the agency and the client about it. "However," he wrote, "they seem to be satisfied and they are paying the bill." He must have had that communication with Wade Advertising and Miles Laboratories by phone. Milligan's letter caused Strotz to think about Joe again. The potential loss of an influential audience was important to this radio executive, important enough that this time he decided to write to Walter Wade, telling him, "I am confident we can secure the support of the National Council of Women, as well as other similar groups, of this program if they could see their way clear to change the M C."[26] Apparently Wade ignored Strotz, or perhaps he rebutted him orally. There is no correspondence about this. Undoubtedly, he countered Strotz successfully. Joe remained.

Joe's difficulty with his lack of formal education appeared to ease over time. There may have been several cries from the audience about his intellectual flubs, but there are no damning letters from large, influential groups. As prescribed by Beardsley, the production staff had the responsibility to give Joe some tutorial help to prepare him for each broadcast. Every week, when the staff had completed the upcoming show's questions, he met with Eliza Hickok, the chief researcher for the program, for coaching sessions. They met on Tuesday and Wednesday afternoons. She explained the questions and the answers to Joe. Then she coached him on avoiding all the possible errors that might erupt. Eliza described these sessions as "hilarious affairs." She would assume the roles of all five Quiz Kids, and give Joe the wrong answers to the questions scheduled for that week.[27] Even though he needed her coaching every week, Joe's contribution to the program as a friendly and trusted quizmaster trumped his discomfort with erudite material.

There were other contributions Joe made. During the planning for each week's program, John, Eliza, and Joe would meet with several staff members

At the start of each week the staff reviewed the last broadcast and started planning the next. (From left) Rachel Stevenson, John Lewellen, Riley Jackson, Joe Kelly, Roby Hickok (courtesy Eliza Hickok Kesler).

at the Wade Agency to review the questions that she and Rachel Stevenson had selected and edited for the program that week. This was a conference held weekly, filled with "ideas, suggestions, criticisms." Often, Joe's experience working with children gave him a unique ability to offer a better idea about how to ask a question on the program.[28] He was, after all, a professional broadcaster — a well-seasoned announcer and emcee.

Lou hired Eliza to be on the *QK* staff in October 1940, a few months after the initial broadcast. But she had been an unofficial member of the staff for several weeks leading up to her being hired.

She was born and raised in Cedar Rapids, Iowa. Her father taught political science at Coe College, a local and well-respected school. When Eliza was in elementary school, some 25 years earlier, she and a group of her friends had formed an unofficial group of bird lovers they called the Zoo Gang. Her friends gave her a nickname, Rosebud, but soon shortened it to Roby. The nickname stuck throughout her life. She encouraged it. Remarkably, when she was an old woman, practically everyone who knew her still called her Roby, even those who knew her casually. A young waitress at her country club's restaurant, where she dined frequently even at the age of 95, referred to her as Roby.[29] Naturally, all her colleagues at the office used her nickname. Some of the Quiz Kids did, too.

When she was a student at Coe, she majored in journalism and wrote freelance articles as a college correspondent for the hometown newspaper, the *Cedar Rapids Gazette*. Upon graduation in 1931 she worked as an attendance clerk at McKinley junior high school in Cedar Rapids, where the soon-to-be-famous artist Grant Wood was the art teacher. Eventually the *Gazette* hired her as a staff reporter, feature writer and women's editor. She stayed for three years. In 1938 she moved to Chicago to matriculate at the prestigious Medill School of Journalism at Northwestern University where she earned her master's in journalism. She earned her degree in the summer of 1940. In August she began looking for a job in publicity, finding that the sidewalks of Chicago could be "as hard on one's morale as on shoe leather. The only difference," she reported caustically, "is that you can get your shoes resoled while you wait."[30]

One day she saw a job possibility advertised in the newspaper that interested her. The listing was at Louis Cowan Productions, so she went to the office on South Michigan Avenue. Lou had had a sign painter put the words "Quiz Kids" on the door just below "Louis G. Cowan & Company." Roby didn't know what "Quiz Kids" meant. Joe Bailey interviewed her, and although he was impressed with her samples of her writing, did not offer her a job. Instead, he speculated that they might need a person who was comfortable doing research because "the girl who is doing it now may leave for New York."[31] Although it was not the work that she was looking for — she wanted to work as a publicity writer — Bailey had offered a glimmer of hope, and it was heartening. Roby knew that she had to face reality: jobs in broadcasting and advertising were almost nonexistent. It was true that the economy was beginning to turn around after the Depression; nonetheless, the national unemployment rate was still at nearly 15 percent in 1940.[32] It didn't matter if she didn't get an ideal job initially as long as it held the real possibility of reaching her goal.

Meanwhile, at Bailey's request, she sent him a letter that was both her résumé and job application. In it, she wrote not only about her experience as the publicity director for both the Community Chest and the Junior League of Cedar Rapids, but also about her background in working with children in Cedar Rapids, when she presented and explained educational films to 10,000 school children in 28 public schools in Cedar Rapids.[33] Bailey was impressed with her. He wrote a note to Lou Cowan attached to her letter, saying that he had interviewed her and he thought she had an "excellent background; good personality.... We might keep this on tap for when and if."[34] When Lou read Bailey's memo, undoubtedly he felt the strike of a sympathetic chord with Roby; her interests and experience with children and education, publicity and public relations, were similar to his own. It was an uncanny confluence of empathy and opportunity.

At the end of Roby's interview with Bailey, he told her that she should return in about two weeks. She saw this as an encouraging sign and was thrilled. She didn't (or couldn't) wait; she was excited about this prospect. She returned in ten days.

Then Roby began going to the *Quiz Kids* office nearly every day, agreeing to help (without pay) wherever needed; she was too shy to ask for compensation.[35] Finally, Lou hired her as a full-time staff member. Bailey and Lewellen defined her job, assigning her to multiple responsibilities. Her primary duty was to select questions from a pool submitted by the program's listeners for Joe to ask the Kids on air.[36] Shortly, she became an integral part of the staff, and in less than three years Bailey promoted her from chief researcher to assistant program director. From the beginning Roby juggled a variety of duties — writing publicity and press releases (the job she really wanted), re-writing questions to ask the Kids on air, and researching the answers. Naturally, when listeners sent in questions, they included the answers. Still, Roby had to be sure that the answers were correct and think of all the possible answers to a question so that Joe would know whether the Kids were right or wrong.

Researching answers was not an easy task. There were no computers and search engines to provide detailed information in an instant. This research was particularly difficult if they had to write a new show when they traveled. They carried research materials with them, looking like a "modern Parnassus on wheels." It was part of the planning to take two typewriters and encyclopedias, Bible concordances, history and literature books, and world almanacs. If Roby and John or Rachel needed further details, they would call local sources: libraries, newspaper offices, Bible schools, universities, and chambers of commerce. Even in Chicago they would call the public library, specialty magazine editors, and faculty at the University of Chicago. It appears that they used these sources frequently enough that their contacts became friendly colleagues.[37]

A simple answer to a question submitted for use on air was never sufficient, because Joe needed extra information at his fingertips. The Kids were encouraged to amplify on a simple answer to a question. Often they amplified anyway, without any prodding from Joe. So, for Roby this meant that thorough research on the answers and some surrounding information was required. For example, if the question was "Who was the Prime Minister of England during the American Revolution?" Joe would need to have a full explanation. More than knowing that the minimal answer was Lord North, he should have "the dates that he lived, his attitude toward the Colonies, and a brief sketch of the American Revolution." But Joe needed to know even more. "If the children happened to tell who preceded and followed Lord North, and about King George III and Queen Charlotte, and the taxation on the Colonies, Joe would have that information" on his answer card.[38] Roby was humorously self deprecating about her role on the staff, describing her status in the organizational hierarchy as "low man on the factotum pole."[39]

Once she had completed her research she wrote the final questions, then

John edited them. Finally Roby turned to the most important duty, tutoring Joe Kelly to help him with pronouncing words he didn't know and with questions and answers for the program airing that week. In addition to those two important responsibilities, Roby had the task of serving as a nurturing but punitive "den mother" to the Kids both in the studio and during their many personal appearances.[40] They turned to her when they had questions. They expressed their fears to her, and needed comforting when they were feeling uncertain or sad. She also had to calm down any of them if they were in the middle of a childhood temper tantrum. She traveled with them when they went to other cities to broadcast the program. She was both their confidante and their authority figure. Sixty years later, at her death, Joel Kupperman, considered by some (even Roby) to be the most memorable of the Kids, recalled her wit and her charm as a fond memory.[41]

Roby needed help shouldering all these responsibilities. She got it when Rachel Stevenson joined the staff to research the correct answers to the submitted questions and, of course, to add details in case the Kids offered supplementary information to direct answers. This research was invaluable to Joe Kelly and to the staff who decided the validity of the answers while on air in order to tally the final scores at the end of each program.

Rachel was born in Cody, Wyoming, in 1906 and graduated from Rice University in Houston with a degree in liberal arts. She was involved with a professional players' production at the University of Chicago, where her husband was "stationed." Her abilities impressed her colleagues so much that they thought that she should work full time in theatre, professionally. She replied that she "didn't want any job unless it's fun."[42] So her allies took it upon themselves to recommend her to Lou Cowan. Lou called Rachel and described *QK* and the children. Rachel considered the possibility of working on the production staff. As she began thinking about her potential career change she saw a cartoon depicting the oracles in ancient Greece. They used children as oracles because they were innocent and had no pre-formed political ideas. It was a subtle coincidence. She thought the child-oracles were just like the Quiz Kids: adults asked the children questions and the Kids answered them.[43] She wrote a letter to Lou describing the child-oracles. She also sent him a copy of a book about the methodology of academic research. She thought the submitted questions weren't always intriguing enough for use on radio; they had to rewrite or edit them. "We had to make them interesting," she recalled.[44] Lou hired her to work under Roby doing research about the submitted questions. As well as researching questions and their answers, Rachel helped select suitable Kids from the pool of prospects that Roby and John interviewed and tested.

of the questions were, they had to balance them with humor. Used as a subliminal tool, the humor helped to keep the show interesting and light-hearted so that formal education would be more acceptable to a mass at-home audience. Just as school teachers do in a public school classroom, they made the learning interesting, entertaining, and appealing to the Kids and adults who were listening at home, thus subtly encouraging and promoting the value of education to a large heterogeneous audience. The subliminal message was that retention of sophisticated knowledge was acceptable, and therefore so were the children — "the eggheads" — who displayed their erudition. Nonetheless, Rachel came to a different conclusion about *QK*. She thought that "it was strictly an entertainment program. It was for adults, rather than for children. People liked the idea of seeing smart children answer [difficult] questions."45

☞ *To raise a number to the 5th power you multiply it by itself four times. The 5th power of 2 is 2 times 2 times 2 times 2, or 32. And the figure 2 is the 5th root of 32. What is the 5th root of 4 billion, 954 million, 209 thousand, 207?*

When Rachel arrived for her interview with Lou, he wasn't in. Instead, Joe Bailey interviewed her, just as had Roby. Bailey, Lou Cowan's *éminence grise*, was Lou's friend during their university days. After he earned his undergraduate degree Joe enrolled in law school, graduating with a specialty in radio law (now called entertainment law). He joined a law firm in Chicago, but Lou wanted Bailey to work for him. It made sense for Lou to hire Bailey, to advise him on legal matters and eventually to work as his office manager, too. Lou trusted Joe and his judgment explicitly. Bailey's duties covered a wide range, some of them everyday tasks. He managed the staff, was the director of human resources, wrote or reviewed legal contracts, and wrote letters to the kids informing them of the details of upcoming travel or any payments due to them in addition to their war bond earnings. Because of Bailey's legal education and his role as a trusted employee, he was an important member of the close-knit top echelon of staff who worked behind the scenes with Lou to set policy and make other major decisions.

Other key players behind the scenes were the advertising agency's directors and copywriters, who wrote the Alka-Seltzer commercials (delivered live on air). In those days, advertising agencies played a significant part in producing and directing the radio shows that their clients sponsored. One outstanding producer at Wade was Forrest Owen. In later years Owen downplayed his duties for the *QK* programs. But in that era of live broadcasting, his job was essential. "Even though my title was producer, my duties were almost mechanical. I had to make sure we got on the air on time, and off at the right time, considering the fact that the commercials were live and that the Kids were unscripted," he recalled.

Forrest had a long and illustrious career in broadcasting and advertising. When he came to Chicago to find work he had difficulty landing a job at a radio station as an announcer, so he decided to go into production.[46] He subsequently found a job in Toledo as a radio production manager, and eventually went to work for a small advertising agency there. He had moved to Toledo to learn his craft, always with Chicago in mind. From Toledo he was able to get a job working for Walter Wade's agency in Chicago.

He was 24 when Wade hired him as a replacement for a producer who was leaving to serve in the army. Wade made it clear that when the former producer came back, Owen would be out of a job. Wade assigned him to produce *Quiz Kids*. In those days the title of producer was misleading. "Lou Cowan was the real producer," Owen explained. He said that if he had the same duties on a radio program today as he had had on *QK*, his job title would be program director.[47]

Forrest Owen did a good job with *QK*, outstanding enough so that the Wade Agency promoted him. They gave him the responsibility of moving to the West Coast to produce the *Lum 'n' Abner* program that Miles Laboratories sponsored five nights a week and broadcast from Los Angeles. Far from having to leave his "temporary" job at the end of World War II when the former *QK* producer returned, Owen remained with Wade. He eventually became president of Wade Advertising.

☞ *The hands of a watch stand at 11 o'clock. Forty-eight hours later how many times would the minute hand have passed the hour hand?*

From the beginning, Lou wanted to market *QK* as much as he wanted to get it on the air. He always tied the two concepts of marketing and broadcasting together, so he was determined to find a smart promoter who understood his thinking and could offer creative ways to help. Enter George Kamen. If Joe Kelly knew how to further his career by appearing in key roles on other programs at the same time he was the Chief Quizzer, or by writing songs and radio scripts, George Kamen knew how to promote *QK* to its best advantage.

Kamen had a sterling track record as a merchandiser and licensing guru and was the right promoter to carry out Lou's wishes and to create new marketing and merchandising ideas. As a young man, George went to work for his uncle, Herman "Kay" Kamen. Eventually, Kay charged him with running the European operations for his company. In the spring of 1940, when the Nazis were threatening to invade France and occupy Paris and the rest of the country, George closed the European office in London and its satellite in Paris and moved back to the United States. He worked from Kay's New York office;

shortly thereafter he established his own company with his own clients. George absorbed the techniques and style that his uncle's famous company practiced. He learned well. It was no surprise that when he formed his own company his style emulated that of his uncle and mentor.

Lou hired him to promote the show. George excelled. He exhibited a sparkling creativity when he employed various merchandising, marketing, and licensing deals. He blossomed to be one of the more valuable players behind the scenes for *QK*, but he was never a member of the staff.

Even though his primary duties were as a marketer and merchandiser, Kamen interacted with the Kids, when it was appropriate. He was warm and generous. The Kids liked him. Evidently he was easygoing and avuncular. In an unprompted gesture, Kamen sent Van Dyke Tiers a congratulatory note when he graduated from high school and at the same time received the news that the University of Chicago had accepted him with a full scholarship. Another time George sent a brief bread-and-butter note to Van Dyke along with a box of wooden matches for Tiers to add to his "collection."[48] Tiers recalled that Kamen habitually wore several, sometimes as many as eight, watches at the same time. Often he would wear four wrist watches, a lapel pin that was a watch, a tie clasp watch, cufflinks watches, and other unusual timepieces. Van Dyke was interested in this eclectic display because he was fascinated with watches and how they worked.[49]

Claude Brenner, who "graduated" from *QK* in 1944 and enrolled at MIT, recalls that when he was a young adult he visited George at his New York office. In his conversation with George he expressed his unhappiness with how his classmates at MIT reacted to his having been a Quiz Kid just a few years earlier. He was uneasy about his relationship with his peers at MIT because they made him feel as if he were different than the rest of them (they often called him "Quizzie" as a derogatory nickname). Kamen took exception to Claude's feelings of insecurity. He thought that Brenner should revel in his "difference" and nothing about it should make him feel wary. "You *are* different," said Kamen. "Remain as different as you are, otherwise you'll simply be one of the crowd. If people remember you for your difference, you'll succeed."[50]

Previous to his work for *QK*, George had built strong relationships with department stores and children's clothing manufacturers throughout the United States. He worked with manufacturers of games, too. He learned the fine points of his profession by working for and observing his uncle, Kay, and his outstanding efforts for Walt Disney. Kay Kamen was legendary in the fields of marketing, merchandising, and licensing. Long before he signed an exclusive arrangement in 1932 to merchandise Walt Disney products, he had set a standard in licensing that was unprecedented. His contemporaries often described him as the man who invented product licensing, not just for Disney, but with ideas and techniques that other companies followed with great success.[51] It's little wonder that Lou Cowan wanted to use George Kamen to promote *QK*. George had learned well from his uncle. Lou realized that he brought to retailing the same flair that Bernays brought to public relations. It didn't matter to Lou that George's company was in New York.

By 1940 radio had brought popular culture to a large national audience with speed and immediacy. And that audience was growing. In 1940 there were 52 million radios in homes, offices, and automobiles. Radio had become a universal medium.[52] As well, Lou Cowan aimed his seemingly never-ending stream of ideas at promoting the program with a mix of sophisticated marketing, public relations, and showmanship. The range of experience from the production staff came from their deep understanding of mass culture and communications. Joe Kelly's years in vaudeville and minstrels and his piano playing and song writing were manifestations of the dissemination of popular culture. Roby Hickok's and John Lewellen's prior work as reporters in print media was reflective of their knowledge of mass communications, as was Forrest Owens's on-air directorial work. As refreshing and superb as the brainy Quiz Kids were, they needed the help of marketing and publicity to make *QK* a success. The brains behind the "brains" were essential to building that success.

ANSWERS

The line is from Washington to Cleveland. Cleveland was the president in 1896.

The answer is 87. Richard Williams answered this, correctly, in four seconds. His explanation was: the 5th power of 90 is 5 billion, 904 million, 900 thousand. The 5th power of 80 is 3 billion, 276 million, 800 thousand. So, the answer has to be between 80 and 90. Because the number in the question ends in 7, any number in the 5th power ends in the same number as the number in question. So, the answer is 87.

Forty-four. Between 12 o'clock and 1 o'clock the minute hand doesn't pass the hour hand, so in any 12-hour period, it passes the hour hand only 11 times. Thus, it passes 22 times in 24 hours, and twice that, 44 times, in 48 hours.

3

How to Become a Quiz Kid

☞ *Use other words to describe what you would be doing, if you gave a goober to a gibbon, some pemmican to a ptarmigan, and a wallop to a wapiti?*

After the debut, the staff followed the guidelines for selecting prospective Quiz Kids that Lou established that spring. Now, these guidelines were more important than ever. Before the first broadcast Lou took the suggestions for prospects from Sidney and Pence, and interviewed all of the future Kids himself. Sometimes, as it was with Joan Bishop, the three of them conducted interviews together. But there was a limit to who these three could suggest as potential Kids. Even having Walter Wade and Joe Bailey conducting a search was limiting. As soon as *QK* went on the air Lou and his production team had "a lot of applicants."[1] After the first broadcast there were 250 children asking to be Quiz Kids.[2] During that first year of QK broadcasts "over 50 children a week applied to appear on the show."[3] Of those 50 applicants, Bailey would audition only two. Only one out of 25 who auditioned survived the cut.

Their applications usually came from teachers. Parents rarely wrote about their children. Sometimes children would take the initiative and write about themselves. Of course there was always the unplanned application. Ruth Fisher's father, on a train from Chicago to New York, by chance met Lou, who was on the same train. During their informal conversation, probably about Lou's work, Fisher described his bright daughter, Ruth, concluding that he thought that she would be a stellar Quiz Kid.[4] Lou must have been impressed. Shortly after, in October 1941 Ruth made the first of her six consecutive appearances on *QK*.

At first, Joe Bailey interviewed all the aspirants, and if promising, he would give them a questionnaire to complete. That system didn't last long. When he became swamped with interviews, he changed the sequence and the office would send a questionnaire to all the prospective Kids automatically. Joe reviewed their completed forms. If he thought the questionnaire showed promise, then he would invite for an interview those children who showed the most potential. More than just confirming knowledge of their specialty, Bailey's assessment of the children as would-be panelists included determining the extent of their general knowledge, as well as their ability to react orally, given that they would be answering on live radio. The only strict limitation was that a candidate could not be over 15 years old.[5] With the number of applicants flooding the office weekly, there was no doubt that Lou would not be spending his time interviewing as he did with Joan Bishop and the Kids selected for the first broadcasts, so it was critical for the staff to follow his guidelines for selection. Within a year, John and Roby interviewed prospective Kids, too.

Richard Williams, his parents, and his brother started listening to *QK* just a few weeks after the first broadcast. They were impressed with the scholarly knowledge of the Kids, so Dick, who was ten years old, and Glenn, five years older than Dick, tried to answer some of the questions faster than the Kids on the panel. There was no ulterior motive; they just wanted to compete for the fun of it. Evidently Dick did well as they tried to outdo the Kids on the radio, but it didn't enter their minds or their parents' to submit his name. Instead, in middle of July 1940, a high school teacher in East Chicago, Indiana, where the Williams family lived, wrote to the *Quiz Kid*s office recommending him.

The letter must have been persuasive, because Dick received a questionnaire from the office at the end of July, just as the family was leaving for a vacation. They were going fishing for walleye pike and smallmouth bass at Lake Itasca in Minnesota. Dick remembers that he "filled the form out hastily and cursorily and my folks didn't give it a look." He took the questionnaire with him as they took off for the lake in the family's new Pontiac. They left home early that day. When they stopped for lunch in Tomah, Wisconsin, he mailed the questionnaire back to Chicago.

It's a long drive from East Chicago to Itasca, and the family, as do many families in the United States, whiled away the time playing mildly competitive games that they devised for lengthy car rides. Usually they were tests of observation. In one, which the two boys called Horses, the object was to count, identify, and categorize by color the number of horses each saw on his side of the road. Another game was to look at signs: billboards, advertisements painted on barns, motor vehicle road signs, even Burma Shave signs, and find as many letters of the alphabet, in sequence, as they could.

On this vacation, Richard's parents tried a new diversion to offset the monotonous 650-mile ride. Richard described it: "This was our first trip with quiz books — books with lists of 20 questions on your choice of subjects, answers in the back. Dad [was] driving, [so] Mom asked the questions from the passenger seat, Glenn and I each wrote down our choice, Mom wrote down hers and Dad's. Mom checked the scores, usually about 19 for her and Dad, 18 for Glenn, 17 for me."

In early August when they returned from Minnesota there was a letter for Dick from Joe Bailey. Joe invited him to come to the *Quiz Kids* office for an interview.

He met with Joe shortly after. It was a brief meeting, only lasting 15 to 30 minutes. If Bailey was interested in him, he didn't say, even though it was a pleasant and friendly conversation. After the meeting Richard received no correspondence about it or any evaluation of his chances of being selected. "But if any actual invitation [to be on the show] was extended it was to my parents, not me," he concluded. A couple of weeks later he heard at the end of a *QK* broadcast the announcer saying that he would be on the following week, September 4. Richard was "flabbergasted and delighted."

He described his first appearance as a Kid. "The kids sat behind school desks facing the emcee [who was] 30 feet across the platform. On my big day, I knew a number of the answers but was too shy to raise my hand high enough for him to see. So he called on other kids."[6] Richard answered only two questions. "I did identify Cotopaxi, an [Ecuadorian] volcano, and what constellation Frank Buck should be identified with — Ursa Major."[7]

As Lou told the story, "Richard was a shy boy and he was hesitant about raising his hand when he had an answer." By the end of the broadcast he was "almost ready to burst into tears."[8] Even with his two answers, the *QK* judges that day — John Lewellen, Roby, Bailey, and Lou — ruled that he didn't score high enough to be invited again.

Polly was furious about that. She thought that Richard hadn't had a fair chance. She insisted that Lou put him on again. Lou didn't want to, but he did it to pacify her. It was the only time when a family discussion altered the decision of the judges. Richard returned seven weeks later. This time, "suitably coached about shooting my arm straight up,"[9] he scored high enough to remain on the panel for six more weeks without losing. After another short break in his appearances, he returned at the beginning of 1941. He blossomed, and became the show's resident math wizard.[10]

During his interview with Bailey, Richard was surprised to see how few people there seemed to be in the office. "There were just Bailey, John Lewellen, Roby, and Lou. I suppose there were some other people there who were clerical. But it was a small office."[11]

Richard's questionnaire was probably simpler than the one that was used two years later. The newer version was comprehensive and had evolved into a document that Roby described as a "cross between an aptitude test and a deed in escrow." No matter how many times it may have been revised during the history of *QK* it attempted to remain current and highly selective. It asked the applicant to list favorite books, hobbies, the subjects he excelled in at school, subjects he had studied beyond the school requirements, the magazines and newspapers he read, the symphonies and operas he knew, his extracurricular activities, offices he had held in school, honors he had won, his favorite sports, and his ambitions. On the last page, he was asked to write a 250-word essay on "Why I Want to Be a Quiz Kid."[12]

☞ *If you were to make a baseball would you know how many seams to put on it?*

When children wrote the initial letter to the *Quiz Kids* office expressing the desire to become a Kid, the letters were sometimes amusing as well as informative. In 1942 Joel Kupperman wrote that he was five years old and he liked to play with numbers. He explained that he could multiply "in his head" any number up to 100 by 98 or 99, that he was facile with fractions, and could determine the average of a list of numbers. He reported that he knew about things other than numbers, but that he liked numbers "the best." He thought it was fun to fall asleep counting numbers every night. He added a postscript, an unintentionally humorous non sequitur, to his essay: "My grandfather has teeth that he takes out at night but he is smart."[13]

Richard Banister answered the questionnaire query that asked if he had ever made radio or other public appearances. He answered yes, but offered details to his reply, writing that he had "said two words in a play for the old ladies' home."[14]

There was more to determining future Kids than grading their questionnaire or an interview with Bailey. There were the intangible aspects of personality clearly defined by Lou. They were looking for bright children, children with self assurance, an upbeat personality, a sense of humor, and an intellectual and social composure, tempered with a large helping of humility. They wanted the children to be charming and unassuming. They didn't want children who were arrogant. A prospective Quiz Kid should have certain qualities. Roby identified seven. What they looked for was "poise, quick thinking, general information, originality, sense of humor, a good voice, and modesty."[15]

The production office was just as emphatic about the characteristics they didn't want. They rejected categorically any children with stage mothers, the so-called Hollywood mothers, who were always trying to push their children ahead in show business. John Lewellen was insistent about that. "We won't take a cocky kid," he said. He included parents in that edict. "Also eliminated were the kids of cocky parents: many were excused because the parents were so 'pushy, predatory, and disruptive' that they were certain to cause trouble."[16]

Rachel Stevenson, who became the chief researcher for the program after a suitable training period with Roby, said that there was something more than intelligence that made up the fabric of a Quiz Kid.

What made a Quiz Kid? The answer came partly from the children's home environment, just as Paul Cowan observed that Lou and Polly encouraged intellectual exploration when he and his siblings were growing up. So it was with the families of the Quiz Kids. Jack Lucal's mother explained that she and her husband encouraged stimulating questions at dinner. Sometimes these conversations became heated debates, often ending with the entire family of four lying prone on the floor with the encyclopedia on the floor, too, opened and spread out as they looked for answers.[17]

There were also immeasurable aspects in the prerequisites for being selected. The staff probed for individuality. "We chose children not only because they were smart, but because they had personality. If they didn't have personality, no matter how smart they were, they weren't Quiz Kids."[18]

Dick Williams seemed to be the exception. With his shy demeanor it was surprising that Joe Bailey wanted him on the show. He must have seen something in Dick's personality that he found appealing. Even before the interview, how do we account for Richard's invitation, given the brief answers he submitted on his questionnaire? Richard wrote that years later Roby remarked to him that she admired Joe Bailey for having invited him in for the interview, given that his questionnaire replies were so sketchy and sparse.[19] Based on his "almost blank questionnaire," Roby thought that Joe Bailey must have had a crystal ball to have foreseen that Dick would eventually become known as "The Super Quiz Kid."[20]

As the selection process evolved it became a well-organized system, with several hurdles established to determine first-rate Kids. After the interview was an audition at an NBC studio staged as an authentic broadcast. Sound engineers tested the voice qualities of the applicants and Bailey spent an hour asking around 150 general questions on history, geography, science and literature, with a few reasoning and trick questions added to replicate a *QK* broadcast. The final test was a two-hour private interview. It was a far cry from Dick's 15 minutes.

As straightforward as the testing process for selection was, some of the children turned it around. When Bailey interviewed Ruth Duskin, she thought it was a game, so she fired riddles back at him. During his first meeting with Bailey, Harve Fischman identified the largest U.S. president as William Howard Taft, saying that he weighed 332 pounds. Then he added to his answer by revealing that Taft once was stuck in his White House bathtub and had to call for help in order to be extricated. As soon as he was rescued he ordered a larger tub to be installed.[21]

With the fertile minds that all the applicants had, Joe Bailey realized soon enough that he could predict that the Kids could be unpredictable, during his selection process and eventually on *QK* broadcasts. That was really his "crystal ball." Throughout the interviews with the prospective Kids, it was as if the sound of Lou slapping his knee during Joan Bishop's interview began to reverberate in Bailey's ears as a signal that told him he had found a new Quiz Kid. Just as Lou had recognized, the predictable unpredictability was exactly what Joe hoped to find.

What made the candidates unusual was their difference in attitude toward learning. For many children, in the Forties and even today, traditional learning is onerous. Too often they don't understand why they have to learn about some seemingly lofty concepts. "Why do I have to study Latin?" they might cry in the 1940s. "What good is reading the poetry of William Blake?" they might ask today; "I want to be a computer programmer." For the Kids, the quest for knowledge, pure and simple, was limitless and self generated. They would try scientific experiments. They read deeply about the subjects that interested them. They had an unusual ability to remember what they read in great detail, and could express those details succinctly and demonstratively. For them, learning was a hobby.

Lou was no longer involved in the everyday details of finding new Kids. He had created the parameters for selection; now he had other things to think about. At the same time that the staff was working hard at finding and selecting Kids, Lou had already moved beyond that. As soon as the program was launched, he started putting more of his ideas into action. Immediately, he turned to George Kamen. Lou's Whirlwind was about to begin.

ANSWERS

Giving a peanut to an ape, feeding compressed dried meat to a bird, and slapping a deer.

There are many stitches on a baseball, but there is just one seam.

4

The Whirlwind Begins

☞ *An automobile and an airplane were having a race. The car averaged 95 miles an hour, the plane flew at 102 miles an hour. The finish line was 190 miles west of the starting line. Which finished first if there was a north wind of 20.09 miles an hour, and would the winner have time to sing "Nearer My God to Thee" before the loser arrived?*

Within a few days after the first broadcast, newspaper and magazine radio columnists in Chicago began to write about the show and to praise it unequivocally. In other cities they were equally ecstatic. Robert Stephan of the *Cleveland Plain Dealer*, in his radio column published the day after the debut of *Quiz Kids*, thought that the knowledge that the Kids had was "amazing." He suggested that the *Information Please* "oldsters" should listen because he thought that the Kids answered some questions that their "elder quiz brothers" might have missed, and that the Kids put the oldsters to shame.[1] It didn't take long to convince him that *QK* was a winner. After listening the following week he called it the "top show find of the summer."[2]

Even more effusive was the *Boston Globe* when it reported that the Kids had clearly changed radio. According to the *Globe*, theretofore radio programs had confined young people in their teens and under to opportunities for routine childish performances. Now, *QK* showed "its adult superiors how to take a brain-twister program by the tail and twist it until it cried Uncle."[3] But critics are critics, and usually they find something to criticize. The *Billboard* was delighted with the program but offered a negative appraisal when they speculated that the producers might have given the Kids the answers beforehand. Nonetheless, they modified their conclusion by saying that they had "reliable assurance" that the show was legitimate and that the Kids were aboveboard.[4]

Perhaps *Billboard* simply did not believe the unqualified admiration for the show expressed by Norman Siegel, who wrote the daily radio column for the *Cleveland Press*. Siegel thought that the Kids were offering palpable competition to *Information Please*. Writing just one week after the debut of the show, he reported to his readers that 7-year-old Gerard Darrow with his knowledge of birds outshone John Kieran, considered by some to be the most well-informed panelist on *Information Please*. He thought that the only flaw in *QK* was using Joe Kelly as the Chief Quizzer because Kelly's track record in radio defined him as a popular middle-brow moderator, and not very well educated. *Time* magazine went even farther in their description of Kelly's low-brow demeanor. They referred to him as a "*National Barn Dance* hayseed."[5] Siegel, suggesting a replacement for Kelly, thought that "somewhere in Chicago there must be a 10- or 12-year-old" who could put the Kids through their mental paces.

Of course, Siegel didn't analyze correctly the subtlety behind Joe Kelly's role. He didn't know or understand Walter Wade's reason for having a Chief Quizzer like Joe. Walter reasoned that Joe was someone with whom audiences could identify, given the barrage of detailed knowledge spewing forth from the children. Their seemingly casual erudition was simply intoxicating as well as possibly intimidating to adults. But this intimidation, real or imagined, could have destroyed their interest in listening to the show. It could turn them off, and they might turn off the show. Nonetheless, despite his mildly negative criticism, Siegel preached to his readers that they should listen to it and learn a "few things you should have known years ago."[6]

Then, Siegel reversed himself. Six weeks after writing this enthusiastic praise of the program and the children, he expressed his doubts about the validity of the show. He thought that the Kids might have known the answers before they went on air and that they had rehearsed the questions and answers.

He based his conclusion on the fact that during the August 16 show, Gerard Darrow answered one part of a three-part question about how to determine the age of various living things in nature: turtles, trees, horses, and rattlesnakes. Asking a three-part question was customary. Frequently, Joe would assign a different Kid to answer each part. More than one of them raised their hands to answer the question. They were all so eager to answer. Joe had a choice. By directing each part to a different Kid, Joe was keeping the program lively because that there was some variety in the answers. He kept the show democratic. He spread the opportunity to answer among several Kids, and thus, extend the final scoring more evenly.

For the question about establishing the ages, Gerard only answered the part about turtles, explaining how to verify their age by examining the placement and combination of spots on their under-shells.[7] Just before the show went off the air, Joe Kelly complimented Gerard on his knowledge. But Gerard, always forthright, said that he knew the man who submitted the question. Siegel must have heard the program with Darrow's enlightening answer and his subsequent casual identification of the source of the question. Suddenly, he was skeptical. In fact, the next day, August 17, he wrote about his suspicion in his usual column but with the section about Darrow set in sobering bold face type to get his readers' attention. He cautioned that he and "a number of other dialers [listeners]" had serious doubts about the whether *QK* was as unrehearsed as it claimed to be.[8]

Siegel wasn't the only disbeliever. Rita Danforth of St. Louis, Missouri, wrote a letter to *Movie and Radio Guide* expressing her curiosity about Gerard's slip and offering her opinion. She heard Gerard's admission. She said that she knew other people who thought that someone must have fixed the program. However, Danforth still believed that *Quiz Kids* was really "on the square." Responding to her letter, the editor of the magazine assured her that Darrow's slip did not imply that the show was dishonest.[9]

When Lou Cowan read Siegel's critical column he phoned him and invited him to come to Chicago at the expense of the show, so that he could do as much reportorial investigation as he wished to support or renounce his doubts. Siegel came to Chicago and observed the pre-show rehearsal and warm-up as well as the show itself for August 23, exactly one week following Gerard's innocent remark. Using the word rehearsal could have been misleading. The rehearsal did not include questions for the program. Jeff Wade of the Wade agency, Walter's son, led the rehearsal, which consisted of the opening and closing of the program, performed by the announcer and Joe Kelly. It included the announcer's recitation of the Alka-Seltzer commercials for the show.[10]

The entire rehearsal period started 30 minutes before the show went on air, with its goal of getting proper voice levels, achieved by having the Kids and Joe do a little informal bantering. It was also a technique that allowed the Kids and Joe to get reacquainted and comfortable, especially important when there were new Kids on that week's program. The last few minutes of the rehearsal were devoted to having Joe ask the Kids two or three difficult warm-up questions.[11] These general questions were comparable to those that Joe would ask them on the show. There was no relation to the specific things that he would ask during the actual broadcast. This question-and-answer session was to create the environment of the program, and to get the Kids ready. The staff had to be sure that nothing that they used in the warm-up session would be on that day's broadcast or any other *Quiz Kids* broadcast in the future. After they used them, Roby kept the questions in a reference file so that they wouldn't repeat them during future warm-up rehearsals or actual broadcasts.[12]

Siegel also sat with Joe Bailey during the broadcast and assisted him with the scoring. He went back to Cleveland, probably Saturday. His column for

Joe always put the Kids at ease. (From left) Joe Kelly, Van Dyke Tiers, Ruth Gloria Fisher, Harve Fischman, Julia Marwick, Mary McHugh (courtesy Quiz Kids, Inc.).

Monday, August 26, changed his disbelieving comments about the show in his earlier column. He wrote a new column devoted entirely to *Quiz Kids*, this time citing his observations and his role as temporary assistant to Joe Bailey. He offered this as proof that he had no doubt about the show's authenticity in his description of the August 26 broadcast. In fact, his column was most admiring of Gerard and his knowledge as he humorously juxtaposed his precocious erudition with his dismissal of the mundane acts of daily life, citing the fact that at the age of eight Gerard still couldn't tie his own shoelaces.[13]

Even during the planning stages of the program Lou anticipated that audiences would question its authenticity, especially after hearing the reactions from various prospective sponsors. So, he invited several prominent educators, unimpeachable in their professional stature and ethics, to be guests on the program. These guest speakers not only vouched for the honesty of the program, but reinforced its value in the process of educating children. Still, audiences were amazed at how the Kids answered questions; they thought they had rehearsed the answers. One listener wrote to ask, "In a country that has a national food and drugs act for inspecting what goes into our stomachs, why isn't there some provision for inspecting what goes into our ears? What do you mean by trying to foist adult child impersonators onto an intelligent radio audience?"[14]

Not as indignant, but certainly just as doubtful, one woman wrote to Lou that she heard Gerard sing verse after verse of "Three Little Fishes" on a *QK* program, with no sign of stopping, apparently ignoring frantic pleas from the production staff for him to end. She didn't seem to be annoyed with the length of his vocalizing; her complaint was about her analysis of what his singing represented. "I thought Gerard's song was so cute, but I don't see how you did it with a child so young," she wrote. "You must have had to rehearse the question and answer for hours!"[15]

Further proof of the authenticity of the unrehearsed nature of the show came on a program one day when just five minutes before airtime, Darrow became ill and could not perform. Fortunately, Richard Williams was present at the broadcast. It was probably John Lewellen who asked him to substitute for Gerard. He did, and earned the second highest score for the day.[16] With Dick's high score coming from his impromptu appearance, it should have been clear to anyone doubting the honesty of *Quiz Kids* that there had been no prior coaching or rehearsal.

Even Siegel's firsthand observation of the program, the reassurance of *Radio and Movie Guide*, and the last-minute stellar performance of Richard Williams when he substituted for an ailing Gerard were not convincing enough for many of the at-home listeners. They continued to believe that the show had a full script, including the questions and answers, and that the Kids knew them beforehand. Of course, there was a script, but it was for Joe's opening and closing statements or any commercial or public service announcements that he made during the broadcast. The program's announcer was primarily responsible for reading the customary opening salutation and closing signature as well as any Alka-Seltzer commercials. Still, some listeners just didn't believe that the Kids, who were so fast with the right answers, were unrehearsed.

Lou had anticipated this reaction. His method of countering this negative feedback, having guest speakers state in well-scripted statements that the programs were unrehearsed, was included in the format even for the June 12 Utley audition. The production team had prepared the way for the persuasive campaign to follow once the actual broadcasts began.

Utley began the "program" by saying that the producer was presenting the program to "illustrate perfectly the effectiveness of our democratic school system." He continued by describing his awe after seeing the difficult level of the questions. "I've been poring over these questions for the last five or six hours and I have no shame in confessing that they've sent me scurrying to the 30-volume encyclopedia and the unabridged dictionary. But the Kids ... they've had no such chance. Each question comes to the Kids fresh as a daisy."

Toward the end of the "program" he introduced the guest, Dr. Harold Miller, president of Middle West University. Utley said that Miller had interviewed "our children and has been with them here in the studio ever since." Miller attested that he "knew for a certainty [that] these children had no advance knowledge of the questions. Their performance has been amazing and truly a splendid tribute to our American educational system."[17]

It was a practical use of a lesson that Lou had learned as an undergraduate in Laswell's class at the University of Chicago. It is the basis of persuasion, used in political campaigns and speeches, in government, in courtrooms, in business, in fact wherever there is a speech or presentation in which the object is to persuade an audience. Repetitions of a viewpoint, repetitions of a claim, repetitions in an appropriate environment, are attempts to convince and persuade an audience to take action or to modify its thinking, or to follow a cause. If the speaker can't convince the audience the first time, eventually he sways them as a result of the repetition of the viewpoint he's promoting. At every *QK* broadcast, even years later, Joe Kelly repeated that the show was unrehearsed, that the Kids did not hear or know the questions before airing.

As well, this viewpoint was often a key element in the comments from the guest speakers, especially those who were educators, who stated unequivocally that the quiz was legitimate and that the Kids were untainted. Although we have no evidence that tells us who wrote the educators' prepared speeches, the primary emphasis in their statements was education and how the Kids exemplified its value, rather than a preemptive alibi for honesty. It does not sound as if professional speech writers wrote their comments; they sound as though they wrote them themselves. John Lewellen and his staff may have edited them.

The production staff was pleased at the end of the first show: The Kids were effervescent, and the audience at the Merchandise Mart was enthusiastic. The conclusion from those present was that the show was viable. But immediately after that première Lou knew that as much as everyone present in the studio during the broadcast was delighted, there was no way to know exactly how many people were listening. And he didn't know what those who did listen thought of the program. That information would be the actual determination of its feasibility. Sponsors decided whether or not to continue to pay for radio programs (and later, television shows) based on the size of the at-home audience.

In 1940 there were several professional sources for that information within the broadcasting industry. Starting in the 1930–31 broadcasting season the Cooperative Analysis of Broadcasting (C.A.B.) was the first company to offer a way to evaluate the size of the home audience for radio shows. C.A.B.'s method was direct. They performed a home-audience survey and reviewed the results, revealing them in an established ratings system that determined the size of the audiences for the most popular radio shows. The C.A.B designed its rating system to help stations and networks establish, maintain, or increase the fees they asked of advertisers. At that time generally one advertiser would sponsor an entire program, and announcers would read commercials live, on air. There were no planned spot commercials as we know them today.

By the 1935–36 broadcasting season, the C.E. Hooper Company surpassed the scope of the C.A.B. and became the leading radio audience research service. Hooper was the preeminent monitor during most of the golden age of radio (between 1930 and 1950). Their employees surveyed households by telephone. They asked respondents what programs they were listening to at the time of the call. It was a method that was different than the C.A.B. model. Then Hooper assigned a numerical rating to those shows with the greatest number of listeners based on a calculated formula they had devised. As a result, radio stations and program producers could command higher fees for those shows that were more popular. Their assumption was that the more popular shows had a larger audience. For producers, and it follows, the program's sponsors, audience size mattered.

It was only natural that Lou, his collaborators at Wade, and Miles Labs wanted an immediate reading on the size of the audience for that first program. They wanted to find out how many people were listening to that first show, immediately. But that was impossible at the time. There was one simple, however incomplete and unsophisticated, method to determine the effect and involvement of listeners to that first program: the incoming mail after the broadcast. After the first week *QK* was on the air, listeners wrote 2,607 letters to Louis Cowan Productions; by the third week there were 5,920 for the week. After the first month the weekly mail totaled 15,213.[18]

Because Joe Bailey ran the *Quiz Kids* office, he had to face this problem. They needed help. Lou realized that they had to get "a whole office to handle it." Bailey started hiring. He employed nine people quickly — two who replied to every incoming letter, six people who opened and read all the incoming mail from listeners, and one administrative assistant, "sort of an amanuensis."[19] As Richard Williams described, it was a small business office, apparently a common system in production offices for radio programs. *Lum and Abner*, the popular network radio comedy program aired during the same years as *Quiz Kids*, had an office of just three people: the creators and its performers Chester Lauck and Norris Goff, and a secretary who, after looking at all the mail, gave it to the two stars to read and answer as they saw fit.[20] They received a lot of mail each week but not the huge volume that was received by the *Quiz Kids* office.

Many of the letters to *Quiz Kids* expressed the enjoyment felt by listeners, and most of them offered questions for consideration for future shows. Listeners submitted questions in their letters for two good reasons. First was the thrill of four seconds of fame on the radio as Joe Kelly would read their names and home towns when he announced that the production staff had selected their questions to use on the program. Second, the chance to win a Zenith portable radio was a strong lure in those days even though its intrinsic value was not very great.

Zenith introduced the first portable radio in 1924. In 1940 portable radios sold for less than $40. If listeners submitted questions for the Kids that were used on the program, Zenith would send them a portable radio, and if the Kids couldn't answer the question, they sent a radio and record player they manufactured as one unit and worth considerably more. Even in 1940 when the country finally appeared to be emerging from the Depression, $40 was an enviable weekly salary for the breadwinner of a middle-class family. A typical family considered it frivolous and financially irresponsible to spend nearly an entire week's income on a radio, especially a portable radio rather than the usual sturdy receiver normally placed in the living room. Understanding that the perceived value of the prize was greater than its actual value should have dissuaded listeners from vying for one (even though it was free). Just the opposite was true. Excitement ran high from the anticipation of winning such a prize because of its association with a national radio program and its famous panel of children.

Not all of the mail addressed to *QK* contained questions for consideration. Some of the letters were critical of the show, pointing out pronunciation mistakes that Joe Kelly made and other slight errors that listeners heard during the broadcasts. Still, this growing volume of mail was clear evidence that there was a radio audience that was actively involved. They were not passive listeners; they respond emphatically.

Involvement is the real goal of every broadcast producer. Sponsors welcome this involvement because it means that their program has an emotional appeal for its listeners, and thus they would most likely want to listen each week. Of course, this was fertile ground for the Miles Labs advertising efforts because they would be more likely to persuade repeat listeners to buy the products advertised every week. Such repetition of a message, such as a radio commercial, is a basic tenet of persuasion.

By the end of the fourth week as a result of the flood of letters to the *QK* office, Lou, Wade Advertising, and Miles Labs concluded that the listeners at home were more than curious; the incoming mail meant that *QK* was a hit, even though it didn't have the number of listeners anywhere near the top 20 shows for the 1939–40 season, led by the *Chase and Sanborn Hour* (Edgar Bergen and Charlie McCarthy, with a 34.6 rating), the *Jell-O Program* (Jack

Benny, with a 34.1 rating), and *Fibber McGee and Molly* (a 30.8 rating).[21] In that era of advertising-dominated radio, until the first years of the 1950s, it was customary for sponsors to list their names first and the stars or hosts of radio shows followed. The names of quiz shows, variety shows or situation-comedies were listed in second position.

Naturally, broadcasting executives scanned the ratings weekly and were attuned to the slightest change in their standings. Lou Cowan was no exception. One week, in a page of suggested on-air announcements to be broadcast live about *QK* that was released to local radio stations (called a "Courtesy Announcement for all Blue Network stations"), Lou called attention to the progress of *QK* showing the Hooper rating that week with a one-sentence, boxed-in notice at the top of the announcement, entitled "How we doin'?" He announced, "we slipped [0].3 on C.A.B. but the competition slipped 2.6 and 1.4."[22] The release did not name "the competition." Even though Hooper had been the dominant force in audience research for nine years, Lou's release still cited the C.A.B. as the source of this audience evaluation.

Lou knew that Zenith radio giveaways and high-scoring Hooper ratings as methods to build an audience were not enough to satisfy Alka-Seltzer. He understood that Miles Labs would like to see a significant amount of fan mail, too. He apparently pushed for it. Subsequently, Joe's script for the program frequently emphasized an appeal for mail from listeners. At the same time, throughout the industry there was a gradual decline in merchandise offers on radio programs. Within three years after the *QK* debut, the number of sponsors who offered merchandise to listeners had "dwindled almost to extinction." Miles was one of the few sponsors that continued to offer merchandise—*Billboard* counted them "on the fingers of one hand"—when they awarded the Zenith portable radio to listeners who submitted questions that were used on *QK*.

Just as Joe Kelly would ask for fan mail, all the network programs increased their pleas for fan mail. So energetic was Joe's request that the Blue Network identified *QK* as one of the four programs on their network that was "credited with substantially aiding" in increased letter writing by listeners.[23]

The growing volume of mail each week produced another idea for audience-building that was both inspired and sophisticated. As well as letter-writing, why not offer another way for listeners to send their questions for possible on-air use to the *QK* production office? But in those pre-email days, other ways to communicate were limited and more expensive than sending a letter (first-class postage was only 3 cents between 1940 and 1950). The production staff had to be creative to solve this problem. By the end of August 1940, they learned that their work on this project had paid off. They were able to announce that at-home listeners could send their questions for consideration by telegram via a special arrangement with the Postal Telegraph Cable Company. When the telegraph service agreed to the deal, they did not tell the staff first. They sent the initial announcement of the cooperation between *QK* and the telegraph service to Charles Beardsley at Miles Labs: "Congratulations. Quiz Kids on NBC Blue Network is indeed the radio sensation of 1940. Because of the public's great interest in this unusual program, special Quiz Kids Postal Telegraph message blanks are available at Postal Telegraph offices for your listeners' questions."[24] Giving Beardsley the news first was a social nicety in the world of business that was both flattering and persuasive. We can see Lou's dramatic flair working the marionette strings above this.

The telegraph company had designed each telegram blank with a photo of some of the Kids on it, the Chicago address pre-printed, ample room for a question and its answer, and the *Quiz Kids* logo as another opportunity to identify the brand. It was a quick, direct, and easy alternative that allowed listeners to act on their ideas for questions without having to find the correct mailing address, an envelope, or a stamp. To keep the cost low for *QK* fans, Postal Telegraph charged night rates for these messages.

Everything was happening quickly. It was the normal state of operations in radio. On the second program after the start of their first long-term contract, the announcer informed listeners about the telegram alternative.[25] This unusual promotion reinforced the perception of the stability of *QK* within the insecure environment of show business. Within the world of radio professionals, the Postal Telegraph promotion dramatically reinforced the panache customarily associated with Lou's reputation as a master showman.

The atmosphere was not completely euphoric at the Louis G. Cowan Company in the weeks following the program's successful debut. Still disquieting was Joe Kelly's employment status, his two-week contract, dictated by Beardsley. It was Beardsley's careful move to save face if Kelly did not perform to his expectations, even though he had insisted that Joe remain after his shaky performance on the debut program. Careful listeners to the first few programs heard Joe laughing frequently during the show, a sure sign of his nervousness about his minimal formal education and its inadequacy when confronted by these brainy and well-educated children. Often, as an adjunct to his laughing, he would ease his academic discomfort by mildly citing his own ignorance about the answers to some of the questions. His humility did not exude confidence nor did it suggest job longevity, although he did become more self-assured as the show increased in popularity. It took some time, but gradually he achieved a measure of self confidence.

At the end of that first month on the air, Joe's job security continued to be uncertain; he was still on Beardsley's prescribed two-week trial. A couple of weeks later he started to become comfortable in his role, with concentrated tutorial help and guidance every week from Roby. (Joe had to be reminded frequently that Shakespeare was, indeed, dead.)[26] Roby had the ability to put Joe, and the Kids, at ease with her intelligence, good nature, and unflagging humor. Her ability to finely tune a phrase in her letters and prose to a pinnacle of understated humor translated well into her spoken words, calculated to deconstruct any seemingly insurmountable tasks that she and her colleagues and associates faced.

With Lou's guidance, the staff continued to build the show's popularity and growth. Lou concluded that there was so much interest in the show and so much publicity that other sponsors couldn't help paying attention to it. Almost immediately after the debut, *Quiz Kids* got "another offer for the fall season."[27] But Miles Labs liked the show, too, and Lou stayed with them. So well was the show received by the at-home audience that Miles Labs signed *QK* to a 52-week contract for the new season at $2,500 weekly for production costs, with the show to be aired on a new day and time (Wednesdays at 7 P.M. Central Time, starting September 4, 1940, on NBC's Blue Network).[28] But *Billboard* must have just estimated the cost. The contract stipulated a weekly fee of $3,000, triple what Miles Labs had paid during the summer replacement schedule. The weekly budget included salaries for the staff, office expenses, and the cost of the bonds for the Kids each week.[29] Alec Templeton returned to his regular Friday evening schedule.

The production staff was so confident that Miles would offer them a permanent contract that one month before the new contract began, they changed the different remuneration between the top three scoring Quiz Kids, who received a $100 bond, and the remaining two, who earned a $50 bond. Now, every Kid would receive a $100 bond no matter how the scoring went.[30] Robert Stephan, the radio columnist for the *Cleveland Plain Dealer*, was a champion for this equality from the beginning. Striking a critical note in his first review of *QK* on the day after its debut, he thought that all five of the Kids should receive equal awards. "They not only richly deserve them," he said, "but children are also so very conscious of success or failure [that] it seems cruel to make a public distinction."[31]

The one-year contract with Miles included Joe Kelly. It was a validation of his ability and an elimination of his preliminary fears. Indeed, Roby's weekly tutoring obviated his feelings of incompetence. It didn't matter that *Time* belittled his lack of a formal education and called him the *Barn Dance* hayseed; the fact remained that the Kids liked him. The audience in the studio and the larger, unseen audience in their homes did, too. Children listening to the program at home believed Joe and trusted him. Shortly, after school started in September, children overwhelmed him with phone calls (to his home). They wanted help with their homework. They had heard him on *QK* and expected him to know all the answers to their homework problems.[32] Parents sometimes called as well, with the hope Joe's answers could provide them with unimpeachable answers to their children's homework questions.

Other magazines did not share *Time*'s disparaging opinion. *Radio Daily*, a trade periodical, reviewing the first show of their first permanent contract, wrote that Joe managed to "put the youngsters through their paces with an ease and thoroughness that keeps the show moving along swiftly."[33] Now Joe could take comfort in his own broadcasting abilities, knowing that *Time* wasn't the only source for critical analysis.

> ☞ *We're searching for a word. To find it, work an arithmetic problem. Use the numbers suggested by the following words: begin with duodenum. Divide by a bicuspid. Then, divide again by a tricep, and what kind of "ology" do you have?*

The first broadcast was aired a week after the beginning of the customary blistering summer months, usually felt no less in Chicago than on the vast, open farmlands of the Midwest. The week leading up to the broadcast high temperatures in the city were hovering around 70° F, comfortable, but warm.[34] Lou remained cool, as always. He had formed many of his plans before the debut; he was prepared. Now, he and his staff had to start acting on them. Lou remembered the advice of his onetime mentor, Edward Bernays: promote the program at every opportunity, and as frequently as possible. He turned to his list of priorities, John Lewellen's "Tuesday Ideas."

Within seven weeks after the June 28 broadcast, Lou had an ambitious merchandising program in place. That he had contacted George Kamen just after the program's debut and hired him to be the exclusive licensing representative for *QK* was the right move at the right time. By the end of August, less than two months after the debut, there were hints that there would be a series of movie shorts about the program and a number of *QK* products available for sale.[35] At the same time as Lou was forming plans for the movie shorts, George contacted Whitman Publishing and Saalfield Publishing to begin licensing and publishing relationships. The result was that Whitman published a series of games for children, and Saalfield produced children's books with a *QK* theme.

During the following year, in 1941, Saalfield produced a book of cut-out paper dolls with illustrations of several of the Kids as the dolls, both boys and girls. Children who owned the dolls could change their clothing by attaching the additional paper cut-out wardrobe articles with the tabs that protruded from the cut-outs.

Not all of the ideas and opportunities came from George, Lou, or the production staff. Parker Brothers had an idea for *QK* and they approached George with it. The famous games company was just as aggressive in their pursuit of their market as Lou Cowan was of his audience. Parker Brothers historian Phil Orbanes explained that it was the usual procedure for Parker to contact any radio show whose characters or concept matched their product lines. Radio shows that had "graduated" from summer replacement status to a regularly scheduled contract for the season were of great interest to the games company. When Miles Labs signed the new contract with Lou it meant that *QK* had emerged successfully from its category as a temporary, short-term summer replacement. It would be customary for representatives from the Chicago office of Parker Brothers to approach Kamen with a licensing proposal for a Quiz Kids game that they would produce and market. If nothing else, this was concrete evidence that the program was already visible in the cultural landscape.

Quiz Kids cutout paper dolls (author's collection, Jason Gardner Photography).

QK was a perfect fit for Parker Brothers. The game company's proposal was to produce a game that they named "Quiz Kids Own Game Box." Lou and George had every reason to listen to a proposal. It made sense for them to accept this opportunity because Parker Brothers was the largest game maker in America. They were preeminent from 1910 until the end of World War II. When Parker Brothers offered a contract, George's responsibility would be to negotiate it for Lou.

Parker Brothers and George concluded the licensing contract rapidly, in time for the toy company to go into production at the beginning of 1941. They introduced the game at the New York Toy Fair in February 1941. It was listed as no. 215 in the 1941 catalog for the fair with a suggested retail price of $1.00. The Game Box contained six games. Parker Brothers most likely culled them from their archive of games that were either appropriate or that they could modify slightly for inclusion in this boxed collection. The terms

"Quiz Kids Own Game Box" (author's collection, Jason Gardner Photography).

of the agreement would specify that the contents of the game or any *QK* logo marks used on the game or its box would have to be acceptable to the Louis G. Cowan Company.

Typically, such a licensing arrangement would involve an advance against royalty. They would compute royalty payments at five percent of the wholesale price. Parker Brothers would have paid the advance on signing the agreement. At that time they usually paid an advance of $500; they would consider subsequent annual advances the fee.

The amount of the fees was determined mathematically. Although there are no copies of the contract between Parker Brothers and the Louis G. Cowan Company, the toy company usually produced 25,000 of any games of this type. The contract assumed that Parker would sell all of them; therefore they would have generated $12,500 in gross revenue, at the wholesale price. The royalty on this revenue would be $625 for the year. To be conservative, Parker Brothers would pay $500 as the advance against royalty. Once they reached sales of 20,000 games, then they would start paying additional royalty.

They manufactured the "Quiz Kids Own Game Box" in 1941 and 1942, but discontinued it from 1943 to 1945 because of materials shortages and limitations caused and enforced by World War II. They went back to producing it again in late 1946. When the game was re-introduced, it sold for $1.50 at retail and continued to be popular. Parker Brothers manufactured it continuously until 1951, when they discontinued it because of receding sales. Typically a game will lose its appeal to its audience before its namesake radio program has lost its own appeal to its audience.[36]

Whitman began publishing *QK* products, too. As quickly as 1941, Whitman produced the "Quiz Kids Radio Question Bee" game. It was a deck of cards with questions "actually used by the Quiz Kids on the famous radio program." Accompanying the game were the answers. That way, children could play a simulated *QK* radio program at home, with one of the players acting as the master of ceremonies (i.e., Chief Quizzer). The game consisted of 36 cards, each with a question on both sides. Just as Joe Kelly did, the M.C. would read each question aloud and call on the player who raised his hand first. In 1941, the World Publishing Company published the *Webster's Quiz Kids Dictionary*. Lou Cowan wrote the preface, and there were photographs and brief profiles of seven of the Kids.

By 1945, Whitman had published the third set of question bees. In 1947 they turned to fiction and published a book called *The Quiz Kids and the Crazy Question Mystery*.

Saalfield published books and collections of typical *QK* questions and answers, not with the level of difficulty that was usually the norm on the program, but nonetheless challenging to some children. The books were in cloth-bound and paper-bound (magazine) formats. As well, other manufacturers produced a range of promotional items including pins, pin-backed buttons, a brass locket and pendant, and an electric "quizzer" game. Most of these were not from manufacturers that had the cachet or popularity of Parker Brothers.

Just as Norman Siegel reported in his August 26 column, it appeared that the *QK* staff was preparing for a series of short films about the program. He said that a major Hollywood studio would produce them. On September 17, 1940, just three weeks later, three of the Kids — Cynthia Cline, Gerard Darrow, and Van Dyke Tiers — went before Judge John F. O'Donnell in Chicago. He designated them as wards of the state of Illinois. O'Donnell appointed their parents to serve as their guardians. It was a confusing legal maneuver, but evidently he had to make the parents their legal guardians in order to validate "possible contracts between the kids and 'flicker' producers, who are likely to film movie shorts."[37] Still worded as a possibility, there was no public announcement that plans for the movie shorts were definite.

The marketing of the program began to work. Week after week the popularity of *QK* continued to grow, as did its audience. Respect for the children and their knowledge produced an unplanned variety of opportunities for publicity. Some were so subtle that they were completely subliminal, unlike the usual placement of publicity in newspapers at that time. In the late fall of 1940 with the winter solstice approaching, Pence James, who often reported about everyday concerns, wrote a newspaper article about some people in Chicago who wanted to know how cold it would be if it were twice as cold as zero. They had asked their friends for the answer, and James asked the head of the city's weather bureau, who said that there was no answer.

Several other theorists offered solutions, among them a physicist at De Paul University and one from the University of Chicago. All of the answers were complicated, their logic hard to follow. Pence, always a champion of bright children, turned to Van Dyke Tiers, whom he had recommended to Lou, and in fact was one of the original Quiz Kids. Van Dyke's answer was surprisingly simple. He stated that at zero degrees Fahrenheit there are 32 degrees of cold. Therefore, he concluded that twice as cold would be 32 degrees below zero.[38] Aside from its value as publicity, it was an exhibition of practical logic based on knowledge that Van Dyke and some of the Kids applied to everyday problem solving. This reliance on Van Dyke within the context of a larger, albeit frivolous, concern was a testament to the intelligence of the Kids and the value of learning and its application to problem solving. Whether or not calling on Van Dyke to solve this problem was spontaneous or the result of subtle publicity is unknown. If it was spontaneous, it was clever. If Lou had planned it, it was brilliant.

At the same time as Van Dyke and the other Kids were astounding Chicagoans in late fall with their problem solving, the *QK* staff had been working for at least three months on ways to expand the show and its audience. Lou wanted to broaden the way in which his staff found new Kids for the show by finding prospective Kids from other cities. Nagging him was the reaction that had been in the forefront of pessimistic advertising agencies and sponsors earlier in the year, before Miles Labs agreed to sponsor the show. "You can't find the Kids" seemed to be their mantra. Many of those prospective sponsors in the spring of 1940 rejected the show because if there were to be two new Kids on the show each week, they thought that it would be impossible to continue to find bright children who would meet Lou's requirements after the first few shows.

Initially, *QK* recruited potential Kids only from Chicago and its neighboring areas. Shortly after, they included the outlying communities in their search. The vast population of Chicago and its surrounding suburbs increased the probability that they could find a large contingent of bright, affable children who would fit the requirements. On the chance that the pessimists were right, Lou and the staff began to explore ways to search for new Kids. One thought was to look in other cities. The idea, although logical, was impractical to carry out. How would they do it and keep costs low, too?

George Kamen had the answer. He presented a streamlined and inexpensive way to recruit prospects that would not only find new Kids from cities throughout America, but would increase interest in the show and at the same time add new listeners in those other cities and their surrounding areas. All this was with a minimal expenditure for the production company or for Miles Labs. George wanted to create an elimination contest among school children that would add excitement and drama to this expanded search.

There was more. George added a marketing fillip, with Lou's enthusiastic approval, that would keep costs low. He would arrange with local department stores to subsidize this search for bright children who lived in their region. These department stores would pay the costs of producing a series of events, actually contests that looked and sounded like authentic *QK* radio programs, complete with difficult questions and live audiences attended by local residents. What's more, the department stores would be responsible for the details of producing the contests, not just pay someone to follow the guidelines established by the 8 South Michigan staff and Kamen. The NBC network would not broadcast these simulated local *QK* programs.

The stores would offer licensed Quiz Kids merchandise as prizes to the frontrunners. A process of elimination would produce the final winner, the brightest local child, whose ultimate prize would be an invitation to travel to Chicago to appear on the national *QK* show along with the other four Chicago Kids that week. On the network broadcast, the local Kid would earn the $100 defense bond, as did the regular panel, and had the chance of continued appearances on the national program under the same terms established for all the Kids: the opportunity to return based on their scores on the program.

At the same time the stores were running the contests, they would promote *QK* products vigorously via local advertising. Promotion of this plan by department stores meant wide publicity for *QK*, and for the store. Kamen pointed out an added dimension to the publicity that was highly attractive. He assured the stores that participated that Joe Kelly would mention them on the network radio show in Chicago. George's plan for "importing" a new Kid eliminated virtually all costs for both the Cowan Company and for Miles Labs, including the cost of sending the bright youngster from another city to Chicago.

This was George's strength: creating marketing plans for selling licensed merchandise for his clients. Kamen was an old hand at creating programs like this. He was able to see how to tie in commercially licensed products, in this case, *Quiz Kids* books, games, clothing, and even birthday cards, alongside the overall promotion for his clients. *Variety*, with its usual journalistic bombast, described the licensed products as part of "a hundred other things which are being manufactured under the 'Q.K.' imprint."

Stores recognized that these local contests would attract a lot of recognition for them in their own community. To participate in Kamen's plan they were required to undertake considerable local promotion in newspapers and on local radio and other costs. The stores awarded $50 in prizes for questions used in the local auditions, and another $50 in prizes to the winners. Department stores were required to pay for the cost of the trip to Chicago for the winner along with one parent, usually the child's mother. They had to buy at least 500 gold-filled *Quiz Kids* keys, which resembled Phi Beta Kappa keys, to be given to the non-winners. The keys were similar to the pins that each of the Chicago Kids wore.

Quiz Kids birthday card (courtesy Cynthia Cline Newgarden, Jason Gardner Photography).

When a famous national radio program mentioned them on air, the local department stores would enjoy the attention. They concluded that it was worth the expense because it would enhance their image in their community and add to local pride. Clearly, Kamen's plan was pure marketing and merchandising genius, well reasoned and visionary.

The *Milwaukee Journal* offered the first opportunity to try George's plan. The newspaper's Goodfellow Fund, one of several still existing throughout the United States as a Christmas charity usually associated with a local newspaper, was to be the recipient of the proceeds of an elaborate five-day Thanksgiving holiday entertainment planned for the general public. The *Journal* wanted the Quiz Kids to make an appearance. The participation of the Kids was far more than their usual basic publicity effort, with their appearance covered by photographers and journalists. The Kids were part of the entertainment; they would perform a simulated 30-minute *QK* radio program that looked and sounded like their normal weekly network show. George and Lou accepted the invitation.

Kamen and the newspaper made the initial plans. The Kids were to appear in Milwaukee on Monday, November 18, 1940, as guests of the *Journal* and the local Parent Teacher Association at the Milwaukee Auditorium, now named the Milwaukee Theatre.[39] Milwaukee is only 92 miles from downtown

Chicago, so it was a relatively uncomplicated trip, similar to several publicity appearances for civic organizations that the Kids had started to make: they could get to their destination by car, do their performance, and return home that same day. Still, the trip was a grand adventure for the Kids. It was also the result of careful planning by Lou, George, the staff, and the newspaper. As well, this was to be their first travel from Chicago and a way to test the realities of traveling with the Kids.

The Milwaukee Auditorium accommodated 13,520 people and was a symbol of civic pride. The city of Milwaukee had built it in 1909, one of many such municipal buildings erected in the early years of the twentieth century by enterprising American cities for the express purpose of housing national political conventions. For the remainder of the year or years between conventions these imposing public buildings were available for other large functions: a space for meetings, lectures, theatrical events, conferences, trade shows, and speeches by local and visiting notables where a huge public audience could gather.[40]

This November 1940 extravaganza sponsored by the *Journal*, and named the Aqua Star and Style Show by the newspaper, was a combination of an aquacade and fashion style show and was something new in entertainment in Milwaukee.[41]

Admission cost 55 cents, 85 cents, and $1.10, with all seats reserved. Opening Sunday night, November 17, the show's five-day agenda consisted of seven performances—two matinees and five evenings—culminating on Thanksgiving, November 21. The opening night audience of 3,500 cheered "lustily." Many of the women in the dress circle wore ermine, silver fox, mink, velvet and glittering sequins, creating an apt counterpart for the fashion show offered during interludes of the aquatic performances.[42] Swimmers included performers from Billy Rose's two 1940 World's Fair aquacades, one in New York and the second in San Francisco, and featured Buster Crabbe, the 1932 Olympic Gold Medal winner and former movie portrayer of Tarzan (he appeared only once in that role), giving an exhibition of the evolution of swimming.

Each performance had a different theme: formal wear on opening night, campus clothes, men's fashion, town and country wear. The Kids performed during the Monday matinee, which featured apparel of special interest to clubwomen.[43] NBC did not broadcast their performance. For all practical purposes it was another local appearance, even though it did not take place in Chicago or its immediate environs. Of course, the primary difference between this event and most of the non-broadcast appearances that they usually made was that this was a test of Kamen's assertive effort to find new Kids.

Four Kids traveled from Chicago: Gerard Darrow, Jack Lucal, Cynthia

Cline, and Geraldine Hamburg. Joining them was "a special quiz guest," Jerome Cornfield, 11, a prodigy from Milwaukee, who at that tender age was a student in high school.[44] Cornfield described his experience as the "outstanding event" of his childhood.

When the staff chose him to be a guest Kid they did not follow the usual, well-established selection procedures. Although he had written a letter to Chicago expressing his interest in being on the show and subsequently completed a questionnaire, there was no preliminary interview, no probing of his personality and demeanor to see if he fit the subjective requirements established by Lou and the staff. He simply received a phone call shortly before the date of the show. Someone on the *QK* staff told him that they had selected him. The staff had taken a shortcut. They did this at the last minute. Jerome concluded, even at the time, that they were "in a hurry."[45]

The Milwaukee show appearance by the Quiz Kids was somewhat different than their usual radio show format. There was no need to be as probing in the selection process for Jerome Cornfield because the *QK* "show" was not a broadcast, not a contest with scoring and points for them to earn. There were no winners or losers; it was just an appearance with the Kids answering the usual variety of difficult questions. None of the Kids received the defense bond as they did the end of each network show. Even without the surge of adrenaline brought on by the competitive environment of their usual weekly radio appearance, it was exciting for the Kids. They had traveled to Milwaukee and had lunch at a downtown hotel, with *Milwaukee Journal* reporters asking questions and taking voluminous notes accompanied by the newspaper's photographer undoubtedly punctuating the queries with the staccato pop of the flashbulb on his Graflex Speed Graphic camera. For Jerome, part of the excitement was having lunch in the hotel, something he had never done before. Lunch and the appearance with the Kids was enough of a reward for him.

Gerard was blasé about the lunch. He ignored the traditional turkey luncheon and only ate three hard rolls as his entire meal, plus a small cup of ice cream for dessert. He was not interested in the conversation flowing around the table, but appeared to be bored, except when the conversation switched to birds. Then he woke up and chattered like a magpie.[46]

For the rest of the Kids, perhaps an additional excitement was more for the boys than the girls. After lunch when they went to the auditorium for their appearance, the boys entered separately from the girls, via the stage entrance. Their path to the Green Room took them through the large community dressing room where some of the professional showgirls and models were changing outfits in preparation for their next entrance. They were in various stages of undress, and some were completely topless. This made a lifelong impression on Cornfield, understandably a more vivid and longer-lasting mental image than many of the other details of that day when he was a guest Quiz Kid.[47]

Of course, George's main responsibility during the months preceding this trip was carrying out his plan. He had to sell the recruiting and merchandising program to retailers across the country for future consideration. The appearance of the Kids at the Aqua Star and Style Show was a coincidental first step for George. The next step was harder. But George had prepared well, and was able to move ahead immediately.

The day after the Kids' appearance, Boston Store, a Milwaukee department store with a 40-year history as a leading midtown retailer, announced its contest. The store's presentation was enticing, and a little grandiose: "Who Is Wisconsin's Quiz Kid?" it asked. The terms of the contest in the search for a Quiz Kid from Wisconsin followed Kamen's product marketing guidelines, offering the simulated Phi Beta Kappa key to 500 children as an "honorable mention," *Quiz Kids* buttons to all participants, $50 in prizes for 24 semifinal winners, $50 in prizes for parents, brothers, and sisters for their questions if used on the network program, and 10 Zenith radios, as a special enticement to pupils in local schools to get them to submit questions, and with that have the chance to win radios for their classrooms. Kamen offered this variation of his merchandising plan to school classes who met certain requirements.[48]

The advertising for Boston Store in the *Journal* that day spelled out in detail the terms of the Wisconsin contest. A day earlier, on the same day as the Kids appeared at the Aqua Star and Style Show, Edgar Thompson reported the news about the new contest, describing Milwaukee as "the first city honored by the 'Quiz Kids' program," recognizing that this local competition was one of several in an ongoing effort that Kamen would set up in "larger cities throughout the country." The department store would select 125 potential finalists, with contests at various levels eventually resulting in one winner. The winner of the Boston Store contest was to appear with Milton C. Potter, superintendent of Milwaukee public schools on the January 22, 1941, network show.[49]

At the same time they were testing the plan in Milwaukee, Lou and George had started to determine the feasibility of expanding this idea nationally. They hired Manny Reiner, a former publicity executive for Monogram Pictures in Hollywood, to arrange for more department store tie-ins. By the middle of December 1940 approximately 60 stores nationally were interested in participating. As a result, George and Lou planned to expand the plan after February 1, coinciding with the introduction of the Parker Brothers game.[50]

This quick Milwaukee trip, taking only a few hours of one day and appearing on the surface to be so simple, set the tone for a plan of action that evolved from it, either by design or by coincidence. A variation of this planned action continued for the next 11 years, and it became a major element in the history of the radio program. The Milwaukee trip had been only the first tiny step in the plan. The next step was already in progress.

ANSWERS

The plane would arrive six minutes before the car — plenty of time for the pilot to sing the song. (One of the Kids answered this question in less than three minutes, without using a pencil and paper.)

The word is biology. Duodenum suggests the number 12; a bicuspid suggests the number 2. A tricep suggests 3. Thus: 12 divided by 2 is 6, divided by 3, equals 2. The prefix bi- means the number 2. Therefore, the word is biology.

5

The Quiz Kids — Selected Short Subjects

☞ *There is one United States president besides George Washington whose birthday we celebrate as a legal holiday in all the states and territories. Which one is it?*

There was no more delicate, evasive wording about the possibility of the Kids making movie shorts as there was in September when Cynthia, Gerard, and Van Dyke appeared in court and became wards of the state of Illinois. Newspapers and trade publications had been reporting that a plan for the Kids to make movies was tentative. Siegel's column at the end of August reported it as a rumor. For the *QK* staff, making the films was not speculation. The project was definite even if all the details hadn't been set or a contract signed.

Most likely before the Milwaukee trip in November, and probably before the court appearance in September, the staff started working on the logistics of the trip. They had to. There was no comparison between the intricate preparation for this new trip and the simpler details behind the Milwaukee appearance. Undoubtedly, the Milwaukee trip represented a good test for the staff and the Kids. As they finalized the film project, it was apparent that it would require a major travel itinerary encompassing numerous components, even though the Kids would be away for just one week. The specifics and decisions that the staff had to make seemed endless: selecting which of the Kids were to go, getting permission from their schools for their prolonged absence along with giving assurances that the children would keep up with their homework, scheduling train travel, making plans for local travel, arranging for the Kids' parents to accompany them, deciding which staff members would go, booking hotels, planning meals, and organizing publicity to appear in newspapers and magazines. It was a complicated task.

Finally, the film shoot was a firm reality; a date was set. In January 1941 the Kids traveled to New York to make two movie shorts and to meet New

York City mayor Fiorello LaGuardia, who wanted to greet them and welcome them to Manhattan. Paramount Pictures produced these films in New York City. They expected to release the first film of a planned series of six during the autumn of '41, the second film shortly thereafter. The remaining four films were to be made later in the year and the studio would release them in a predetermined schedule. Each of the Kids received $150.00, not bonds, from the production office for every short film that they completed.[1]

Making short films about the program made more sense than making a full-length feature. These films, which would run for eight to ten minutes, were a perfect vehicle for the Kids and their talents. There was no need to have a script writer (there were no commercials, other announcements, guests, or scheduling to manage as there were on *QK* each week), and there was no need for a plot. Basically these films were shortened versions of their weekly broadcast, so that the staff constructed the film "scripts" in the usual manner from their archive of questions already submitted by the at-home radio audience. Typewritten questions and answers for Joe's cards were the primary pre-production requirement for the films.

Short films were in a format that movie audiences had already accepted and enjoyed. Showing them as part of the entertainment was a customary practice for movie exhibitors in the 1930s and 1940s. Exhibitors ran them as part of the program, consisting of one or two feature films, a newsreel that was a visual presentation of a newspaper presenting a variety of topics in addition to the news stories, a comedy, sometimes a cartoon or two, or one episode of a continuing 12-part adventure serial, and a short film featuring a famous swing band. These short films altogether were part of the entire entertainment program at movie theatres. Theatre owners usually called this supplementary program of non-feature films "selected short subjects."

Some theatres only showed newsreels. But they often featured short films as part of a one-hour program. They repeated the program continuously. These newsreel theatres were usually located in large cities at or near train or bus stations where travelers or commuters or others with extra time could go to the newsreel theatres as a distraction or time-killer while waiting to depart on public transportation, or while waiting for their next scheduled activity to begin. It was a popular way for sales people to rest and relax when they had time between business appointments. They could keep up with news and current affairs and be entertained in less than an hour.

Toward the end of December 1940 Lou went to New York by himself.[2] Why he made this trip is not clear; it could have been to make final arrangements with Paramount and to make certain that there would be a minimum of travel problems during the upcoming visit by the Kids. There is no diary or appointment book to offer concrete evidence, but based on a promotional plan from NBC for the upcoming year, he seems to have met, as well, with Bertha Brainard in NBC headquarters at 30 Rockefeller Plaza. Bertha Brainard was head of programming for the network.

Going to New York was important for Lou, as it was for the Kids when they followed at the beginning of January. It was their first extended trip together to another city, requiring them to stay at a hotel and have meals for several days. Lou wanted to be certain that the plans that the staff made were adequate. His early trip to New York to finalize the details of the film shoot was a good opportunity to check on other details — hotel accommodations, meals, publicity for *QK*, and tourist-site brochures for the Kids and their parents. It was important for Lou to have this extended trip with the Kids well-planned. Lou was his own advance man. Now, with this experience in New York, he could delegate and direct with authority others on the staff to do this advance work for any extensive trips they might have to take in the future. With the staff charged with doing this preparatory work, he was able to focus on more ideas to make *QK* grow.

For some of the Kids this trip at the beginning of the New Year was their first visit to New York, and we assume that they were excited about seeing the largest city in America. Not necessarily. Cynthia Cline was more excited about meeting Fiorello LaGuardia than she was about seeing the city. She was not in awe of Manhattan. "After all," she recalled, "I came from Chicago, and that was a big city, too."[3] Six Quiz Kids, each with one of their parents, were on the New York trip, along with Joe Kelly, John Lewellen, Lou and Polly, Roby, George Kamen, and two people from Wade Advertising.

They departed from Chicago on the *Twentieth Century Limited*, New York Central Railroad's showcase train, on the evening of January 3. Lou wanted the whole entourage to feel excited and at their best. So, he planned the trip with his usually exquisite sense of style. He chose this train specifically; he wanted to make this an adventure for everyone: the Kids, their families, and the staff. He wanted the excitement to start immediately. The train ride was an adventure unto itself.

The *Limited* started service between New York and Chicago in 1902 and featured speed and luxurious comfort for first class and business travelers between these two major cities. Passengers boarded the train in Chicago and New York City walking on plush red carpets specially designed for the *Limited*. (This distinctive luxury, really a marketing effort by the New York Central railroad, evidently is the origin of the phrase "red carpet treatment," presently stated as "on the red carpet," such as on Academy Awards night.) The original *Twentieth Century Limited* offered a barber shop and secretarial services. On boarding in New York, the railroad gave carnations to male passengers (for their jacket lapels) and presented perfume and flowers to women.[4]

Early the next morning, January 4, at a regularly scheduled prolonged stop in Albany, New York, before the final southbound whoosh to Manhattan, Kamen brought a group of men from a children's clothing manufacturer aboard to distribute several articles of clothing for the Kids to wear in New York City. These were samples of a new line of children's wear, the beginnings of a "Quiz Kids collection," that manufacturers would sell to department stores throughout the country. Not all of the Kids had samples to wear.[5] The manufacturers hadn't completed the full line yet; these samples were just clothing and accessories for girls.

The paper cut-out dolls book depicting the Quiz Kids, both boys and girls, that Saalfield produced the following year subtly promoted the idea of a line of juvenile clothing. The book shows dolls depicting the Kids. It was easy to cut the dolls and the articles of clothing out of the book. A child could change the clothing for the dolls; each article of clothing had tabs so that the child could attach the interchangeable clothing to any of the dolls. Clearly this was George's merchandising handiwork: tying together the marketing for manufacturers with department store promotion and paper-doll cutouts reflecting the *QK* clothing line. The details of the promotion all fit together: the book, the clothing design, and Kamen's abilities in department store merchandising.

Later, another manufacturer, the Kaynee Company, produced a line of boys' clothing, primarily sport shirts and other clothing items. To help promote the Kaynee line, George and Kaynee produced commercials for the clothing with the Kids and Joe Kelly reading the copy live during regular network *QK* broadcasts. One commercial started with a few bars of the program's musical theme ("School Days") on the organ and then, with the music fading down, Joe Kelly intoned, "Here they are—radio's famous Quiz Kids!" as if the commercial were an actual *Quiz Kids* program.

This commercial featured Richard Williams, Gerard Darrow, Jack Lucal, Van Dyke Tiers, Jack Beckman, Claude Brenner, and even though it was about boys' clothing, Cynthia Cline. Cynthia's role seemed to reflect what the advertiser wanted to present as the carefully worded edict that every mother should make when they politely admonished their sons to dress tastefully. Her pronouncement was a mother's viewpoint, as Cynthia says judiciously, "It's awfully nice to see boys dressed neatly." Kelly supports this matronly homily by saying that he thought that "all the little girls in the country agree with you." Consistent with Kamen's supercharged style of promotion, the commercial featured a contest that offered a free book of limericks along with an application blank for a boy to write an essay about "Why I Want to Be a Quiz Kid." Boys from anywhere in the United States could enter, and the winner, no matter where he lived, would have the opportunity to be on a future *QK* show.[6]

After that early morning interlude in Albany, the train continued southward without interruption other than its regularly scheduled stops. By midmorning, the train eased into Grand Central Terminal with its roster of Quiz Kids and their entourage. All the Kids — Joan Bishop, Cynthia Cline, Gerard Darrow, Mary McHugh, Van Dyke Tiers, and Richard Williams — were arranged on the platform according to height; the girls were in the back because they were taller. The publicity efforts by the staff in Chicago in the weeks before the trip paid off. Newspaper and magazine photographers met the train when it pulled in and shot photos of them on the train and on the platform. As usual, the Kids were cooperative and unassuming.

While they were getting ready for the cameramen, a young man came toward them leading a pretty, young, blonde woman, looking pert in a black coat and leopard-skin hat, carrying a muff and wearing an orchid. He said that the blonde's name was Yvette and that she was a professional singer. He tried to infiltrate her into the group photograph, obviously to gain free publicity exposure for her. But Kamen shooed her and her manager away quite firmly.[7] It was a crude and amateurish attempt at promotion, compared with the professional dexterity that was the norm for *QK* publicity. The Kids, not even giggling, stood quietly, exhibiting detached interest as they observed the young woman and her manager.

After the brief photographic session they walked into the station. Gerard discovered the marble floors at Grand Central Terminal. He began to run and slide on them triumphantly, finding the polished marble perfectly suited for his gliding. His recent history of self-travel was less perfect. Gerard had a badly scratched chin as the result of an unsuccessful effort to ride a bicycle, a gift he had received at Christmas.[8] After this publicity session at the train station, the Kids and the entire group went to their hotel, the Beaux Arts Apartments on East 44th Street in Manhattan, where they checked in. The Kids faced the press again; this time there were newsreel photographers (there were four newsreels made of the Kids).[9] They answered questions about themselves and about topics similar to those that they usually encountered on their radio program. The reporters couldn't stump them, even though there was some hesitation about one question. They knew locations of islands and populations of cities. But they appeared stymied when someone asked them to identify the president of Brazil. One of the Kids finally said, "Vargas." When asked what they would like to do in their free time while in New York, all six said that they wanted to visit "the museums, the Aquarium, the New York Zoological Park and the Statue of Liberty." Van Dyke said that he wanted to see Charles Chaplin's film *The Great Dictator*, because it "just vanished in Chicago."[10]

Richard Williams, contrary to Cynthia Cline's indifference, was excited

Arriving at Grand Central Station, New York, January 1941. (From left) Richard Williams, Gerard Darrow, Van Dyke Tiers; (top row from left) Cynthia Cline, Joan Bishop, Mary McHugh (courtesy George Van Dyke Tiers).

about coming to New York. He was more pedestrian about the tourist attractions he enjoyed. He remembers seeing Radio City and the NBC studios at Rockefeller Center, a popular tourist attraction similar in appeal to the NBC studios in the Merchandise Mart back in Chicago. He also recalls that George Kamen took him to the Horn and Hardart Automat at the southeast corner of 42nd Street and Third Avenue, a short walk from the Beaux Arts. For the rest of his life, the visit to the automat remained prominent in his memory of that trip.

Horn and Hardart Automats in their time were paragons of self-service, popular and famous for being inexpensive fast-food restaurants. The interior of the 42nd Street establishment was a riot of shimmering glass and chrome, designed in classic Art Deco style and rivaling the lobby of the iconic Chrysler Building, one block to its west. The décor of the restaurant was not unique; the interiors of the entire chain were in that same style.

The restaurant offered various dishes placed behind small window-covered sections adjacent to coin-operated slots (accepting nickels only). Just a few nickels inserted into an adjacent slot followed by twisting the knob next to it a half-turn caused the window to open with an audible click, allowing you to take out the dish of food — a main course, perhaps, or a salad, or dessert. This self-service concept fascinated Richard for its efficiency and democratic nature.[11] In contrast, the Beaux Arts featured a more formal restaurant, still relatively inexpensive but significantly more costly than the automat. The most expensive meal at the Beaux Arts cost at least 65 percent more than a meal at the Automat. At Horn and Hardart a customer could eat a meal for less than $1.00. The menu at the Beaux Arts featured a complete four-course dinner ranging in price from $1.00 to $1.65.[12]

Richard was more impressed with the little technological wonders of the automat than the cost of its food. When he inserted a nickel for hot chocolate he was mesmerized. So he neglected to put his cup under the spout, and the chocolate flowed freely, onto Richard, onto a woman standing next to him, and almost immediately onto the floor.[13]

During the interview by reporters at the Beaux Arts on the day they arrived, the discussion turned to Washington, D.C., where the Kids were going the following week to meet with Eleanor Roosevelt. Paramount had arranged this publicity event at the White House.[14] When asked by reporters, the Kids said that they would ask Mrs. Roosevelt if she would compare living in the White House with living in Hyde Park, N.Y., her husband's hometown. Van Dyke said that he wanted to ask President Roosevelt about the defense program. And Cynthia said that she wanted to ask him about his basic formula for foreign policy. The press conference ended after that, but the Kids continued their conversation, talking about "the war, aid to England, and Whither Now America?"[15] Immediately after, they faced individual interviews.

As the series of individual interviews began, someone realized that free-spirited Gerard had disappeared. There was a frantic search. Someone found him in the lavatory writing a letter to his cocker spaniel, Rusty. Darrow's note said, "Dear Rusty, I am in New York. I am having [a] good time. I have a surprise for you. Love[,] Gerard Darrow." The surprise for Rusty was dog candy. Strangely, he signed his full name. Usually he signed his more formal letters, in an exhibition of unspoiled playfulness, Gerard D→.

Gerard Darrow was unique, uninhibited. Generally a quiet, well-behaved child, once he started talking he couldn't stop. He was "just about as high as a fire hydrant and twice as overwhelming when he turns himself on full force." Because of his vast knowledge of birds, he was already lecturing on ornithology in Chicago's high schools. He wrote poorly, was bad at mathematics, and said that he hated school. He also said that he was more devoted to swimming than he was to geography.[16] Reluctantly, he agreed to enter first grade. Gerard said that he consented "only to learn to read."[17] Given his intelligence and ability to focus, it's surprising that he hadn't learned to read at home, well before the customary age for school enrollment.

Roby and Gerard (courtesy Eliza Hickok Kesler).

Shortly after the second session with the press, the Kids went to their appointment with Mayor LaGuardia. LaGuardia had invited them to City Hall to meet them and take the opportunity to have his photographers take pictures with the Kids. Cynthia recalls that he was charming, as he normally was with children. After shaking hands with the Kids, the mayor boasted that the kids in New York could match their precocity. The Quiz Kids were incredulous. The mayor challenged them, asking, "Do you want to take them on?" Silence. Then, as usual, Gerard, who did most of the talking, murmured hesitantly, "I don't know." It was unlike the self-assured confidence he exuded when asked about ornithological subjects. But he bounced back. He queried the mayor about what was the hardest part of his job. La Guardia, with a quick-witted politician's teasing response, replied, "Answering little boys' questions."[18] After a short period of conferences among themselves the Kids accepted the mayor's challenge. LaGuardia declared that the contest between the Chicago Kids and New York's juvenile geniuses could be a public or private contest.[19]

The next day, Sunday, George invited Cynthia and her mother and, in fact, all the Kids, their parents, and Lou and Polly, to brunch at his hotel. Perhaps as a tribute to Cynthia and her inclination to write verses spontaneously, his invitation was playful and rhymed. His poetic rhythm may have been awkward and some of the rhymes forced, but the message was charming and effective. He typed it on stationery from the Lombardy hotel, where he was staying, a reasonable walk from the Beaux Arts:

Mayor Fiorello LaGuardia wanted to meet the Kids in his office. (From left) Gerard Darrow, Van Dyke Tiers, Richard Williams, Cynthia Cline, Joan Bishop, Mary McHugh, LaGuardia (courtesy George Van Dyke Tiers).

> Please come to my breakfast
> 'Bout ten thirty, it's brunch,
> So bring appetites
> And bring all the bunch,
> We're going to have fun
> And I'm positive that
> You'll like dropping my coins
> At the odd Automat.
> You won't have to answer
> A quiz or a thing
> Or smile for the press,
> No one needs to sing —
> Except just one quiz
> And this is no joke,
> "Who'll eat so much
> That I'll simply be broke?"[20]

The Kids stayed at the Beaux Arts for five days while working on two filmmaking sessions, Monday and Tuesday. Paramount's studios were in Astoria, Long Island, just across the 59th Street Bridge from Manhattan. These two short films were essentially two *QK* radio shows, but running far less time than the usual 30-minute weekly broadcast. Each Quiz Kids film ran for 11 minutes.

Leslie M. Roush produced and directed the films. The Kids were in excellent hands with Roush. He was a capable filmmaker who specialized in making documentaries and short films. During his career of more than 20 years in Hollywood, Roush made 50 short films with 26 of them of famous big band jazz or musical performances. They were a forerunner of music videos.

His other short films featured a range of subjects, characteristic of documentary filmmakers: sheep ranching in Montana, the training of a circus performer, the business of renting male escorts, a travelogue about Nairobi,

The Kids at the Beaux Arts Hotel. (From left) Cynthia Cline, Van Dyke Tiers, Richard Williams, Mary McHugh, Gerard Darrow, Joan Bishop (courtesy George Van Dyke Tiers).

Playing with their "Own Game Box" at the Beaux Arts. (From left) Gerard Darrow, Joan Bishop, Van Dyke Tiers, Cynthia Cline, Richard Williams (courtesy George Van Dyke Tiers).

and an early morning disc jockey who specialized in requests from milkmen, truckers and others who were up and about during the "lobster shift" (between midnight and 6 A.M.).[21] As well, Roush made 11 short films written and performed by Robert Benchley, the famous humorist and sometime actor, often known for his wry, satirical essays appearing in *The New Yorker*.

Roush shot enough footage to enable himself to cut and edit it into two films. Paramount released the first in theatres September 12, 1941; the second, December 5, just two days before the Japanese attack on Pearl Harbor and the formal entry of the United States into World War II. Roush filmed three additional short Quiz Kids films at two more sessions — one in August 1941 and the last in early spring of 1942. He made just five films instead of the six that were originally scheduled. The studio released each shortly after production was complete. Roush shot the first film from that initial Astoria session at the beginning of 1941 in Cinecolor, an early process for making movies in the 1930s. Technicolor eventually replaced the Cinecolor process.[22]

The second short was in black and white, but the remaining three were in Cinecolor.

The Monday session began in the morning. Traffic clogged the streets in Astoria: trucks, taxis, cars, and buses. Overhead, the elevated Number 7 subway train, screeching along, was just as dissonant as the El outside Joan Bishop's rehearsal room in Chicago. Each of these modes of transportation that morning in New York was trying to push through to its destination, emitting impatient shrill warnings to the world surrounding them, a cacophony of horn-blowing and brake squealing that might startle the most aurally challenged observer. Just two weeks after Christmas, it seemed that everyone was ignoring the annual holiday pleas for peace on earth and goodwill toward men. Monday always appeared to be the busiest and noisiest day of the week. Astoria was, along with Long Island City, located at the core of the factories and warehouses that made up the industrial zone of New York City.

Inside Paramount's studios it was infinitely quieter. Still, it was fast moving and exciting, especially for Roby. She was so busy writing that her typewriter gave out. "You see," she wrote facetiously, "my old Remington, used to a rather dull routine, couldn't stand the whirl of New York and died a quiet death in the director's office of Paramount studios." She thought that making the movie shorts was the biggest thrill she had ever had. She thought it was like the romantic notion most people associate with Hollywood: "directors in yacht chairs, directors yelling 'cut' and 'quiet.'"[23]

But this wasn't a cinematic re-creation of Hollywood. No fragile egos to be calmed. No nervous actors, fretting over their costumes or makeup or their barely memorized lines. Leslie Roush was relaxed and calm. There was no rehearsal, no preparation for the actors. There didn't have to be; the actors were the Quiz Kids, and no preparation was necessary. It was just another performance for them. One reporter described the overall mood as "a rare one for any set. Everyone was in high good humor." Even the parents looked delighted, and "parents of movie children seldom look delighted." No one seemed to be frantic. People spoke casually, quietly. There was no harsh voice yelling, "Quiet, please," or "Quiet on the set!" There was only the low warning bell to signify when a scene was to start, or that it had just ended.

It was an ideal atmosphere for the Kids. They were not at all flustered; it was familiar, like their weekly broadcasts. The Kids were having a good time. Between shots they played a piano that was in the studio, singing in dubious harmony. They dashed around the set in an ad lib game of trying out each other's seating on the set, their own impromptu variation of musical chairs. They took the whole experience in stride, not talking about the film or about their performance, boasting about how many right answers they had, or complaining about the answers they missed.

On the set for the film shoot, January 1941. (From left) Joe Kelly, Cynthia Cline, Van Dyke Tiers, Gerard Darrow, Richard Williams, Joan Bishop (courtesy George Van Dyke Tiers).

The actual shoot was a game for them, too, even though Joe asked some tough questions. Joan answered the music questions quickly, apparently without effort even when Joe sat at the piano and played one bar of a song and asked them to name it. Cynthia knew about dancing, the boys knew the answers to the most assorted questions. None of them thought that the questions were too difficult.

Lou was calm, too. He sat on the sidelines the entire time, enjoying the action, enjoying his "children." At the end of the shoot on Tuesday he reckoned that of 40 questions, the children had missed only four or five. He was proud of them. He beamed with delight.[24]

The only difficult part was Joe Kelly. As much as Roby's adventures with her dying typewriter were problematic, Joe proved even more so. In her coaching session with him before the film shoot, she primed him for a question for the Kids about Einstein's theory of relativity. She phoned him the night before the shoot and told him to "brush up" on the subject. When he arrived at the studio, he confessed that he hadn't had time to read about the theory. Roby took him aside and in a few minutes he had the "stuff down cold." But when he talked about it a few minutes later he talked about apes and monkeys. Somehow he had confused Einstein with Darwin. Roby worked with him more. "When we got through this time, we had not four dimensions but eight. He multiplied them."

Joe, even with his lack of formal education, was still likeable. At an earlier tour of the Miles Labs plant in Indiana, Joe's usual sense of humor compensated for his lack of intellectual depth. He called an audience of all Alka-Seltzer employees "Fizz Kids."[25]

After completing their shoot on Tuesday, they had time for some sightseeing before doing their regularly-scheduled broadcast Wednesday evening.[26] Thursday, January 9, they left for Washington and the White House.

Quiz Kids broadcast from NBC studios, New York, January 8, 1941. Cynthia Cline, Van Dyke Tiers (courtesy George Van Dyke Tiers).

Shortly after they arrived at Union Station in Washington early that afternoon, a capital guide thought he could best the Kids. He asked if any of them could tell him "who was the first president of the present United States?" Richard answered almost immediately, saying that it was William Howard Taft. The guide was impressed with how quickly Richard responded.[27]

The White House expected six Kids. The Kids and their entourage were a formidable group of 18 (the two people from the Wade office had returned to Chicago). Among the six children, Mary McHugh was a stand-by; the others were five of their mothers, Van Dykes's father, Joe Kelly, John Lewellen, Lou and Polly, Roby, and George. When they arrived at the White House Thursday afternoon they had to wait for a short while in a small, private room. Mrs. Roosevelt was in a meeting with the wives of the Supreme Court justices. The Kids passed the time in their usual style, minutely inspecting and examining everything around them with intense curiosity—furniture, paintings, and small objects. On their way to the little waiting room, the grandeur of the White House generally impressed Joe Kelly. But when a guide took them on a detour into the room where the president gave his fireside chats, he said that it was the "oval room." Joe, always ready with a pun, turned to Roby and said about Roosevelt, "This is where he probably drinks his Ovaltine."[28]

Categorizing their examination as "inspecting" is a mild way to describe their activity. The Kids went right to the furniture and decorative items on shelves and table tops. They touched and picked up antique and priceless vases, plates, and other items; crawled under furniture to scrutinize it more carefully, to delve into their construction and the details of the craftsmanship involved.[29] They examined the framed portraits on the walls, most likely to add to their continually expanding knowledge of American political figures and thus to their repertoire of historical trivia. Van Dyke went to George Washington's portrait, the painting that Dolley Madison saved in 1812 when the city of Washington was under attack and the White House itself was on fire. He wanted to look closely to see if Washington was wearing the false teeth that had been made for him by Paul Revere (Van Dyke concluded that he was). They didn't intend their extreme physical activity to be mischievous, or to destroy these objects. It was the exact opposite. They simply admired them. They appreciated their value, and they basically wanted to learn more.

Mrs. Roosevelt's meeting elsewhere took a little longer than she expected, so on her direction an aide led everyone on a tour of the public rooms of the executive mansion. A few minutes after they completed this mini-tour and returned to the little waiting room, the First Lady came in, warmly greeting the Kids and the entire group.[30] She complimented the Kids. She thought that they were wonderful. The First Lady revealed that the first family enjoyed playing their own quiz game, saving the hardest questions for the president. "He usually gets the answers, too," she said.[31]

When Mrs. Roosevelt asked about the special Quiz Kids badges that the six of them wore, each in the shape of a Phi Beta Kappa key, this was an unrehearsed cue for Cynthia. She offered her key to the First Lady. Mrs. Roosevelt accepted it but said that she didn't deserve it. After telling the Kids that the president was interested in ornithology, Gerard took off his key and held it out to Mrs. Roosevelt. "This is for your husband for the fine work he is doing," he said. The First Lady laughed heartily.[32]

The Kids fascinated her; they looked quite normal and natural. Her schedule dictated only a limited session for this meeting; she actually wanted to spend more time with them. The next day, Friday, they visited with U.S. Senator Charles Wayland Brooks of Illinois.[33] They attended a session of Congress and a photographer took pictures of them with both Illinois senators. The Kids explained to the adults in their group "what bill the senators were talking about, who they were, and how a bill was passed." Roby thought it was wonderful having the Quiz Kids along to explain the process and identify the senators who were debating that bill. Later they visited more conventional tourist attractions: Arlington National Cemetery and George Washington's house at Mount Vernon. The Kids had gathered around the iron grating surrounding George and Martha Washington's tomb and were giggling loudly. Roby came over to find out why. Van Dyke pointed to the patch of rust-colored cement at the bottom of the tomb. He chuckled. "It looks as if George seeped out a little."[34]

They left for Chicago and home late that afternoon.[35]

On the train back to Chicago, everyone was in high spirits, the Kids especially, with much hilarity among them. Their pranks reached a climax at night while their mothers slept in upper berths on the Pullman car. It sounds as though Roby joined the Kids in their mischief when she declared "what fun it was to leave mama stranded in upper 6 while you hid the step ladder in the men's room."[36] It's no wonder that the Kids liked Roby. She was a disciplinarian, but with a clear understanding and belief of practicing polite decorum. She was tolerant of childhood pranks. Apparently they amused her. She accepted their underlying spirit, knowing that the Kids meant no real harm. All told, it had been a rigorously scheduled week, but infinitely enjoyable. Everyone — the Kids, parents, and the staff — was pleased.

The Kids pulled practical jokes through the years of travel on trains, sometimes hiding the ladder on their Pullman car. Joel Kupperman on the ladder (Photofest).

☞ *A man goes into a butcher shop and sees that hamburger is on sale for 30 cents a pound. He orders a pound of the meat. While the butcher has his back turned to grind it, the man takes two quarters that the butcher carelessly left on the counter. He pays for the meat with the two quarters, and walks out with the hamburger and his 20 cents' change. On his way home he feels guilty, and returns to the store. How much does he owe the butcher?*

On the same day as their arrival in New York, January 4, back in Chicago there was an announcement of another exceptional publicity idea of Lou's. With their issue of January 6, 1941, the *Chicago Herald-American* would publish a daily feature column called "Beat the Quiz Kids." It was a simple idea, but it required intricate planning and coordination. Clearly, Kamen and the staff, with the participation of the Kids, had been working on the idea and its execution for some time. The questions appear to be those that Joe Kelly might ask on broadcasts. Most likely they were from the pool of questions submitted by listeners but not used on the program. Roby and Rachel could have just styled them on those questions.[37] King Features Syndicate offered the possibility to distribute this feature to their network of newspapers throughout the United States.

To promote this new column, the *Herald-American* featured a contest for school students in the Chicago area. The contest ran for seven weeks. Students were encouraged to write questions for the Kids and mail them to the newspaper. The newspaper would read the entries, and the best five questions earned cash prizes for their creators. Each of the five students with the best questions each week would receive $20.

Each "Beat the Quiz Kids" column was illustrated with a posed photograph of one or more of the Kids doing household chores, at play alone or with their friends, doing things with family members, playing with their pets, riding their bicycles or on roller skates, playing sports, being photographed in standard publicity poses, appearing at various locations in Chicago, or doing other usual "human interest" activities, adroitly staged to help photojournalists shoot images that were visually interesting. The most difficult part of this simple idea was the logistics of arranging the photography used for each column. From their appearance, many of the photographs taken indoors look as if they were shot in a photographer's studio, probably that of C.M. Frank, who was the primary photographer used by the *QK* staff. Frank's studio was convenient, just a few blocks from the *QK* office.

Edward Bernays used low-key techniques to promote the Diaghilev ballet troupe, and these photos and the question-and-answer contests were made to be equally disarming. Overall, they were examples of understated public relations. The photos illustrate that these precocious, "brainy" Kids were perfectly normal in their daily activities, just as ordinary kids were throughout Chicago, or anywhere in the United States. The photographs look as though they were styled to help deconstruct the erroneous and common notion that intelligent, precocious children were nerds — strange creatures who were set apart from the activities of the rest of the world. The visual message was that the Kids were children just like other children.

The questions in the columns covered a range of topics, just as the radio program did, so that children (or adults) could take the quiz, individually or together. The newspaper printed the answers on a different page that same day. The column appeared six days a week for the seven-week duration. The response to the newspaper quiz was so lively that King Features agreed to continue with the "Beat the Quiz Kids" column in newspapers in several other cities. By the end of April little more than three months later, King had placed the column in more than 20 newspapers nationally, including the *New York Journal-American*, *Milwaukee Sentinel*, and *Boston Herald*.[38] In all, the idea of a column was, by any standards of evaluation, an inspired publicity campaign.

☞ *If you had to write a check for eleven thousand, eleven hundred and eleven dollars, how would you write it?*

There was little or no time to rejoice in the success of the New York and Washington trip. John and Roby plunged right into the next projects, which were more intricate to plan than anything they had experienced before. The trip to New York opened the possibility of new ideas for Lou. As usual, he was percolating ideas for the future as a result of the successful filming of the shorts. Usually his concepts were clearly and simply stated but often more intricate and more sophisticated in execution than they appeared to be. For everyone who worked on Lou's new ideas, there were increasing responsibilities added to their jobs each time. Now, as he revealed two new projects, it was understandable that the stakes were higher. The rewards were, too. Actually, there was no time to ponder any question about whether or not the staff was prepared. As always, they simply had to jump in and work on them as they came through via Bailey or Lewellen. Right now, they were committed to move ahead with these two projects. They started immediately.

ANSWERS

Calvin Coolidge. But the question, "Which one is it?" is ambiguous. "Which one is it" can refer to either which president's birthday or which legal holiday all of the states and territories celebrate. The answer to the latter is July 4, Independence Day; the only federal holiday celebrated everywhere. Therefore, this leads to the answer to the other possible question: which president's birthday is it? The answer is Calvin Coolidge, who was born July 4, 1872, making his birthday and the national holiday a joint celebration. The ambiguity of the question was an indication that this may have been a trick question, and a difficult one, at that. For a perceptive Quiz Kid, this ambiguity offered a clue to the answer, that it might be a trick question. To answer the question correctly, the Kids had to know that every state celebrates this holiday on July 4, and that Coolidge was born on that date.

He owes the butcher 50 cents. Ethics or morality aside, solve this as a pure arithmetic problem. To simplify the problem and the answer, assume that the man only had one dollar in his pocket when he entered the store. If he didn't take the butcher's 50 cents and paid for the meat with his dollar, he would have received 70 cents change, and he would have had only 70 cents in his pocket when he left the store. But, when he paid the butcher with the money lying on the counter and received 20 cents change, he had $1.20 in his pocket when he left the store. He should have had only 70 cents. So, $1.20 less 50 cents is 70 cents. Therefore, he owes the butcher 50 cents, the amount that had been lying on the counter that rightfully belonged to the butcher.

You would write it as twelve thousand one hundred and eleven.

6

Rising Stars

☞ *Shakespeare had favorite names for characters in his plays and used them over and over. What name did he give to these characters: Who was the daughter of a French king in one play, lady attendant to a princess in another play, and wife of an English king in another play?*

Upon their return from New York and Washington, the Kids resumed their normal family responsibilities, returned to their customary schedule at school, and continued to meet the mounting demands of the weekly program. As *QK* grew in popularity, requests increased for their appearances at local and regional events, both educational and civic. It seemed that everyone wanted to hear and see these preternaturally bright kids. People wanted to witness their thinking and their erudite ad libs. It didn't matter if their spontaneity was an attempt to clarify and expand on another Kid's answer. Their contributions, sometimes breathlessly delivered, often led to an intelligent and informal interaction with Joe Kelly. Audiences loved the dialogue between Joe and the Kids and the Kids with each other. When they corrected one another's answers with nitpicking improvements, they sounded completely innocent, even though they might have been masking a competitive denigration. Intellectual nitpicking was endemic among them.

There was a danger in letting the Kids set the tone for the show with their knowledge, and for Joe Kelly to assume the role of an uneducated rube. In the early months of the show, Joe's self-deprecating attitude as a member of the unwashed masses led one radio fan magazine to conclude that the shows sounded unsophisticated and amateurish. Roby worked hard on a publicity campaign to destroy the perception of amateurism. The goal was to place the Kids "in the professional class."[1] Her output of publicity releases included anything outside of the *QK* "classroom" that identified the Kids as more than simply adept at remembering the facts that they absorbed from their voluminous reading.

Gerard lectured about ornithology at a high school in Chicago, but he had been doing that before he was a Quiz Kid. We have seen how just a few months earlier, in November, Pence James called on Van Dyke to solve a confusing problem related to air temperature, which he did using basic mathematics and uncommonly mature logic and reasoning. His clear logic was impressive and the demand for his appearance continued to increase as 1941 unfolded. The Art Institute of Chicago invited Cynthia to submit a sketch to them, which she did with great acclaim from the museum's staff and the general public. Invitations for the Kids to appear either individually or as a group were escalating. Their knowledge as well as their rising star-power had a seductive appeal. They were appreciated for their grasp of a variety of subjects just as respected teachers were appreciated for their understanding of various academic disciplines. The National Audubon Society made Gerard a member and the Chicago Academy of Sciences made him a life member because of his sophisticated interest in ornithology.[2] More than just coming to the NBC studios each week, the Kids were busier than ever. Requests for their appearances were increasing.

A week or so earlier in New York when the filming of the shorts had gone well, Lou and his youthful counterparts at Paramount were euphoric with plans for future film projects for the Kids. However, breathless excitement is a common disease in show business, usually cured by the bitter pill of budget considerations. In the movie industry there was always the concern about film projects exceeding their budget. The emphasis on accounting was so predominant that it was known to stifle creativity. The predominant fear of failure among Hollywood's stone-faced senior executives practically overshadowed everything else. Still, the New York exhilaration appeared to be genuine, enough for Paramount's Hollywood studio to make specific plans.

With the New York producers exuberant after the completion of the short films, high spirits about *QK* surfaced in Hollywood, too. There was talk by the Paramount studio of trying to revamp Gerard Darrow into a featured juvenile for films to come. With atypical understatement, *Billboard* announced Paramount's thoughts about Gerard just 11 days after the Kids returned from Washington.[3] The announcement seemed to be confirmed rather than just a manic speculation. Paramount's invitation for Darrow and the Kids to make screen tests in Los Angeles set off the *QK* staff in preparation for the trip.

On the West Coast extravagant ideas started to pop, insinuating that there was more to this excursion than a simple trip to Hollywood. Several studios approached Lou about buying or investing in *Quiz Kids*, perhaps calculating imagined profits generated from his radio property. Lou refused. MGM and Universal Studios made specific offers, but Lou wasn't interested. Nonetheless, he admired Joe Pasternak, a successful producer at Universal. Pasternak wanted "to do a picture" featuring the Kids. MGM had a more dramatic and probably more lucrative offer. The studio wanted to buy *QK* outright. But Lou was not enticed. He "didn't want to do business that way."[4]

More appealing to Lou was the programming idea that Bertha Brainard conceived at the end of 1940. She wanted to have the Kids featured on a Jack Benny show, on one of his scheduled Sunday evening broadcasts from Los Angeles. It was customary for radio performers and other celebrities to "visit" radio programs, to be guest performers at little or no pay.[5] Reciprocity among radio performers was acceptable and expected. Producers and star performers simply viewed this as a way to promote themselves and their own vehicles. Because Benny's show was among the highest rated comedy shows in the country, an appearance on his show was the tastiest plum in the pie, worth plucking anytime.

She set up the specifics of the deal to present to Jack and Lou.[6] So it would have been logical for Lou to meet with her in December to discuss those details on his quick trip to New York before the Kids traveled to Manhattan for the Paramount shorts.

At the beginning of 1941, after all the praise for *QK* in newspapers and magazines, the undercurrent of capricious audience interest still worried Lou as it would any radio show producer. His show appeared to have strong national appeal. The response by the listening audience, based on the thousands of letters that came in each week, helped to confirm it. Still, Lou was not convinced that the audience would remain enthusiastic once the initial excitement about the show subsided. His experience in producing radio programs during the years before *QK* undoubtedly had taught him about fickle audiences. The increasing flow of mail from listeners was only a superficial indication of audience interest and not enough evidence to predict any palpable long-term loyalty. The fascination with brainy kids would undoubtedly be short-lived.

Transience was a basic fact of life in producing any radio program. So was the need for a continuous effort to build an audience. It was always on Lou's mind, no matter how much mail flowed into the office or how many laudatory articles there were in the press. Making a good impression with an audience was an ongoing and demanding need, the focus of the producers and their staffs on every radio show throughout the broadcasting industry, even the most successful. It was how radio programs helped to ensure that their sponsors remained their benefactors. In tandem with any efforts at increasing the number of listeners was the pervasive concern of how to keep that audience interested enough so that they would want to "tune in next week."

The usual solution practiced by radio show producers was to make each show fascinating enough to hold the attention of its listeners and thus to entice them to listen to the next broadcast. To capture prolonged attention from repeat listeners created a weekly tension that was always nagging away at every production staff. The whims of a listening audience created a severe uncertainty that was present after every broadcast. It never slackened for the whole life of a program. Certainly the Hooper ratings, read compulsively by producers, added to this never-ending tension. A loyal audience for a commercial radio show was just as important to its sponsor, reinforcing the possibility of repeat business for the sponsor's products or services. Such dependability from a listening audience was a determining factor that could help ease the tension felt by the radio program's production office. For the *QK* staff it was no different. They expended great effort to keep each broadcast interesting, lively, and as memorable as possible to keep their audience faithful, their ratings up, and their sponsor happy.

The *QK* staff was creative enough to solve the problem of stimulating week-to-week interest without needing Lou's help every day. For most shows, audience size at the end of every 13-week segment was of primary importance, an even greater tension-builder. Sponsors would calculate audience size and its relation to product sales as part of a formal review to determine if they wanted to continue their contractual obligation and financial support. Lou was aware of the real meaning behind audience size when he declared that sponsors didn't really pay much attention to ratings. He told Walter Selden, "The thing that sold our show was the sale of the product more than anything else."[7]

Sales of Alka-Seltzer actually increased during the summer of 1940 when *Quiz Kids* replaced Templeton. Walter Selden reported that this may have prompted Miles Labs to offer the full contract in September.[8] Selden, not missing an opportunity to add a little lighthearted humor to the reason why Alka-Seltzer sales had climbed, suggested that maybe the *QK* audience, overwhelmed by the intellectual content of the show, "just got more headaches after listening to your program."[9]

Any long-term contract between the sponsor and the producer was only a guideline. It was based on performance, reviewed and judged regularly. These reviews after every 13 weeks by Miles Labs were included in the contract for the show to be aired on a regular NBC schedule starting in September. They determined whether or not the program would continue for the next 13 weeks. This kept the staff and the producers in an ongoing state of anxiety, culminating in each of the quarterly evaluations. Every 13 weeks the tension among the staff built to a live-or-die intensity. Roby remembered clearly, "We were all very nervous, at each review, not knowing if we were going to have jobs the next day."[10] In the 1940s, a radio season was 39 weeks, plus a 13-week hiatus usually during the summer months, thus completing a full calendar year. The annual calendar, defined as "the season," was based on the assumption that a show's audience dropped in the summer.[11] Sponsors believed that "families went on vacations and therefore did not listen to their favorite radio programs while away from home."[12] Coincidently, the 39/13 schedule paralleled the customary public school calendar, beginning in September and ending in June. Replacement shows would fill in during the summer months, just as *QK* was the summer replacement for Alec Templeton during the previous summer.

There were exceptions to this schedule, and *Quiz Kids* was one of them. When they began their first one-year agreement with Miles, there was no hiatus; they were to be on air for a full 52 weeks. The rise in sales of Alka-Seltzer during the summer of 1940 suggests that Miles structured the full contract because of that rise in sales. But the downside of this 52-week contract was that Miles gave them four reviews a year, rather than the three reviews that other shows had to face during their 39-week seasons. As precarious and nerve wracking as the quarterly review was, bypassing the traditional summer break offered a slight advantage to producing the show in the summer. Schools were not in session, so it was easier for the staff to book publicity appearances and other extracurricular activities for the Kids, providing ample opportunity for additional creative attempts at audience-building.

Roby had the additional burden of helping to keep enthusiasm for the show at a peak by virtue of her publicity and press releases. On the surface, these efforts at promotion may have appeared to be superficial, but they were vital and crucial to the life of the show. It was a responsibility for which she was well prepared, given her experience as a newspaper reporter in Cedar Rapids and her graduate studies at Northwestern University. There is no explicit evidence that shows that Joe Bailey included the deep-seated ramifications of writing press releases in her job description when he interviewed her. He must have realized that it wasn't necessary; she understood the seriousness of this responsibility.

Lou's challenge went beyond the weekly pressure felt by his production staff to produce a good show. His task was to look at the larger picture, to build a national audience for his radio show. That's what he wanted and that's what Beardsley at Miles Labs wanted.

One solution was to expand the idea of the Milwaukee trip to build an audience by traveling to nearby cities with just a core group of Kids, no more than a one-day trip from Chicago, and giving live performances to large audiences. They would present the Kids in the *QK* format. If it worked in Milwaukee, there was no reason why it couldn't work elsewhere. It was a fascinating and apparently simple idea, but emphatically more difficult to plan and carry out than focusing on making each show interesting. But Lou and Joe Bailey would have realized that even if the "Kamen Variation," that enlightened chess-move concept to tie in product marketing at local department stores with the search for new Kids, sweetened the pot by increasing the listening audience the result would still define *QK* as a strong regional program from the Midwest.

Another solution was to travel with the show to other cities nationally and give live performances. There was precedence for this idea. *Vox Pop*, the national network radio program, did just that. Its format was to travel each week with only two interviewers and a producer and ask the "man on the street" his thoughts about a variety of topics. *Vox Pop* traveled to its audience, to their hometowns, setting up a temporary broadcasting hookup, often in hotel lobbies, train stations, and other public gathering places. They even set up in the lobby of the NBC studios at 30 Rockefeller Plaza, asking for the opinion of men and women as they traveled to New York from cities around the nation.[13] In 1939 *Dr. I.Q.*, a radio quiz show, adapted this unusual format. *Dr. I.Q.* did not broadcast from a traditional studio, but traveled from city to city and broadcast from large concert halls and theatres. The audience was composed of residents from the surrounding area.[14]

More inspiration to travel may have come to Lou from a source closer to home than *Vox Pop* or *Dr. I.Q.* WLS in Chicago reached out to audiences other than those who listened to the *National Barn Dance*. *Barn Dance* booked the stars of the show for appearances at state fairs, farming festivals, outdoor amphitheaters, and opera houses all through the Midwest.[15] It wasn't quite the same as the other two shows; these were performers on the show traveling to make individual appearances rather than the entire show going on a tour.

Traveling nationally with the show was historically a show business tool applied to radio, a variation of the on-the-road tryout performances before opening night in legitimate theatre. These appearances by the Quiz Kids in other cities would vary. They would be guests on another radio program as a self-promotion effort. Or, they might make an appearance for a civic organization to help them with a worthy community cause just as they had in Milwaukee, or perhaps to promote the values of education as they did weekly on NBC.

They would do their weekly broadcast from other cities around the theme of their appearance to benefit a local civic group when the subject was appropriate to be on the air and when the performance coincided with the established NBC schedule. Now, these audiences could see for themselves what they had been hearing at home in their living rooms each week.

These live performances were also attractive to audiences who had only heard about the Kids but had never listened to the program. Attending a broadcast or a live performance by famous performers has always been an exciting experience. The *QK* production staff knew that it was unrealistic to expect with smug confidence that the existing listening audience, and especially new listeners, would be attracted enough to cause them to tune in just because they had heard about these intelligent Kids or read a newspaper article about them. To believe that their fame was sufficient reason for people to interrupt their normal domestic activities to listen to this program was a passive and arrogant conceit. Such smug passivity was guaranteed to shorten the life span of *QK*. Lou's concept about taking the show to the audience was a more active, more assertive idea.

When it was apt, and to keep costs down, Lou understood that he could use George Kamen's sharp merchandising skills when the show traveled. As in the Milwaukee experiment, but perhaps not as structured, in other cities a department store or a consortium of local department stores would subsidize them, all arranged by Kamen. Although Lou's main interest was to advance the show, Kamen at the same time saw some of these trips as another way to help promote sales of *Quiz Kids*–licensed children's clothing, games, books or any of the rest of the *QK* line of products that George was pushing. The young production staff from Wade was amazed at George's tenacity and focus. George was older than they were and the producers from Wade were still in their twenties. But they looked up to him in awe because "the only thing on his mind was department stores and how to promote to them."[16]

Most important, it appears that Lou did not conceive of these trips only to market licensed merchandise, although George's elimination contests with simulated broadcasts could have been an easy way to structure a future travel schedule. The imminent introduction and release of the Parker Brothers "Quiz Kids Own Game Box" and the planning of the *QK* clothing line was enough ammunition for George and Manny to make a reasonable sales pitch to their network of department stores.

As clever as the Kamen Variation was, George designed it specifically to sell products. Lou thought more broadly than that, even though he welcomed and encouraged licensed product marketing for his program. Lou's vision was about enlarging the scope of the program, not just trying to sell a collection of *QK* games, toys, books, and clothing. Promotional products usually have a short life, especially those marketed for children. If that was the only reason to travel, then audiences might become wary. A local audience could come to the cynical conclusion that *QK* had come to town just to market licensed products of temporary and questionable value, and the reputation as a program that emphasized the value of education would be tarnished.

If they explored the idea of a national travel tour for *Quiz Kids*, it was ruled out quickly. Taking *QK* on the road was complicated. Instead of just traveling with two or three performers as was common with *Vox Pop* and *Dr. I.Q.*, John had to take the entire cast, Joe Kelly, the Kids and at least at one parent for each, Roby, and sometime Rachel Stevenson. It wasn't practical and it wasn't easy.

Bertha's concept was a stroke of good luck because it would take *QK* to the West Coast, regardless of any ideas that Paramount may have suggested. She added an additional twist in her plan to make it even more appealing. She scheduled the Kids on with Benny, followed by Benny's appearance on a West Coast *Quiz Kids* broadcast. The Brainard plan was the key to a long-term solution for increasing the national audience that Lou was seeking, although it wasn't apparent at the time.

Bertha's plan made Paramount's idea of a screen test for Darrow the secondary reason for the trip. Undoubtedly, Lou saw Bertha's plan as an opportunity to expand his broadcasting property within a larger framework than making a film or two with Paramount or any other studio. Her plan dangled a lure more enticing than the supercharged interest by Paramount and the other film studios. There were more long-term benefits to be realized for *QK* with Bertha's concept than any benefits derived from having Gerard appear in a movie, or even a series of movies. Benny's network show held the promise of a big break for *QK* because of its vast nationwide audience. It offered immediate and increased exposure on the West Coast at the same time. It was a dazzling way to attract new listeners and to reinforce the loyalty of those who already tuned in. After appearing with Benny, association with him would elevate *Quiz Kids* to a new level of respect among at-home listeners and radio professionals.

Once Paramount revealed their plans in *Billboard* during the first weeks of January, there was a rapid increase in the agenda for other events surrounding the visit to the Jack Benny show. The first happened within a few weeks. By the end of January Walt Disney agreed to a proposal to be a guest on the *QK* show that was scheduled shortly following the Benny broadcast. Normally, Disney made few personal appearances. He had good reason to be on *QK*. He was working on two features, *Fantasia* and *The Reluctant Dragon*.[17] The *Reluctant Dragon* featured a Quiz Kid–like character, and so a tie-in with the Kids would be good publicity for both Disney Studios and *QK*.

But the Brainard plan raised questions that had to be answered before Lou could accept it. Most likely he was excited about the idea when he first heard it, but we don't know if he agreed to the deal immediately when he met with her at NBC headquarters or if he wanted to think about these other issues, and perhaps discuss them with John and Joe Bailey after he observed the Kids during their travel to New York and the White House. He had to consider if there were any problems and pitfalls to the long travel schedule implied in Bertha's plan. The trip to Los Angeles would keep the Kids away from home longer than they had been before. Of course, Lou didn't wait very long to decide. Being a good executive, before telling Bertha his decision he would have met with Lewellen and Bailey a day or two after they returned from Washington to hear their opinion and analysis of the New York-to-White House trip. We can only assume that when asked, they were just as excited as Lou about Bertha's plan and agreed with him that they should move ahead with it. As abbreviated an itinerary as the New York-to-Washington trip had been, it gave them a practical view of what was entailed in the more extended itinerary of a trip to the West Coast.

The basic concern from Lou was whether or not the Kids could handle such a prolonged trip. There's no doubt that John and Joe Bailey would have thought that the Kids could. This time, it was experience that was the basis for their response, not just a sycophantic "yes" in order to mollify the boss, as John probably had given on that Tuesday afternoon nearly a year earlier when he heard Lou's excited bombardment of ideas for the show. Understandably, then, Lou was thrilled. Their encouragement meant that he had the genuine support of his key staff, and he was able to move toward a firm decision quickly about traveling to the West Coast. The exact date when *QK* agreed to the guest appearance on Benny's show is inconsequential. More important is what appearing on his show represented, and Lou, understanding the implications very well, took the opportunity gladly.

While Lou was trying to determine what problems may occur on this trip, there was one that Lou or John didn't have to ponder. The broadcasts from New York and Washington during the previous month were proof to NBC that the performance of the Kids while traveling with the show would present no major problems. They could adapt; they could perform anywhere.

But, first things first. As soon as everybody returned from Washington, John and Roby had to focus on a different trip, one that took chronological precedence before they could dedicate most of their efforts to this trip to Los Angeles. It was the solution to another of the Tuesday ideas having to do with *QK* and the use of school teachers as a way of expanding the listening audience. Lou wanted to emphasize the educational value of the program, aside from mere entertainment, as a reason for families to tune in. We have seen how college professors and administrators praised the Kids when they were guests on the program. Lou wanted to have the recommendation from schoolroom teachers in addition to those highly respected leaders in the field who were guest speakers on his show.

Luck was on Lou's side once again. The opportunity to reach school teachers arose quickly, just as the opportunity to search for new Kids had emerged when the Aqua Style and Fashion Show approached *QK*. The National Association of School Superintendents, a component of the National Education Association, invited the Kids to perform at their 1941 national convention in Atlantic City, New Jersey. The teacher's group had scheduled the convention for the last week in February. Here was Lou's chance. He was happy to agree to it. There wasn't much time after the Washington trip for John and the staff to arrange for this new trip, but it was a significant project, worthy of delegating time to, because the Kids were to appear in front of an audience of thousands of educators from all over the United States.

As they started to work on it, Lou and John decided that to make this appearance especially memorable, the Kids would do more than just a performance of their usual question-and-answer radio show. They were going to try a special format that they would introduce and test on a unique local radio show in Chicago, February 21, just four days before the Kids would appear at the NEA convention.

Using this special format in Atlantic City, the Kids were going to compete with some well-educated adults in a show that Lou and John designed to create dramatic audience appeal. On the February 21 program in Chicago John would introduce the unique format. The Kids would compete with five of their parents. At the convention they would use the same format and battle five educators. There was a significant unknown in presenting this format at the convention. The Kids and their intellectual abilities were well known. So was that of their parents. Lou thought that the parents of these precocious children were "very smart," too.[18] There was little concern that the February 21 duel would misfire. But there was no way to gauge the abilities of a panel of the five school superintendents who were going to compete against the Kids. Of course they couldn't be pre-qualified as the Quiz Kids selection process did the children who Joe Bailey interviewed. This enhancement of having the Kids joust with the educators was exciting for Lou and John. It followed the Bernays public relations doctrine of infusing publicity with dramatic flair.

Creating dramatic flair can be hard work. "Next we go to Atlantic City to pit the kiddies against five school superintendents," Roby reported in a letter to her family a week after the return from the White House. "I'm busy now working on that show, getting [gathering] questions about butterflys [sic] and woodpeckers which we hope will throw the educators."[19]

As usual, everything had to be completed quickly. The teachers' convention in Atlantic City was the week following the Quiz Kids–Parents show. The staff, working closely with the convention's planners, had arranged for two performances by the Kids, not to be broadcast, but similar to that of their scheduled radio program. It was a natural way to illustrate the educational value of *QK* at its best, and an inducement for NEA members to register for this convention, thereby increasing revenue for the NEA.

The planning for this trip was a greater challenge to the staff than the trip to New York and the White House. It was especially difficult for Roby because she had to do research for five shows that the Kids would present during one week. There was the Wednesday network show on February 19, the February 21 special broadcast with their parents, two performances on February 25 at the convention, and their network show the next day, February 26. To prepare for these five shows, Roby's schedule was more crammed than ever, with no let-up in the frenetic pace she had experienced on their trip to New York and the White House. Her new portable typewriter had a vigorous workout.

If the 11,770 school administrators, who gathered from across the entire United States and registered for the meetings and events, were excited about the wonderful Quiz Kids and their performance, audience-building would likely result.[20] When they returned home, they would tell their colleagues, their families, neighbors, and friends about the unbelievable performance that they had seen in Atlantic City. Such word-of-mouth corroboration would go a long way toward increasing the radio audience in their hometowns. The recommendation of school teachers, usually considered to be trustworthy, was a subtle way to reach that goal. It was the primary benefit of the appearance. The shows by the Kids in Atlantic City were of ultimate importance in establishing additional professional and authoritative support to a grassroots audience of established listeners and new listeners throughout the nation for subsequent broadcasts. There was a lot to keep everyone at full throttle when they came back to Chicago from Washington.

There were these two new projects — the trip to Atlantic City and the West Coast venture — and as always, the weekly radio program.

The Kids were busy with other things leading to the February 21 show, but outside the realm of the NBC broadcasts. The *Herald-American* set up the "Beat the Quiz Kids" column as a contest that allowed any school children in the Chicago area to submit questions for the February 21 show. Questions were judged and selected by a panel. The winners were to receive cash prizes from the newspaper. To keep "Beat the Quiz Kids" fresh and current each day, Joe Bailey asked the Kids to answer a series of questions that he would send to the newspaper for the column. This was "homework" for the Kids. Roby and Rachel compiled their answers and determined their scores shown as a percentage of "correct answers." Each day the scores attained by the Kids were displayed in that day's column so that readers could use the average score of the answers from the Kids as a benchmark with which to compare their own scores. Clearly, these were questions that Joe Kelly had not used on the program. With the same ethical consideration, the Kids were on their honor to answer the questions for future publication in the *Herald-American* without the benefit of any new research in sources they might have at home, or from libraries, or other places. As well as answering questions submitted to the newspaper, the Kids were required to go to photography sessions to pose for pictures that were displayed each day in the newspaper at the top of the "Beat the Quiz Kids" column.

It appears that this homework for the Kids continued only to the end of the newspaper's contest. King Features continued to run the "Beat the Quiz Kids" column after the newspaper promotion. Each column still showed the percentage of correct answers from the Kids. But it would have been unreasonable to ask them to continue answering the questions after the promotion. This suggests that the questions in the column after the conclusion of the seven-week contest came from the production office files of questions that Joe asked on air, so that the staff just had to compile the percentage of correct answers for publication in each column that the Kids had given on their broadcasts.

The newspaper promotion contest concluded Friday, February 21. That evening the special *QK* program format was aired with the five Kids — Cynthia, Van Dyke, Jack Lucal, Dick Williams, and Gerard — competing against their parents. There is no conclusive evidence that this show was considered to be a test, but it had all the appearances of a two-program trial because of the proximity to the Atlantic City performances. John and Lou thought that there would be a significant increase in listeners on that Friday evening because of the great interest in the newspaper contest. Even if there was no increase in listeners, there was no harm in trying it on this broadcast; it was aired only to the local Chicago-area audience. The syndication of the newspaper contest in Chicago and other cities by King Features most likely helped create excitement about the contest and for this special program throughout the Chicago region, just as the syndicated column did, and would continue to kindle interest for its national audience.[21] For the February 21 broadcast the production staff, as advertised, used questions from those submitted by local school children to the *Herald-American* during the previous seven weeks.[22] As with the questions submitted for the network broadcasts, they were edited and shaped by John, Roby, and Rachel.

Reporting in their newspaper the day after the broadcast of this "Quiz Kids Versus Parents" program, the *Herald-American* concluded that their parents were intellectually gifted, too, performing just as well as the Kids. "In short, the five Quiz Parents proved one thing: the Quiz Kids are just chips off the old blocks, nothing more ... nothing less." The newspaper, with more than a dollop of restraint, still managed to be effusive in its praise.[23]

The entire *QK* production staff thought it had been a success, so well-received that they categorized it as a format that was both entertaining and audience building. It worked. It looked like a winner. In retrospect, the real sizzle of the Quiz Kids–Parents show was that both the studio audience and the listening audience liked it. Lou appreciated the effort made by the parents. He thanked them with a note that he wrote to each of them the day after the show, describing this special program as a "family party" that made the Quiz

Kids–Parents episode a rare radio show.[24] Now, they were ready for Atlantic City.

This appearance at the teachers' convention was another demanding, shakedown cruise to prepare for the West Coast trip, and to see how the Kids would adjust to a travel schedule with the added stress of appearing in front of large audiences. Normally there were live audiences at their weekly programs in the Merchandise Mart, usually around 150–200 people.[25] The Milwaukee appearance in November had been before several thousand. To perform in front of nearly 12,000 in Atlantic City was a different matter, especially an audience that was so sophisticated and critical about education, and whose recommendation to the folks in their hometowns could make or break interest in future network *QK* broadcasts. In 1941 marketers called this form of recommendation word-of-mouth advertising. The same concept is practiced today by businesses using social media as the method of getting an audience to spread the word.

These educators in Atlantic City could be difficult to convince. When faced with children with reputations that exceeded the norm, such as those of the Kids, teachers would be especially observant, critical, and perhaps skeptical. To gain approval, the Kids had to be sharp. If they were, they would hear the roar of encouragement, delight, and applause from a large audience. It could be awe inspiring, if not fearsome. If they failed, it was an opportunity lost. Of course John could predict that the Kids would do well in such a setting. But he wanted to make sure, and so the staff chose the brightest and most affable Kids to go on this important trip.

The group left Chicago for Atlantic City from Union Station on Pennsylvania Railroad's *The Advance General,* one of the railroad's luxury "all-weather fleet," at 2:30 P.M., Monday, February 24, 1941, arriving in Atlantic City the next morning.[26] The Kids and their entourage stayed at the venerable Marlborough-Blenheim hotel on the Boardwalk. It was a brisk 10-minute walk south to Convention Hall on the well-trod 2" × 4" planks placed in a chevron-like pattern, where the Miss America beauty pageant was always held, and where the auditorium was so ample that during the 1930s it was often converted to a full-size football field, easily accommodating indoor professional games. It was the first site for indoor football. In that role, Convention Hall was a predecessor to today's "weather proofed" domed stadiums.

The teachers' convention was an important annual event for educators and, as usual, attracted many notable speakers for its opening session. Among them was Governor Harold E. Stassen of Minnesota. Even at this politically benign event, talk about war was inevitable and significant. Dr. John W. Studebaker, U.S. commissioner of education, said at the opening session that if Germany were to defeat Britain, the United States must either abandon democracy or else carry on the fight to a successful conclusion.[27] Thomas J. Watson, president of IBM; Harvard University president James Conant; Isaiah Bowman, president of Johns Hopkins University; and several prominent educators, writers, and high ranking officials in the field of education from President Roosevelt's administration were featured speakers throughout the weeklong convention.[28]

The same day as their arrival, February 25, the Kids did both planned performances. The one with the five administrators went well. Once again this intriguing special format, the Quiz Kids–Parents, was a hit as it had been in Chicago when Lou and John introduced it just four days earlier. The trial runs of this special format were justified in the acceptance by their audiences. The Atlantic City panel performed well enough to negate any previous concerns that Lou or John had, and was further proof of the success of this formatting variation. John speculated that they could use it repeatedly. This was the era when broadcasters would make decisions based on their gut feelings. There were no focus groups or extensive market tests before rolling out. If they thought it would work, they just tried it. Sometimes they failed. This time, they succeeded. The special program, now having been offered twice, in Chicago and in Atlantic City, appealed to Alka-Seltzer, too. Lou remembered that "the show was so good, as a matter of fact, that the sponsors want to do it on the network [shows]."[29]

The "Quiz Kids Versus" as a unique program was worth considering as a format with an unlimited number of configurations, earmarked for special events. It was an easy and attractive vehicle to use when the program traveled to make appearances for special events in and around Chicago or to other cities. Putting the Kids against a local panel had the elements of drama and promotion that made it an enticing draw both for live audiences and the listening audience, when broadcast. Now it was no longer a Quiz Kids–Parents show, it was more flexible: a Quiz-Kids-Versus-Another-Panel performance.

The Kids' second performance on February 25 was that evening, part of the entertainment for the attendees at the convention, including the commercial exhibitors. This postprandial show appears not to have featured a competitive panel as the morning's had. It was just the Kids in their customary radio show format. Milton Cross, radio's "voice of the opera," was the master of ceremonies for the evening's program, and of course, Joe Kelly remained as Chief Quizzer for the Kids. The National Broadcasting Company Orchestra performed, as did mezzo-soprano Gladys Swarthout, the "distinguished star of opera and screen," singing a selection of six songs by American composers, one of which, "The Ragpicker," by John Sacco, was composed specifically for Swarthout. Notwithstanding her fame, and in the tradition of theatre, show business, sports, music, or any program with multiple individual performances (as it had been in vaudeville), the featured performers, the stars, always appeared last. They were considered to be top billing. In Atlantic City the Kids had top billing, without exhibiting any of the ballyhoo often exhibited by performing acts, usually as a facet of self-promotion. That the Kids appeared as the final performers on the Atlantic City program was ample proof of their predominance that evening.[30] They were rising stars.

The next day the Kids had a day of sightseeing, followed by their regularly scheduled Wednesday broadcast that evening, this time from Atlantic City, with a guest appearance by Admiral Richard E. Byrd, the famous polar explorer, on an NBC feed from New York. Thursday was the return home travel day. They arrived in Chicago at 8:30 A.M. Friday, February 28, early enough so that it wasn't necessary for any of them to miss school that day.[31]

The trip was a success. The Kids-vs.-superintendents face-off went well, and the itinerary went smoothly, as it had in New York and Washington the month before. It was a conceptual feather in Lou's hat, too. More than any other performances or performers on the program that Tuesday night in Atlantic City, *QK* was illustrative of the convention's traditional and customary theme of advancing the value of education.

Immediately after returning to Chicago, John, Roby, and Rachel went back to work on the Paramount–Jack Benny trip. In letters to her family in Cedar Rapids, a continuous stream of personal correspondence that primarily discussed family and social matters, she sometimes included news about her job, as many people do in their letters to family and friends. In one, she reported that the Kids would be on Benny's show, suggesting that this appearance would help Lou's goal of increasing the national listening audience for *QK*. Roby described the invitation to appear on Benny's radio show as a priceless opportunity to give the show "a terrific boost, as Jack Benny has the highest ratings in the country."[32] Roby referred to the impending appearance on Benny's show as an invitation; she must not have known about Bertha Brainard's plan.

It was full steam ahead to prepare for Jack Benny. The deadline was imminent. Deadlines always seemed imminent in radio. For John and his staff, the clock was ticking, as it was in June 1940 in the weeks before the opening broadcast; as it was at the end of August when their summer replacement contract was about to expire and there was no guarantee that they would continue beyond Labor Day; as it was in November in Milwaukee, when the rush to enlist Gerald Cornfield without the usual selection process clearly demonstrated the frenzy to meet that deadline; and as it just was before the trip to Atlantic City preceded by the significant February 21 broadcast. It seems as though the production office segued from one crisis to another as a matter of course. Now, at the beginning of March, was another crisis. This new critical deadline was the most important to the life of the program since the June 1940 debut.

Adding to the planning, this trip was different because there was more than the usual level of excitement surrounding it, in Chicago by the staff, for the children, and on the West Coast. Both Paramount and Benny ignited interest among the Hollywood film and radio communities to a frenzy of anticipation about meeting these already legendary children. Everyone was waiting for them, excited about actually seeing these up-and-coming stars.

This time it was no longer a simple matter of putting four Kids in a car and driving two hours to Milwaukee. The stakes were higher and the payoff was a larger national audience for the show. And so, Lou and the staff devoted a major portion of their time preparing for the trip. They knew that to plan the mechanics of travel just by relying on the success of the New York, Washington, and Atlantic City trips was a mistake. Their recent experience in travel with the Kids showed them that they had to be fastidious about the fine points in their schedule. They had to anticipate anything that might go wrong, based on what they had experienced during the previous five months of taking the show from Chicago to New York, Washington, and Atlantic City. As long as they planned the minute details of caring for the Kids and the itinerary, traveling with them was viable. They always had to keep in mind the difficulties that might crop up, especially with this highly charged group. They had learned that even when the children weren't performing on a *QK* broadcast or appearing before an audience they were always self-assured, intellectually unpredictable and infused with a high level of energy and curiosity.

Their curiosity seemed to overshadow everything else, requiring more than just tight scheduling. Their natural inquisitiveness could affect even the simplest of plans. They were polite children, but their questioning often went beyond the range of other children and many adults. The Kids were often just on the borderline between cute and exasperating. Their enthusiasm led to pranks, just as it did with children who weren't as intellectually precocious. The Pullman car ladder trick was an apt reminder. To describe them as reserved was an ironic understatement. When planning future trips, the production staff had to recall their visit to the White House, and how the Kids began actively scrutinizing their surroundings with a tactile curiosity, turning over precious vases, peering closely at irreplaceable framed art, and crawling under priceless furniture for a close examination. Roby, John, and Joe Kelly had to consider any possibility and try to prepare for it.

In their active search for information the Kids were always well-mannered but never shy. The fear of making gaffes in no way dampened their actions. Gerard was the quintessential illustration. Of course, they conformed to the social requisites of the day that placed an emphasis on gentility. Even so, their deep-seated curiosity led them to actively, but always accidentally, bend the social rules in their quest for knowledge. Overall, their decorum was respectful. It appears that their parents didn't hamper them by making them conform to strict social niceties that adults usually imposed upon children at that time as a way to reinforce lessons of acceptable behavior. Their upbringing emphasized good manners. Clearly, such polite etiquette was an underlying criterion in selecting children to be Quiz Kids, even the most outwardly inquisitive children. As they became more famous each year, their civility remained with them. John K. Hutchens, writing in the *New York Times*, was impressed: "They are always polite, even to people from the newspapers and magazines who come around and ask questions they must have heard a thousand times before."[33]

Considering all of these factors, and the earlier assessment by Lewellen and Bailey, Lou concluded that the most important revelation about organizing an extended travel schedule with this large group was that it was manageable by his production staff without his strict supervision. Lou no longer had to see to all of the pre-trip details. His experience as the advance man for the New York trip allowed him to pass those responsibilities to John and his staff. Lou felt confident enough in their abilities that he left most of the details of planning to them. He was convinced that the Kids could thrive in any kind of publicity effort that Roby mapped out for them and that they could handle the prolonged, tiring scheduling of interviews by newspaper and magazine reporters, as well as long interruptions to their normal academic and family activities. Tiring as it was for the Kids to be interviewed and pose for photo sessions, it was a necessary demand in creating publicity for the show.

Free of their commitments to Atlantic City, when the staff resumed work on the West Coast trip, it seemed that every day there were changes in scheduling. Originally the plan was to leave for California on March 16 and to return to Chicago March 28; they would be gone for just 12 days. The Kids were to appear on Jack Benny's program probably on March 23, with Gerard as the featured Kid. After the guest appearance by Walt Disney, for the rest of the time in Hollywood there would be photo sessions with Hollywood stars and personalities. This was a quick trip, by contemporaneous definition, because travel by air wasn't common (or affordable) yet. But Benny changed the date of their appearance on his show, and rescheduled it for April 6. Consequently, Lou or John changed the appearance by Disney and the departure date from Chicago with final departure set for two separate days between March 29 and April 2. As usual, the Kids and the production staff would travel in luxury.

The new itinerary had John leave for Los Angeles with two children and two parents on March 29 so that there would be enough time for Jack to work with them for his April 6 show. Roby would follow with three of the Kids and three parents Wednesday, April 2, immediately after that week's *QK* program. She was anxious about being completely in charge of the April 2 broadcast because John would be in California.[34]

Prudently, the staff designated travel on the Union Pacific Railroad's *Challenger*. The *Challenger* was a train marketed as offering economy service combined with fast and comfortable travel between Chicago and several major cities on the West Coast. Union Pacific called it "Everybody's Limited," offering full Pullman service in an attempt to reignite business from passengers who couldn't afford to travel because of the Depression. Food service on the line was "three meals for under a dollar a day." Train travel was fast for that time: Chicago to Los Angeles in just 39 hours and 30 minutes.[35] Choosing travel on the *Challenger* was both a conservative and expeditious choice by the staff, because it was a combination of thrift, speed, and comfort for the Kids and their entourage.

Lou had a different point of view predicated, as usual, on exquisitely planned marketing. Roby knew how Lou thought; no detail and no possibilities escaped his marketing sensibility, even something as ordinary as making plans for travel. He had established a precedent when they took the *Twentieth Century Limited* to New York. She knew that he would want the Kids to travel on the *Super Chief*, even though it was an "extra fare" train. The perception encircling the *Super Chief* was one that projected success, an aura surrounding the Kids and the program that Lou wanted to cultivate. Lou would take any opportunity, no matter how subtle, to buff the image of the program, to promote it to its fullest.

The surcharge added to the standard fare on the *Super Chief* added to the perception of luxury that attracted celebrities and notable passengers, allowing them to distinguish themselves from ordinary travelers. As well as defining a caste system, it was pure vanity. By the late 1930s the *Super Chief* was the flagship train of the Atchison, Topeka, and Santa Fe Railway, the so-called "Train of the Stars" because of the many celebrities who traveled on it between Chicago and Los Angeles. Technologically different, too, it was the first diesel-powered all–Pullman sleeping car train in the America. For Lou, the surcharge was insignificant when he considered the value of the publicity surrounding such elegant and fast travel. It was the same reasoning as the decision to take the *Twentieth Century Limited* to New York.

Once again, the itinerary changed just before the planned departure. Benny was coming to Chicago to be the emcee at a benefit for Greek war relief, one of several efforts to help the civilian population of Greece and its army, which had defied the Italian takeover of their country in a war with Italy that started in October 1940 and continued almost to the end of April

1941. The growing intensity of the European war, especially the Battle of Britain (the air war between Germany and Great Britain), prompted many relief organizations in the United States to try raising money to aid European countries. In February there was a stage show, with radio personalities, but not broadcast, to raise money for the Save the British Children Federation. Canada, too, needed relief. A week earlier, on February 14, a show in Toronto for the benefit of the Canadian War Finance Radio Committee featured George Burns and Gracie Allen.[36]

The Chicago benefit for Greek relief was at the Civic Opera House on Wednesday, April 2. It was not a broadcast. Coincidentally, the benefit was on the same evening as the regularly scheduled *QK* network broadcast at the Merchandise Mart, just seven blocks from the opera house. Appearing on the same program with Benny were Gerard Darrow, who made a short appeal for Greek aid, and Cynthia Cline, who had written a poem for the occasion.[37] A benefit staff member translated her poem into Greek, and Cynthia memorized it in that language so as to recite it to the assembled audience. She was hardly aware of the events around her. She completely focused on giving a good performance. She had practiced reciting her poem repeatedly right up to the point when she was waiting to go on. She still remembered it in Greek 70 years later.[38]

On the same program that evening were Ed Wynn, Bob Crosby and his band, and Blackstone the magician, among other performers. Admission was $10 for orchestra seats, and $250 for boxes. Movie stars donated several items for auction as an additional effort to raise funds: Lionel Barrymore donated one of his etchings; Deanna Durbin, a handbag; Mae West donated a four-foot doll; Walt Disney, an original *Fantasia* painting; and Bing Crosby, a scarf. Benny auctioned his own violin and Philip Levit, a real estate dealer from Chicago, bought it for $35. Marlene Dietrich donated a slightly used lipstick![39]

The next day, Benny, the Kids and their parents, the production staff, Benny's writers and his male secretary from Australia took the streamliner, *The City of Los Angeles*, to the West Coast. All the planning was now a reality. Excitement was in the air; the Quiz Kids were going to Hollywood.

ANSWER

All these characters had the same name: Catherine.

7

Hooray for Hollywood

☞ *A pilot flying an airplane that can fly around the world in 24 hours leaves New York at noon. What time is it when he flies over China?*

As confident as Lou was, his decision to take the Kids to Hollywood must have produced a strong current of worry flowing beneath his usually calm manner. His primary reason for this trip was to build the audience for *Quiz Kids*, even though newspaper radio columnists were full of praise for the program, suggesting that the audience was growing rapidly. One reporter opined that the program and its precocious youngsters were making radio history within a few weeks after its debut with "their popularity continuing to grow week by week."[1] The forthcoming appearance on Jack Benny's program was a wonderful opportunity to reach a vast number of people west of the Rockies, many of whom may have heard of the program but not actually been able to listen to it.

There must have been several questions in Lou's mind to ignite any anxiety he may have felt about the broadcast with Benny. How would Benny's writers portray the Kids? Would they show them as nerds? Would the Kids only have a few minutes of time on Benny's show, more like a brief, figurative handshake, easily forgotten by his vast audience? Would their intelligence be respected or ridiculed? Would he be able to make a contribution to the script not as a writer, but perhaps as a guiding presence or editor? Worrisome questions, even to calm, gentle Lou. Of course, Jack Benny's show was a situation comedy, and the creation of jokes and gags was of primary importance. Usually his writers handled anything serious within the context of the script as lightly as possible.

Roby was anxious about the trip, too. The plan was for her to write newspaper articles about the Kids as they visited the movie studios, were guests at the parties with Walt Disney and Jack Benny, and attended other events during their two weeks in Los Angeles. Each day she was to wire her latest article to the Chicago newspapers for release. Rather than performing her normal duties as a researcher, script writer, and mentor to Joe Kelly, she thought she would be doing plenty of writing on this trip, and that this responsibility would be predominant. This was more to her liking. Still, with all the previous experience she had with the show, she was nervous. She thought that this trip was her "big chance."²

Finally, Lou and John and Roby realized that the stage fright bubbling beneath the surface of their thoughts would disappear because the Kids would prevail. Lou and John reminded themselves that in the shaky first broadcast the previous June, the Kids carried them through. There was no reason to doubt that they would do it again. The children had proved it in New York, at the White House, and once again in Atlantic City. Undoubtedly Hollywood would be no different. Leaning on that conclusion calmed their anxiety.

When the *QK* group boarded the train at Union Station, they discovered that Benny was traveling with three companions: his two writers and his secretary. It had been an intense week for Jack, more than his usual frantic schedule of creating a weekly radio show interspersed with frequent benefit and charity performances. He had brought along his writers to Chicago so that they could write a script for Jack's weekly program on the following Sunday. It was to be a quick trip, and the writers had to squeeze in their work during odd moments in order to meet the usual deadline back in Hollywood. (They had been clever about promoting this Chicago trip beforehand. On his radio program before this trip they wrote the customary jokes about Jack Benny's miserliness. More than just a reference to the penny-pinching foibles of his radio character, the writers put some flesh on the description. They primed the pump. For this trip to Chicago and the Greek benefit, there was a teasing speculation about how he was going to share an upper berth on the Pullman car with his three colleagues so that he wouldn't incur any additional expense.) They left Los Angeles Monday, April 1, arriving in Chicago in time for rehearsals for the benefit. Their return to Los Angeles was to be with the Kids and their group.

Everyone had to follow the agenda precisely because *The City of Los Angeles* departed from Chicago to Los Angeles every third day in April 1941, only ten times a month. The first scheduled departure was at 6:15 P.M. on Thursday, April 3, to arrive in Los Angeles 39 hours and 45 minutes later, Saturday, April 5, the day before the broadcast. The entire group had to be on that train; the next departure was on Sunday, April 6.³

Compared with Jack and his few cohorts, the Kids and their entourage seemed more like a safari. As usual on extended trips, they traveled with a large retinue. Their train left Chicago Thursday, the day after the Wednesday *QK* broadcast and Jack, Gerard, and Cynthia's performances at the Greek benefit. There were six Kids—Gerard Darrow, Richard Williams, Claude

Brenner, Jack Lucal, Joan Bishop, and Cynthia. The sixth Kid was a pinch hitter, at hand on long trips in case one of the five became ill, or if there were another reason for a substitution. In addition to four of their mothers, the group included John Lewellen and his wife, and Roby. Lou was already in Los Angeles.[4] Joe Kelly and his wife were to travel later — probably Sunday, April 6 — because of his ongoing commitment as the emcee for *National Barn Dance* every Saturday evening. Leaving the day after *Barn Dance*, Joe would arrive in Los Angeles on Tuesday, allowing enough time for Roby to coach him for the regular Wednesday *Quiz Kids* program to be broadcast from Hollywood. By then Joe was familiar with the coaching sessions; he knew what to expect, so that when necessary Roby could cut back on the time allowed for coaching.

Roby was thrilled with the prospect that she and John would be working with Jack's script writers, Eddie Beloin and Bill Morrow. In her youthful fantasy about this trip, she thought that she was lucky to be part of this process.[5] Fantasies rarely come true, however. John and Roby's primary duties were the same as they were in Chicago, focused on creating *QK* broadcasts and the ensuing publicity surrounding them. It was solely up to Jack and his writers to create the overall theme of the program. John and Roby's involvement with writing the script for the program was only as consultants about the questions for the Kids, and the unique way they wrote them. Other than that, they were only observers of the process of creating a hit radio comedy. Still, it was exciting for Roby, as it would be for anyone who understood the difficulty of writing new material each week, especially comedy material for a mass audience. She learned that the popular image of comedy writers was far from the truth. Writing comedy was not a hilarious team effort of jokes and pithy remarks tossed back and forth. It was serious business. More than serious, she thought the atmosphere around Benny's writers was grim. These funny men were completely somber, like "a mortgage committee meeting of the Union League Club."[6]

Eddie and Bill sat in the lounge car with Jack and used this travel time to focus on the April 6 broadcast. This intensity of creativity was normal for them. The only difference was their surroundings: they were working while riding on a fast train, with all of its inherent distractions. Apparently they had experienced the same situation on the train eastward from Los Angeles at the beginning of that week as they prepared Jack's script for the benefit. They were used to working in unorthodox surroundings; they could take the train in stride. But they had larger problems than the unusual environment of a train ride.

Try as they might, they couldn't find a way to blend the Kids into the program's usual format. They just couldn't make it work. It had seemed like a good idea to have all the Kids on, but now that this trip was a reality the writers had serious doubts. Jack had doubts, too. Faced with the reality of creating a script, what was so funny about bright children?

Even if they managed to write a program that was acceptable, Jack worried that the Kids wouldn't be able read the script well enough. He thought he had made a big mistake by including all of them, rather than just one or two.

Originally the plan had been for Gerard to appear on the broadcast alone, with the script written around him. The idea was to show how smart Gerard was and how dumb the rest of them (Benny and his cast) were.[7] Then Benny changed the plan, and Joan Bishop was going to appear with Gerard. Travel plans changed, too. John Lewellen was scheduled to leave Chicago on March 29 with the two Kids and two parents (Joan's mother and Gerard's aunt), allowing enough time to work on Jack's April 6 show. Roby and the rest of the group would follow after the regularly scheduled broadcast in Chicago on April 2. Sometime during the last two weeks of March, Jack changed the plan again, probably because of his commitment to the Greek war relief show. Now, all the Quiz Kids were on the same train with him the day after the benefit at the Civic Opera House.

Frustrated by the apparent inability to weave all the Kids into an episode of the Jack Benny program, the children's appearance seemed to be in doubt even as they were barreling toward California. Roby couldn't decide if they should get off at the next whistle stop, or to stay calm and just order another round of ginger ale for the Kids. She wasn't sure how Miles Labs would react if Benny changed his mind. Fortunately they weren't relying only on Benny's decision; they had planned to go to the West Coast anyway. The excitement of appearing on Benny's show had added another layer of stimulation, albeit a major one, to the anticipation of this trip. If Benny withdrew his offer, it would be troublesome, because Miles Labs had agreed to pay for all their expenses. Without Benny's show, Miles might have withdrawn their agreement to foot the bills. Roby's fears were premature. Both of the Beardsleys, Charles and Arthur, came to Hollywood to join the entourage, as did Walter Wade and his wife.[8] With the arrival of the Beardsleys and the Wades, the expenses, paid by Miles Labs, had been justified.

If Benny canceled the appearance by the Kids, it would be an unfortunate setback, but apparently not a deal breaker. Between the interest in the Kids among several movie studios, the *QK* broadcasts emanating from Los Angeles, and a schedule of social events that would promote *QK* similar to those that they frequently attended in Chicago, there were more than enough reasons to undertake this trip. These social events were the result of some scheduling by Walt Disney, Jack Benny, and some movie stars. This trip would be an important contribution to audience-building. Even without the appearance on Jack's program several media outlets would feature their visit to Hollywood, providing them with more publicity nationwide toward their ultimate goal of increasing their listeners.

The fear of cancellation disappeared later that day. Benny finally hit upon something funny that he could use with the Kids. He was sitting in the lounge car, taking a break from working on the script, when he found himself next to Gerard. Young Darrow was reading Shakespeare's *Hamlet*. Jack was reading the comic section of a Sunday newspaper. He thought that the contrast was ironic, and amusing. The child should have been reading the funnies; he should have been reading Shakespeare's play. He asked Gerard a few questions about *Hamlet*, but he didn't understand the answers. With that, he felt the spark of an idea, the solution to the problem of how to have all the Kids on his show.

He gathered the other Kids together and asked them what they were studying in school. They were happy to tell him about Cicero, Thomas Jefferson, the Dutch East Indies, Stonewall Jackson, dinosaurs, Rip Van Winkle, adjectives and adverbs. Jack went back to his writers at the other end of the lounge and had a consultation. They agreed, and became energized once again. They began to rewrite the show.

Jack's idea was to have four of his cast, Mary Livingstone, Dennis Day, Phil Harris, and Don Wilson, compete with just four Quiz Kids. (Jack Lucal was not going to be on the April 6 broadcast.) The episode would be a variation of the QK Versus format, only this time with some of the customary Jack Benny gags woven into the script.

Benny would be the Chief Quizzer, of course. He would ask the questions alternately of each side, the Quiz Kids and the Benny Kids. And he would keep score. The writers named Benny's "kids" the Jell-O Kids. It was an obvious promotional ploy, acceptable for that era in broadcasting. It was particularly difficult for Benny and his writers to write dialogue (i.e., questions to be asked) for these precocious children. The writers couldn't write the usual array of gags and jokes for the Kids. That would have been tantamount to belittling them.

The writers had already developed the comic foibles to create the stage personalities for Jack and his cast that they used regularly each week, such as Benny's perennial 39-years-old age, his penury, and his vanity. They characterized Phil Harris by his fondness for drinking, whereas they drew Dennis Day as a perennial naïf, with overtones of stupidity. Eddie (Rochester) Anderson's character had jokes written to fit his role as Benny's on-air housekeeper, valet, driver, errand runner, and general factotum, etc. These facetious characterizations led to creating familiar gags each week. The radio audience loved them and relied on them as predictable comic interludes.

The basis of Jack's idea was to create a contrast between the intelligent answers that the Kids gave to questions, and the answers that Benny's cast would give to simplified variations of the same questions. In writing the script, they would use a series of lowbrow radio gags as answers to these watered-down versions of the erudite questions, but aimed at providing the expected laughs at the expense of the cast, not the Kids.

A new problem emerged. How could the writers devise suitable questions for the Kids? They didn't have the experience or the resources to devise such questions. John and Roby could have helped, but someone had a more creative solution: ask the Kids to write their own questions. Benny was willing to try it. He asked the Kids individually what they'd like to say. The questions that the Kids suggested were not the same as those on a usual *Quiz Kids* broadcast, but they were sufficient. The new idea seemed workable.

They reached Los Angeles Saturday morning at 8:00, as scheduled. The script was ready and a rehearsal was held that same afternoon. The Kids, Roby, and John had just enough time to check in at the Hollywood Knickerbocker Hotel, refresh themselves and get to the rehearsal. The rehearsal was on the sun porch off the living room at Jack's house. For Cynthia Cline those rehearsals in the home setting, more intimate than at a broadcasting studio, were one of many highlights of this trip. She remembers that Jack's wife, Mary Livingstone, was gracious and pleasant, and the entire Benny cast was down-to-earth and personable.[9]

Everyone laughed at the gags, the Kids read the script well, and Benny and his writers smiled with relief. A second and final rehearsal Sunday morning, the day of the broadcast, was a surprise for Roby. The writers had edited and rewritten the script. She was amazed at how they transformed the script in just two days, from the last version completed Friday on the train, to the final version for the Sunday rehearsal. It had been "cropped, clipped, and manicured" to shape it into a show more to their liking. Her excitement about the prospects of working with the writers, or at least seeing how they worked, was well justified.

The show started with its usual format for the first 15 minutes. Don Wilson announced that Phil Harris's orchestra would play the opening theme, attaching a different and mild tongue-in-cheek or punning title to the music as he did each week, such as "Silver Threads Among the Brass Section," "Wyoming, Why Do You Begin with W?" or "The Vine Street Viggle." Benny's cast "arrived" for each episode singly, and their dialogue with Jack was primarily jokes that played on their radio characters. (It was a format that many radio comedies used; Fred Allen used the same on his weekly walk along "Allen's Alley," meeting with his cast of characters, each doing their comic turns.) As usual, each episode of the Jack Benny program allotted time for

Jack Benny and the Kids arrive at Union Station, Los Angeles. The next day the Kids were on his show. (Front, from left) Benny, Gerard Darrow, Richard Williams, Claude Brenner. (Rear, from left) Joan Bishop, Cynthia Cline (courtesy Cynthia Cline Newgarden).

musical entertainment, Dennis Day sang a song each week, and Phil Harris and his orchestra played a jazzy arrangement usually at the middle of each program.

After Dennis sang, just over nine minutes into the program, Jack introduced the Kids, just as he had announced that he would on his previous week's program. His introduction was serious and tasteful with none of the gags that he sprinkled throughout his usual scripts. "For our featured attraction of this evening, and our cultural contribution of the season," he declaimed, "we have with us tonight four youngsters from one of radio's most popular programs that comes to you every Wednesday night from Chicago: the Quiz Kids." He continued, explaining that the Kids were on the show to "match wits" with his cast. "What's going to happen to us shouldn't happen to Einstein," predicted Mary. Furthermore, Jack announced that he would be the quizmaster. He went on to say that the following Wednesday, he would be quizzed as a guest on *Quiz Kids*.

Before he could continue, Rochester interrupted him with a "phone call." This was a device used to signal his entrance for that episode. Rochester said that he had something important to report. Carmichael, Jack's resident polar bear, had just come out of hibernation from his place in the cellar, he said. Jack was doubtful. He thought that it was impossible for the bear to wake up so early in the year; he needed two more weeks to lie dormant. He asked Rochester what happened. Rochester told him that when the gas man went down to read the meter, Carmichael had heard him and seized upon him. Jack asked him what happened, and Rochester said that he didn't know but he doubted if they would "get a bill this month."

Jack thought Rochester's description was silly, and that the bear wouldn't hurt a fly; he was just playing. "Yes, but where's the man?" Rochester asked. Jack told him not to be so pessimistic. Carmichael was pretty hungry after sleeping all winter, so he instructed Rochester to give the animal a big dinner, but not to let him eat too fast because this would be his first meal. "Second meal," said Rochester, "Where's the man?" As Rochester was to end his phone conversation with Jack, he paused to ask him if he was really going to have the Quiz Kids on the program: "They're supposed to be pretty smart, aren't they?" "They're brilliant," Jack replied; "they know everything." "Well," said Rochester, "ask them what happened to the gas man." It was a typical joke-filled introduction of a cast member, and basic ammunition for humorous reference later.

After a 50-second jazzy upbeat song by the band, it was time for the Kids to appear. Jack's writers used a subtle fillip to characterize them. The Kids were on for nearly all of the last 15 minutes of the 30-minute program. Benny started by asking Gerard if all the Kids were present. Gerard said that they were. "Well, here we go, folks," said Benny. It was time to introduce the competition. "The Quiz Kids versus the Jell-O Kids," he declared, "May the best team win." Following the script exactly as it had been written, Gerard interrupted and corrected him immediately, by saying, "May the *better* team win."[10]

With Gerard's five-word sentence Benny's writers not only created a gag, but captured the essence of the Kids. It was their nature, individually and as a group, to correct the slightest errors they heard or saw, even in their off-air daily lives. It was as if they were school teachers constantly and persistently correcting their students (everyone else). With their fund of knowledge, they were critical of everything and everyone. There was no arrogance about it, though. They seemed to be trying to instruct those around them, not scold them or appear to be superior. They offered their criticism with good humor, with no malice intended. Just as they were with their curiosity about the physical world around them, they weren't shy — they would speak up no matter who or what needed remediation.

Roby wasn't immune to their criticism either, although they were more hesitant and more polite with her. Several days later, on their way to the MGM studios, she pointed to a large white building on a hill and asked, "Wouldn't it be fun to go to the Griffith Conservatory when we come back? You know — to look at the stars and planets and hear a lecture. Wouldn't it be fun?" she reiterated, almost demanding a reply. The Kids didn't answer. They were silent. Roby looked at each one, searching for a response, but the Kids appeared to be looking intently out the window. Finally Claude, with his clipped British accent, turned to her and said, gently, "It would be fun, but you do mean *ob*servatory, don't you?"[11]

After Jack announced that this show would be a competition, he mimicked Joe Kelly by saying that he would call the roll, letting the Kids introduce themselves as they did on their own show. Then he had the Jell-O Kids introduce themselves in the same manner as the Kids, with the insertion of predictable ironic jokes ("I'm Philip Harris. I'm six years old and I attend the Hollywood Recreation Bowling Alley").

The assumption that many people made was that all the Quiz Kids were under 10 years old; generally they thought that they were much younger. Because it was radio and the home audience couldn't see the Kids, when there were very young Kids on, the audience thought that they were all that young.[12] To foster this misconception, newspaper and magazine reporters wrote about the younger Kids, emphasizing their abilities. It was much more newsworthy and dramatic to write about the wondrous precocity of a seven-year-old than about those who were approaching or already in their early teens. On their first appearances on the program, Gerard was seven, as were Joel Kupperman and Ruth Duskin. Lou apparently encouraged the idea, too. He wanted to be sure to have Joan Bishop on the first program in June of 1940 while she was still 12. Lou knew that it was more theatrical to have young children on the program, and Lou was always looking for the dramatic twist. Perhaps that's why Joe Kelly, probably under Lou's direction, emphasized the accomplishments of the youngest Kids on the broadcasts.

Jack Benny's Jell-O Kids did nothing to dispel the notion that all the Kids were under ten. After Phil Harris stated that he was six years old, when the rest of the Jell-O Kids introduced themselves, Mary Livingstone said that she was six, too. Don Wilson claimed to be seven, and Dennis Day reported that he was just one year old! He explained, "My mother dropped me off." The only Quiz Kid on the program that evening who was actually at such a tender age was Gerard, who was still seven. The ages of the other three ranged from 11 to 15.

After the introductions, Jack proceeded to the questions. Two of those that he asked the Kids had been suggested by Claude and Gerard on the train a few days earlier. During his session with Jack in the lounge car that day, Claude had proposed that Jack should ask him for the Latin names of the five classes of fish in order of their development, such as the Cyclostomata and the Elasmobranchii and the ganoid fish. Gerard offered this: A coleopteran, a *Musca domestica*, and a Lepidoptera were having a bit of a tête-à-tête on a screen door. Now if you suddenly appeared with a fly swatter, one of the parties would leave quite hastily. Who would it be? On the show, when Gerard replied to his question, he gave the correct answer (the *Musca domestica*, the common housefly) and then amplified his response by translating the other two Latin names into English (beetle and butterfly). It was a replica of the kind of extended response frequently offered by the Kids on their own show.

The writers came up with the gag questions for Jack to ask the Jell-O Kids. These were comic variations of the serious questions that Jack asked the Quiz Kids just a few minutes earlier. After Gerard's question about the housefly and the subsequent definition of Lepidoptera, Jack asked Dennis: What fly would you associate with butter? That's a little tough, so I'll put it this way, he explained. Butter is associated with what fly? Dennis didn't know, so Mary answered correctly. Jack took great pride in awarding a point to the Jell-O Kids. There was the obligatory difficult math question, answered correctly by Richard Williams, with his explanation of how he determined the answer.

Following Richard's math question was Claude's entry in the field of ichthyology. After Claude answered his question about the five orders of fish, Jack asked Phil Harris how he would spell fish. Phil answered, F-I-S-C-H. Jack said: That's right — Joe Fisch. I know him well. That's another point for the Jell-O Kids, he announced with loud and forceful pride. At some point Benny declared that there was a tie score, so that there would be a final question. He had the orchestra play a song and asked Joan to identify its title and whether or not it was classical or popular. Joan didn't know the answer to either part of the two-part question. Jack asked Phil its name and he didn't know either. He promptly asked a few members of the orchestra, who didn't know the title of what they just played. Benny knew the name, and promptly declared that the Jell-O Kids had won the competition. At that point he moved toward the end of the show and offered some solace to the Kids. "Tough luck, Quiz Kids, but you lost fair and square."[13]

The broadcast went well that night. Eddie and Bill successfully blended the Quiz Kids into the Benny format. The Kids performed as Jack had hoped they would. They did not appear to be giving a perfunctory reading, but injected life into the words. They did not deviate or make any embarrassing mistakes, either. Lou, John, and Roby must have been pleased. Benny was. He said that it was his funniest show in years. He cast aside his previous doubts about the abilities of the Kids. He concluded that these bright children could be entertaining and that they could read the script as well as the professional actors in his cast. He was so pleased that he invited the Kids to appear as guests on his show each Sunday for the next two weeks.[14]

Of course, this meant that the Kids would have additional air time during their two weeks in Los Angeles. Lou and the Beardsleys must have been ecstatic. The Kids would broadcast their show twice and appear once as Benny's guests, all previously scheduled. Now, they would have two additional appearances on Benny's show. Benny recorded his radio broadcasts in 1941, but not before airing. He recorded each program live as he broadcast it. If it had been a few years later, when broadcasting technology became more sophisticated after World War II, Benny would have taped the three broadcasts in advance all in one day and released them at the scheduled times.

Fortunately, when Benny extended his invitation for two more weeks, it didn't present a problem for the *QK* travel schedule or budget. When Lou planned this trip, his schedule included a stay until Sunday, April 20, to accommodate various movie studio appointments and screen tests. But when Benny extended his invitation by two more Sundays it created more difficulty for the writers than for the Quiz Kids. The writers had to produce two new scripts featuring the Kids. If the first show was problematic, writing two new episodes would be daunting. What could they possibly do to keep the next appearances by the Kids interesting, without sounding as though they were simply *QK* broadcasts? Would they have to create two new QK Versus the Jell-O Kids contests (the winner of two of the three would be the champion)? That choice was too repetitive, perhaps too boring, and too difficult to make interesting. Would they have to create new adventures for the Kids with Jack and his cast? As bright as the Kids were, they were not actors, even though they were more than competent on the April 6 broadcast. As funny as they might be occasionally on their own show, they were not professional comedians.

Benny and his writers solved the dilemma. In fact, their solution exceeded Roby's expectations. With the two extra appearances on their show, Benny's creative team did more than simply write additional scripts featuring the Kids. They extended a natural, believable, story line that emanated from the April 6 show. They tied together the three appearances as a continuing story — in effect it was a three-act play with a beginning, middle, and an end. It offered Roby a rare insight into how Jack Benny created the leading comedy show on radio in 1941.

The schedule of events for the week after Jack's April 6 show started early the next day. On that Monday, April 7, Walt Disney had a midday welcoming get-together for the Kids at his studio. It was a boisterous party. The pace was frenetic at this first Hollywood bash for the Kids. Everyone wanted to meet them and to speak with them. Three months earlier, in January, their boisterous press conference in New York at the Beaux Arts had been sedate compared with this.

Even though they were the honored guests and the focus of attention, the Kids were in awe of all of the notable people who were present and were just as excited about meeting them. The Disney party guests from Hollywood were so thrilled about meeting them that they gathered around the Kids asking them questions and wanting to know about them. At the same time, newspaper reporters, magazine writers, and studio publicists reporting on this lunchtime party converged on them. The pop of flashbulbs sounded like a miniature fireworks display as photographers worked as rapidly as they could, shooting the Kids from every angle.

Conversely, the Kids were star-struck at Disney's party. They were the visiting celebrities, but Hollywood and its denizens still fascinated them. As many people still are, they were movie fans. They bought autograph books and took them to the Disney party as well as the various parties and social events they attended during the following two weeks, collecting hundreds of autographs among them. Cynthia's book — leather-bound — has 50. Richard Williams still treasures his.

Many of the signatures are of people long forgotten by contemporary film enthusiasts, but there are many notables of the day who still remain memorable. The guests were practically a Who's Who of 1940s Hollywood. Among them were Eleanor Powell, Red Skelton, Sonja Henie, Milton Berle, Don Ameche, Betty Grable, George Raft, Bob Hope, Paulette Goddard, Charles

Boyer, Edgar Bergen and, of course, Charlie McCarthy. It wasn't easy for the Kids to get signatures at these parties where they were the guests of honor. The Kids realized that their autographs were in great demand, too, because the other party guests crowded around them to ask them to sign their books. Roby called it a "Signature Social."[15] Apparently acquiring autographs was one of the social and cultural mores of Hollywood society in 1941. The movie celebrities had autograph books, too. It was ironic. Famous actors were in a throng around the Kids. What made this atypical was that the fans of these actors, eager to get their autographs, usually mobbed them. Trying to handle the requests for their autographs, the Kids had a hard time breaking away to expand their own autograph collections.[16]

To compensate for this difficulty, the Kids probably kept their autograph books in their pockets for the entire time they were in Hollywood on the chance of a random meeting with more of their screen idols, or other famous people connected with the movie industry. Richard always had his handy. Keeping his autograph book with him almost backfired. A few days later, during the warm-up for the April 9 *Quiz Kids* broadcast, John and Roby noticed that Richard had a little book sitting on his lap with a pencil tucked in it as a place marker. They thought it might appear to be a reference book. Before the program started John asked him for the book, explaining that it might look suspicious, appearing that Richard needed to look in the book for help with answering questions. The studio audience would think he was cheating. Not so. Richard simply wanted to make sure he got Walt Disney's signature in his autograph book — the little book that was on his lap. Disney was the guest celebrity on the show. Instead, John gave Richard's book to Disney, who signed it during the opening commercial.[17]

Lunch, served at Disney's party, included such whimsically named dishes as Snow White Salad, a Duckie Fruit Plate and Grumpy Delight.[18] Dessert was ice cream and a slice from a 200-pound cake made for the occasion.[19] The Kids dashed around, trying to get autographs. But they were so overwhelmed with requests for their autographs that they nearly didn't get any food. "Everybody else ate and we were sort of hungry," reported Roby.[20] Disney's animators had illustrated the menu. Playing softly in the background was recorded music from several Disney films. After lunch, Disney showed two of his new films, not yet released. First, he presented the Kids with an elaborate introduction. When he asked them to come on stage, none came. He called for them again, still no one appeared. As usual, the Kids were exploring, and Roby and John found them in the men's and women's restrooms.

The first film Disney showed was an unfinished Donald Duck cartoon (it was animated, but still in black and white). This was followed by a short about a character named Baby Weems who was born with superior intelligence, a

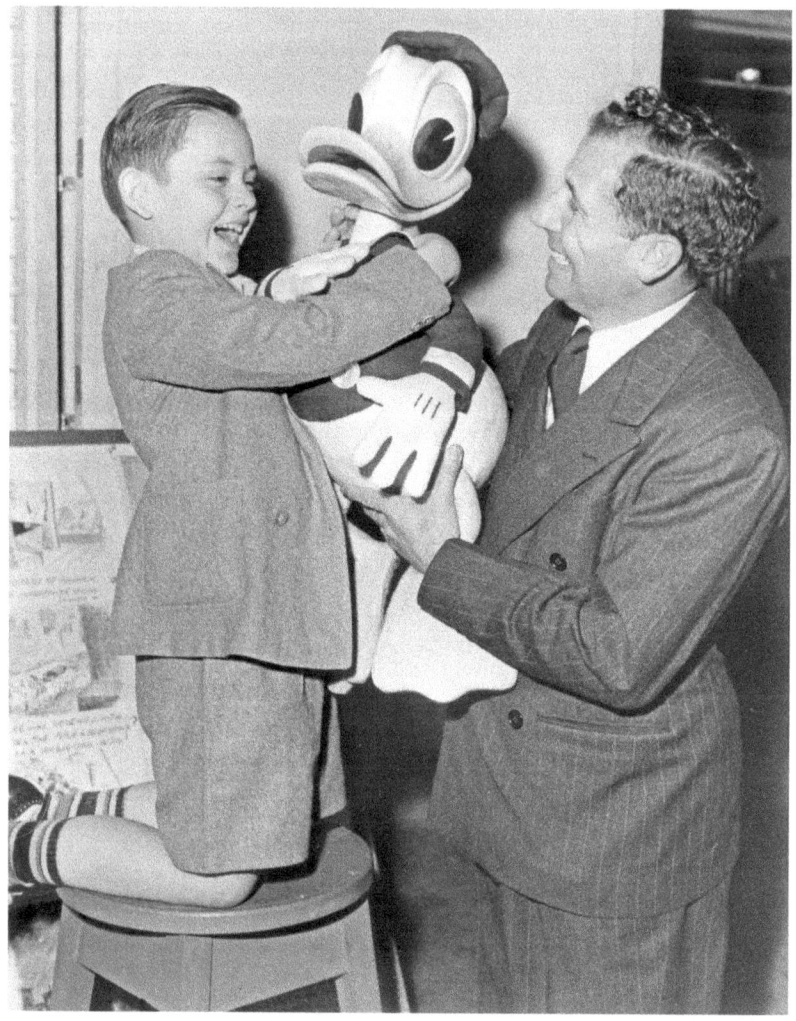

At Walt Disney's party for the Kids, April 1941. Gerard clutches a Donald Duck doll, a present from Walt Disney. Clarence Nash, the voice of Donald, looks on (Billy Rose Theatre Division, The New York Public Library for the Performing Arts, Astor, Lenox and Tilden Foundations).

thinly-veiled reference to the Kids. The short was to be a film-within-a-film sequence in the Disney film *The Reluctant Dragon*. The Baby Weems sequence was appropriate for this occasion; it suggested the *Quiz Kids* broadcasts. Between the two films a magician performed. He asked for volunteers to come on stage, and Gerard and a child actress who appeared in the film of *The Virginian* volunteered. While on stage, Gerard was up to his usual uninhibited, attention-getting actions. He mimicked the magician visually by pulling imaginary objects out of the air. The audience was delighted with his antics.

Disney had invited several movie stars and their children, including Pat O'Brien and his children, Robert Young and his children, George Burns and Gracie Allen with their son, Bing Crosby and his two sons, Joan Blondell and her son, and Joan Bennett and her daughter. The accumulation of so many A-List actors suggests that this was a major Hollywood event on that day.

After showing the new films, from 2:00 to 2:15 NBC aired a special live broadcast that featured Walt Disney and the Kids. The announcer explained that they were standing at the "entrance to the Sound Effects Stage of the Walt Disney Studios." This theoretical setting helped create a little bogus story to promote his cartoons and films. It was as if the audience — the radio audience — was standing with the announcer, eavesdropping on this special event. The announcer, Buddy Twiss, said that Disney and the Kids were on a tour of the studios and would be arriving "any minute." This program would be different for the Kids, he clarified. On their own program, they answered "just about every question on any subject that you can mention." Now, instead of answering questions, Twiss explained that the Kids would ask the questions. No doubt, he intoned, the Kids would challenge Disney and his staff. Always inquisitive about everything, the questions that the Kids asked explored the intricate workings of producing and making animated movies.

Disney took them to the sound effects "stage." Because this was a radio broadcast, Disney used a device that would produce a memorable and somewhat comic effect, fanciful as it was. He assigned each sound effect to a special "drawer." As he opened each of the "drawers," they produced the appropriate sound. The sound effect continued until he shut the drawer. It was akin to turning up the volume on a radio, then quickly twisting the volume knob to mute it when desired.

Then he introduced the Kids to his various characters, Donald Duck, Pluto, Goofy, Minnie Mouse, and others who were supposedly in the middle of making the voice-over sound track for a new cartoon. On this broadcast each actor who normally performed the various voices for the cartoons played his character. One of the Kids noticed that something was missing from the introduction of the actors. The actor who played Mickey Mouse was not included. "Who does Mickey Mouse?" our inquisitive Kid asked. A small, high-pitched voice in the background said, "I do." It was a revelation for the Kids, and perhaps everyone else in the audience: Walt Disney was the voice of Mickey Mouse.

Then Cynthia asked Clarence Nash, the voice of Donald Duck, the technical details of how he made Donald talk. The answer was a way to explain the fine points of creating the sound of voices in cartoons. Disney actually wrote this portion of the script. As well, he included how he made sound effects for the band as a background sound effect when his cartoon characters would sing a song in any of the cartoons, with an on-air song as an aural illustration. After this brief musical interlude, there was a standard radio sign-off, summarizing what the program had been and concluding with a mention of the Blue Network as its creator. In retrospect, this little broadcast with the Kids was a clever, if not always subtle, way for Disney to promote his new films.

If the luncheon party and the activities of the past few days had been hectic, the next two weeks were just as frantic. Fortunately in March, before they left Chicago, Roby, John, and Joe Bailey had written the *QK* program for April 9 with Walt Disney's appearance, so that it was not a pressing task after Benny's Sunday show on April 6.[21] Still, there was no pause in the activities. There were personal appearances and parties that brought about a demanding pace just as equal to that of the usual preparations for the weekly broadcast.

The Kids got baby chicks as gifts at the party. (From top left) Joan Bishop, Cynthia Cline, child star Jane Withers; (bottom from left) Richard Williams, Gerard Darrow, Jack Lucal, Claude Brenner (Photofest).

In the week following the first Benny broadcast, after Walt Disney's party for the Kids, there were screen tests scheduled at MGM, and meetings with Twentieth Century–Fox about a screen test for Gerard. Roby wrote about her hectic schedule describing these events in a letter wishing her family a happy Easter (March 13 that year). A little purple journalism had seeped out of her new typewriter as she acknowledged that she probably wouldn't have time to send them Easter gifts, because she hadn't "budged" out of her hotel in five days.[22]

As evidence, she reported that at that moment she had five "important calls pending," including one from Jane Withers, "the movie star," about a party she was hosting for the kids. Jane Withers was only 15 years old and a child star at Twentieth Century–Fox, successful enough so that the prospect of the Kids being the featured guests at her party was appealing to them as a plum social event, and just as appealing to Lou as another avenue for promoting the program.[23] Roby reported that while she was waiting for the call from Withers, she was expecting a call about where in New York to send photographs taken during Disney's party (Roby had sent a chauffeur to Disney's studio to get them). A short time before writing this letter, she had a meeting with someone from *Time* magazine and arranged another room for a writer and reporter from *Modern Screen* magazine who were going to give the Kids a movie quiz to be featured in their magazine. "These are just some of the things I've done in the last hour," she wrote, breathlessly. "The phone has just rung again and the appointment was set for Joan Bishop's audition for Bing Crosby's show," she noted. In addition to planning and arranging time for the Kids as a group, she had to supervise their individual plans.

She reported that the heightened pace continued that morning. The Long Beach Chamber of Commerce called (for the third time) to try to get her to agree to having the Kids as their guests at a hummingbird farm and to appear at some club. Earlier, Charles Beardsley had stopped by her table at breakfast to say that they must see the Douglas airplane plant on Monday (April 14). The phone rang again and someone wanted the Kids to judge a children's writing contest. Then Lou called from Palm Springs, where he was working at Jack's weekend house with the writers and Jack preparing the Sunday, April 13, Jack Benny program. His call was to give her the outline of that Benny show so that Roby could write a press release (at the same time handling all these other tasks) to *Time* magazine and other publications. The next night, Saturday, Gloria Jean, the child actress, was giving a party for the Kids, with the Jane Withers party scheduled for Sunday. Joan Benny, Jack's daughter, was giving one on Tuesday, April 15. In her typical understated manner, Roby describes herself as "sort of busy."

Later, the reporter and photographer from *Modern Screen* magazine interviewed the Kids, took photos, and gave them the quiz that was to appear in the next issue of their magazine — 20 questions about contemporary movies. Only three of the 20 questions stumped the Kids. (In trying to identify who played the Lone Ranger, Gerard thought it was Tom Mix.)[24] The reporter was "scared to death" of the Kids. She had been at the Disney party for them. Gerard had three live baby chickens that the magician at the party gave to him after pulling them out of his pockets. Apparently, the magician's gift signaled that he was willing to forgive Gerard's mimicry during his magic act. The reporter asked Gerard what he was going to do with the chicks. He looked at her and said, slowly, "I'm going to *eat* them." She was horrified. "Eat them?" she cried. Gerard nodded. She began begging him not to, so he turned to her and said, with disgust, "I'm not really going to eat them."[25] Gerard was exercising his shock techniques. He was often flamboyant, complete with outrageous statements or actions, and a wicked sense of humor to match.

In reality, there was no chance that Gerard would eat the chicks. The thought of eating birds, fish, or any other animals was distasteful to him. His interest in them was purely scientific. For a break in their hectic schedule, Charles Beardsley took the Kids fishing to a trout pond near Los Angeles several days later. Between them they caught 40 fish. Afterwards, they were preparing to eat some of the fish. Gerard and Richard couldn't. The thought of actually having a meal with their fish made them ill. That evening, several hours after the fishing expedition, Richard was still upset about the whole idea.

After the fishing trip, they were to go to a lion farm.[26] It was Gay's Lion Farm, in El Monte, 13 miles east of Los Angeles. Gay's raised lions to supply the demands of circuses, zoos, and movie studios.[27] Undoubtedly, this was the source for the MGM lion, Slats, who died of appendicitis in 1927, and his look-alike successor, Jackie.[28] They also visited the hummingbird aviary. Both of these visits appeared to be promotional appearances, much like those they made in Chicago, complete with photographers and reporters interviewing them for articles that they released shortly after to various publications — local, national, and trade-related. The lion farm visit seemed to be an opportunity for MGM, with their abiding interest in child actors, to ally themselves with the Kids.

The Kids didn't have much free time, but when they did, they worked on their school homework and explored the Hollywood public library in the process. Joan Bishop practiced on a piano off the main lobby of their hotel. The Kids played a vigorous tournament of ping pong every day in the hotel's sun roof— Richard was the undisputed champion among them.

It wasn't only the staff who tried everything they could to promote the Kids. Their hotel in Los Angeles, the Hollywood Knickerbocker Hotel, sent a reporter and photographer from their in-house newsletter staff to shoot pictures and interview them about what they liked about the hotel (their answer: the sun roof and ice cream). They were going to use the presence of the Kids at the hotel as the basis of an article in a national hotel trade association magazine promoting their establishment. The photographer was Bert Kopperl, the famous Hollywood celebrity photographer who had worked in New York for *Time* magazine in the 1930s with Margaret Bourke-White, the renowned photographer for *Life* magazine.[29]

A few hours after their April 9 broadcast the Kids actually heard themselves on their own show. They had done the broadcast at 5 P.M., but only 1,300 people in all of California heard them — those in the studio audience. *QK* was actually on air at 8 o'clock. Eager to hear themselves, the Kids gathered around the cigar stand at the Knickerbocker, where Emmy, the clerk, had a small radio turned to their program, listening as she worked. The Kids stopped to hear it, excitedly identifying their own voices, and maybe even a little disappointed and deflated about how they actually sounded, especially Claude, who kept saying, "I *cahn't* sound like *that*. *That* is simply *awhful*."[30] (Claude, who was born in South Africa, hadn't lost his accent.) Gerard was indifferent to the broadcast. As soon as Joe Kelly came on to start the program, Gerard went to the magazine rack in the lobby and sat cross-legged on the floor, reading a comic book. When other hotel guests came over to him to ask him how he knew the answers that he gave on the show, he didn't look up. He ignored them. He just sat and continued to read the comic book.

Not everything in their itinerary pertained to movies. Just as it was at the beginning of their New York trip, reporters asked them what they wanted to see in Los Angeles. Gerard wanted to see the La Brea tar pits. Cynthia wanted to go to the Los Angeles Museum to see "little Esau." Perplexed by her choice, the reporter asked her to explain. She told him that little Esau was a small mammoth found in the La Brea pits. Jack Lucal, whose ambition was to be a priest, said that he wanted to see the San Juan Capistrano mission (Groucho Marx was his second choice, and Carmen Miranda, his third). Joan Bishop, along with Cynthia, included two famous nightclubs ("a peek at Ciro's") and the Brown Derby, and to meet the teenage star Deanna Durbin (they got their wish: Cynthia and Joan had lunch with her two days after the April 6 Benny broadcast). They wanted to see the Hollywood Bowl, and of course, to meet Cary Grant. Claude wanted to meet Mickey Rooney. Gerard, adding to his wish to go the La Brea pits, added Catalina Island, the Bird Park, and the San Diego Zoo to his wish list.[31]

Act Two was broadcast the following Sunday, April 13, Easter Sunday. As they had planned in Chicago a month earlier, Jack's appearance on *QK* was to be three days after his Easter show on April 13. Eddie and Bill created a logical continuation of the first appearance the previous Sunday. This time, only Gerard, Richard, and Claude were on the program. They appeared on nearly the entire 30-minute segment.

The plot revolved around Jack's anxiety about his appearance on *QK* three days later. To prepare, he had Mary Livingstone ask him questions, none of them very difficult. He couldn't answer any of them. Embarrassed, he tried to rig the upcoming *QK* program. He asked Claude to help him during his imminent appearance by not answering some of the questions. Claude declined, saying that it wasn't ethical. Benny continued to try with the other two Kids. He asked Gerard and Richard for their help by remaining silent when they were asked questions. They declined because of ethics. Jack was in a tizzy, with answers and questions floating around in his mind. He asked Rochester to eavesdrop on the Kids to hear what they were talking about or to observe what they were reading so that he could be prepared, so that he could have an advantage. Then Jack asked Rochester to take the Kids down to the cellar to meet Carmichael, opening the opportunity for a continuation of the "Where's the man?" joke. After dinner, Jack realized that he was tired. He wanted to sit and rest for a few minutes before going to bed. He fell asleep in his chair, and had a dream, with a nightmare about appearing on *QK*. Rochester woke him, telling him that he had been having a bad dream. Jack decided that it was time to go to bed, he said goodnight to Rochester, and Rochester replied, "Good night, Boss." End of show.

After the final commercial, with just 20 seconds remaining, Jack thanked "the makers of Alka-Seltzer, Lou Cowan, and the Quiz Kids" for appearing on his show. He announced that the Kids will be on his show the following Sunday, too. He also promoted *QK* by saying, "Folks, if you think I had a nightmare tonight just listen in Wednesday. These kids are murder."[32]

That Wednesday, April 16, the Kids did a doubleheader. At 8:00 A.M. all six Kids, this time including Cynthia, were on the list of speakers and performers at the Los Angeles Breakfast Club, a weekly gathering of local civic leaders and businessmen. This weekly meeting was on a local radio station, KFWB, created by Sam Warner of Warner Brothers. The pre-meeting announcement and program suggested humorously that if the recipient forgot "to get up on Wednesday morning, he should listen in on KFWB from 8:00 to 9:30."[33] This breakfast club was not the famous radio program from Chicago, *The Breakfast Club*.

For his appearance on *QK* that evening Jack described himself as being six years old.[34] He wore a wig with long, child-like curls, in a hair style that was reminiscent of Little Lord Fauntleroy, more common for young boys in the early twentieth century than in the 1940s.[35]

Staying with the program's format, Joe Kelly introduced the Kids by first name, and asked them to identify themselves by full name, age, and the name of their school. Joe introduced Benny as Jackie. Benny said, "I am Jackie Benny. I am 6 years old. I didn't have a chance to go to school at all. I was just a poor boy and I used to stand on the corner selling papers barefooted in the winter and I used to say, 'Extra! Extra! Paper here! Get your paper.'" Kelly admonished his embellishment of his on-air identification by asking him to be quiet. "And incidentally," he asked Jack, "where are your curls?" Jack wanted him to repeat the question. Finally, sounding exasperated, Jack replied that they were on his lap because "they got hot."

In an unplanned gesture, a few minutes after his entrance, he had removed his wig. When he took off his curls, he shed his prepared script, too, with his "they got hot" answer. It was an obvious ad lib. Throughout the show, Jack commented about the questions in a low, conspiratorial tone of voice, making excuses for his ignorance, claiming that he knew the answer to math questions but had made a slight mistake in calculation, or becoming adamant about the correctness of his answer to a question about politics, even though he was wrong. He interrupted Joe frequently. Joe asked him to be quiet repeatedly as if he were an unruly child. As he did with the Quiz Kids, Joe disciplined him gently. His "quiet, please" to Benny was a gentlemanly scolding. Exasperated, Joe finally said to Jack, "I'm beginning to think that you're getting into what little hair I've got left." Jack, never missing the chance to ad lib, and in a manner fit for a Friar's Club roast, replied by saying that he could always tell Joe where to shop for a toupee.

Although Jack and his writers had a copy of the questions for the Kids before the broadcast, for several days Jack's creative team worked on what jokes Jack could make between the questions. It was difficult for them because *QK* was an unrehearsed show in the usual sense; there was no script for the Kids. Their script was the questions that Joe would ask. But no one could write or predict what the Kids might say when they answered the questions.

So, the gags prepared for Jack by his writers might not work, after all. Eventually they wrote jokes that they put on small cards for Jack to hold while they were on air, similar to Joe's question-and-answer cards. But if the Kids didn't know the answer to a question that Jack's gag was about, or if they elaborated on their answer at length or went on an entirely different tangent, as they did frequently, Jack's prepared jokes were of no use. Shortly into the show, Jack realized that. He ignored his notes and began to ad lib as often as possible for the remainder of the half hour. It was with his ad libs that he got his biggest laughs from the studio audience.

Normally, one of the writers at Wade Advertising or on the *QK* staff at 8 South Michigan would write continuity — a script — for the announcer, with the introduction to the program, any informative messages about future scheduling, Joe Kelly's opening and closing remarks, and his dialogue with a scheduled guest.

The only thing that Benny appeared to have prepared before the program was a question about Fred Allen, referring to the well-promoted, and fictitious, feud between the two radio comedians. The question that Joe asked the Kids was to compose a second line to the first line of a two-line rhyme. The first line was, "Fred Allen has a funny show." Jack interrupted. "I'm going home," he declared. After the Kids recited their second lines, Jack contributed his conclusion to the verse. It was more than a second line:

> Fred Allen has a funny show,
> How he does it I don't know.
> His jokes are old, his gags ain't funny,
> He ought to be paid in Confederate money.

At the end of the program Joe announced that each Kid, as usual, would receive a $100 U.S. savings bond, but there would not be a bond for Jack Benny. Instead, he would get a Zenith portable radio. "Maybe you can learn something listening to *QK* every Wednesday night," Joe advised him. "Well, at least I can hock the radio," Benny replied, to end the program.[36]

Their social activities continued at the same pace after Benny's Act Two broadcast with the Kids on the following Sunday. The Kids took a bus tour on a standard sightseeing vehicle, complete with a guide who spoke into a microphone. True to form, the Kids argued with him on practically every statement he made. When they stopped at the zoo and got off the bus for a brief tour, Gerard told the other tourists who were on the bus that some of the signs on the bird cages were misleading. With a flourish of understatement, he said that he knew about birds. Challenging his claim, a woman in the group of tourists spoke up. "Well, my little man," she asked, "can you tell me what kind of feathers I have on my hat?" "Yes, ma'am," Gerard answered, "dyed chicken feathers."[37]

During their last weekend in Hollywood, the Kids visited W.C. Fields at his home. When they arrived, they saw some of his clothing hanging at one of the living room windows, airing. Dick Williams asked Fields if he was selling these clothes. "No," replied Fields, "this is a tailoring establishment." The Kids then raced across the lawn, picked rose blossoms, and each of them plucked a banana from Fields's banana tree. Cynthia asked their host if the bananas were good to eat. Fields replied that they weren't. Gerard asked him if the bananas weren't so good to eat, perhaps he could tell him where to get a drink of water. Fields was incensed. "My boy," he exploded, "the last water around here came with the spring rains and the grass soaked it all up."[38]

☞ *The words armed assault in United States newspapers this week failed to disturb either the police or the United Nations Security Council. Why not?*

Toward the end of their first full week in Los Angeles, they visited MGM and were guests on two sound stages so that they could see how the studio actually made movies. Originally their visit to MGM had been planned for the day before, but the plans fell through. Screen tests had also been planned for that day at Universal, Paramount, and Twentieth Century–Fox, but those studios canceled, too. All the studios, even Paramount, which had expressed such strong interest in the Kids, required them to have the screen test first before they would consider them, a standard practice in Hollywood. Gerard already had a two-page script for his test at Fox. Roby thought that because of his usual iconoclastic performances on *QK* broadcasts, that he should write his own script for his screen test. In fact, after the *QK* broadcast on April 9, someone asked, "Who is Gerard's script writer? Wasn't he wonderful?"[39]

Because the four studios canceled the appointments, Roby was in charge of 14 people that afternoon (the Kids, parents, and other members of the entourage). She took them to an ostrich farm and then an alligator farm. She loved this outing, partly because the children floored the guide at the alligator farm by asking questions that upset his prepared talk. The guide memorized his speech word for word and zipped through it so quickly that he couldn't stop. No one could get a word in, not even to ask a question. Naturally, the Kids had lots of questions. The guide kept talking faster; they didn't stand a chance. But they managed it. Claude derailed the guide when he asked him how much an alligator's brain weighed. The guide looked pale, and said, between the lines of his speech, "I've never been asked that before." When they saw the Gila monsters, the guide stopped and told them he would spell it for them. The Kids were polite and didn't react. They also didn't give him the Latin name for it, or any other esoteric information that they usually had at their command.

Gerard was thrilled because he sat astride to ride the same alligator as Dorothy Lamour (his favorite actress) had ridden in a recent movie. All the Kids rode him, holding on to a little harness. The alligator's name was Billy. When Gerard was on him, Billy decided to go into the water, and Gerard kept pulling him back, as if he was reining in a horse.[40]

Their visit to MGM for their screen test was the next day. Afterwards, they visited two sound stages. First, they saw the filming of a scene for the comedy *Lady Be Good*. Of course, Cynthia, Joan, and Gerard were familiar with the process because of their experience in New York three months earlier when they made the shorts for Paramount. Nonetheless, the Kids disrupted the filming, just by being themselves — curious and inquisitive — climbing, examining, peering, and asking. When they came on the set the actors and the crew gave them an ovation. They were filming a scene in a café with Eleanor Powell and John Carroll, and as usual there were multiple takes. It didn't take long for the Kids to learn the dialogue. They were able to recreate the scene word for word, with the same verbal inflections that the actors used.

When there were breaks between shots, the technical crew, Eleanor Powell's stand-in, and other crew members gathered around the Kids and asked them all kinds of questions, from riddles to quotations. Each time the director, Norman Z. McLeod, was ready to start the next shot, he would call for the crew and would always find them bunched around the Kids. After shooting the scene, the cast and crew posed for photos with the Kids. When Gerard was introduced to Eleanor Powell, they shook hands, and he bowed very low, saying that he was glad to meet her. Then he turned to Roby and in a loud whisper he asked, "Who is she?" Unconstrained at eight years old!

The Kids were on the set for an hour, but then Gerard and his aunt Bessie went to Twentieth Century–Fox for his screen test while Roby and the rest of the group went to sound stage 18 to visit the Marx Brothers and to observe the shooting of their new film, *The Big Store*.

During the few days after they arrived in Los Angeles, when reporters asked the Kids who they wanted to see in Hollywood, they invariably answered: the Marx Brothers. Jack Lucal had the worst case of Marxitis. He would lope around like Groucho, tilted and on the bias, and pretend to chase girls as Harpo did.[41] He confessed to the reporter from *Modern Screen* a few hours before going to MGM that his ambition was "to be a priest and to try to keep Groucho Marx in the movies."[42] (He did become a priest, but there is no record of any attempt by him to extend Groucho's film career.) As soon as they walked onto the Marxes' set, the first person they saw was Groucho, standing with one foot resting on a white, velvet chair, with his right hand stuck Napoleon-like in his Prince Albert coat. Chico came over to the group and Roby told him that they were the Quiz Kids. He called to Groucho after the shot, and Groucho, still in character, walked in his usual bent-over stage style toward them and said in pure flywheelian, "Get 'em out of here, they're too smart." The Kids, as usual, brought everything to a halt. The Brothers stopped filming and called their families so that their own children could talk to the Kids on the phone.

The Kids were eager to try their own quiz on the Marxes. Called the "Sanity Test," they devised it on the train to Los Angeles, and started testing people when they checked in at the Knickerbocker. Their brilliant memories intact, the Kids had recalled a *QK* mid-broadcast Alka-Seltzer commercial delivered by announcer Marvin Mueller seven months earlier. The Sanity Test was almost an exact replica of that Alka-Seltzer commercial:

MUELLER: While our Quiz Kids are relaxing for a few moments, how about a little quiz of our own? I'll ask you some questions, then you answer them. After that I'll tell you your answers. Are you ready? Well, name any number from one to five. Now name any color. All right — name a piece of furniture. Now, let's see — your answers were three, red and chair — or am I a poor guesser? Now, here's one more. What remedy do you think of when you are troubled with a headache or acid indigestion?[43]

The Quiz Kids' test determined the "sanity" of everyone who was willing to participate. They tried it on Jack Benny, Don Wilson, Rochester, various producers at MGM, Walt Disney, and several others.[44] They asked Chico if he would take the test. He agreed to it and they proceeded.

They asked him three questions. First, they asked him to name a color, quickly. Chico replied, red. Second, they wanted him to name a piece of furniture. He said chair. Third, they asked him to tell them a number between one and five. He said four. The kids concluded that he was one-third insane, because if he were sane his answers would have been red, chair, and three. (Eleanor Powell had tested sane. Roby didn't. She answered: green, davenport, and two.) Fascinated by the test, Chico went around the set insisting that the crew must take it. He had a slightly different version: Name a color between red and blue. Name a piece of furniture. Name a number between five and six.[45]

Later, Roby told a reporter from *Time* magazine about their meeting with the Marxes, and the next morning the reporter went to see Groucho to try to verify the rumor that he was retiring from movies. The first thing Groucho asked when he saw the reporter was "What is 2 and 2?" He began giving him the Sanity Test. He said that he had picked it up from the Kids.[46]

The Kids were thrilled with the Brothers, and the Brothers seemed just as excited about seeing them.[47] There was a photo session with the Kids and the Brothers, their director, and their producer. Out came their autograph books. The three Marx Brothers signed. Groucho signed his name in Cynthia's book, followed by the words: "a dope" and Harpo, always of few words, surprisingly illustrated his signature with a simple line drawing of himself playing the harp.[48]

Just Claude, Richard, and Gerard were on Jack's show for April 20, but their dialogue only occurred during the last ten minutes. The script started with a subplot. Jack was so depressed about his poor showing on *Quiz Kids* the previous Wednesday that he didn't want to face the ridicule that he thought was certain when he did his own show. Mary Livingstone claimed that because of his depression he attempted suicide by hanging himself. (He said that he fell off a ladder and a rope entangled him.) He entertained thoughts about running away and joining the French Foreign Legion to avoid any mockery from his cast or acquaintances. Finally, he relented and agreed to do his show.

There were the usual jokes about his performance by members of his cast during that first 20 minutes, but they were mild jokes, not mean-spirited. The major plot of the script occurred during the last 20 minutes: he was going to drive the three Kids who had stayed with him for the past three weeks to the railroad station so that they could join the others for their return to Chicago. The plot explained that when Jack invited the Quiz Kids to be on his show for two additional weeks, he invited Claude, Richard, and Gerard to actually stay at his house. He didn't want them to have the expense of staying at a hotel.

On this final program with Jack, there was no dialogue with the Kids exhibiting their usual fount of knowledge; it was simply a typical Jack Benny radio program, with the Kids having some lines that were part of the overall scenario. The usual jokes prevailed: Benny as a miser, his 1927 Maxwell car (it was the voice of Mel Blanc, who was also the voice of Carmichael), and his perennially youthful age — "There I was with those little kids and I couldn't answer one question. And me, 34 years old." After dropping off the Kids at Union Station, Jack was sad. He said that he hated to see the Kids leave. He was crazy about them and would miss them. He wondered what he would do when he came home and they weren't there. He wondered what he would do in his spare time. "Just look for the gas man," suggested Rochester.[49]

This last joke about Carmichael and the gas meter man was the end of the program. It was the elliptical ending that tied together the three acts created by Beloin and Morrow. This miniature well-made play provided a little insight into what made the Jack Benny program so popular. This well-constructed plotting was a delight for Roby.

With the last Jack Benny show completed, everyone could breathe easier. Jack was so enamored with the Kids that he gave each of them a gold wrist watch from Trabert and Hoeffer, retailers of luxurious jewelry in Beverly Hills. Each watch was engraved individually. The back of Cynthia's watch displays "To Cynthia from Jack Benny."[50]

The past three weeks had been filled with a busy schedule for the Kids, the production staff, and the parents. Their calendar was always full, with little time off. For the staff it was the usual hard work. For the Kids, it was demanding, but nonetheless they had a good time, traveled to new places, and went home with long-lasting memories. It was a pattern that would be repeated many times in the future whenever the Kids traveled, even though future travel might not take them to the center of the glamorous life associated with Hollywood.

It looked as if Lou's gamble with this trip was going to produce the anticipated results. Certainly *QK* had a saturated exposure in California and the western states for those three weeks. There was also superb national exposure because the Jack Benny program was broadcast on the Red Network, admittedly the network of the nation's largest stations. Jack and his cast had cooperated fully on this venture, perhaps even beyond what Lou and Miles Labs had hoped.

If Lou, Walter Wade, and the Beardsleys thought that the exposure on Benny's show reached their goals, Walter in retrospect six months later thought differently. In a letter to Niles Trammel he emended their after-show euphoria with the cold facts of ratings. "In fact," he wrote, "if you check back, you will find that Jack Benny's rating profited by it [the Kids as guests] far more than the Quiz Kids."[51]

Later in the 1940s the Jack Benny program began using as its closing music "Hooray for Hollywood," a song that had been introduced in the 1937 film *Hollywood Hotel*. The lyrics are a satiric comment on the excitement and magnetic pull that the movie industry had on Americans in those Depression and post–Depression years. But hooray for Hollywood, not as a song title but a simple declaration, was an apt summary that Lou, the Beardsleys, and Walter Wade would have given immediately after this trip.

The next day, back in the real world, the Kids returned home, still traveling in style, this time on the always superlative *Super Chief*. As usual, the train moved at high speeds, giving proof to its description as a streamliner. On the train John and Roby moved at top speed, too, working on constructing the questions for the show for Wednesday, April 23, two days later.[52] Even after the whirl of social events, promotional appearances, and movie auditions during the past three weeks in Never-Never Land, for Roby and John there was no let-up. The pace was still killing, with little or no time for them to relax and enjoy this elegant train ride and peer out the generous observation windows as they glided through the western states and into the heartland's prelude to Chicago.

They knew that they had just Monday and Tuesday to create the show for Wednesday. They were as prepared as they could be. When they had to write a new program while on the road, they traveled with their "great, big iron suitcase" containing books for research.[53] They could carry only a limited number of books. The library of reference material at the South Michigan office usually was comprehensive enough for fine-tuning most of the listener-submitted questions. On this train, in fact any time they traveled, the reference materials in their iron suitcase were minimal. What's more, working on the train, they couldn't call any local sources for verification as they usually did when they traveled. As they began working on the new program, even with all of the limitations and interruptions of their surroundings, John and Roby were confident. They knew that even while on the train, they could devise a new script in time for the upcoming broadcast.

What they didn't know was that within four days they would learn that Lou's plans for promoting *QK* and the staff's hard work for the past several months to carry out those plans had paid off. Right on schedule, the *Super Chief* pulled in to Union Station late Tuesday night. *Quiz Kids* had arrived.

ANSWERS

It would be the same time in China — noon. The earth spins at 1,000 miles an hour. The pilot is flying at the same speed, so he's flying with the hour.

The police and the United Nations were not disturbed because Armed and Assault were the names of two famous race horses scheduled for a match race. Assault pulled up lame after a workout earlier that week, and the story was in the Chicago newspapers. The Kids were expected to know more than what they needed to know for their school studies, or for their individual extracurricular interests. Sometimes Joe asked them on air about everyday events reported in newspapers, news magazines, or radio news programs.

8

Soldiering On

☞ *If you have $1.15 in coins and are unable to make change for either a dollar, a half dollar, a quarter, a dime or a nickel, what coins do you have?*

Back from Hollywood, the Kids had no trouble readjusting to their normal routines even though they had been stars in the make-believe world of Hollywood for the past two weeks. John and Roby reentered the flow of their real world without any letdown, either. There was no harsh descent from the excitement of Hollywood. On the contrary, while they were in California some exhilarating news had burst forth in Chicago. On April 12, *Billboard* magazine reported that *Quiz Kids* was the winner of the Chicago Federal Advertising Club's 1940 award as the outstanding network show produced in Chicago.[1] *Radio Daily* awarded *QK* a statuette for best new program of 1940.[2] A few days after the advertising club's award, *Movie-Radio Guide* honored the program with statuettes for the best children's program of 1940 on NBC Blue.[3]

Now, with the staff arriving from Hollywood, the Michigan Street office was complete and once again brimming with feverish activity. Added to the excitement of the advertising club's accolade was more heady news. *Billboard* revealed a second honor that they added to the glistening reputation of *QK*. Two days following the first Chicago broadcast after the homecoming, the magazine announced that they had given the Louis G. Cowan Company a special award for outstanding "exploitation" of a single program (*QK*) for 1940. "Exploitation" was the word used by the magazine, as was the custom in 1940, to describe promotional efforts. Lou's peers in Chicago already recognized and praised his virtuosity as a promoter. Now, his reputation was emerging from his geographically limited fame into one of national awareness among professionals in radio. Personal satisfaction aside, what that meant for Lou was that *QK* had "arrived." The renown of the program had become national, not just outstanding in the minds of a handful of local or regional radio program analysts and critics. There was no doubt that the recent exposure on the Jack Benny program would add another reason for the growing preeminence of *QK* in the months to come.

Lou was delighted because his colleagues understood the thinking and planning behind his promotional efforts, as well as their execution. This special award was the result of a survey, part of the magazine's overall publicity and exploitation survey each year. There is often a negative connotation to the word exploitation. It can mean using another person for one's own profit. Alternatively, it can mean, simply, the use of advertising or publicity. The latter definition applies to the survey and awards given by *Billboard*. The magazine's survey asked professionals in the field to select their choices for excellence among advertising agencies, radio stations, television stations (even then, when television was still an embryo), and press agents.

The award noted that *QK* had only been on the air since the previous June. The announcement of the award signaled that what made Lou's efforts so outstanding was that the debut of the program was at a time when radio listening was at a low tide, yet with the force of Lou's publicity efforts *QK* burst forth and became "nationally prominent in a very short time." *Billboard* cited specifics. As well as normal methods of promotion — announcements, contests, signs on trucks, and other details — the award cited the "Beat the Quiz Kids" column, special broadcasts, and guest appearances by the Kids at various functions. The magazine described the specific efforts of the *QK* production office: working closely with radio stations by helping them with promotion for the show, setting up miniature *QK* broadcasts, and with George Kamen's connections, licensing stores to conduct local elimination contests as a way of finding new prospective Kids. Promotion also included merchandising items such as *QK* pins and buttons distributed by department stores.[4] As well as promoting the show to build an audience, this award meant that Lou had won the ultimate respect from his peers. At the same time, the recognition of his abilities in Chicago and the surrounding region helped to enhance his reputation and thus to build his awareness nationally culminating in the award from *Billboard*.

The award did not affect Lou's behavior. He took it in stride; he did not act self-important. In fact, during the week following the announcement, his agency placed an ad in *Billboard* in response to the announcement of the award. It was appreciative, thankful, and businesslike, infused with humility and gentle irony. Signed by Lou and nine other staff members, the ad stated that winning the award was a great honor, but that it created a predicament for them. They had been trying to find a suitable expression of appreciation comparable to this "outstanding distinction." Acknowledging their devotion to their ongoing work for their public relations accounts, the signers stated that it was much easier to write and produce radio shows than the task of adequately expressing their feelings about winning this award. Simply put, they were proud to have won it. The ad stated that they wrote this "note" as a straightforward and direct statement of thanks.[5]

The exploitation survey revealed that extensive use of personal appearances by radio performers personalized the relationship between the performers and their audience, especially when the audience could see these performers in the flesh at theatres, fairs, conventions and other avenues of exposure.[6] This was exactly what the Quiz Kids had been doing since the Milwaukee appearance in November. This identification with audiences was natural for the Kids, both on the air and at personal appearances. It was not a planned or rehearsed dynamic. Personalizing the relationship with the program's listeners was a subtle factor and a benefit embedded in the act of building its audience.

What was refreshing about the publicity for *QK* was the way in which the staff worked. There was no blatant ballyhoo, couched in bombast and arrogance. It was soft sell, reflective of Lou's own personality traits. When he called on potential sponsors a year earlier to sell *QK*, his soft-sell approach was akin to the characteristics of his new quiz program. The publicity staff did not dictate to reporters how to write newspaper copy about them. They worked closely with personnel at various publications so that any publicity that they disseminated was more of a joint effort than an arrogant directive from the *QK* office. Roby, or anyone who worked on behalf of *Quiz Kids*, did not oversell the program or boast extravagantly about it. Traditionally, press agents, anxious to make a placement and thus satisfy their bosses in New York or Los Angeles during their "short assignments," often practiced such loud and blatant methods. These traveling promoters might arrive from New York or Los Angeles to a smaller city, spend a short time with the local media, and leave within a day or two to travel on to the next city. There was no depth to their relationships with local media. The most respected publicity agents considered this method tasteless and unnecessary in the 1940s. So did Lou when he established the standards for his staff. They established an "entente cordiale" when they worked with local or national magazines and local newspapers.[7]

There was no time for the troops to sit back and bask in the light glowing from these two awards. Everyone soldiered on. They had to. Initially, after the over-the-top debut of *QK* the previous June, there was a great demand for personal appearances by civic and charitable groups in and around Chicago. In the "Beat the Quiz Kids" columns, there were photos of the Kids in various locations, staged to show how they performed ordinary family chores. Or there were photos of them taken when they appeared at various locations in Chicago. But these photographs and their appearance at events were purely self-promoting. Did Lou and his staff set up these personal appearances? Or were they the result of requests by others? Clearly, the staff created the promotion materials associated with "Beat the Quiz Kids." It is uncertain how many of the actual ideas they generated for other appearances. We can conclude that after their return from Hollywood and their newfound prominence from the awards given to them by broadcasting industry peers, requests for their personal appearance increased. It was clear that the staff did not generate all of these requests, because they were increasing in quantity and variety. Roby alone was the entire publicity staff. She would not have had the time to create such a broad campaign with the variety of invitations that they received. She and a few other staff members were too busy working out the details for a rapidly growing schedule of personal appearances by the Kids.

The day after their return from Hollywood, Cynthia received a letter from Joe Bailey. He informed her that she was to appear on Bill Stern's network broadcast three days later, April 27. Stern, a famous NBC sportscaster with a vast national audience, would interview Cynthia, Gerard, and Claude on his network sports program, *Sports Newsreel of the Air*, this time broadcast at NBC's Studio B at the Merchandise Mart. There was no apparent reason for the appearance of the Kids, other than Stern's unembellished statement that he was "in Chicago to present the world famous Quiz Kids." It was unlikely that his reason for being in Chicago was just to include three Quiz Kids on his program. It's more likely that there were other reasons he broadcast from the Merchandise Mart. Seemingly, the appearance of the Kids was simple publicity, probably arranged by the staff at 8 South Michigan.

Nonetheless, the three Kids made a brief appearance. Stern asked them during his 63-word introduction to the program if they would write some two-line verses that they could read at the "close of our interview." After reporting on the results of major league baseball games that day, followed by a commercial and his usual human-interest feature, Stern introduced the Quiz Kids segment with an intended pun. He said that in the past he had presented some unusual personalities, but the Kids were "in a class by themselves."

After asking Claude about sports in his native South Africa, he turned to Cynthia to ask her favorite sports. After naming them, she said that on the train to California just a few weeks earlier, the Kids had devised an indoor sport: the Sanity Test. She tried it on Stern. Stern did not exhibit the sense of the ludicrous that Chico did when the Kids tested him on the set of *The Big Store*. Stern took the test seriously, and passed. He was, by definition, completely sane. At the end of the interview, there is more evidence that Roby or John planned, or at least managed, this appearance. They offered a wry ending to the interview. Stern closed the segment by thanking the Kids, offering them good luck, and finally saying goodbye. In unison, as they did on *QK*, the Kids said, "Goodnight, Mr. Stern."[8]

On May 15, less than two weeks after the announcement of their exploitation award in *Billboard*, the Kids made a quick trip to St. Louis. There, six of the Kids entertained 1,006 members of the National Association of Broadcasters at a dinner banquet concluding their four-day annual national convention. Undoubtedly, their recent awards added luster to the NAB appearance. More than just a topic of curiosity, they were stars now. Lou's peers in broadcasting welcomed them with heightened enthusiasm beyond what they might expect normally at such events.

More gratifying than the awards was the practical result of all the staff's hard work. Miles Labs renewed their contract for another 52 weeks of network broadcasting on NBC Blue. The new contract began October 1.[9] At this point 62 Blue Network stations nationwide carried *Quiz Kids*.[10] Miles agreed to sponsor the program for $3,000 weekly for the term of this new contract. These weekly expenses were for the cost of actors, musicians, writers, directors, royalties, prizes, and other production costs. Although it was a significant raise in income for the Louis G. Cowan Company, it still paled in comparison with Jack Benny's $18,000 weekly.[11] Lou's characterization of their $1,000 weekly budget for their summer replacement status as being "low even for 1940" was applicable a year later even to this tripled amount.

☞ *The letters F, D, and R (Franklin Delano Roosevelt) begin the names of three of the political parties, which have been successful in electing their candidates to office of president of the United States. The fourth party begins with the letter W. What are these four parties?*

The inauguration of the Lend Lease program, signed into law on March 11 to promote the defense of the United States by supplying war material to Allied nations — weapons, equipment, even ships — meant that the nation's stance of neutrality was over, even though there would be no formal declaration of war for another nine months. Within a short time, the U.S. Treasury Department enlisted *Quiz Kids* to help in defense work, with a specific responsibility to help raise revenue via the sale of bonds. It was a small beginning for the radio program's notable participation in war-related activities to raise revenue. Eventually the efforts of the Kids extended to 1945, when the war ended, and for several months after, into 1946.

The Treasury Department's program to sell bonds — called Defense Bonds — went into effect May 1, 1941. The department had already reached out to *QK* before that date because just one week later, May 8, the Kids made a special recording to promote the sale of bonds and stamps. The record, played in high schools nationwide, urged students and faculty to purchase, or influence the purchase of, these bonds and stamps for defense. The Treasury Department determined that the potential listening audience for this recording was three million. Alka-Seltzer donated the services of *QK*.[12] And NBC's recording division recorded this special *QK* program. The revenue from the sale of bonds from the recording helped pay for various defense activities, such as Lend Lease, before the actual declaration of war. After December 7, and for the duration of the war, the bonds were renamed War Bonds, and continued to be earmarked to pay for the cost of the war. The revenue from bonds was one of a myriad of ideas germinated by the Treasury Department during the years between the outbreak of the war in Europe and the involvement of the United States as a participant in the global war that evolved from it.

At the same time that *QK* was working on the Treasury Department's bond initiative, at the request of the Department of the Army, John was preparing to originate some of the regularly scheduled Wednesday broadcasts from military bases as a morale booster for enlistees and officers. Their travel experience during the past six months made plans for future personal appearances for the Treasury feasible, and was of great value when the Army Department approached them, too. Fort Meade, near Washington, D.C., was to be one of the first ventures in their patriotic travel schedule.[13]

But the first documented appearance at a military base was closer to home. *QK* traveled to Fort Sheridan, an army induction center in the Highland Park suburb of Chicago, for its May 28 network broadcast. Highland Park is only 28 miles from midtown Chicago. This broadcast was a morale booster for new recruits processed at this mobilization, training, and administrative center. General J.L. Homer made the introduction to the *QK* program for that last Wednesday in May 1941. The guest observer was Major General Charles H. Bonesteel.[14]

☞ *Instead of sailing the seven seas, name the seven seas surrounding the Dutch East Indies.*

Two thousand University of Chicago alumni (both Lou and Joe Bailey were alumni) returned to their campus on June 7 for an annual event that the alumni association titled Alumni Assembly. They heard William Morgenstern, director of the alumni foundation, report the results of their monetary contributions. That year was notable because it was the university's 50th anniversary celebration.[15] The schedule of social events starting at 11:30 A.M.—lunches, speeches, entertainment, and dinner. The afternoon session featured the Kids; they jousted with five distinguished University of Chicago professors for a QK Versus session. It was a repeat of the audience-pleasing Quiz Kids–Parents sessions in February, the competition a few days later with school adminis-

8. Soldiering On

During an appearance at Fort Sheridan, the Kids bounced around in a military vehicle. (From left) Jack Lucal, Harve Fischman, Paul Sigmund, Richard Williams, Gerard Darrow (Billy Rose Theatre Division, The New York Public Library for the Performing Arts, Astor, Lenox and Tilden Foundations).

trators in Atlantic City, and the recent Jell-O Kids event in Hollywood (of course, without gag writers' input).

This time the QK Versus contest was significantly more dramatic and more erudite. First, the competition was composed of University of Chicago professors, known for their profound knowledge in various academic disciplines: psychology, French, economics, mathematics, and medieval history. Second, the audience included many of the academicians' former students, who would relish seeing how their former mentors would function in the world outside their classrooms. The contest started at 3:30 P.M.; it was insular, not a radio broadcast.[16]

Fourteen hundred alumni, anxious to see the Kids battle the faculty, were jammed into the auditorium at Mandel Hall. This audience actually overflowed into the building's corridors. The president of the university, Robert Maynard Hutchins, was a featured speaker. He digressed from the solemn recitation of the financial status of the alumni's largess as he went on to introduce the next event at the assembly. He apparently had no illusions about why an excited overflow crowd had come to an otherwise ordinary reading of finances. "I suppose you all came to Mandel Hall to see the Profs showed up by the kids," he predicted. During the laughter and applause that followed, the curtains on the stage opened. Two tables were at opposite sides of the platform. Seated at one were the Kids, wearing red caps and gowns. The professors, dressed in their traditional, somber black caps and gowns, were at the other. After a reasonable period of intellectual jousting, Hutchins's forecast came true. The score: Quiz Kids, 275 points; professors, 140.[17]

Aside from the usual difficult questions, the last question of the session was about the cost of a fur coat. This question was later described as a "whooperdoo, killer-diller."[18]

☞ *Would it be more economical to buy a fur coat at one store for $300, or a second coat just like it at another store, if there were $40 between the price of the second coat and the price of a third coat, three-fourths of the cost of the second being equal to two-thirds the cost of the third?*

The most significant event during the week following the University of Chicago appearance was the announcement, according to *Newsweek* magazine, of a precocious one-year-old in the news (Dennis Day again?). It was the magazine's sly way of introducing and noting the first anniversary of *Quiz Kids*, "among the most successful and publicized" of the "current wave of question-and-answer programs." Citing their one-year skyrocketing history of appearances with Jack Benny and at the White House, and their list of distinguished guests, the Chicago *Herald-American* noted their help with charitable movements — Bundles for Britain, Community Fund, March of Dimes, Boy Scouts, Red Cross, and the Greek War Relief. The newspaper suggested facetiously that during the past year "they have answered so many questions that instead of needing an encyclopedia they could write one."[19] More specifically, by the end of 1941, there had been 54 Quiz Kids competing on the broadcasts during that calendar year. Among them, they had answered 89 percent of the questions asked of them. *QK* awarded nearly 1,000 portable Zenith radios to listeners from 46 states and the District of Columbia, whose questions they used on the program.[20]

Featured on this birthday broadcast of June 25, 1941, were Kids who had appeared on more than ten programs. Instead of the usual panel of five Kids there were seven, those who had the best records during the past year — Gerard, Jack, Richard, Cynthia, Van Dyke, Joan, and Claude — each well known and respected by avid listeners. Fifty-five other Kids who had appeared on the broadcast during the past 12 months joined them. The guest observer was Dr. Harold Swanson, who was the guest observer on the first broadcast. After the close of the program, they had a more traditional birthday party at the Hotel Stevens in Chicago.[21]

As well as the sparkling and dramatic travel schedule for the year, their usual grassroots travel agenda continued to fill rapidly. Three days after the birthday broadcast, the Kids were on their way to the Miami (Ohio) Valley Chautauqua grounds for a personal appearance. It was a quick trip. They left Union Station Saturday, June 28, and returned to Chicago at 6:30 A.M. Monday. The usual contingent of parents or other chaperones accompanied them. Only John Lewellen from the *QK* production staff traveled with them this time. He alone was in charge. They were to be part of the entertainment for the opening day of the 1941 Chautauqua season, the first of a series of eight Sunday programs featuring an opera star, a congressional representative, and the former mayor of Narvik, Norway, during the course of the summer. WLS broadcast this Chautauqua program; it was not a scheduled network *QK* program.

This time the panel included Joan, Van Dyke, Richard, Gerard, and Harve Fischman. The reports of their triumph at the University of Chicago alumni gathering must have left a deep impression outside the city, in the region. The Dayton, Ohio, newspaper described them as "five children of the air who can answer more questions correctly than a board of college professors."[22] Traveling with them was Philip Dickerman, age 7, a musical prodigy who was to be their piano accompanist. Because of his normally child-like short legs, when he sat at the piano his feet could not reach as far as an adult's might. Philip used a special extension on the piano pedals so he could reach them when he played.

Joe Kelly was the Chief Quizzer. Joe, as his usual schedule required, had to emcee the *National Barn Dance* Saturday evening, so he did not accompany the Kids on the train; he flew to Cincinnati Sunday morning. The distance by car from Cincinnati to the Chautauqua grounds is only 33 miles, giving him more than enough time to get to the area and appear with the Kids that afternoon.[23]

There was no slowdown of extracurricular activities after the Chautauqua session, even though it was the usually hot Midwest summer. On July 25, Gerard was in Cleveland as a guest of the Cleveland Zoo at a banquet, attended by 400 businessmen, to help open their campaign to raise $25,000 "for a bigger and better zoo." Earlier in the day while on a tour of the zoo, Gerard hung around the alligator cage for so long that the zoo's superintendent asked him jokingly if he wanted one. Gerard did; he had been saving his money for an alligator for two years. He picked out a small one and took it with him to the banquet to show off his new pet.[24] Naturally, when asked the usual ornithological questions, he answered easily (*What plants eat animals?* ... "The sea anemone eats fish." *How many toes have a two-toed sloth?* ... "Ten." *What bird wears "glasses" and looks clownish?* ... "The spectacled eider, a member of the duck family.") So immersed in his knowledge of birds and fish and insects, when asked a hypothetical question that day, relating ornithology to international politics, he was perplexed. "Is there a bird large enough to carry off Adolf Hitler?" asked a newspaper reporter. Instantly Gerard responded with sincere curiosity by asking, "Who's he?"[25]

Major Lenox Lohr, president of NBC from 1935 to 1940 and since then the president of Chicago's Museum of Science and Industry, invited the Kids to a luncheon at the museum on July 29. He arranged for a tour of the museum after lunch. Two days later, July 31 Riverview Park had designated the day as Quiz Kids Day. The park's administration invited the Kids and their parents "to join in the fun" for the afternoon. Riverview Park was an amusement park within the city limits of Chicago with "rides and games and plenty of excitement for all."[26]

Toward the end of August, it was back to New York for the Kids to complete two more shorts, their contractual obligation to Paramount. They did their scheduled Wednesday broadcast from NBC at 30 Rockefeller Plaza. New York Mayor Fiorello LaGuardia was the featured guest. The Kids actually did a doubleheader that evening. An hour after the *QK* broadcast the Kids appeared on *The Treasury Hour*, a regularly scheduled program conceived by the United States Treasury Department as one of many efforts promoting the sale of bonds to pay for the rapidly increasing costs of manufacturing matériél for defense (and eventually war). This series featured well-known entertainers from radio and movies. The popularity of the Treasury program (or perhaps the Kids) was so great that people stood in line outside the theatre just to enter and be part of the audience during the broadcast. Gatecrashers tried endless ploys. Among them, 20 women claimed to be the mothers of the Kids.[27]

On the Treasury program, the Kids performed in the always-entertaining QK Versus format. Their adversaries were five well-respected educators from the New York area. The Kids had taken on the University of Chicago panel in June; now their prey was the East Coast intellectuals. It was a short appearance by the Kids, judging by the low score of the contest; the Kids won 60 to 25.[28] As they had in January, they followed their trip to New York with a trip to Washington. En route, they stopped for a few days at Fort George G. Meade in Maryland near D.C., to entertain officers and enlisted men. They stayed at the fort for three days. The Kids reveled in learning about the equipment on their tour of the base. Always inquisitive, they were doing "most of the quizzing" the first day. As always, they were being kids just having fun.

Directed toward a waiting car for the beginning of their tour, Gerard challenged the other Kids. "Last one in is a sissy," he declared, goading them to race to the car.[29] The Kids, both boys and girls, were fascinated by the workings of a French Seventy-five, a 75-mm field gun. Some arms experts thought that it was the first modern artillery piece. Unusual for that time, the two girls in the group of Kids, Betty Swanson and Edna Heenan, a local contest winner from Richmond, Virginia, were interested in the workings of the artillery.[30]

Someone interrupted Gerard's breathless investigation of the camp with a request for him to describe the characteristics and family history of the oscillated blenny. He did, in his usual dispassionate manner. In fact, he was more interested in the maximum effective range of the Seventy-five. And Gerard asked if he could ride in an airplane or a tank. He begged the driver of their car to ride over the adjacent training grounds so he could have a really "rough ride." Tuesday evening at the fort's recreation hall the Kids entertained the assembled officers and enlisted men with another QK Versus performance, in a match with five officers. Before they left for Washington, the Kids admitted that as well as volunteering to entertain soldiers, they were "getting plenty of entertainment themselves."[31] On to Washington on Wednesday, to end this trip with their regularly scheduled broadcast, this time from the Mayflower Hotel in Washington, over WMAL, the local NBC station.[32]

Paramount released the first of the movie shorts the Kids had made in New York at the beginning of 1941 in September with understandable fanfare, boldly displayed in a *Chicago Herald American* "Quiz Kids Special" section. On September 3, the film had its world premiere at the Chicago Theater. Both regular theatregoers and invited guests were in the audience. Just as in a Hollywood opening, at 6:45 P.M. before the film viewing, there was a red carpet event (the newspaper, in mundane 1941 phrasing, called it a "sidewalk broadcast"). At the same time, inside the theatre a 15-minute warmup for their regular weekly show was held, broadcast from the stage of the Chicago. The panel was composed of the same Kids who were in the short: Richard, Joan, Van Dyke, Cynthia, and Gerard. Joining the festivities were 67 other boys and girls who were Quiz Kids at one time or another. The entire group sat on the stage for the broadcast, wearing caps and gowns. The five panelists wore white; the other Kids wore maroon. With dramatic flair, and as a sign of respect, the theatre's ushers wore caps and gowns for this gala evening.

The audience that evening included notable local educators and civic and religious leaders, as well as Mayor Edward Kelly (no relation to Joe Kelly). Leslie Roush, the film's director, a Paramount Pictures vice president, and John Balaban, head of the Balaban and Katz theatres, were prominent audience members. Balaban and Katz had built this luxurious theatre in 1921. It was the first large, lavish movie palace in America, paving the way for other ornate movie palaces originating from a similar blueprint in many cities in the 1920s throughout the country. The Chicago was the flagship of the Balaban and Katz chain. There was the usual promotional deal-making between the theatre's owners and WLS. At least 70 Balaban and Katz theatres were actively promoting *QK* and the *March of Time* radio programs on WLS. In return, WLS furnished on-air tie-in announcements informing its audience when these shorts were playing in various theatres in the chain.[33]

Paramount was not above getting down to the mat. They were just as active in trumpeting the short directly, resulting in their ability to get free publicity in Boston. Marty Glazer, the publicity chief for the studio, traveled to Boston and arranged a tie-in with the local Fenway theatre chain. He arranged free publicity in newspapers. The analysis of his efforts after the fact showed that the free newspaper coverage allotted to promoting the *QK* movie was the largest free publicity to date in newspapers for a movie short in the Boston area. At the same time, another publicity effort helped. A week before the opening of the short, scheduled for October 9, Jordan Marsh, a Boston department store, conducted a *QK* contest, under George Kamen's direction.[34] The Fenway theatres and the store cooperated in boosting each other. Theatre lobby cards on easels called attention to the store's contest. The department store placed several ads in local newspapers. The ads included "reminder lines" about the short film at the Fenway theatres. Large window displays at the stores tied in directly with the film. As well, Glazer managed to orchestrate free publicity by tying in with the local NBC station by means of on-air spot announcements on the *QK* broadcast, and four other announcements placed every day for 19 days.[35] There was more. Hovey's department store in Boston was having an anniversary sale (to "celebrate" 108 years in business). Among the featured sale items were black rubber raincoats and "helmets" for boys, lined with cotton and with *QK* questions and answers, presumably printed on the lining. The normal price was $2.99; the sale price was $1.99.[36]

The rest of the schedule for the movie premiere in Chicago continued to be formal. At 7:35, after the radio program, was the screening of the film. At 10:00 the audience saw another stage performance by the panel of Quiz Kids, answering different questions than those asked of them at 7:00, but this follow-up performance was not on the air. After this performance was a second showing of the short.[37]

Billboard thought the film was "cute and interesting," but the reviewer thought that the short could have been more interesting, or at least more natural, if the set had been different. In the film, the Kids sat along a wall in large chairs with high backs. Joe Kelly wore a cap and gown and sat at a desk on a platform. The reviewer thought that that the chairs were so prominent that they were incongruous and detracted from the naturalness of the scene. He suggested that perhaps the Kids could have been sitting at desks or in ordinary chairs to make the setting more real.[38]

Two weeks later, it was back to the Milwaukee Auditorium where the Kids had performed at the Aqua Stars and Style Show the previous November. This time they were part of the entertainment along with Laurel and Hardy at a dinner on September 17 during the 21st Annual Convention of the American Legion Auxiliary. Once again just four of the Kids were on the program — Dick Williams, Harve Fischman, Joan Bishop, and Margaret Merrick. The emcee was movie comedian Joe E. Brown.[39]

That same evening in Chicago during their regular network broadcast, Cynthia Cline, one of the original Kids, became the first to "graduate" from the program. This was her last performance, and Miles Labs gave her a wristwatch, a gift in honor of her time on the program.[40] For both Cynthia and her mother, the few weeks preceding and including her last broadcast constituted a grand exit from *QK*. Just six weeks earlier Mrs. Cline, Richard Williams's father, Jack Lucal's mother, Van Dyke's father, and Gerard's father were the "Quiz Parents" on the August 6 broadcast. Claude Brenner was the Chief Quizzer, and Gerard was the guest observer.[41] The show was a variation of the well-received special Quiz Parents broadcast at the culmination of the "Beat the Quiz Kids" contest. This time, however, the panel consisted of only these five parents; none of the Kids were competing.

At the end of September Joe Bailey wrote to six Kids — Harve Fischman, Richard, Van Dyke, Gerard, Jack Lucal, and Joan — and asked them to submit 10 questions (and the answers) in their "own favorite fields," to be used as a "two-page spread" in a future issue of *Liberty* magazine. "It might be well for you to submit a few additional questions so that we can easily select 10," he suggested. Bailey asked them to respond as "early as they possibly can." Van Dyke replied on October 5, six days after Joe wrote his letter. The Kids received $25 each for their efforts.[42] The result of the request from Joe produced enough questions so that the magazine had an article with 40 questions and answers. *Liberty* entitled the spread "It's Their Turn Now: A Quiz by the Quiz Kids."

It was probably an easy task for them, if the prompt response by Van Dyke was any indication of the difficulty of the assignment. For the casual observer, the questions appear to be difficult. The submissions by the Kids were of the same caliber, and just as creative, as those familiar to anyone who listened to the Wednesday broadcasts. It could be that someone edited, or even rewrote them. Most likely, it was John and Roby in their customary fashion. Joe Bailey hinted at that possibility in his letter when he said that the staff would select those for publication. John and Roby would not have released the questions from the Kids without adding their creative input just as they did when listeners sent in "raw" questions for consideration each week. No matter what the format, radio or print, they were always careful about how they devised questions, editing and re-editing until they were pleased with how they sounded and felt they reflected the standards established by Lou. Nonetheless, the Kids created the questions, and even if John and Roby edited them, they provide an insight into the capacity and range of information that the Kids had at their fingertips.

1. The life of what great composer was saved by a button?
2. Who wrote (1) the Firebird Suite; (2) Firework music; (3) Ritual Fire Dance, and from what suite does the last come?
3. What turtle defends itself like a skunk?
4. Where do we get isinglass?
5. You are invited to attend a party to be held at the Dartmouth, the Beaver, and the Eleanor. Please come in costume. What party would you attend and what would you wear?
6. Who was the first president of the Chinese Republic?
7. If 20 Quiz Kids met, and each one shook hands with each of the others, how many handshakes would there be in all?
8. The English names of ten chemical elements begin with the letter "C." How many can you name? Six correct out of ten would be a good score.
9. My brother has longer legs than I have, so when we go downtown to the movies he can get there while I am going two thirds of the way to them. After the show, he gets home when I am still three blocks from home. How far do we live from the theater?[43]

Meanwhile, plans for another book from Saalfield Publishing were coming to fruition. George Kamen had licensed Saalfield to publish a *Quiz Kids* cutout doll book. The book used likenesses of the Kids as the dolls. Dolls were accompanied by other headless doll figures with tabs on them so that children could cut them out and change the clothing on the Quiz Kid dolls by placing the headless figures — the wardrobe — over the dolls. Joe Bailey informed Cynthia that the production staff, probably Lou, John, Roby, and Joe Bailey, had selected her as one of the eight Kids to appear in the book. She was paid $25 to have her photo taken by the *QK* usual photographer, C.M. Frank. She had to make the appointment herself to go to Frank's studio for the photo session. Bailey thought that Cynthia "would look nice in a skirt and short-sleeved sweater" and that she should wear her hair in a soft natural hairdo "just the way you wear it every day." She was not to wear a hat in the photographs. Saalfield wanted the photo session completed during the first week of October.[44]

8. Soldiering On

Bailey's suggestions to Cynthia outlining how to dress were not spontaneous. Lou had defined an image for *Quiz Kids* that included how the show sounded on air, how the Kids traveled, and how Joe Kelly and the Kids looked. Now that the invitations to travel were increasing, Lou's guidelines became more important. More than just a few hundred people in the audience seated in Studio E would be seeing the Kids. He was clear about how they should look when they appeared in public.

Lou's design of the program was noticeable in subtle ways, too. Years later, Ruth Duskin Feldman concluded that Lou had carefully orchestrated the show. She thought that it was not just a fluke that just as she was approaching puberty and decided to stop going on trips with the Kids, *Quiz Kids* discovered Naomi Cooks. She realized that it was "too convenient to be coincidental" that she resembled Shirley Temple and that Naomi looked like Margaret O'Brien, "each at a time when that particular child star was the cinema darling." Ruth recognized that both of them were encouraged to wear pigtails "until we were eleven."[45]

Bailey's dress-code directions to Cynthia didn't matter after all. Saalfield changed the original plans for illustrating the doll book. Instead of photos, the illustrations were drawings, in color. There were at least two editions of the book. The first doll book featured likenesses of eight of the Kids, Richard, Gerard, Cynthia, Ruth Duskin, Betty Swanson, Joan Bishop, Joan Alizier, and Mary Claire McHugh. The second version shows four Kids on the front cover.

November was a busy time for personal appearances by the Kids, busier than ever. The intensity and frequency of their appearances still seemed to increase exponentially. Perhaps because of their continually increasing fame, it seemed as if every few days they made a personal appearance.

At the beginning of the month, with only two days' notice, the Kids made a 5-minute recording for an Association of Motion Picture Advertisers luncheon. The association held their event sometime later that month. Presumably, the luncheon was to be in Los Angeles. The recording was "Paramount's contribution to the entertainment" at the luncheon. The recording studio making the record was familiar to the Kids: the World Broadcasting Company in Chicago, where Lou had made his demo records. It was not a burden for the Kids to get to the recording session. It was a quick session, notable because it was a clear indication of how familiar and comfortable the Kids were with broadcasting.

It was easy for them to walk in, make the recording, and leave. By November 1941, they had the experience to be able to do this calmly and professionally. Joe Bailey's letter, written November 4, asked the Kids to be at the studio on November 6 by 4:20 P.M. He promised that they would be finished with the session by 5:00. He included a script with his letter so that the Kids could "go over it in advance."[46]

The script was in the *QK* broadcast format. The answer that the Kids gave to each question was a gag and not to be taken seriously. The jokes were references to the film industry. The script was loaded with predictable, lowbrow jokes, like the annual dinner for a college fraternity, or a show business gathering, where the speakers' putdown humor is used to encourage a sense of community within the group.

The real theme of the AMPA meeting was short films, so it was logical to have a recording made by the Kids, even though it was a counterpoint to any serious events in the business agenda of this convention. The recording was to be purely a slight entertainment, a little audio dessert on the lunch menu.

The jokes had no literary allusions, no high aspirations. Of course, Joe Kelly was the Chief Quizzer, and the Kids — Van Dyke, Cynthia, Claude, Harve, and Gerard — introduced themselves as they did on the radio program. With his tongue firmly planted in his cheek, Joe said, "This program is *absolutely* unrehearsed." He first asked the Kids to identify the outstanding company in the motion picture industry. In unison, the Kids replied that it was Paramount Pictures Incorporated. "You see, folks," Joe commented ironically, "absolutely unrehearsed." The script was short, just five pages, with references to industry leaders, films, movie studios, and disreputable movie press agents.

At the middle of the month NBC commemorated its 15th year in business with a weeklong anniversary celebration culminating in a three-hour marathon of entertainment on a radio program produced by the network and broadcast on the evening of November 15. To make the program attractive, the roster of artists appearing on the show included practically every performer heard regularly on their Red and Blue networks. The Quiz Kids were part of the entertainment, as well as 36 other famous radio performers (among them Jack Benny and Don Wilson, George Burns and Gracie Allen, Bing Crosby, Lum and Abner, and Edgar Bergen).

The emphasis of this program was on the entertainers, rather than congratulatory speeches from radio executives. *Variety* concluded that this marathon was an improvement over their tenth-anniversary show, where the speeches from executives were long-winded. This time any speeches were "slipped in between the acts," and were brief. The speakers included David Sarnoff, the president of RCA, Niles Trammell, president of NBC, two of NBC's well-known announcers, and several officials from the Roosevelt administration. The European war crept into the festivities as a sober grace note of nationalism added to the entertainment at hand. Speakers "stressed the part played by American radio in the defense objectives and national unity." Both Secretary of the Navy Frank Church and Under-Secretary of War Robert Patterson alluded to the course the United States was pursuing because of the Axis threat. Niles Trammell reported that NBC recently had withdrawn its man in Berlin because the Nazis insisted on using him for propaganda purposes.[47]

The next day the Kids made an appearance at a meeting of the North Shore Evening Club in Winnetka, Illinois. Joe Bailey said that their participation would be relatively short, "from approximately 8:00 to 9:30 P.M."[48] Two days later Gerard Darrow was the emcee on the November 18 broadcast of *The Treasury Hour*. This unusual broadcast emphasized a "youth angle," so it was appropriate to have Gerard participate. He was the most famous and the most identifiable Quiz Kid at that time. With the program's emphasis on youth, understandably, Walt Disney was a guest on the broadcast, too.[49] Nearly all the AM radio stations in the United States carried *The Treasury Hour*. There were 831 AM radio stations in the United States in 1941[50]; in comparison, the Federal Communications Commission reported that in 2004 there were 4,781.[51]

Clearly, when the Kids returned from Hollywood the program became a stalwart within the professional radio community. By the end of November, it was no longer just a common assumption that *QK* was a mainstay of American popular culture. It became official. The Princeton University Triangle Club lampooned *QK* in a satirical skit, one of 25 dealing with subjects of world and national interest as they staged its 53rd annual stage production entitled *Ask Me Another* at the McCarter Theatre in Princeton. For the first time this venerable student-written satirical production abandoned its tradition, the conventional musical comedy format, in favor of a topical musical revue. The club kept its tradition of featuring an all-male kick line in drag.

After the opening performance at the McCarter the troupe took the musical on a national tour during the winter holiday season.[52] Large audiences in New York and Mansfield, Connecticut, on the weekend before Christmas greeted frisky performances with enthusiasm. The *New York Times* reported that the skits scrutinized "practically all of the foibles of our contemporary world." The sketch "What Is Your Favorite Radio Program" lampooned *QK* and was among the notable segments of the show. Other targets for their satire were Ernest Hemingway, Tin Pan Alley, and the German High Command. The newspaper conceded that the skits were "all done in a friendly fashion, however, and no one is the worse for it after the jesting is over." The "traditional chorus of maidens not so fair, with frames as willowy as oaken trunks" titillated the audience.[53] It would bring back memories for Lou, as he recalled his work with the Black Friars.

The Kids were busy with other tasks. The *Quiz Kids Magazine*, managed by George Kamen, was planning to distribute autographed copies of a Saalfield publication, *Quiz Kids Quiz Book,* to winners among the magazine contributors. Joe Bailey asked Van Dyke to "drop in sometime" to autograph books, "since your picture appears on the jacket of the book along with those of the four other Kids who participated in the first movie short." Bailey seemed casual about his request, even though November was a month of frenetic activity. He did not want Van Dyke to make a "special trip for this purpose," but he had hoped to get the autograph by December 1. His deadline was flexible, seemingly without urgency. "A few days later will be all right," he said.[54]

The staff scheduled more appearances for December. On November 28, the Kids received an invitation to perform at a luncheon for a group of 4-H Club winners who had traveled to the International Livestock Exposition sponsored by the International Harvester Company. The luncheon was December 3, at an armory in Chicago, giving the Kids just five days' notice.[55] It was to be a busy day: the Quiz Kids appearance at the 4-H Club luncheon was followed by their regularly scheduled broadcast that evening.

On the surface, this International Harvester event did not look significant, certainly not in the same league as their recent travel to Hollywood, New York, and the White House, and their visit to the United States Senate. This corporate invitation looked innocent enough, and perfectly natural, another in the long schedule of appearances at civic events. But maybe it was not as casual as it seemed. It could have been that Lou encouraged this simple luncheon performance by the Kids because he thought that there was a potential association with Harvester for the public relations part of his business.

Harvester was an important company at that time and would have been a welcome addition to the roster of public relations clients for the publicity arm of his business. International Harvester as a prospective client was more than a regional business success; the company was national in its scope and at that time almost at the pinnacle of its dominance in its field. After all, this was the Midwest, and any major company whose business was in the thousands of miles of farm belt radiating from Chicago would want to be associated with a service firm in that agricultural hub, especially one with an enviable record of success. This luncheon event may have opened an opportunity for a business relationship. Perhaps the spark of this idea may have lit the tinder at the Louis G. Cowan Company a short while before the livestock expo. Maybe it was simply coincidental that Jesse Miller, Jr., age 11, had been a one-time Quiz Kid two months earlier on the October 1 broadcast. Jesse's father was a die shop foreman at International Harvester.[56]

The day before the appearance at the luncheon, Bailey wrote to Van Dyke again, telling him of another event. Alka-Seltzer had asked the Kids to donate their time with a personal appearance at the Chicago Youth Exposition. Joe Kelly had consented to contribute his time, as well.[57] The expo was at the Sherman Hotel in Chicago. It was a five-day exposition beginning December 8. It was the same day that the United States entered World War II. The Kids appeared on Thursday, December 11, as exemplars of that day's theme "Youth in Education Day." They started at 8:15 P.M. Joe explained, "Our part of the program will be preceded by a 15-minute program [of songs] by a choral group." The Kids put on a 25-minute show, mimicking their usual broadcast. Bailey promised that they would be able to leave the hotel by 9:00.[58]

Less than a week later, December 17, the customary *QK* broadcast aired from the U.S. Naval Training Station in Great Lakes. Joining the Kids to entertain both the live audience of naval personnel and the mass audience listening on their radios across the nation was Lieutenant Commander Eddie Peabody, playing the banjo. The naval station's male chorus was on the program, too. With three such appearances at military bases within seven months, it was clear that the War Department valued the appearances of the Kids as a morale booster at military posts. This was the first of three military visits in 1941, each broadcast on their network program.

This first year, these personal appearances, as frequent as they were, were just a preamble for the next 12 years. The Kids' travel schedule during the four years of the war would expand considerably because of the escalation in their performances at military bases and their other work for the Treasury Department.

If the minutiae of their schedule for the past 12 months seem to be intense and infused with many details, I have included them because they give us an informative glimpse of the first full year of this radio program, and the intense effort needed to produce and promote it. Subsequent years were just as industrious and fast moving.

Often, people who met Roby commented to her that she had an easy job. She only had to appear at the studio a half-hour before the broadcast and then go home immediately after, a total of one hour of her time. After all, she had no script to write, they said. The "script" was the questions for the Kids, all submitted by listeners. At the end of a broadcast, she didn't have to return until the following week. So, what was the big deal? An easy job, well paid. Enviable.

In fact, she was busy all day, six days a week; some weeks, seven. Her duties as researcher; publicity writer releasing stories, photos and biographies of the Kids to "eight hundred newspapers"; and as a scriptwriter were the customary duties of her job. There were more. She arranged appearances for the Kids at hospitals, orphanages, civic events, and the frequent appearances that did not fall into any predictable category. She coordinated the script and the music with the pianist who was to play the music questions on air, assuaged the "ambitious parents" of children who were not *QK* prospects, and auditioned prospective Kids.[59]

Occasionally the prospective Kids were unusual, aside from their intellectual abilities. Less than a year after America entered the war, she interviewed two refugee children from Germany who had been part of the Kindertransport mission that placed nearly 10,000 German-Jewish children in the United Kingdom nine months before the European war began in 1939. Roby's description was terse, but no less telling; "This morning [Saturday] I came down [to the office] to interview two refugee children from Germany. Jewish — escaped to England — went to school there — and now are the most American Americans I've ever met."[60] There is no further comment about whether or not these two children became Quiz Kids.

The rest of the production staff was equally as engaged, as the popularity of the program escalated rapidly starting with the first week of 1941. After the first trip to New York the Kids were increasingly occupied with the broadcasts and the expanding schedule of appearances elsewhere. When they returned from Hollywood and the show with Jack Benny, requests for their appearance increased. The planning for these personal appearances was difficult and time consuming, adding even more complexity to the normal requirements of producing a weekly program. By the middle of 1941, these requests poured in nearly every day. Toward the end of the year at the start of a new season and a new contract, there was an even greater increase in requests for personal appearances. Any lingering thoughts about the transitory nature of the radio audience could easily have started Lou and Joe Bailey thinking about reviving the idea of taking the program on a nationwide tour to continue building their audience. But a tour would be costly, far exceeding any reasonable budget. They realized that they didn't have to think about touring. Bertha's plan of personal appearances with Jack Benny, and the thinking behind it, could be the solution about how to travel. There were enough requests for personal appearances throughout the United States to keep the Kids on a busy itinerary. The Kamen Variation could be the answer to how to pay for the expenses of such active travel. In December, the invitations continued pouring in even after Pearl Harbor and the declaration of war. There seemed to be no stopping these requests.

Just looking at their schedule for this one busy year gives us a picture of how these activities, and the fame of *Quiz Kids*, increased beyond the expectations one might have for a hit radio program. It took a lot of energy to handle each of these special appearances. The effort was worth it. Indeed, the calculated effect of heightening the awareness of the *Quiz Kids* by virtue of these special appearances worked. Evidently, John and Lou considered these

Ruth Duskin on a pile of mail from listeners (courtesy Ruth Duskin Feldman).

invitations desirable publicity and not a chore. As more requests for appearances started coming from all over the country, they were evidence of a growing national listening audience.

It was an active audience, too. Listeners at home connected to the program in ways that might seem incredible today. More than submitting thousands of questions as possible brainteasers for the Kids, they wrote hundreds of personal letters declaring their adoration of the show, offering criticism, and asking the Kids for favors. The mail engulfed the staff. The letters had become a mountain.

ANSWERS

You would have a half dollar, a quarter and four dimes.
The four political parties are Federalists, Democrats, Republicans, and Whigs.
The seven seas are: Arafura, Banda, Coral, Celebes, Java, Timor, and South

China. (Note: After World War II, the Dutch East Indies was renamed Indonesia.)

It's better to buy the first coat. If ¾ of the second is equal to ½ of the third coat, then ¼ of the second is 2/9 of the third. Therefore, ½ of the third minus 2/9 of itself (the same as ¼ of the second) leaves 1/9, the difference between the cost of the second and third coats, in relation to the third. Thus, if $40 is the difference in cost, 9 times $40 is the cost of the higher priced coat, $360, and the second coat would be $320.

Answers to *Liberty* magazine questions

1. *Handel, while dueling with another musician, Mattheson.*
2. *(1) Igor Stravinsky, (2) Handel, (3) De Falla from El Amor Brujo.*
3. *The musk turtle emits an oily secretion that has an unpleasant odor.*
4. *From the swim bladder of the sturgeon (and other fish).*
5. *You would attend the Boston Tea Party and would wear the costume of an Indian. The Dartmouth, the Beaver, and the Eleanor were the names of the three English ships attacked.*
6. *Yuan Shih-Kai.*
7. *There would be 190 handshakes. The rule is, subtract one from the total number of Quiz Kids—19 (a person would not shake hands with himself), multiply it by the total number—20—and divide by two.*
8. *Cadmium, calcium, carbon, cerium, cesium, chlorine, chromium, cobalt, columbium, copper.*
9. *Nine blocks. Since I walk two thirds as fast as he does, when he gets home I still have one third of the way to go. This one third is three blocks. Therefore, the total distance is nine blocks.*

9

Box 1100

☞ *Two articles of wearing apparel that women wear next to each other we spell with the same four letters. What are they?*

On the first broadcast of *Quiz Kids* there was an announcement that asked at-home listeners to submit questions for use on future programs. Lou established this request for questions on the demonstration records, stated clearly even during Clifford Utley's audition on June 12, 1940. In making the plea for entries, the show's announcer gave the audience the mailing address: post office box 1100 in Chicago.[1] When thousands of letters arrived after the first show, and the quantity continued to increase each week, the staff was delighted, as was the production team and Charles Beardsley. Almost instantly, *QK* was a familiar entity, certainly at the Chicago post office. And the show's recognition showed an exponential increase. Within a few weeks after the June 28 broadcast, no postal box number was required. Listeners had decided to simplify the address on their mail to the program. Thus, the postal service accepted and was able to deliver mail addressed to:

> Quiz Kids
> National Broadcasting Company
> Chicago, Ill.

QK continued to grow in popularity and familiarity. The show's announcer told listeners of another new, simplified address. For the staff, it was another informal way, a milestone toward success, to measure the popularity of the program. No street address was needed, no post office box number, not even the broader destination of the state of Illinois was part of this streamlined address. Now, you didn't have to remember very many details; you could write to the program with just three words on the address section of the envelope:

> Quiz Kids
> Chicago

Among the questions submitted by listeners each week, starting immediately after the first broadcast, were fan letters to individual Kids. To answer their fan mail, or for any other letters or social notes that the Kids wanted to write, each Kid had a quantity of personal stationery, actually social note paper measuring seven by five inches. Of course, with the heightened sense of style established by the production staff, it would have been remiss if there were no envelopes to match. The paper was an expensive laid stock. With a great sense of discreet style, each sheet had printed on it, in cerulean blue ink, the program's logo and address and the name of the child. So unpretentious and classic was this stationery that it would have been acceptable in the upper echelons of polite, white-glove society.[2]

No one could calculate how fast the Kids were to become famous. Lou and the staff knew that if the show was a success, the Kids would become celebrities. But they didn't realize how quickly that would happen. Lou's whirlwind catapulted individual Kids into nationwide recognition almost immediately. They became household names, symbolic peaks of knowledge and education. This was to be expected; the program was lively and appealing. The enhanced status of the Kids brought about the trappings of celebrity adoration similarly enjoyed (or despised) by actors and actresses in radio and movies. Because the press lionized them, their fans clamored for their autographs. Ruth Fisher Henoch recalls that even though she was a Quiz Kid for just six weeks, she was a celebrity; people asked for her autograph. Before being a Kid, as a hobby she had sought autographs of famous people. Once, by chance, she saw Eddie Cantor coming out of a theatre in Chicago and got his. But when she became a Kid and people began asking for hers, she realized that she didn't deserve such adulation. In fact, she concluded that the entire practice of asking a celebrity for an autograph was unimportant. It changed her own outlook on being a famous person. "That experience," she remembers, "ended my autograph hunting days forever."[3]

One measure of their fame was their fan mail. People from all over the United States wrote to them; the quantity and variations of fan mail increased with each passing week. Cynthia Cline Newgarden believes that the fan mail she and the other Kids received is an example of informal cultural anthropology. She describes the fan mail written to her as "a good indication of what people were thinking at that time."[4] As well as the usual letters proclaiming undying adulation, the Kids often received some with unusual gifts accompanying them.

Richard Williams received skates wrapped in a "priceless" sweater from a fan in Vancouver.[5] Someone sent a Portuguese half-dollar. Another sent three gilded wishbones. An enigmatic crocheted doily tumbled out of one letter. An amateur geologist sent some rocks, while a more sentimental writer sent a dozen pressed leaves. Most of the letter writers wanted the Kids to identify the objects on air, not considering the fact that this was radio and the feasibility of identification would be better via television, even though that medium was not widely available until nearly ten years later, at the end of the decade.[6]

Roby was amazed by the generosity of the show's listeners. She took an inventory of gifts sent in by listeners, and it produced an eclectic, somewhat strange list: neckties, rings, lapel pins, puzzles, a wasp nest, baseball mitts, walnut meats, a bushel of apples, handmade bath mats, chocolate cakes, butterflies, and some grapefruit.[7]

More typical fan mail without these extraordinary enclosures came from both children and adults. Some were reflective of fantasy-like wishful thinking, while others were simply expressions of joy or congratulations. Understanding the social and cultural meaning of these letters, Cynthia has kept her fan mail. Some of it expresses frustration, their writers desperately seeking to succeed in show business or the arts, and expecting her to be helpful.

Arthur Inman of Boston asked for a favor. For 10 years he had been writing a book of poetry that had to do with memories of his boyhood. He wasn't sure that his memory of his childhood thoughts reflected accurately the thoughts of someone "between the ages of five and thirteen."[8] So he asked Cynthia if she would take the time to look at his manuscript and give him her opinion. Of course, what Inman perhaps didn't realize was that in 1940 Cynthia was 15, certainly not a child any longer, and her memory of childhood thoughts was subject to the same elusiveness.

Some of Cynthia's fan mail came from lonely people who were looking for correspondents (the term "pen pals" wasn't in general use during the early 1940s). Some people made presumptuous offers. Others were trying to sell something. One man asked for an autograph to add to his "growing list of Prominent Radio People," and included a self-addressed, stamped envelope and blank slip for "your convenience."[9] He added humbly that if she didn't want to comply, she should simply mail an envelope he enclosed and thus he would understand that she did not want to reply.

A few of these letters included one dollar in cash so that Cynthia could buy Christmas Seals on behalf of the correspondents. One, Charles E. Pecker, wrote four letters between September 11 and November 27, 1940, and sent a $1 bill twice for Cynthia to make the Christmas seals purchase as his representative. Pecker also hoped that NBC would make a recording of her singing so that he and other listeners could buy it, and in that way "we could listen to you whenever we liked."[10]

Charles Bullock of Buffalo, New York, congratulated Cynthia on her "remarkable ability in composing those poems during the program" and asked her for a copy of the poem she wrote on air during the August 16, 1940, broadcast. He expressed his appreciation in advance if she sent it, and even more so "if you wrote it yourself," probably a sly request for her signature.[11]

Martha Ann Dieffenbacher of Havana, Illinois, who was Cynthia's age, offered a brief autobiography and asked Cynthia if she would reply to tell her about herself because Cynthia's life would be "interesting whereas I have been boring." At the same time she was self-deprecating when she reported that the student body voted her as All American Girl but said she couldn't understand why they chose her. She thought that perhaps because her peers wanted to get out of school early, they voted for her in a hurry.[12] Her letter was a plaintive request, asking naively if Cynthia would be her friend.

Another of Cynthia's fans was Johnny Mandel, who became a successful and famous composer and arranger. Mandel was a high school student at the time he wrote to her in 1942. He was born the same year Cynthia was.[13]

At the same time there were outright pleas for money or other commercial favors. Mrs. William Pfeiffer of Pontiac, Michigan, said that she was "forced" to sell her bound volumes of *National Geographic* magazine, from 1906 to 1941, and thought Cynthia might buy them. She wanted to sell them for $500.[14] Thinking that Cynthia was a prospective buyer was completely misguided. Certainly none of the Kids was rich; in fact, they came from middle class families, cautious about spending money, still affected by the economic fears created by the Depression, as were many Americans in the early 1940s.

The restraints about spending money were not important to everyone. Mrs. Stanhope Philips of Ventnor, New Jersey, sent $50 in Defense Stamps. She wanted to divide the stamps evenly among five of her "favorite" Kids. Lewellen thought that she would be pleased if the five Kids wrote a thank-you note to her.[15]

In 1940 shortly after the war began in Europe, there was an increase in American manufacturing for export to countries already feeling the strain of war-related shortages. There was also some unusual activity from women who created and worked in true "cottage industries," knitting sweaters and gloves and socks at home under the tutelage of a civilian master knitter and guided by the clothing patterns designated by the Department of the Army. Once completed, the government distributed all these articles of clothing knitted in 1940 and 1941 to American soldiers in England, before the formal entry to the war by the United States.

Mrs. Helen DeVeaux Baker of Jacksonville, Florida, decided to write and ask the Kids to create verses, specifically "a four-line sentiment to enclose with a scarf-helmet I am knitting for the boys Somewhere [sic] in England."[16] She thought that these "sentiments" might boost the morale of "the boys." The letter was addressed to the Quiz Kids and delivered to Lou's office but must have been passed along to Cynthia because of her proclivity for writing poetry.

Sometimes Joe Bailey would ask the Kids to answer certain fan mail because he understood the value of good public relations. Bailey asked Cynthia to write to a 14-year-old boy because it was an opportunity "to cheer up a little fellow who has had more than his share of misfortune." The boy was blind and walked with crutches from the age of seven; two weeks earlier he had split a bone in his leg and was confined to bed for five weeks.[17]

Another unusual request came from a fan in Hood River, Oregon, who asked if one of the Kids could select "a name for her little black kitten." Bernice Cranston, the *Quiz Kids* office manager, assigned this request to Cynthia, with the understanding that the listener neglected to say whether the kitten was male or female, therefore Cynthia should submit an androgynous name. In a postscript, Cranston asked Cynthia to let the *QK* office know what name she suggested because it might make a nice public relations story for the Hood River newspaper.[18]

No matter how glamorous a career or profession might be, there are always the ordinary details that are associated with it. Movie stars have to wake early in the morning, often before dawn, to go to the set and have their makeup applied, sometimes sitting for hours in the process. Professional athletes have to undergo a program of rigorous exercise as part of their jobs, sweating and grunting just as the rest of us do, or make appearances at corporate and civic events and luncheons where they have to make motivational speeches. Famous and successful people in a multitude of vocational disciplines have to answer their mail or do other ordinary and time-consuming tasks. It's the lackluster and sometimes tedious part of being a success. Faced with their own success, and with the support of a sensitive production staff who worked with them from behind the curtains, the Quiz Kids rose to the challenge just as they did orally on air, with the trappings of style and the patina of charm.

Considering the program's increasing recognition, it was almost a foregone conclusion that Miles Labs would renew its contract. The continuing and increasing volume of mail was evidence that the program's audience was increasing and the show was growing more popular across the nation. The horizon seemed boundless.

ANSWER

The two articles are shoe and hose. Joe Kelly announced that he saw the hands of the Kids raised instantly — in less than a second; they probably raised their hands before he finished asking the question.

10

Quiz Kids, Too?

☞ *Where on the present day map would you place Carthage, Troy, and Babylon?*

There was an underlying tension at 8 South Michigan during the spring and summer of 1941, a counterpoint to the exhilaration everyone felt after returning from Los Angeles and receiving the awards from the trade publications. These industry awards were a validation of the program's rapidly growing popularity. But anxiety tinged this sparkling accomplishment. Competitors to *Quiz Kids* had begun to surface in other cities.

Usually the stations aired these *QK* clones only locally or regionally. Boston logged in first. Friday, October 18, 1940, only six weeks after *QK* began broadcasting with its first 52-week contract with Miles Labs, *Ask the Children* made its debut on WBZ-WBZA, an NBC Blue Network show. Selden Loring, a New England author, was the emcee. The show featured five children under age 16 recruited from schools in the greater Boston area. Each child received a bank book with a deposit in his name for appearing on the program. The three who scored highest received a larger deposit than the other two. The highest scorers would appear the following week along with two new children. The Hudson Coal Company of Scranton, Pennsylvania, sponsored the show.[1]

In December, *Variety* reviewed *Recess Time*, a local quiz program on WSCH in Portland, Maine, with children as participants. The program made the startling claim that it was the first to probe juvenile intelligence with aired questions and answers, starting in 1938. Broadcast from the State Theatre in Portland, it was part of the usual Saturday movie exhibitor's offerings to attract an audience of children. Apparently the emcee asked the assembled audience of children the questions, and awards were dispensed throughout the program.

Despite the outrageous claim that seemed to be baiting *Quiz Kids* for a reaction and perhaps some free publicity in the process, Harry Botwick, the house manager at the State Theatre did not exhibit any greater aspirations other than to produce a "keyed-up kid attendance." The possibility of duplicating the format "excited considerable interest among other northern New England exhibition circles." More than 20 exhibitors had visited the show in the previous month. All of them came "to decide whether it could be duplicated on and out of their own premises as a potential weekend business builder."

The quiz portion was ordinary and "cut from [the] customary bolt of cheesecloth." Based on the applause that greeted Botwick when he appeared onstage (he was the emcee, too), *Variety* concluded that he was more responsible for the success of the show than any interest by other exhibitors in duplicating the program.[2]

In December a "carbon copy" of *QK* called *Kid Wizards* began broadcasting on WHN, an independent, local New York station. The program ran for 30 minutes on Tuesdays at 9 P.M., a day earlier than *QK*. It appears that their Tuesday schedule was an attempt to entice the New York audience to switch from the Chicago *QK* to the local program. WHN thought it had potential as a real competitor, so they introduced it and continued running it as a sustaining program (that is, without a sponsor). The producer and WHN had high hopes that a sponsor would be interested once it began to gain an audience. Louis L. Wolff, a child psychologist, was the emcee.

Kid Wizards had a permanent panel of three children, augmented by one or two new panelists each week. NBC suggested to Lou that he use this same format, closer to the *Information Please* model at the time of the first *QK* broadcasts. Lou rejected the idea emphatically.

Kid Wizards had a unique way of selecting a pool of prospective questions for the panel. They chose new panelists based on questions submitted by hopeful panelists, somewhat different from the way *QK* would select questions from those submitted by the at-home radio audience. Only young listeners could submit questions for possible use on air by *Kid Wizards*. If their questions stumped the panel, the producer would invite them to be on the show.

One critic portrayed the show cynically. He thought it would appeal to an audience that wanted to describe the contestants as "ain't-he-cute-he's-only-six." Listening to the program on the last day of 1940, this critic thought that the youngsters were strong only in specialized areas (one youngster was particularly adept in his knowledge of Gilbert and Sullivan). To be expected, the majority of the panelists were strong in science. They were uneven in their knowledge of general information, "assuming there was no advance coaching." More specifically, this critic said that they habitually stumbled on "the simplest questions on general subjects." What's more, the critic thought that Wolff had not familiarized himself with the questions in advance, a problem that *QK* solved when each week Roby would coach Joe Kelly extensively.

On the show of December 31, 1940, one of the children had to correct Wolff for thinking that "Chico Marx plays the harp, instead of the piano."

Kid Wizards paid listeners $5 for each question they submitted that the production staff selected for a broadcast. If a question remained unanswered the listener would receive a dictionary in addition to the invitation to appear on a subsequent show.[3] WHN's gamble paid off. By February 25 *Kid Wizards* attracted a sponsor, Consolidated Royal Chemical Corporation, advertising its Vitamized Yeast Foam Tablets.[4]

Two months later another competitor emerged, this time on the NBC network, as well. It was the first network radio show to originate in Seattle. Its name was *Kids of the Week* and it was a half-hour broadcast. The basic idea of the show was similar to *QK*; the panel of children could speak about any subject introduced by the moderator, Doris Sederholm. One major difference was that there would be no audience present in the studio during broadcasts. The producers reasoned that although a studio audience would add excitement to the program, it would result in more pressure for the kids. The panel consisted of two age groups, one ages 10 to 12, the other 12 to 14. There were six panelists — three boys and three girls. First aired locally on Sunday, April 27, on KJR in Seattle, it was scheduled weekly thereafter for four weeks before moving to Hollywood and the NBC Pacific Blue network. The Lime Cola Company of Sylacauga, Alabama, sponsored the show.[5]

It was a bitter drink for the Wade Agency to swallow. The agency acted quickly. Immediately after the first broadcast Wade protested vigorously to NBC. After all, *Kids of the Week* was a network show, not a local show like *Kid Wizards* or *Ask the Children*. NBC agreed that the program had too much in common with *QK*. The network decided not to carry it on Pacific Blue even though they had scheduled the show to start on that network the following week, May 4. *Kids of the Week* only aired once. After NBC yanked this West Coast upstart, Lime Cola's advertising agency, Davis and Pearson, sought legal redress for breach of contract.[6]

In 1940, complying with NBC's broadcasting requirements, Lou's concept was different enough from *Information Please* so that there was no demand for redress from its producers, advertising agency, or sponsor once *QK* was established and broadcasting.

By the spring of 1941, Wade and Lou must have decided that these upstart competitors were getting to be distasteful, if not threatening. They decided to take action. Joe Bailey protested this sprouting of competitors in a phone conversation and letter to NBC. He cited several stations which "in our opinion, infringe upon the established format and content" of *QK*. In addition to *Kid Wizards* and *Ask the Children* he listed 21 stations from the Blue Network, as well as CBS and independent stations from around the country, that were the culprits. Even though Joe's letter sounded indignant, he meant his list to be thorough and informational. He recognized the limitations of his exposé; saying to the network, "You have no control over" the stations that were not NBC stations, but he was listing all 23 "for your information." Joe's list was wide-ranging:

NBC (Blue Network)

School Kids Kwiz, KECA. Los Angeles
Junior Wizards, WBOE, Cleveland
Pop Corn, KEX, Portland, Oregon
School Kids Quiz, WAKR, Akron
Dr. I.Q. Junior, NBC (Red)
Junior Quiz, WCFL, Chicago
Greenwich Time Quiz Kids, WJZ, New York
Quiz Kids, WEAN, Providence, R.I.
Quick Wits, WRNL, Richmond, Va.
Acree's High School Aces, WGN, Chicago

Other Network Stations and Independent Stations

Master Minds of Tomorrow, KTBS, Shreveport, La.
Kiddie Kwestion Bee, KRIC, Beaumont, Texas
The Kids Quizaroo, KSFO and KNX, Los Angeles and San Francisco
The Little Red School House, WGY, Schenectady, N.Y.
Mr. Dodge, KRLD, Dallas
The Young American Club, KROK, Rockford, Illinois
Stump Us, WKBW, Buffalo, N.Y.
Children Are Also People, CBS
Quiz Kids, WSTP, Salisbury, N.C.
Kids Quiz, WICA, Ashtabula, Ohio
I.Q. Kids, WATL, Atlanta[7]

Reacting to Bailey's list, Jules Herbuveaux, the production manager for WMAQ, the NBC outlet in Chicago, sent a memo to Sidney Strotz with Bailey's letter attached. Herbuveaux was practically sneering in his memo to Strotz. He wasn't sure what NBC could do to clear up the situation, but he thought that "a lot of the trouble is the catch-penny promotion methods [i.e., calculated to sell quickly without concern for quality] that Cowan has used in a number of towns." He gave as an example a recent phone call he had received from the NBC representative in Washington, D.C. asking if it would be possible to have a local department store do a one-time-only *Quiz Kids* broadcast. Apparently, Cowan, under Kamen's initiative, had used that department store for promoting *QK*. The store must have benefited from the promotion noticeably. Naturally, they wanted to try to repeat that success with their own version of a QK program and a corresponding promotion. They contacted NBC's Washington representative to ask permission. The representative called Herbuveaux about the request, realizing, and saying in plain language, that the store "wanted to cash in by buying a one-time shot on our [Washington] station." The Wade Agency refused to allow it. Herbuveaux realized that the store "would then go to another unaffiliated [with NBC] station and try to put on an imitation." He thought that some of the programs that Bailey listed as infringing on the format and content of *QK* might be the result of such practices.[8]

Strotz replied that NBC had no control over the two Chicago stations mentioned by Bailey, probably because they were independents. But he did offer some relief, saying that he was going to ask the NBC Station Relations Department to stop the practice "where stations involved are affiliated with our Blue Network and are carrying 'Quiz Kids' commercially." He thought that Wade could probably bring as much pressure and influence on these stations as NBC could.[9]

As he promised, on the same day he answered Herbuveaux, Strotz wrote to William S. Hedges, NBC vice-president with the responsibility for station relations. He asked him what action NBC could take with their affiliated stations about the *QK* competition. Strotz named only seven from Bailey's list of 23, all of them Blue Network stations.[10]

In July 1942 WSNY in Schenectady, New York, announced that it was broadcasting a quiz program locally with children as the panel. Its format was an obvious copy of *QK*. Called *The Book of Knowledge*, this 30-minute program featured five children competing with each other. Just as required by *QK*, the panelists had to retire by the time they reached their 16th birthday. WSNY aired the program in cooperation with the Grolier Society, publisher of *The Book of Knowledge*. The publisher awarded an encyclopedia to the contestant who scored highest and sent another to the listener who submitted "the best weekly question for discussion."[11]

In Toledo, Ohio, another quiz show with children was *Dr. I.Q., Jr.*, a variation of the NBC network show *Dr. I.Q.*[12] The juvenile version became a staple of the NBC network, and enjoyed a longevity that the other competitors to *QK* did not. Jimmy McClain, the original host of *Dr. I.Q.* at its debut in 1939, and Lew Valentine were its emcees from 1941 to 1949 when it went off the air.[13]

Sporadically, throughout the history of *QK* many other people or groups produced adaptations of the program. These variations stemmed from the show, but most of their producers did not intend to broadcast them. They used either of the two basic *QK* formats: a panel of four or five children or the Quiz Kids Versus format. It was easy to set up the program. There was very little, if any, expense; a table and four or five chairs for the panels. Gowns and mortarboards were optional. Primarily used to entertain, a school faculty would produce a duplicate *QK* program in its school auditorium, a business group could feature it at a business meeting, civic groups might have their version, or it was a powerful attraction at local fund-raising events in any one of a number of cities.[14]

Of course the Kids repeated it innumerably themselves. The success of the Quiz Kids Versus format at the Atlantic City teachers' convention and the suggestion by Miles Labs to use it on network shows made it easy for Lewellen to use it time and again during the next 12 years in many variations. The Kids continued to compete with their parents on Mother's Day or Father's Day. But John also used this format to have the Kids compete with college faculties, members of the U.S. Senate, Army Air Corps pilots, civic groups, radio news reporters, intellectuals, soldiers and sailors, businessmen, politicians, and school teachers; in fact, any group with specialized knowledge or erudition that apparently could be a challenge for the Kids, even the "cradle crew," the nickname suggested by the *Chicago Tribune* to describe the youngest, newest Kids who competed on one show with "old" Kids.[15] The format, even when lampooned by Jack Benny when the Kids were on his show, was a great attraction. John repeated it several times both on air and when the Kids traveled and their appearance was not to be broadcast.

In May 1941 Joe Bailey and Walter Wade voiced their concerns about these imitators of *QK* broadcasts. It's understandable why they were so vociferous in expressing their frustration to NBC. They had worked hard at building an audience and they were protective of it; any hint of encroachment on their territory raised their hackles. But by August, it appears that Bailey and Wade Advertising had put these intrusions from unaffiliated stations in perspective, leading Bill Hedges at NBC to "assume that the matter had died down." Bailey and Wade were now probably more sanguine in their thinking about *QK*. They realized that these imposters in local and regional markets were to be considered flattering, their damage to the *QK* market more trivial than significant.

In the last quarter of 1941 after the euphoria of Hollywood and the association with Jack Benny's program, the entire *QK* production staff and the Kids were busier than ever. Their dance cards were full. There was almost no time to relax, to bask in the sunshine of their recent successes. By any measure, in the competitive world of broadcasting and the continuous fight to stand out from the crowd, *QK* had won the battle. But the real war was just beginning.

ANSWER

Carthage is in Tunisia, Troy is in Turkey, and Babylon is in Iraq.

11
Any Bonds Today?

☞ *Which of the following states seceded from the Union in the Civil War: Maryland, Louisiana, West Virginia, Missouri, Arkansas, Kentucky?*

There was no interruption of activity for *QK* and the staff after the declaration of war by the United States in December 1941. At the beginning of 1942, Joe Kelly wrote the words and music to a popular song he titled "Just Ask the Quiz Kids." Famous Music Corporation, at that time the music publishing division of Paramount, published it.[1] On the cover of the sheet music is a photo of the Kids and Joe taken during the filming of their first short for Paramount. The lyrics are about the knowledge that the Kids exhibited each week. The words tell a little story in a problem/solution format. Joe stated the problem immediately: the Kids answered questions that have "worried me since I was a child." Generally, the lyrics reinforced the popular misconception that the Quiz Kids were invincible; that if you didn't know something all you had to do was ask the Quiz Kids, because they knew the answers to everything.

His song was a flashback to his youthful days as a teenage dance band leader and songwriter. He wrote this song for family entertainment. But it was also a clever way to promote the radio program, because the last eight bars were a blatant request to tune in to the weekly *QK* radio program. Specifically, if there was something puzzling the person singing the song or the audience listening to him, the solution was easy: Just turn on the radio and listen to *QK* for the answer.[2] The photo on the front cover was a subtle and visual way to promote the Paramount shorts.

By 1942, Kelly had become famous, too, not just from his popularity with listeners of *National Barn Dance*. His name in the region surrounding Chicago became so well known as a result of his work on *Barn Dance* and *QK* that the *Chicago Sun* newspaper hired him to promote their comic section by reading the comic strips to children on WLS, just as Mayor Fiorello LaGuardia would do on radio station WNYC in New York during a newspaper

Joe Kelly published a song about Quiz Kids (author's collection, Jason Gardner Photography).

strike three years later. Joe read the "funnies" seven days a week: six 15-minute programs weekly, and a half-hour reading on Sunday.[3]

Once again *Billboard* gave its award for outstanding single-program exploitation to the Louis G. Cowan Company for promotion of *QK*. *Billboard* specified 11 accomplishments that occurred throughout the year, saying that Lou and his staff had never missed an opportunity to promote the program, handling it cleverly throughout the year. Among those cited was the technique of placing the Kids on other radio programs having audiences different than their own to attract listeners who hadn't heard *QK* previously. The seeds sown by Bertha's plan had grown into healthy plants and were starting to blossom.

Examples noted were the Jack Benny broadcasts and Benny's reciprocal appearance on *QK* in Hollywood in the middle of April 1940; the appearance of the Kids on *The Treasury Hour*, broadcast on CBS, an NBC competitor; and the world-premiere of their short films — "the first time in film history" that a short film was given this Hollywood world premiere treatment. It hadn't been reported as such, but most likely the premiere was complete with searchlights crisscrossing the sky. The *Billboard* award revealed that there was a concerted effort by Lou to encourage parodies of the Kids by film and radio personalities when they appeared as guests on network benefit performances.

Billboard took into account the special programs on which the Kids were competing with college professors, and where the parents became Quiz Kids. Of course, the merchandising of products was included. An off-the-cuff count by Lou amounted to 15 different products: Quiz Kids hats, coats, dresses, two types of games, fountain pens, greeting cards, sweatshirts, sweaters, shirts, cut-out dolls, and books, all handled by George Kamen.[4] Personal appearances at army camps and naval stations, even before the war began, were a significant factor in the excellent promotion of the program, the magazine noted. (All of the examples cited by *Billboard* occurred before the war began.)

Beyond the elements of focused promotion, there was the need for intelligent public relations by the *QK* staff. They had to take great care in all of this audience-building promotion to avoid presenting the Kids as abnormal, conceited brats. Occasionally, the staff had to take "prompt and smart action" to head off "adverse public reaction" whenever negative criticism appeared in an educational publication. The magazine concluded that it was tougher to "accomplish this ballyhoo" for 1941 than the previous year, because the program had been on the air for seven months before the evaluation period for the 1941 awards (January 1–December 31, 1941) and thus was competing for public notice with established programs. Because *QK* was no longer a novelty, the production staff "had to do extensive planning to exploit the program as successfully as they did."[5]

To be expected, *QK* itself was the subject of evaluation, too. *Variety* reported at the beginning of the year that NBC had announced on the show's recent broadcast that the Kids, 54 of whom had appeared by the beginning of 1942, gave correct answers to 89 percent of the questions asked of them during 1941.[6] The *New York Times* explained with some detail, facetiously, that the 11 percent difference between the correct answers and perfection from "those terrifying little sages, the Quiz Kids," was due to the fact that the Kids missed, as they referred to them, some easy questions: How do you make a cheese soufflé?; What is the difference between a Percheron and a Clydesdale?; What was the nickname of Edward the First of England?[7]

There were more significant conclusions than the percentage of correct answers from the Kids. Joe Kelly reported at the close of the broadcast on April 8 that a survey by the *Journal of Education*, "the oldest teachers' magazine in the United States," described the effects that the radio program was having on the Kids. Their survey showed that the "87 Quiz Kids to date 'definitely benefited' by the experience." The magazine concluded that the Kids had improved in voice, poise, and mental alertness, without becoming egotistical. The Kids also had improved their ability to express themselves and to get along with other children. Kelly thought that the most admirable trait revealed by the survey was that "when they lose, they can stand up to defeat like good sports."[8]

Notwithstanding, entry to the war did not interrupt or diminish the civic requests for appearances by the Kids. When the production office sent letters or memos to the Kids, there was little or no reference to the war. But it was still uppermost in people's minds. As a respite from thinking about the war, the *Chicago Tribune* invited the Kids to visit a farm that the newspaper owned near Wheaton, less than 30 miles from Chicago, to give them an opportunity to "soak up a little barnyard lore."[9] It was a bucolic day, away from the noise and frenzy of the big city, with its new focus on the war. It was a brief return to a quieter environment.

With all their sophistication, the Kids were still big-city kids, just as parochial as children from rural surroundings who come to a large city with no preparation for adjusting to its customs. Often when Joe asked the Kids questions about farm and country, they were inexpressive, or they just guessed, sometimes with embarrassing consequences. When they appeared at a livestock show in the fall of 1940 the Kids were asked the question "On which side would you milk a cow?" One of the Kids answered, "The outside." We have to imagine that this response was either an urban wise guy answer, or simply an uninformed guess. This trip to the newspaper's working farm was a way to "get rid of a blind spot in their brains."[10] They had no first-hand experience with life on a working farm.

Gerard knew a lot about flora and fauna, but that was mostly textbook knowledge. This rustic visit was more about getting hands dirty and shoes muddy. Even Roby, who was probably closer to farm life, having moved to Chicago from Cedar Rapids, a smaller city adjacent to the Iowa Corn Belt, wondered at her muddy shoes — shoes more appropriate for a stroll on the sidewalks of the Magnificent Mile of Michigan Avenue than a mucky slog through a reeking barnyard.

This one-day trip was an education for the Kids, a chance for them to get away from the classroom, to ask questions and, as always, try to satisfy their curiosity by asking questions and diving in to a tactile exploration of their surroundings. It was the first visit to a farm for most of the Kids. They romped through the pastures, swarmed over fences, insisted on petting every animal they saw, and examined equipment and machinery. Gerard spent most of his time wandering in the woods, inspecting and classifying the trees, shrubs, and birds he observed. Harve Fischman and Richard Williams asked pointed and interesting questions about everything they saw.

What the Kids didn't know about farm life sometimes produced amusing results. The peacock that roamed with the turkeys brought on cries of delight from the youngsters. Mistakenly, they identified it as a pretty "colored chicken." Joel Kupperman saw a pile of hay outside one of the dairy barns. He couldn't resist running and jumping right into it. Triumphant in his dive into the stack, and climbing up to its top, he shouted his success to the rest of the Kids while bouncing up and down on the pile. But it wasn't a stack of hay, it was manure: one big pile of cow shit. Later while observing some newly born calves at the dairy, he took off one of his gloves, offering a friendly, grimy finger to one of the calves. The calf wrapped its tongue around his finger; Joel squealed with delight. He wanted his mother to come look at the calf that "thinks I give milk."

By the end of the day, one of the children summarized the trip by boasting that the Kids from now on would "be able to answer any farm questions and we won't make any of the silly mistakes we did last year."[11]

The next day, Saturday, Roby and John were back at the *QK* office. Before they had a chance to settle in there was a new and apparently urgent request for an appearance; this time the war had something to do with it. As soon as they walked in, someone from the Navy radio school called and wanted both of them to "come right over" because they wanted to "set up the children taking the recruiting exam for the navy's technical radio school."

Two months earlier, the Army Air Force made a similar request, asking if six of the *Quiz Kids* boys could take the aviation cadet test. Each side had its reasons. The army wanted to evaluate the difficulty of their test for young men who were considered "intellectually superior." The Kids wanted to know "if the army could stump them." The test questions came from several disciplines, including mathematics, spelling, current events, history, and physics. The president of the aviation cadet examining board administered the exam. Of the six Kids, only one, Harve Fischman, failed. His weakness in math dropped him to a grade of 65. Passing grade was 80, and the highest possible grade was 150. Van Dyke scored highest, with 131. Their average score was 101. No doubt Fischman's low score had a dampening effect on their average. Even with Harve's dreadful 65 pulling their average down, they did better than the recruits. The average score of cadets ranged from 99 to 100.[12] The air corps gave the test to young men, ages 18 to 27, to determine whether they were fit to become aviation cadets. The examination session lasted two and one-half hours. Most of the Kids thought the test was easy, verifying their own complacent prediction that they would pass. Claude Brenner said that he had a little trouble with one or two definitions of words, but thought the rest of the test was "fairly easy." The examination was "a snap" for Van Dyke, who was more certain in his evaluation. He thought that the vocabulary was extremely easy.[13]

The navy was aiming at a different goal, with the Kids as the focal point. The technical radio school recruited boys just after they graduated from high school and enrolled them in a three-month intensive technical program with a curriculum equal to the difficulty of college courses. For nearly 15 hours every day, the recruits underwent a grueling schedule. After they completed the three months of intensive study, and if they passed the course, the navy would assign these newly minted technicians to crews on war ships as "expert" radio operators. The Kids would take the same exam as the prospective recruits. Once again, John and Roby were confident that the Kids could pass the entrance exam. The navy planned to release the story nationwide.[14]

There was no explanation of the thinking behind the navy's plan for releasing the test scores made by the Kids. It's possible that the navy thought that the publicity from having the Kids take the exam would result in young men wanting to enlist in the radio school program. But, to have the Kids take the exam and then release the outcome might result in an unpredictable reaction by young men throughout the country. Would they think that the test was too difficult, and decide that they didn't want to pursue the opportunity? To qualify for this training program, did they have to be as smart as the Quiz Kids just to pass the entrance exam? It would be intimidating and actually embarrassing if they failed. Or, might they think that because they were a little older than the average Kid, they would have little trouble passing, and therefore that the exam was manageable, and the navy's radio school was still attractive?

Perhaps young men didn't think about these possibilities, either positive or negative. The excitement and patriotic fervor rampant among young people at the beginning of the war often clouded sensibilities and put a complete blindfold on rational logic. Perhaps they would think simply that they had happened onto something exciting and glamorous; they could ally themselves to the fame and intelligence of the Kids. That reasoning, added to the adventure of an important job with a lot of responsibility from the first day they reported to their shipboard assignments, had a seductive appeal. But it was not for John or Roby to question the possible manifestations of the navy's publicity program; their only responsibility was to shepherd the Kids to the exam and get them home.

When John and Roby arrived, the navy school revealed the depth of their planned day with the Kids. Roby thought "it was terrific." She thought that it was a look into the future of broadcasting and the changes to come in mass communications after the war was over. The school had a pioneering television department. In 1942, television was a medium still considered a breathtaking novelty because it rarely was seen outside the centers of broadcast communications in New York and Hollywood. When the Kids appeared at the school to take the recruiting exam, they were also to be on television, with the "head of the WAVES" (Women Accepted for Volunteer Emergency Service), a recently established military component of the navy for women, established by Eleanor Roosevelt. It was a parallel military service to the WAAC, the Women's Auxiliary Army Corps, created just three months before the navy's program. Presumably, the navy would film this television performance too, for dissemination, just as the *QK* shorts had been. Prominently displayed at the navy television studio were "movie reels" that suggested that possibility. So hectic had these past 24 hours been that Roby didn't notice until she and John returned to 8 South Michigan that she "came back to the office with manure still on [her] shoes" from the visit to the *Tribune* farm the day before.[15]

John agreed to the navy's proposal and the school acted quickly. October 29, 1942, five days after the preliminary meeting with Roby and John, the Kids took the navy recruiting exam.[16] There is no documentation that shows the results, but we can assume that John and Roby were correct in their belief that the Kids performed well, as they had when they took the exam for the air corps.

The requests for appearances by the Kids were continuous. Calls from all over the country for personal appearances increased even as the war progressed. There was no letup. It was almost as if the war didn't exist. But it did.

Manufacturing of war material became more intense than before the declaration of war. Understandably, shipyards were building ships only for the navy; aircraft manufacturers only for the air corps; automobile manufacturers were making vehicles only for the military. Other than manufacturing, there were other inconvenient changes indirectly affecting people's lives. Gradually the government took over buildings, hotels, theatres, and other places that it could use to help the war effort.

In Chicago, one such wartime adjustment affected Joe Kelly's emcee role on *National Barn Dance* every Saturday. The program had been broadcast from the Eighth Street Theatre for several years. The auditorium in the theatre was ample enough to accommodate the audience who came to enjoy the program each week. In 1942 the War Department took over the building and turned it into a training camp. The barn dance radio program "was forced" to move to the smaller Chicago Civic Theatre, and thus, to reduce and limit its live audience accordingly.[17]

One visible change that had a direct effect on *QK* came from the Zenith Radio Company. Zenith had to abandon the manufacture of their portable radio because of shortages in materials. Subsequently they temporarily abandoned that prize, which Alka-Seltzer awarded to listeners whose questions were on the program. Instead, those listeners had a choice of either a priority certificate for a post-war short-wave portable, or a $50 war bond.[18]

Even with all the hardships of a war-oriented society, there was nearly full employment. Prosperity had returned, and with it the hope and feeling of personal financial security that had nearly disappeared during the Great Depression. To be expected, the shortages and cutbacks of most basic domestic goods resulted in rationing and restraint as an additional hardship. Naturally there was grousing and complaining, but for the most part the government-organized system of national rationing worked and Americans, with some glaring exceptions, were living better than they had in the terrible decade of the 1930s.[19] As the war and its sobering horrors evolved, the mood in the United States was practically buoyant.[20]

On radio, one of the most visible illustrations of this elevated mood was *QK*. The exuberance of the kids and their thirst for knowledge made them an icon, a bellwether of the future when the war would be over. The fear that many parents had for their children and for the next generation was that this terrible world war would result in a bleak and depressing future for them. On their radio program and at personal appearances, the Kids projected an aura of normality. They were a hopeful symbol of a bright future.

Preparation for the war had been building for years, visibly with the Lend Lease program and other strategies that benefited both European countries in their war with Germany and American manufacturing. The federal government's conscription of men for military service before the war began was a major part of preparing for war, or as a necessity for defense. The government passed the military draft law on September 16, 1940. This was the first time in U.S. history that the federal government conscripted men for military service during peacetime. One month later, October 16, men ages 18 to 36 had to register for the draft, and on that day, more than 16 million men reported to firehouses, schools, churches, and police stations in every community in America to register and give important information about themselves.[21] But starting December 8, 1941, the day after the Pearl Harbor attack, and every day thereafter, thousands of young people throughout the country, men and women, volunteered to join the various military services, or to be involved in war efforts in some way. Conscription took a self-induced leap upward early that morning. Less than 24 hours after the attack on Pearl Harbor thousands of young men throughout the nation, not willing to wait for the inevitable draft, enlisted in the army, navy and Marines. Historian Richard Lingeman reported, "The total for the entire day was three times that of April 6, 1917, when the First World War began."[22] The rate of enlistment in the military was high.

Radio show personnel volunteered for active duty in the military or switched to other work related to the war just as people in other occupations were doing.

The three major executives at the *Quiz Kids* office volunteered to be active participants in the war effort. Actually, Lou offered his services before the attack on Pearl Harbor. He discussed some ideas with a government public relations official, Ed Kirby, most likely as early as September 1941. The success of *QK* and the industry awards for the program, contributed to building his reputation in broadcasting. Among other benefits, it would have given him easy access to Kirby.

Now when Lou spoke it was with a greater authority. His colleagues listened closely. The success of the marketing of *QK* hadn't changed his personality. As usual, he understated his emerging prominence in his field when he said that his success with *QK* "projected him into something of a person known somewhat nationally, within broadcasting," as a radio producer and clever public relations practitioner.

Lou had some general ideas in mind (always). He met with Kirby and "discussed various kinds of things that could be done for the troops" during the war.[23] Kirby was the former director of public relations of the National Association of Broadcasters. It appears that they first met at the 1941 NAB national convention in St. Louis when the Kids were booked to perform at the concluding banquet. By autumn 1941 Kirby was head of the radio division within the federal government's Bureau of Public Relations in Washington. The government established the radio division in April 1941.[24]

Shortly before Pearl Harbor, Lou was in Washington and called Kirby, probably to say that he was ready to serve. Knowing Lou and his ability to create his whirlwind of ideas, he assumed that Lou would have some specific thoughts. He did, and Kirby was interested. Lou began working for him shortly after, focusing on various things that he could do "for the troops." He and Polly and their children moved to New York, where the radio division's offices were established. Lou was confident in the abilities of the *QK* production staff. He turned over the running of the program to John Lewellen with full responsibility to manage *QK*, assisted by Roby and Rachel Stevenson.[25] Naturally, he stayed in contact with John by phone. He came to the Chicago office at least once a month as long as *QK* was on the air.[26]

By the middle of January 1942, *Variety* reported the news of Lou's association with Kirby to the broadcasting industry. The report was inaccurate, however, stating that he was working in the "radio publicity division of the United States Army" as an active staff member and consultant. Along with two other radio professionals, the three of them were to "fill out" the department, leaving no further vacancies. This increased the staff of the publicity section to ten "trained broadcasting personnel."[27] No doubt the reference to the lack of future jobs was to hinder any deluge of job applications from the radio community, filled with personnel traditionally restless in their search for new jobs in this insecure, but always quixotic, world of mass communications. Actually, Lou worked in the radio section at the New York office of the OWI (Office of War Information) where he was the liaison between the War Department and his office. Specifically he worked on the *News from Home* program that the department broadcast via shortwave to military forces stationed overseas.[28]

John Lewellen tried to enlist for active duty, but the War Department turned him down because the military thought that if he enlisted the show might go off the air. They wanted to keep *QK* on because they thought the program was a valuable morale builder for the American public. Forest Owen remembers, "We all heard this story at the time," and that Lewellen reported it to the production staff.[29] There is no documentation to prove that Lewellen attempted to volunteer and was rejected other than his oral announcement to the office, but it is probable. General Lewis Hershey, the director of the Selective Service, advised local draft boards that network and station employees would get "special consideration" in view of the federal government's desire to keep commercial broadcasting functioning at maximum efficiency (during the war) in order to sustain morale and to keep the public fully informed.[30]

Niles Trammel, president of NBC, agreed. He thought that radio's role in national defense was to provide mass entertainment that "strengthens morale, that allows us to return to our serious problems with fresh vigor and a new outlook."[31]

Joe Bailey volunteered, too, and joined the navy with an officer's commission. It was only a short while after going on active duty that the dangers of war became personal for him. The staff in Chicago read in the newspaper that a German submarine had torpedoed Bailey's ship in the Atlantic Ocean. There were only 35 survivors. It took a day or so filled with anxiety to find out, but Bailey was among the survivors.[32]

That summer, *QK* made a significant change in its broadcast schedule. Starting with the July 12, 1942, broadcast, they would air on Sunday, not Wednesday. *QK* never returned to their weeknight schedule. The radio program stayed on Sunday, or Saturday, for the next 11 years.

☞ *In computing averages, what are the definitions of the following: (a) Median, (b) Mode, (c) Mean?*

More difficult than recruiting civilians for military duty and stepping up manufacturing of materials and equipment to wage war was the nagging requirement of paying for it. Among the various financial actions Washington undertook, the Treasury Department created an ongoing promotion seven months before the attack on Pearl Harbor to finance war production by selling savings bonds to the public. On the first day of this promotion, May 1, 1941, Secretary of the Treasury Henry Morgenthau, Jr., ceremoniously sold the first Series E Savings Bond to President Roosevelt. For nearly five years after that auspicious date the Treasury Department sold $185.7 billion in government bonds to help pay for the war.[33] Shortly after the United States entered the war, the department made an appropriate change in the name of the bonds; they were no longer savings bonds. Now they named them war bonds.

An even more intense major effort to sell bonds began in September 1942. The Treasury Department designated eight fund-raising campaigns. Officially, they called them drives. By the war's end, there had been seven War Loan Drives and one Victory Drive. The Treasury announced a final War Loan Drive in August 1945 when the war was over. They renamed it to coincide with the new name for the bonds: victory bonds. This final drive was from October 29 to December 8, 1945.[34] All of these drives, lasting only a few weeks each, were a supplement to the nonstop barrage of advertising on radio, in newspapers and magazines, on billboards, movie screens, and other places where the general public could see or hear them. This continuous exposure to the request for Americans to buy bonds was repetitive and endless, constantly "hammering home the importance of buying bonds."[35]

By now, *QK* network broadcasts were a mainstay of popular culture and had made the Kids a recognized name across America. Naturally, they were a major attraction when they visited military bases. The special recording to promote the sale of bonds and stamps that they had made a year earlier and that had been played only in schools was an initial and successful contribution to the defense and war efforts on behalf of the Treasury. We don't know how much revenue was produced by this recording but it was evidently enough to raise eyebrows in Washington. And so, it was an understandable progression from those initial efforts that caused the Treasury to contact *QK* with a long-term proposal for the Kids. They would use their network program format to make live appearances at war loan rallies.

John and Lou agreed to the proposal, even though neither Lou's Quiz Kids company, the staff, nor the individual performers, including the Kids and Joe Kelly, would receive any compensation from the government for their efforts, not even the cost of travel, lodging, or ordinary meals. During the war, patriotic fever ran high throughout the nation, in all walks of life, and in all businesses. It's little wonder that throughout show business every authorized request from the government for individual performers was met with overwhelming acceptance even though they were not to be paid for their work.[36]

For the next three years, *QK* added appearances at war loan rallies to their travel itinerary, even though travel during wartime was more difficult than it had been before the war. Nonetheless, the Kids, Joe Kelly, John, Roby and Rachel were well prepared to follow a daunting schedule of appearances at bond rallies. The prewar schedule of appearances by the Kids or network broadcasts of *QK* in other cities was apt training for the often-rigorous bond rally and personal appearances schedule designed by the War Finance division of the Treasury Department. For both the Treasury and *QK* these rallies were an opportunity to reap benefits. Plainly, the Treasury Department saw a way to raise more revenue. The benefits for *Quiz Kids* were more subtle, more theoretical, while feeding its ongoing business strategy.

These war loan appearances, in addition to their patriotic contribution, were another way to reinforce awareness of the radio program among audiences throughout the country, just as the prewar travel schedule had. Expenses for their travel multiplied, more than Miles could assume in its budget. George Kamen understood the problem and pitched in to help. He increased his efforts to arrange promotion programs with local retailers to pay their expenses in the cities they visited on the bond tours. This was especially critical for the *QK* production office and the parents of the Kids because of the lack of remuneration from the Treasury Department.

The first appearance by the Kids at a war loan rally was on November 22, 1942, just at the beginning of the First War Loan Drive. Between that date and May 14, 1944, the Kids made at least 13 appearances, spanning the country from the East to West coasts, and raising nearly $36,000,000. That first appearance in November was in Des Moines, where the rally was in conjunction with the weekly *QK* broadcast. As much as John and his staff looked forward to this opening program of the tour, the musicians' union ban created an obstacle to the production of the broadcast.

11. Any Bonds Today?

James C. Petrillo, the president of the Chicago musicians' union, threatened the major American recording companies that his union would go on strike. Petrillo wanted the record companies to pay better royalties to musicians every time their records, recorded commercially, were played to the general public, especially on network radio programs — even those that had any delayed broadcasts, recorded for broadcast at a later time. Petrillo announced that starting at midnight, July 31, 1942, union musicians would strike. He decreed that union members would not make records for any record company.

In the fall of 1942 there were 12 stations on the Pacific Coast who recorded *QK* at 4:30 P.M. (6:30 P.M. in Chicago) and then played the recording as a delayed broadcast in the evening in their time zone when they had a larger audience. To abide by the rules of the musicians' strike, *QK* had to use non-union instruments, and there weren't many that could qualify. Those that could — the sweet potato, the washboard, the musical comb, and several others of that ilk — were limited in their range and appeal.

For the Des Moines war bond broadcast there was a music question that required playing three songs for the Kids to identify as the basis for answering the questions. After considering many instruments that qualified within the guidelines established by the musicians' union, John and Roby finally decided. A musical comb wouldn't do it, nor would a washboard. Instead, they thought a music box might be okay. To make sure they asked the union and a music box was acceptable. So, they bought one in Chicago. John was going to play it on air in Des Moines. He took it home to practice.

To complete the music question Joe would ask, John had to deftly and rapidly change the perforated disks that emitted "My Old Kentucky Home," "Blue Bells of Scotland," and "The Beautiful Blue Danube." John practiced diligently at home until his participation was effortless. Even minutes before the broadcast, to make sure he would perform gracefully, John continued to practice, playing and changing the discs repeatedly. By on-air time, he felt confident.

At the designated time on the program, Joe asked the Kids: "What countries do these songs remind you of?" He then said that the instrument that played the music was an "old fashioned music box" that uses "steel discs instead of records." He wanted to make sure that there would be no squawk from Petrillo. John played "My Old Kentucky Home," which one of the Kids identified correctly, and then the "Blue Bells of Scotland," which was identified with the correct country as well. Joe then revealed that the last song would be difficult. In playing the famous Strauss waltz, the Kids had to identify five countries with which the music could be associated.

When John tried to play the "The Beautiful Blue Danube," a strange sound came from the music box, "a sound that was as unmusical as when Jack Benny's Maxwell is shifted into high" gear. John tried again, repeatedly, but he couldn't fit the disc into its groove and "the Blue Danube refused to flow." After several attempts, Joe conceded defeat, and told the Kids the answer. "I guess the music box broke down," said Joe, finally. Somehow they got through the broadcast from the Shrine auditorium in front of an audience of 6,000 bond buyers who bought $500,000 in bonds that day.[37]

The Des Moines broadcast was one of the less successful efforts. Four months later, in March, they produced $1.2 million at a drive in Philadelphia, Pennsylvania. After that they were producing regularly more than a million dollars at each performance.

In Washington on September 19, 1943, the Kids were a featured attraction at the Third Drive for that region, appearing at Constitution Hall to broadcast their weekly radio program. This bond drive featured a special event, a war show called "Back the Attack," opening on September 9 and playing for 18 days on the grounds surrounding the Washington Monument. There were two shows daily, with nearly 2,000 army men demonstrating a vast array of ordnance, partly paid by the proceeds from the sale of bonds at previous rallies.[38] The Army Department exhibited the equipment in several tents outdoors at the monument to allow viewers to see what their bonds would be buying in the future. With sly irony, the *Washington Post* said that it was for most Americans the first opportunity to look at this equipment; "the Japanese, Germans, and Italians had already seen it."[39] Sponsoring an exhibit of equipment such as this was another way that the Treasury Department promoted the purchase of airplanes, navy vessels, and a great variety of other military equipment. These displays were an effective means of stimulating extra bond sales by "bringing the war closer in spirit to the home front."[40]

Ten department stores in Washington backed the Kids, among them Sears, Woodward and Lothrop, and the Hecht Company. The appearance by the Kids in Washington was only a part of a two-week, intensive war-loan tour they made. It started with a brief war-loan appearance in Elkhart, Indiana, on September 14. (Coincidentally, the corporate headquarters of Miles Laboratories was in Elkhart.) The next day was a travel day, and by September 16 they were in Washington, where they made several appearances at the "Back the Attack" show during the three days before their radio broadcast. They also visited Fort Washington, Maryland, a suburb just south of downtown Washington where the Adjutant General's School was located during the war.[41]

Senator Scott Lucas of Illinois invited the Kids to sit in the family gallery at the September 21 session of the Senate. Senator Carl Hatch introduced the Kids and asked the assembled senators to pay tribute to them as a "distinguished group of citizens." He explained that he listened to *QK* "with a great deal of interest, and to obtain not only pleasure and entertainment, but a great deal of information." But Senator Lucas, in his remarks following Hatch's, described the Kids as not just being from Chicago, but in "effect these young people belong to the Nation and to no particular State." Lucas based his tribute to the Kids on the fact that they were on tour to sell bonds, concluding, "No group of youngsters in America is doing more to promote the sale of war bonds." Continuing with the tribute, Senator Alben Barkley was so enamored of their erudition and amazed by their ability to "accumulate such a vast store of knowledge." He expressed the hope that "some day one or more, if not all of them, may occupy seats as Members of this body."[42]

Three days after their Constitution Hall show, they were in Williamsburg, Virginia, performing at another rally, and four days later in Richmond for a local rally, aired as their usual network broadcast on Sunday, September 26. Added to that itinerary were brief visits to two army bases and the Marine Corps base at Quantico.[43]

Always competitive, *QK* was trying to top its one-day sales to date when they traveled to Detroit the next month. There, they would "attempt to establish a war bond sales record."[44] Although they generated $4,561,000 in war bond sales in Detroit, an admirable total, it was not their most productive during this intense period of activity.

Sometimes just one of the Kids would make an appearance to help promote war bond sales. Toward the end of August, Gerard made a quiet and inspiring solo appearance on behalf of the Treasury. He was a featured speaker at the Chicago Woman's Club luncheon, part of their summer program, where he spoke seriously about war bonds, with plans to conclude his visit by helping the club's war bond committee and its sales efforts. He appeared to be in an upbeat and charming mood.[45] But the pendulum swung three and a half months later.

During their bond drive trip to the West Coast in late fall of 1943, Gerard's eccentricities and his mood swings became problematic. He began to be unmanageable for the production staff more frequently. Always unpredictable, on the air and off, he was often the darling of media reporters, who reported every inconsistent utterance, every nonconformist blip in his behavior. They seemed to overlook the times when his behavior was distasteful. But Lou and the production staff had had enough of it. In San Francisco toward the end of the West Coast bond drive, Gerard refused to cooperate at a press conference, sitting apart and "wolfing popcorn" as the rest of the Quiz Kids acted in their normal, cooperative manner during press conferences. The last broadcast during this trip was on December 12, 1943. Usually, the Kids who traveled on the bond drive tour were the most prominent at that time: Gerard, Richard, Ruth, Harve, and Joel. On December 19 they were back in Chicago for their weekly broadcast. Gerard was not on the program. He never appeared on *Quiz Kids* again.

There was no explanation in the press and there are no letters from listeners inquiring about his disappearance, nor are there any copies of press releases to explain Gerard's sudden departure from the program. But the popcorn incident appeared to be the final straw in the series of embarrassing incidents going back to his outré performance in Fiorello LaGuardia's office. It could have been that *QK* management thought that Gerard's highly specialized knowledge of ornithology was too limited. Most likely management simply dropped him. He was 11 years old, five years younger than the customary graduation age.

After Gerard's departure there was a change in the participants for bond rallies. Only four Kids, all popular and consistent in their program appearances, traveled on bond tours. Up to then, there often were five Kids. Sometimes only four toured and the fifth was a local bright child who filled in. This fifth Kid was always the winner of a local Quiz Kid contest, like those

The core Kids who traveled for the war bond appearances. Harve Fischman, Richard Williams, Joel Kupperman, Ruth Duskin (courtesy Eliza Hickok Kesler).

who had been on the pre-bond broadcasts in other cities since the autumn of 1940.[46]

Their most productive war bond appearance during this 18-month period was at Symphony Hall in Boston on February 20, 1944. Filling the hall to capacity, they sold $3,500,000 before the program began and $3,000,000 more to people who arrived too late to be admitted to the auditorium. Despite their disappointment, the audience still bought bonds. There was no chance of admission by virtue of the "standing room only" tradition in theatres.[47]

Because the Kids were traveling so much and missed school, sometimes for several consecutive weeks, the question of their education came up. But the Kids always had assignments from their teachers; this was part of the planning that the office staff made sure to emphasize. One principal at a school that one of the Kids attended sounded almost lenient. He said that a trip to New York or Boston was worth two months in school. He believed that travel was broadening and was "one of the best ways to get a thorough education in history, geography and a million other things in the most painless manner." Almost after each trip, certainly the major ones, the Kids appeared in the auditoriums of their various schools telling the other students what was seen and learned on their journeys.[48]

In total, by war's end, the Kids performed at bond rallies in 38 cities, raising $120,000,000.[49] At least 21 of these were part of their regularly scheduled broadcasts.[50] Not all the bond rallies were broadcast as network programs. More than the seriousness of purpose, doing performances to help sell war bonds was an exciting time for the Kids. When they appeared in a city for a war bond show, they arrived as celebrities. In Philadelphia, the local NBC Blue station sent a jeep to escort them to their hotel. In Los Angeles and Portland, Oregon, jeeps met the Kids at the railroad station. The area newspapers reported their other activities. In Philadelphia they visited the Liberty Bell. In Washington they were welcomed at nearby military hospitals and forts. In San Francisco, they went to Sausalito to see how war bond money helped build ships. As exhilarating as it was for the Kids, it was equally exciting for local residents.

Similar to the U.S. Senate recognizing in 1943 the efforts of the Kids in the war bond drives, the Treasury Department was grateful for their work throughout the entire war and shortly thereafter. On the October 26, 1946, broadcast the U.S. secretary of the treasury, John Snyder, speaking from Washington, announced that *Quiz Kids* would be presented with the U.S. Treasury Silver Medal Award for distinguished service to the Treasury and the nation as a result of the active part taken by the cast and sponsor in the bond drives. Miles Laboratories had awarded 235 Kids who appeared on the program to that date a total of $165,000 in bonds. The medal was presented on that broadcast by Arnold J. Rauen, director of the Savings Bond Division for the State of Illinois.

☞ *There are 16 "men" on a side, and one of the 16 is a woman. What is the game?*

Music and songs have always been a way to stimulate patriotic enthusiasm, and the Treasury Department encouraged professional composers to write songs with war bonds as a theme. The first song "on a national scale was ... 'Any Bonds Today?' composed by Irving Berlin and donated to the Treasury."[51] With the cooperation of ASCAP during their dispute with the radio networks, musicians could perform Berlin's song "freely and unconditionally everywhere."[52] Radio stations played it repeatedly. Performers sang it at live appearances. Recorded by various performers, including the always-popular Andrews Sisters, it was even the title of a two-minute animated Warner Brothers cartoon shown in movie theaters nationally, with the song performed by Bugs Bunny and featuring Porky Pig and Elmer Fudd.

The Quiz Kids, popular attraction as they were, were just one element in an outstanding roster of Hollywood, Broadway, and radio personalities who made frequent appearances to catch the attention of the public. At the 1943 bond drive in Washington several movie and radio stars joined together to help the effort. Among them were Fred Allen, Lucille Ball, James Cagney, Judy Garland, Harpo Marx, Mickey Rooney and Walter Pidgeon, all considered to be "salesmen worth their weight in gold."[53]

Other special events were just as fascinating. The Treasury Department and their advertising agencies tried many sales ideas during the course of the war. Many of them were merely to reinforce the idea within the public consciousness, such as "Any Bonds Today?" Others, like the rallies, were overt — a direct plea to sell bonds. Some of the promotions were unique, short-lived efforts to produce extra bond sales. In 1942–43 a countrywide tour of a two-man Japanese submarine, captured at Pearl Harbor, was as an attraction, accompanied by a temporary bond sales booth. The *Saturday Evening Post* created a "Four Freedoms War Bond Show" in 1943, on a tour to 16 cities. There were Liberty Ship exhibits at leading seaports. Exhibitions of captured equipment at state fairs in the Midwest and elsewhere were an attraction where people could buy bonds. Kay Kyser, one of Lou's early publicity clients, took his band on a short tour of six cities, temporarily renaming the Kay Kyser Bandwagon with a contemporaneous pun, Kay Kyser's Bond Wagon.

The Treasury Department designated several unique sports events to help sell bonds. Baseball Defense Bond Day in the fall of 1941 and the game between the Washington Senators (the name of the American League baseball team in the District of Columbia at that time) and the Norfolk, Virginia, All-Star

Navy team in June 1943 are just two examples.[54] Monday, June 26, 1944, baseball fans saw an unusual and memorable game with its focus on sell bonds. It was officially a day off for the three major-league baseball teams in New York — but not really. On that day, there was a special game at the Polo Grounds, the home field of the New York Giants. The Yankees, Brooklyn Dodgers, and Giants played against each other. The *New York Times* called it the "zaniest game ever." The goal was to raise a million dollars in bonds.[55] The price of admission was the purchase of a bond. The three teams played successive innings against the other two, then sat out an inning. Attendance was more than 50,000, a respectable gathering even by today's standards.[56] The projected sales were quickly reached and surpassed by eager fans. The event accounted for a total of $56,500,000. Speaking at the game, Mayor LaGuardia announced that $50 million of that total was from New York City's treasury.[57] The remaining $6,500,000 came from admissions.[58] Football games, too, were a way to sell the bonds. The army-navy game in the fall of 1944 was for bond sales, as were several other football games and other sports events.

Enlisting the Kids to help promote the sale of war bonds had an interesting secondary aspect. When the Treasury Department used them, it was an example of the direct application of raw conceptual intellect for practical use. The Kids were precocious, but their knowledge was classroom intelligence, not yet focused on a diverse range of workable ideas with everyday application. Such application traditionally doesn't emerge until adult insight tempers academic ability with purposeful goals. Still, the Treasury Department valued the talent to learn that the Kids exhibited, and saw how their intellectual curiosity would entertain and amaze audiences, as it did on their radio broadcasts and their appearances at military bases. Such broad appeal was enticing enough to attract audiences to attend war loan drives. Throughout America people were infinitely curious about the Kids.

Appearing on national radio, the Kids and their knowledge was entertainment for a vast national radio audience. Their fame from their weekly radio program was a springboard for their efforts for the war bond drives. At the bond rallies they appeared in front of large audiences in their same charming weekly "classroom of the air" format, to help raise money to pay for the war effort. Lou and Joe Bailey didn't have to think about setting up a tour across the country. The Treasury Department did it for them. Even though no one, neither the staff nor the Kids, or the expense of travel, was paid by the government, the office at 8 South Michigan gladly agreed to the deal. Just as Lou and Joe Bailey had discussed at the beginning of 1941, they used the Kamen Variation to pay for travel expenses. It was a perfect scenario.

Forrest Owen recalled that there was no grousing from department stores about the cost. "Everybody won," he concluded. Lou and John and Bailey attained their goal of reaching far-flung audiences as well as satisfying their patriotic urge, the stores gladly paid for the promotion, the Treasury Department benefited from the appearances by the Kids, and audiences were thrilled by seeing the Quiz Kids in action. By buying bonds they felt good about helping the war effort. Everyone on the staff at the *Quiz Kids* office, including the Kids, felt a surge of patriotism.[59]

At the beginning of the war loan drives someone at the Treasury Department recognized the value of the Kids as entertainers and morale builders. The War Department did not want the program to go off the air, because the appeal of the Quiz Kids drew large audiences to the Treasury Department's bond rallies. And so there was good reason, an irresistible ulterior motive, why they wouldn't allow John Lewellen to enlist. Instead, the Treasury Department enlisted the entire cast and staff to help promote war bonds.

ANSWERS

Maryland did not secede. Louisiana did. West Virginia did not. Missouri did not. Arkansas did. Kentucky did not.

The terms used in computing averages and their definitions are: (a) Median means the middle, or that number of a series which has as many numbers preceding as following it. (b) Mode means the most frequent or most common value; in a small number of items the mode may not exist, for none of the values may reappear. (c) The Mean is a calculated average.

The game with 16 "men" on each side is chess.

12

Don't You Know There's a War On?

☞ *Is Pearl Harbor located in the Pearl Islands?*

During the war years, *QK* continued in the same format as it had before the war. We don't hear any difference when we listen to the recordings during those years even though Lou was in New York and did not take part in the details of producing the program each week. John, as Lou had predicted, kept the program running smoothly and within the pattern and tone Lou had established before he moved to the East Coast. John's executive skills were outstanding. His staff admired him. Roby thought he was a brilliant writer. Even the Kids warmed to him from the very beginnings of the program, describing him as a gentle complement to Joe Kelly.[1]

Although the war was usually uppermost in the national state of mind, there was only scattered reference to it on the handful of recordings of *QK* broadcasts that are available from those years. We begin to hear some subtle changes in the program, however. During the 18 months of broadcasts leading up to the war, nearly all the guest speakers were respected educators or public figures who generally spoke about the ideal goals of the American education system and how *Quiz Kids* and the Kids exemplified those concepts. As well, those guest speakers reinforced the honesty of the program, perhaps unwittingly feeding Lou's underlying precept of repetition as an element of persuasion. We have no actual evidence of this. There is no detailed account in correspondence or memo that outlines any direction to the guest speakers for their preparation for their speeches during their on-air appearances.

Based on listening to the skimpy collection of recorded programs from this period and those more plentiful after 1947, we can only surmise that John or Roby edited the speeches prepared by most of these guests to reflect the company's viewpoint. Undoubtedly there was preparation before their appearances. John's personality was so low-key that his pre-broadcast directions to any of the speakers could have been simply a casual suggestion that they might want to stress the key points established by the production office when they wrote their speeches. As we listen to these guest speakers, they were consistent in their praise of the intelligence of the Kids and how it related to the principles of good education, declaration of the honesty of the program, and in their admiration of the sterling ethics of *QK*.

The slight change in programming began after the Hollywood trip in 1941 and was in place by the beginning of 1942. This modification had Lou's fingerprints all over it, with his invisible hands reaching from New York to shape it. Rather than having the majority of the guests on the program from the world of education, now there were more celebrities and nationally well-known people as guests on the programs, augmenting the choice of local or regional educators. Increasingly these high-profile celebrities would become the standard guests, still speaking in reverential tones about the Kids and stressing the values of education. Perhaps it was the sparkling programs with Jack Benny that gave Lou the idea. There is some evidence to support it. It was, as *Billboard* described in their award for best exploitation in 1941, part of the ongoing effort at audience building engineered by Lou.

Bob Hope, Bing Crosby, Jack Benny, Fred Allen, Jimmy Stewart, Tallulah Bankhead, Chico Marx, Eddie Cantor, Gladys Swarthout, Brace Beemer (the Lone Ranger), Maurice Evans (the famous actor best known for his roles in Shakespeare's plays), Smiley Burnette (Gene Autry's second banana), Victor Borge, and Edgar Bergen (with Charlie McCarthy, of course) were among the show business personalities who were guests on *QK* when they broadcast from Chicago. Each, of course, was really there to promote his latest professional efforts — a new film, a radio show, a record, a

Fred Allen visited Quiz Kids on several occasions, and the Kids visited his show, too. Joel Kupperman, Fred Allen (courtesy Quiz Kids, Inc.).

12. Don't You Know There's a War On?

Bob Hope and Joel Kupperman. Hope said that he suffered from "Child Fright," a seizure of terror at the thought of verbal intercourse with a small, intelligent biped (courtesy Eliza Hickok Kesler).

book, an upcoming performance, a nightclub or theater engagement, etc. They actually made *QK* more informal and more entertaining.

Despite their barely hidden reasons for promoting themselves, these celebrities were appealing enough to attract *QK* listeners. It was exciting bait for those who were among the loyal audience each week. These famous guests were attractive enough to entice new listeners, too. Often they replaced Joe Kelly for part of that broadcast, taking over as Chief Quizzer. When Gene Autry was a guest on the program Joe turned over the quizzer duties to him, but before making the transition, he began some good-natured show business banter. "Wait a minute," Joe said, "you better put on my mortar board so you look like a teacher. Come on, let's trade [hats]." Autry replied that his traditional 10-gallon hat might not fit because he had more hair than Joe had. "You're telling me!" exclaimed Joe, "I'm short about three gallons on this hat, Gene. I can't get into it." Autry offered an explanation. There's nothing wrong with the hat, he said, your "head is just getting too big, that's all."[2]

Getting Bob Hope ready for the Kids. (From left) John Lewellen, Joe Kelly, Hope (courtesy Eliza Hickok Kesler).

The escalation of having celebrity guests with its resulting increase in audience probably helped in securing a more valuable contract with Miles Labs when it was time to renegotiate. By the spring of 1943, *Quiz Kids* had 20 million listeners for each broadcast, and Alka-Seltzer paid $15,000 weekly for the program.³

Before the war when someone on the staff had to work on the details of travel to other cities it was like juggling of four balls. During the war the juggler had handcuffs on. Travel to appearances in other cities was more difficult. What had been a simple trip to Milwaukee before the war became a frustration. No more was it an easy drive, with John and four Kids in one car and Joe, Roby, and Rachel in another. Travel by car just wasn't practical, given the rationing of gasoline and tires.

Strict gasoline rationing went into effect in May 1942 on the East Coast and then expanded nationwide in December of that year. Car owners had to glue a paper sticker, approximately three inches high by two inches wide, to their windshields, prominently displaying a single letter of the alphabet. An "A" sticker was for cars whose use was nonessential and usually limited consumption of gasoline to three gallons a week. For the first year of this program, car owners could not drive "A" cars for pleasure. The "B" sticker was for driving essential to the war effort, such as workers in industries that made goods for the military. "B" stickers allowed holders to buy a maximum of eight gallons a week. "C" stickers were for physicians, ministers, mail carriers and railroad workers, "T'" was for truckers, and the rare "X" sticker went to members of Congress and other VIPs.⁴

The alternative was just as daunting. Trying to book public transportation was excruciating. Tourists, business travelers, or military personnel returning home for furlough or traveling to report for duty at new bases packed the trains and buses. There were few seats available for anyone who did not fit into these special categories. What made it more laborious for the *QK* staff was the prerequisite of booking first-rate accommodations on trains, especially on long trips. Pullman service was practically

Quiz Kid Richard Weixler, age 5, and Little Jackie Benny, age 6 (courtesy Eliza Hickok Kesler).

impossible to get. Preparing for a trip to Los Angeles in 1943, Roby reported on the difficulty in getting train reservations. "The movie people called their office here [in Chicago] to get us reservations for Sunday night, but of course there wasn't any space. Now they are pulling strings, ropes, wires and pulleys to get us out there." Making plans was uncertain. Roby had to cancel the idea of visiting her family on a weekend but if another passenger canceled, she would have to be in Chicago to "get packed, everything rounded up to take from the office, deal with newspapers who want to take pictures as we leave." She wrote that she was "afraid to leave town."⁵

Even if a traveler could get a coach seat, it meant sitting upright for the entire trip, overnight or not. Roby felt guilty when she compared her comfortable Pullman room on a train from Chicago to Houston with those of Army WAACs on the same train. The WAACs had to sit upright in a coach car for the entire trip. The *QK* staff traveled well, as usual. "The train, of course, was cool — but so crowded. We had rooms both ways and felt rather uncomfortably unpatriotic. I feel sorry for a carload of WAACs in an un–air conditioned car."⁶ Even with wartime restrictions on travel, it was possible

Some of the most famous names in show business loved to appear on Quiz Kids. (From left) Gerard Darrow, Bing Crosby, Ruth Duskin (courtesy Quiz Kids, Inc.).

to get a Pullman berth, but usually at black market prices with $10 to $50 markups.[7]

No matter how difficult travel was, the frequency of personal appearances by the Kids for the benefit of civic or charitable organizations, aside from the war bond rallies, continued during the war. Just after the first of the year in 1945, Lewellen was planning two *QK* broadcasts in March for the benefit of the Red Cross during their month-long campaign for their war fund. The first, March 11, was from Bushnell Hall in Hartford, Connecticut, where a donation of blood was the price of admission.[8]

The second was broadcast one week later from Constitution Hall in Washington, where the audience consisted of 3,800 volunteer workers.[9] For some time, John had seen this as an opportunity. Earlier, at a war bond program in New York at which Senator Joseph Ball was a participant, John broached the idea of a program where four of the Kids would participate in a "friendly competition" with four senators on their broadcast from Washington. Ball liked the idea, providing the "B_2H_2 projected tour did not interfere."[10]

The B_2H_2 reference was the Roosevelt administration's acronym-like way

12. Don't You Know There's a War On?

Chico failed the "Sanity Test" but the Kids were crazy about him. (From left center) Chico Marx, Gerard Darrow, Claude Brenner, Richard Williams, Margaret Merrick, Joel Kupperman, David Prochaska, Ruth Duskin, Harve Fischman (courtesy Quiz Kids, Inc./Ruth Duskin Feldman).

of describing the Ball-Burton-Hill-Hatch resolution introduced in the Senate in 1943. The goal of the bipartisan resolution authored by senators Joseph Ball, Harold H. Burton, Lister Hill, and Carl A. Hatch was "that the United States should cooperate with other nations after World War II to bring into being a world organization through which the peace-loving nations would pool their strength against lawless or aggressive actions by any nation."[11]

This forward-thinking resolution was an obvious, preliminary stab at the formation of the United Nations. But the senators knew that there might be some resistance by conservative, isolationist voters just as there had been before the war when visionary politicians suggested international cooperation among nations. To help sell the idea, the senate organized a schedule, sending "bipartisan congressional teams on speaking tours" to promote the cause, starting in 1943.[12]

Lewellen thought that "the B_2H_2 group would be a perfect quartet for

(From far left, clockwise) Joel Kupperman, Gerard Darrow, Harve Fischman, Richard Williams, Ruth Duskin, Eddie Cantor (courtesy Ruth Duskin Feldman).

the purpose." As an additional persuasive element in his first letter to Burton, John said that the Kids "would be thrilled to have such a distinguished group on their program, and that they are great admirers of B_2H_2, as is everyone in the country." It was such a broad statement that it appeared just to be flattery rather than a quantitative conclusion. Lewellen recognized this, admitting that that his statement "may be a little strong." The Quiz Kids Versus format continued to be an audience favorite, four years after its introduction in Chicago and Atlantic City. John described that the previous competitions in this format "always turn out to be a lot of fun without embarrassment to anyone." He cited the four competitions with University of Chicago professors. "The same professors," he explained, "were always anxious to participate after the first experience." Lewellen mentioned this detail to "indicate that the contestants always have a good time, and that it [competing against the Quiz Kids] is no ordeal as might first appear."[13]

Once again, as in the preceding four years, the Quiz Kids Versus format was an easy and attractive program to produce, practically guaranteed to appeal to audiences everywhere. By 1945 the format was well established; John had codified it. He sent instructions to the four senators well ahead of the broadcast date of March 18. In it, he outlined the details for that evening: when and where they would broadcast the program and when the senators should arrive ("you should come in the stage entrance and be back stage by 6:45 P.M."). John continued, amplifying the details, trying to cover any questions that may arise. He wrote that their arrival would allow enough time for the senators to meet Joe Kelly and ask any questions about procedure. The preliminary program would begin at 7 P.M. including a playing of the national anthem and a two-minute talk by a Red Cross official. Then Joe Kelly would be introduced and would bring the Kids onstage and introduce them. When he introduced the competing panel (the senators), John explained, "The four of you will walk on stage together and take your places at your table. After everyone is seated and introduced there will be a 'warm-up' session of questions until we go on the air, at 7:30."

In a paragraph that supported the claim that the program was going to be fun, John gave the section a subtitle of "Who Will Win." "Nobody" was his immediate reply. "Although for the sake of interest we will pretend it is a real contest, at the end of the program when the judge announces his verdict, no scores will be given, and through some gag yet to be thought up, everyone comes out on top." Lou decided to alter the rules slightly a few years later when he acted as a "guest judge" for a Quiz Kids Versus broadcast where four Kids were competing with four University of Chicago alumni. At the end of the program, after the scores were tallied, Lou, with a clear display of irony, announced that the score was "obviously a tie, although the Kids have 305 points against the adults 140." "With such impartial judging," observed Joe Kelly, "there's nothing more to say."[14]

As for advance preparation for the senators, Lewellen said that there was only one opportunity. It occurred during the roll call. When Joe "calls the roll he always calls the children by first name and they respond with their full names, their age, their school, their grade in school and their home town." Kelly, he explained, "will call on each of you as 'Senator Ball of Minnesota' etc., and each of you should respond with your full name and any remark you care to toss in, such as 'I'm old enough to know better and I hope my constituents are listening in.'"

Lewellen went on to describe the questions, reinforcing that his staff would select them to avoid professional embarrassment for anyone. "Because they are still immature, the children would sound silly on profound questions of government. On the other hand, a number of questions requiring detailed scholastic information would be unfair, because we have a notion that you men have been too busy at your jobs to review your eighth grade text books recently. Therefore, most of the questions will have a humorous twist." John continued. He promised that they would ask nothing that "could be in any way interpreted as having an adverse reflection on your qualifications for the all-important position you now hold. In other words," he maintained, "the whole thing will be in a spirit of fun and a wise-crack will be just as good as a correct answer."

He also cautioned the senators that Joe would call on the first of the eight contestants whose hand was up to answer any question. He cautioned the politicians to put their hands up fast because "our youngsters have been at this so long they are lightning-fast." He concluded that the senators should not hold back "just to be nice to the children — they'll be doing their best and you do yours."[15]

Of course, the Kids each received their $100 savings bond for appearing on the program. The senators were to receive the same. When offered, Senator Burton declined the remuneration, saying that he would rather have a check for $100 made payable to the American Red Cross.[16] When Burton received it, he forwarded it to his Cleveland chapter immediately.[17] (Ohio was his home state.) We can only assume that the other three senators did not feel the need to profit from their evening of fun on *QK*; there is no evidence to about how they handled their compensation.

Interspersed with requests by local, regional, or national civilian organizations, there was an increase in appearances at military bases and hospitals, munitions factories, and other places where the emphasis was on the war.[18] Some of those visits coincided with their weekly network broadcast, and the programs emanated from those sites, making their visits more exciting for audiences everywhere. When these appearances at military bases during the war were not part of one of their broadcasts, or when those appearances were not war bond rallies exclusively, the role for the Kids was morale building for civilians. At Fort Washington, near Washington, D.C., during their tour for the Third War Loan Drive, the Kids as usual were to perform by competing with seven army officers. As was their custom, they defeated the officers with a score of 210 to 130 before "a howling audience of 1,500 enlisted men."[19] By the end of the war, the Kids had visited 60 army, navy, merchant marine, coast guard, and air corps military stations and hospitals.[20]

Their fame preceded them. Just by having the Kids entertain at a factory or military base was thrilling for those audiences. It was a welcome and uplifting relief for the factory workers and servicemen.

☞ *What stitches would you define in the following expressions: (a) A stitch having a disagreeable disposition? (b) A stitch preceding a fall? (c) A stitch having links?*

After completing the first segment of short films with Paramount at the beginning of 1941, there were several film and radio possibilities that emerged to feature one or more of the Kids. One idea from Paramount was to focus on Gerard in a full-length feature film. Apparently Paramount speculated that he would have appeal as an erudite Mickey Rooney. When the Kids went to Hollywood to appear with Jack Benny in April, Gerard made screen tests at Paramount and other studios. After more failed screen tests two years later, Gerard's guardian aunt, Bessie Darrow, thought that he was not photogenic.[21]

Some Hollywood film production studios tried to lure the Kids again in November 1943 when they went to Los Angeles for war bond appearances and their own broadcasts during a nearly four-week visit. The Kids were enticed by the possibility of multiple screen tests. Perhaps the studios rushed to screen tests because it didn't cost them anything to bring them to the West Coast. They were going to be in town anyway. Joe Kelly was filming *National Barn Dance* at Paramount at the same time, and he would be available for any screen tests along with the Kids.[22]

Harve Fischman, whose long suit was American history, hoped that his adult career would be as a newspaper reporter. Naturally, he wrote for his school paper. When the Kids were in Washington for their appearance at the beginning of the Third War Loan, the *Washington Star* asked him to write his impressions of the District of Columbia. The newspaper actually gave him a desk at their office. As well, the *Washington News* asked him to interview people while he was in D.C. First, they had him submit a list of who he wanted to speak with. Harve submitted FDR, but the *News* told him "to shoot at a lesser light."[23]

Harve's passion for being a reporter prompted another idea from Lou. Just a month before this Washington bond appearance, Lou tried to sell a new program to the Blue Network. His new show would feature Harve as a "child newscaster." When Lou made the proposal, the network was interested — enough to reserve a broadcast time for him to appear five times a week, even before hearing an audition record. Of course, they wanted an audition record immediately.[24] As with many ideas in the business world, this project never came to fruition, and we don't know why. There is no correspondence that offers an explanation.

Of all of those prospective projects in Hollywood there was only one that actually came to be. Universal decided to use Joel Kupperman in a comedy they were making in 1943 with Donald O'Connor, an 18-year-old singer, dancer, and actor, in the lead role. The film featured Ann Blyth, age 15, in her first feature film.

The first serious discussions about the project made it difficult to believe there would be a film made at all. Contract negotiations between the *QK* lawyer and Universal's lawyer were complicated. Apparently each camp had an agenda; they were not always in tandem. At one point, Lou and John were "ready to throw the contract back in their faces." During the tortuous negotiations toward the end of July, Roby spent one weekend visiting her parents, and when she returned she found "a bloodless revolution going on between the lawyers." She sat in on one of the sessions only to be confused by the legal language, especially "the parties of the third part and parties of the second, and the minor [Joel] agreeing to said agreement herein." Roby wrote to her family that she became "panicky amid the hereins." The final written contract totaled 36 pages.[25]

The contract refers to Roby as a "governess," just because "we didn't want to say publicity agent or a program writer." But Universal's Chicago office didn't understand that nuance. They thought that she actually was a governess. They "treated her like a second maid." Roby asked John to tell the movie's director that she had "never been in service ... that I can't serve a formal dinner ... bathe a seven year old, nor can I polish silver." She concluded her argument with a pithy self-description. "Fortunately," she wrote, "I was born out of service and in wedlock."[26]

Despite her new "title" as governess, Roby made plans to write a story every day from Hollywood about Joel and how intelligent people react to the "Hollywood glitter." She hoped to sell the story to the *Chicago Sun*. But she realized that one stumbling block caused by the war could prevent her idea from seeing light. She modified her proposal of the daily article by adding the conditional "if the paper quota will permit." She noted that all the newspapers throughout the war were "yelling for help because they've been cut down on their paper supply."[27]

Joel's movie contract guaranteed him $2,000 a week for three weeks. There were several salary options. If he were to make a second movie, his salary would be $3,000 weekly, $4,000 a week for a third, and $5,000 for a fourth.[28] Although the contract specified that the *Quiz Kids* office would get a percentage of Joel's earnings, Lou gave that fee back to the Kuppermans. Lou thought that the trip might make a family vacation for the Kuppermans.[29] This reimbursement could help pay for the cost of the entire family, including Joel's parents and his sister, to accompany him to Hollywood. Fortunately, Universal scheduled the film, entitled *Chip Off the Old Block*, to be shot in August during Joel's summer respite from school.

In the midst of all this time-consuming digression, the beat at 8 South Michigan continued, just as loud and up-tempo as ever. Three days after appearing before the probate judge in Chicago, who granted permission to

Joel's father to allow him to accept the movie contract, the Kids, including Joel, traveled to Chanute Field in Rantoul, Illinois, 113 miles from Chicago. There, on August 15, on their weekly network broadcast and with 2,000 enlisted men and officers making up the audience, the Kids competed with four soldiers and a WAAC, all college graduates and apparently carefully selected because of their academic achievements.[30]

Meanwhile, Universal wanted to act immediately and get Joel to Hollywood so they could start shooting his scenes. But there was still uncertainty about travel plans. The war overshadowed everybody's thinking and plans. In preparation for travel to Hollywood, the studio called its Chicago office to have their people arrange for train reservations for August 22. But trains were wartime-crowded as usual, with no seats, reserved or not, to be found. Universal tried everything in their arsenal of clout; they pulled "strings, ropes, wires, and pulleys" to get Roby and the Kuppermans to Hollywood. By then, Roby was feeling homesick for the simpler pleasures of being with her family and friends in idyllic Cedar Rapids. She contemplated taking a weekend at home and returning to Chicago Sunday morning. But she was fearful. If there was a cancellation on the train she might only have a minimal amount of time to get ready — to have her bags packed, to get materials she needed from the office, to call newspapers to alert their photographers who wanted "to take our pictures as we leave."[31]

Roby's fears about a fast departure were justified. She and the Kuppermans appear to have arrived in Los Angeles in the middle of the week ending August 29, and the action started immediately at the train station, where Ann Blyth, representing Universal, met them on the platform. Roby was not impressed with doing business in Hollywood. "This town is crazy," she wrote, "We don't know what's up half the time." But she started to change her mind. She began liking California more. It was the first time that she had ever been "enthusiastic" about Hollywood.[32]

Once again, the studio offered more bait when the possibility surfaced of Joel making a movie with Fred Allen in October.[33] Roby reported to Lou and John that *Life* magazine was planning a story about Joel with the theme of "a Quiz Kid looks at Hollywood and is pretty bored by it." Indeed, Joel was bored. Across the street from their hotel was the Chinese Theater, a major tourist attraction because of the footprints of movie stars cast in the sidewalk in front of the theatre. Roby asked Joel if he'd like to go see the famous patch of sidewalk, but he declined, politely.

His sister did go, and the next morning at breakfast Roby asked her what she thought of all the footprints and hand prints. She said that she didn't like it. Joel, with a mouth full of cereal and toast, yelled out, "I told you not to go!" At seven years old, he knew exactly what he wanted. When asked if he wanted autographs of Abbot and Costello he declined again, explaining that it was easy to get them, all he had to do was walk up to them and ask them. What he really wanted, he said facetiously, was Benjamin Franklin's autograph.[34] Joel was consistent in his condemnation of Los Angeles. He sounded like Woody Allen would some 50 years later. Several days after his refusal to go see the footprints of the famous, Hedda Hopper, the legendary Hollywood columnist, asked Joel how he liked Hollywood. "Fine," said the young math shark, "it's only ten percent not quite as good as Chicago."[35]

After six weeks in boring Hollywood, Joel returned to Chicago, and one week later traveled to Detroit with three of the Kids to make a war bond appearance. The fifth Kid was a Detroit-area winner. They were the usual traveling Kids, Joel, Harve, Ruth, and Richard.

In the two decades between the world wars, anti–Semitism in America had surged to frightening levels. Notably, Henry Ford, the Ku Klux Klan, and the radio diatribes of Father Coughlin were the most evident to the entire nation. During these war years, the Nazis were the most visible perpetrators of anti–Semitism in the world. Yet in the United States "it was not the least of the war's ironies that while America fought Nazi Germany in the name of decency, democracy and civilization, American Jews were the victims of a nasty rise in bigotry."[36]

On this trip to Detroit, Henry Ford asked if he could meet with the Kids at his office. Knowing Ford's strong anti–Semitism, Harve's mother suggested that Richard Williams, the only gentile in the Kids group that day, be the first to enter Ford's office. There were a greater number of Quiz Kid regulars who were Jewish, just as three of the four traveling Kids were. When they arrived at a new city, shouts of "Oh, they're all Jews" rang out from the crowds who gathered to see them. Of course this was inaccurate; Richard and many of the other Kids were not Jewish. On another appearance in Seattle, the owners of a department store who had helped finance their trip invited Richard and his mother and the *QK* staff to a plush estate for a social gathering. None of the others in the group were invited. Richard Williams thought that this discrimination was because the others were Jewish.

Lou, especially sensitive to these matters, once asked Roby why all five Kids were Jewish on one of the programs. Roby had no fear about telling Lou the truth. She said, simply, it was because that week they won.[37]

As well as the stark reality of the war, life on the home front was in flux for most of that decade. Noticeable anti–Semitism continued throughout the war years and beyond. Curbs on goods and services made life more difficult. To soothe the discomfort of having to get along with less, "It's only for the duration" (of the war) became a mantra to assuage those severe wartime restrictions. Newspaper articles reporting the growth of juvenile delinquency during the war years, and the magazine columnists dissected and debated the issue, a nagging reminder of perceptible societal change.

Nonetheless, throughout those years *QK* was a Rockwellian portrait of an ideal America, where couples raised "cheerful families who lived in white houses with picket fences in front," and where "children rode bikes or played ball on the lawn outside."[38] Even with all of the reminders of a world savaged by a horrible war, the Kids remained a refreshing fount of youthful optimism.

ANSWERS

No. Pearl Harbor is in the U.S. naval station in the Hawaiian Islands. The Pearl Isles are located south and slightly east of the Panama Canal.

The stitches defined by the expressions are (a) cross; (b) slip; (c) chain.

13

Peace

☞ *What unit of electrical measurement is the reciprocal of itself spelled backwards?*

The most visible change in *Quiz Kids* immediately after the war was the absence of war bond broadcasts, although the Kids participated in bond rallies for five months more, until January 1946. The war was over but the government still had to raise more money to pay for its cost. Just as they had during the war, the Treasury Department issued bonds, renaming the bonds once again. Infused with pride, they called them victory bonds. The Treasury continued to use rallies to help sell them as they had done with great success during the war. For the Kids, the schedule now was not as hectic as it had been, but occasionally displayed remnants of the intense timetable of the war years. Starting in May 1945 three weeks after the war in Europe was over, the Kids performed at bond rallies in several cities, including Dallas, Buffalo, Des Moines, Youngstown, Ohio, and Washington, D.C.

Toward the end of that year at the Washington rally on December 2, 1945, *Quiz Kids* was the primary attraction, or at least the shared attraction. The broadcast featured just four Kids competing with an equally appealing team of four U.S. senators. It was another of the always-popular Quiz Kids Versus programs. The Kids — Robert Burke, Harve Fischman, Joel Kupperman, and Richard Williams — faced off against the four senators, evenly divided between Democrats and Republicans: Joseph Ball (Republican, Minnesota), Glen H. Taylor (Democrat, Ohio), William Stanfill (Republican, Kentucky) and Abe Murdock (Democrat, Utah). The broadcast was from the Mayflower Hotel. The Treasury Department's marketing plan was the same as it had been during the war: admission to the program was only with the purchase of a bond. There were no Alka-Seltzer commercials on this broadcast. To help tally the scores, the judge was another Democrat, Senator Kenneth McKellar of Tennessee. But there was no partisan score-keeping or judging by McKellar. As John Lewellen usually maintained, QK Versus broadcasts were not real contests. He intended them to be a half hour of radio entertainment, great fun and a good time for all, both participants and audience.

Two months before Germany's unconditional surrender, Joe Kelly anticipated the war's end and was looking forward to it with an ambitious idea to start his own business, probably as an adjunct to his radio career. At home, Joe always enjoyed making huge sandwiches with a variety of ingredients. In March 1945 he thought about opening a chain of sandwich shops after the war, and so he put in a bid to buy several old railroad cabooses. His plan was to convert them into the shops. There is no record of what he was going to name the shops. It was an interesting and creative idea, arguably one that came from his belief that the economic prosperity enjoyed by Americans during the war would continue sailing on a steady course after the war ended.

Hedda Hopper, in her syndicated newspaper column, offered a different motivation for Joe's plans. She suggested that Joe was still feeling insecure about his job even though he hadn't received any mail voicing disappointment with his performance since Lucy Milligan's judgmental letter in 1941. With teasing humor Hopper, the famous chronicler of Hollywood gossip, commented that perhaps he was "afraid those kids will grow up."[1] Her remark implied that once the Kids reached maturity and graduated from the program, *QK* would go off the air. If she had understood the program's structure of revolving panelists of Kids, she could not have come to her conclusion. Undoubtedly, she meant her remark to be a sly joke. If we were to take her comment seriously, it would have once again emphasized job insecurity in the world of radio. Programs could go off the air, even the successful ones, and the always nagging fear of unemployment would come true for everyone involved in production.

But Joe wasn't feeling at all insecure about his job. Hedda Hopper's comment didn't really concern him. He continued to do what he thought was right, and Lou agreed with him. He was happy enough with Joe to hire him as quizmaster on a new radio program called *RFD America* that aired from Chicago in late 1947.[2]

Joe's belief that prosperity would continue after the war was the self-encouragement he needed to seriously consider venturing into sandwich shops. He was confident about the future. But the overall state of mind of many Americans had changed after this war. To be sure, people celebrated the end of the war both privately and in public, with large crowds gathering in major cities throughout the nation. After the euphoria of victory had worn off, the mood was different. There was an always-present element of disquiet just beneath any outward appearances, with an injection of fear creeping into thought and conversation.

The dropping of the two atomic bombs over Japan brought about the

Japanese surrender six days after the United States dropped the second bomb over Nagasaki, three days after the first bomb at Hiroshima. The enormity of the destruction caused by the atomic bombs began to generate other questions, other anxieties and fear. This wasn't the first time that a subconscious nervousness began to surface. Six years before the atomic bombs were dropped several American newspapers in 1939 had introduced the element of fear with their reports about the developing work in nuclear fission.

The resultant apprehension was visible enough that Enrico Fermi, one of the physicists working on the Manhattan Project, spoke to the nation on CBS radio shortly after newspaper columnists began discussing the possible devastation that might result from nuclear fission. Representing the War Department's nuclear initiative, his intent was to assure listeners that "there was no cause for alarm." After his radio appearance, the War Department kept the work of this group of scientists under strict secrecy. After a short period of time, most likely because the growing concerns about the escalating European war took center stage, the fear of experiments in nuclear fission subsided.[3] Security still remained tight. So secretive was the work on the nuclear chain reaction that when scientists created the first successful reaction at the beginning of December 1942, Dr. Arthur Compton telephoned James Conant in Washington to report their success. It was a melodramatic, coded message. "The Italian navigator has discovered America," Compton reported. Conant asked, "Is the new country safe to enter?" "Yes," replied Compton, "Columbus finds the natives are friendly."[4] It was the language of spy stories on radio.

After the Hiroshima and Nagasaki detonations the concern was that there might be horrible, long-term consequences for those victims who suffered from radioactive fallout. Even more troubling was the fear in America, and in fact the world, that the release of radiation might spread to people elsewhere in Japan, or even globally.

Still, there was not a widespread fear that doomsday would follow. There was no visible panic. To be sure, the federal government embarked on a public relations spin to lessen any such fear. For the most part, it worked. The message was that atomic energy would improve the quality of life in peacetime, not destroy it. Thus, harnessing atomic energy to help with many of the traditional labor-intensive tasks in a variety of businesses would reduce the amount of work needed to complete long-established manual tasks, resulting in more leisure time for the labor force. Most people came to believe that. Some thought that the increased leisure time really meant that there would be widespread unemployment. Calling unemployment an increase in leisure time sounded like an unadulterated public relations spin concocted for a naïve audience.

Glenn Seaborg, who had been one of the scientists working on the Manhattan Project, was a *QK* guest on the November 11, 1945, broadcast, just three months after the bombing of Japan. There was no pressing reason for him to make an appearance. There had been no unusual news about him. He wasn't on the program to speak about the value of education, as so many previous guests had, often the customary reason for a guest to appear on the program.

Seaborg was a celebrity. The circumstances of his fame were so noteworthy — his discovery of plutonium, and his work on the Manhattan Project — that there seemed to be no reason to think about any hidden motivation or calculated reason that prompted his appearance on *QK*.

It would be a smart move for John Lewellen to think of inviting Seaborg to be on *QK*. It was a plum in scheduling to have him on the broadcast. Seaborg was a star in his own right. Of course he was well-known among the community of nuclear scientists and the Department of the Army. Because of the obsession with atomic and nuclear energy, he was becoming a household name. John thought that his appearance on *QK* would have great appeal for the audience. But there is no evidence that Lewellen invited Seaborg. Nor do we know if Seaborg asked to be on. It could have been either.

Once the schedule for his appearance was set, John reversed the usual format for that Sunday's program, with apparent deference to Seaborg's prominence in the field of nuclear science. Rather than have the Kids answer Joe's questions, he had the Kids ask Seaborg questions.

It was the last half of the broadcast. Immediately after Bob Murphy read the mid-broadcast Alka-Seltzer commercial, Joe set the tone for Seaborg's appearance. His foreword to the introduction of this famous scientist to the studio and the at-home audiences was not casual or brief. It was not his usual style of introduction for many of the other guests, especially those who had established their fame in entertainment, sports, politics, government, or education. This time Joe was serious and somber. No longer was he Jolly Joe Kelly, reading the comics to children on a local radio station. No longer was he the Saturday night hayseed on *Barn Dance*. No longer was he the familiar pre-dawn radio voice for farmers, reciting that day's hog prices, peppered with corny jokes, knee-bangers calculated to wake them and get them in the mood to face another hard day on the south forty.

Joe's preamble was ominous. He shaded his words with the serious dichotomy related to atomic energy, at once optimistic and fearful ("the whole world is rightly curious about the atomic bomb and its grave implications for world peace or world annihilation").

These extremes in thinking about the atomic bomb were not unusual. Eleanor Roosevelt, a month before she became the U.S. delegate to the United

Nations General Assembly nearly a year later, voiced the same concerns. She was present at the welcoming ceremonies for the opening of the United Nations at Flushing Meadows, New York. Upon reflecting on the General Assembly's work for the following two months, she speculated that it was a "terrifying thought that in this room peace or eventual annihilation are at stake."[5]

After Kelly's grave introduction, Seaborg answered apparently in the fashion that Lewellen suggested to B_2H_2 and other celebrity guests who would be participating in the seemingly competitive Kids Versus format. Lewellen must have coached Seaborg on how to answer the roll call, the standard feature at the beginning of each broadcast. Each Kid introduced himself, gave his age, and identified the name of his school. After Joe introduced him, Seaborg didn't give his age or "school," but he explained, with what seemed to be a light touch of humor, that when he was invited to appear on this broadcast, he agreed "on one condition: that I was not in competition with the Quiz Kids." There were a few titters among those who were in the studio audience. They probably thought his comment was ironic, that the Kids would best him in any display of erudition. But that wasn't what he meant. He continued to say that "even though I am not being scored tonight I'm still in competition with their ability to think up provocative questions." He offered that he would do his best to come up with the right answers.

Perhaps remembering the uneasiness prompting Fermi's talk on radio in 1939, the War Department and the army began a vigorous public relations campaign shortly after the United States dropped the atomic bombs. They wanted the campaign to allay any continuing fears.[6] Joe's opening remarks suggested that this broadcast was part of that campaign. Listening to the questions posed by the Kids, they appear to be too sophisticated, too directed to have been ad lib queries. It sounds as if John or Roby wrote them. And they did. Richard Williams recalls that this was "the only time that a question of a guest was planted with me."[7]

Seaborg's answers described both ends of the spectrum, from the fear of the bomb to the preventative measures in place to ensure the safety of the scientists who were working with radioactive material. He described the explosion while adding some perspective. He said that people could feel the force of the explosion 50 or 100 miles from the point of detonation. He gave as a specific example the fact that Milwaukee residents could feel an atomic bomb dropped over Chicago. Making it more personal, he noted that *Quiz Kids* announcer Bob Murphy lived in Milwaukee. Murphy reacted with audible dismay. "What's more important," Seaborg added, "is that the whole downtown area of Chicago could be obliterated by one atomic bomb, including the Merchandise Mart where we are now." For someone who was trying to

Glenn Seaborg talked about nuclear research on the Quiz Kids broadcast, November 11, 1945. (From left) Glenn T. Seaborg, Sheila Conlon, Robert Burke (courtesy Lawrence Berkeley National Laboratory).

minimize any trepidation about nuclear energy his statement was startling; Seaborg was emphasizing the basic fear of total destruction.

Quiz Kid Bob Burke asked him how the military would use the bomb if there were another war. Seaborg outlined several options, with each of them escalating the horrors. He said that they could drop bombs from a plane as they had been over Japan, but that there would probably be a "more efficient way than that." They could shoot them over in rockets.

Even worse, he continued, the bomb "might be disassembled and brought in to this country ... in suitcases." He continued saying that the bomb would be "reassembled to be planted in a back yard, maybe your back yard, or in somebody's cellar and then the saboteur leaves [it with] a time mechanism [that] causes it to explode the next day, the next week, the next month, maybe the next year." His remarks must have brought on a chill to the studio audience.

He followed his horror story with some hope, nevertheless assigning the responsibility for the prevention of war to the Kids and the audience. "It's up to you, Quiz Kids, and also up to the listeners to see that there's absolutely no possibility that there will be a war with atomic bombs. We will have to have international controls which might include inspection to make sure that they are never used. If they were ever used, it would just be a world catastrophe."[8] Historian Joseph Illick, in his 2002 book *American Childhoods*, reflected Seaborg's idea of cooperation as the best prevention for a nuclear war when he observed, "The implication of the nuclear age, even before the cold war, was that international cooperation was necessary, reinforcing the idea that American family members, by working together, provided a model for the world."[9]

Even though Russia did not produce a bomb until four years later, the possibility that they would was a recurring fear. Upon reflection, more than 65 years after that broadcast, Richard Williams doubted that "the American public was yet afflicted with such worries" of fear about future atomic bombings. He claimed that "Russia was four years away" from exploding its first atomic bomb.[10] Richard's analysis comes more from hindsight than foresight. In November 1945 no one knew when Russia would have the bomb — four years later or four weeks later.

Newscaster Raymond Gram Swing reported to his listeners, "The bomb dropped on Hiroshima was in effect dropped on the Russians, since it was not needed to bring the Japanese war to a close, but to establish and demonstrate a vast margin of power superiority over the Soviet Union." In a similar vein, A.J. Muste concluded that the bombs dropped on Japan were "a move in the power struggle between the United States and Russia."[11]

Harve Fischman asked Dr. Seaborg if any of the people working on the bomb in the research laboratories were in great danger of being "vaporized." Seaborg questioned the use of the word vaporized, and ignored its comic-book melodramatic reference. Instead, he answered calmly and seriously by saying that they took every precaution possible in the laboratories and practically no serious accidents took place.

Then there was Richard's question. Richard asked Seaborg if there had been any other new elements discovered, like plutonium and neptunium. "Oh, yes, Dick," he answered. "Recently there have been two new elements discovered, elements with atomic numbers 95 and 96, at the Metallurgical Laboratory here in Chicago. So now you'll have to tell your teachers to change the 92 elements in your schoolbooks to 96 elements."[12]

The scientists hadn't publicly announced the new elements yet; the formal announcement was to be five days later at Northwestern University during a meeting of the Chicago section of the American Chemical Society. The *Chicago Tribune*, using typical newspaper slang, called the announcement of the new elements on *QK* "a noteworthy scoop."[13]

In fact, the scientists hadn't named these elements yet; they still identified them by their periodic table numbers. Arthur G. Levy, a real estate executive in Chicago, wrote to Seaborg, humbly suggesting two names for the elements. He offered Radoreaidium for 95 and Energyradium for 96. He parsed these names, and explained that the prefix had brought to mind "the words Radium, Radar, Radio and Raid." He said that *raid* made reference to the two bombs dropped over Hiroshima and Nagasaki. He stated that the "aid" part of the word *raid* meant that atomic energy should be for "technological, commercial, beneficial, healthful, and peaceful purposes instead of ... the destruction and annihilation of human beings, animals and all other forms of life." Anticipating the discovery of new elements or metallic substances, Levy submitted ten additional names. His creative juices flowing, he even suggested Quizkellyium (Quiz-Kelly-ium), a blunt reference to Joe and the Kids. Apologizing for the length of his letter ("an excess amount of stored up energy"), he asked Seaborg to reply with criticism or approval.[14]

The always-gracious Seaborg did reply, complimenting Levy on his "originality and imagination," but declining to use any of the suggestions, saying that "when we finally come down to the business of choosing names we will feel impelled to rely on the more prosaic and ordinary."[15]

Levy's letter, however long, did not reflect any trepidation he may have felt. It was a well-reasoned effort. Aside from the humorous suggestion of using Joe Kelly and the Kids as the basis of naming an element, the letter offers some insight into the fact that Levy was aware of the implications of atomic energy, both devastating and uplifting. Levy prayed that "a more humane use" would be the result of any work on atomic energy.[16]

Seaborg's description of the distance from the bomb that people could feel its reverberations prompted another listener to write directly to him. Gladys A. Reichard, an associate professor of anthropology at Barnard College in New York, wrote to Seaborg on November 21. She said that she had spent part of the summer in Arizona and New Mexico. She reported that a Hopi Indian, living in Oraibi, Arizona, was at work in his garden on a day that the scientists tested the bomb at Almagordo. He saw the flash and heard an explosion. She calculated the distance from Almagordo to Oraibi and concluded that it was at least 340 to 360 air miles. She explained the reason for her letter: "I write you because I know that the results on the second test were obscure and think this may give you some tangible estimate." She recognized that she spoke as a layperson and not a nuclear scientist. So she added a little humor and softened her correspondence toward the end of her letter: "If this has no value for you I trust you have, as do I, a capacious waste-basket for this note."[17]

It seems that Seaborg's appearance on the broadcast was part of the federal government's public relations agenda. Listening to that broadcast, the overriding message in his comments suggests that he was there to promote arms control and the peaceful application of atomic energy. In contrast with that uplifting viewpoint, Seaborg stated the ominous alternative quite clearly, to suggest that the fear of destruction was enough motivation to support peaceful uses for atomic energy. He assigned serious responsibility to "you Kids and the listeners" to prevent a new war in which countries might use catastrophic atomic weapons.

> ☞ *Suppose you had a pair of balances that are out of balance. You weigh an object on one side and it weighs 10 pounds. You weigh it on the other side and it weighs 40 pounds. What is the true weight of the object?*[18]

World War II may have been over but the intense battle among the Kids, their nitpicking competitiveness, continued and seemed to intensify. When Claude Brenner corrected Roby's mistaken identification of the "Griffith Conservatory" when they were in Los Angeles before the war it was constructive criticism. In general all the Kids tried to instruct those around them by correcting their errors. The kids were charming, funny, polite, and respectful of each other and the adults with whom they spoke.

On the show each week the criticism of the Kids by their contemporaries was different. Beneath their sunny façade was an environment of intense competition — intellectual and social. It was sharp and competitive, extreme nitpicking. Within a few weeks after the show's debut nitpicking was obvious, turning Joe Kelly into a mediator between Van Dyke and Gerard. One of Joe's questions asked the Kids to "define respectively a dodo, a dido, and a dado." Gerard, always confident, answered the first part, replying that a dodo is a prehistoric bird. Joe accepted his answer as correct. Van Dyke disagreed, saying that the dodo is extinct but not prehistoric. Gerard thrust back, and looked to Joe for support as he countered by defending himself, saying that his encyclopedia defined the bird as prehistoric. Joe tried to smooth over the dispute with diplomacy, suggesting that there wasn't much difference. Van Dyke insisted. "Mr. Kelly, I would like to submit to you that all prehistoric animals are extinct, but all extinct animals are not necessarily prehistoric."[19]

Claude Brenner was acutely aware of the competitive nature of the nitpicking during the broadcasts. The Kids tried to come in first in the calculating of scores at the end of each broadcast. "Winning was big for me. It was the business of being a Quiz Kid," he remembered when he was an adult. He eventually "got over it." But when he was on the show, he didn't bond with the other Kids because "these weren't my friends, they were people I competed with."[20]

Quiz Kid Patrick Conlon voiced a similar recollection. "If you got too chummy with the other Kids, you weren't doing a good job on the show." He remembered the intense competitive nature of the interaction with the other Kids for many years. "It got to be unpleasant between Lon Lunde, Joel Kupperman, and me," he said.[21]

We can hear an apt example from a recorded show. Joe Kelly asked the Kids to identify three passages of classical music, played by the organist. They were to give the title and composers' names, and then to spell the last name of each. Lon Lunde's hand was up first, and he answered the question correctly, identifying the composers as Tchaikovsky, Rimsky-Korsakov, and Prokofieff. He also qualified his answer on spelling by saying there were two ways to spell Prokofieff, either ending with a double f, or with a v.

Joel Kupperman, on the panel for that show, interjected a nitpicking criticism, saying that Lunde did not spell the names of the composers with an initial capital letter. As usual, Joe Kelly diffused the tension between the two Kids and moved on to the next question.[22]

Lon Lunde agreed about the nitpicking on *QK*, categorizing it as being competitive. He thought that the show was "meaningless unless there was competition. And I wanted to win." He understood that in order to succeed on the show, you had to survive. Only the strongest Kids, those who could "dope out the answers," would be invited back. Sometimes it didn't take raw knowledge, it took insight and experience. After being on the show a couple of times, "we knew when Joe Kelly was asking a trick question by the tone of his voice when he asked it." He thought that if a Kid managed to survive the anxiety and fear during his first appearance on a network radio show he would come back stronger on the next show. He concluded that "experienced Kids were the strongest."[23] Even being aware of the nitpicking competition of the show and knowing how to survive it, Conlon still wanted it to be friendlier. He regretted the competitive tone of *QK*.[24]

☞ *Who was the first signer of the Constitution of the United States?*

Gradually television was changing the radio industry, and Lou as well. He and his family continued to live in New York after the war and his association with the OWI ended. He announced in an advertisement in February 1946 that he had opened a New York office, an extension of the Louis G. Cowan Company in Chicago, now incorporated as Louis G. Cowan, Inc. He identified the capabilities of his new company as radio production, transcriptions, and 16-mm films. His new company was evolving to packaging his own television properties rather than radio programs that had been Lou's focus during his career to then.

Some time earlier, John Spiegel, Lou's brother-in-law, had an idea that was in tandem with Lou's beliefs about the importance of education. He suggested to Lou that *QK* should do something about relating to school teachers. Perhaps his creative juices had started to flow during that exciting evening that seemed so long ago when his wife, Babette, proposed *Quiz Kids* as the name for the program. Probably his suggestion was more recent than that, knowing Lou's habit of acting quickly on an idea that he liked. Lou would not have waited more than five years to take action.

Spiegel suggested a contest that he called "The Teacher Who Helped Me Most." The contest would be open to children enrolled in any grade in schools throughout the United States. More than just naming the teacher, the students had to explain why these teachers were so special. To enter the contest, they had to write to the *QK* office. Miles Laboratories would award the winning teacher a scholarship for further graduate studies at a college or university. Lou liked it. He thought that it was a good way that they could publicize how poorly teachers were paid, and that the contest could help produce a change.[25]

During the *QK* broadcast of January 27, 1946, Dr. Paul Witty, director of the Psycho-Educational Clinic at Northwestern University, announced and explained the details of the first contest. By this time *QK* had changed the contest's name to the "Best Teacher of 1946," and they called the essay "The Teacher Who Has Helped Me Most." The winning teacher, selected by his or her own students, was awarded a year of advanced study at the University of Chicago, Northwestern University, or Notre Dame. The winning teacher could be any teacher that the student had had. The teacher still had to be teaching, not retired.

The award included tuition, living expenses, transportation to and from Chicago to appear on a *QK* broadcast, and $1,000. The student who wrote the winning letter received $100 in cash; the writers of the next 100 best letters each received $10. A scholarship committee of three academicians to oversee the contest was led by Dr. Witty and included Dr. Ralph Tyler, chairman of the Department of Education at the University of Chicago, and Dr. Phillip F. Moore, dean of the University of Notre Dame's graduate school.[26]

In the second year of the contest, there were more than 33,000 nominations, and the cash prize increased to $2,500 for advanced study at any university. The winner, Aline Neal, age 42, of Jackson, Mississippi, earned an annual salary of $1,900 as a fourth-grade teacher in Jackson.[27] Charles Beardsley, who by then was chairman of the board of Miles, presented the award to her on the June 8, 1947, *QK* broadcast. Joe Kelly interviewed her; she spoke about her 24 years of teaching, 19 of them in the fourth-grade classroom of Duling Public School in Jackson.

She also revealed some startling information about herself. She said that when she calculated her salary for a calendar year of 12 months, it came to $36.54 a week. Because she was supporting her elderly parents, she worked every evening from 6:30 to 9:30 as a ticket taker at a local movie theater.

After her second job she went home by bus, graded student papers and other administrative chores, and prepared lesson plans for the next day.

She told Joe that because she was only able to take courses during summer months, she had not completed her undergraduate degree. Each year she borrowed money from a local bank to pay for her coursework. During the school year she had to pay back the loan and support herself and her family with those two jobs.

When Beardsley presented the award on the broadcast, he announced that the awards committee had adjusted the rules of the contest for her. Originally the award of tuition and money for expenses were for teachers who wanted to work toward a graduate degree. Because Neal needed only a few courses to complete her bachelor's degree, the award was for those undergraduate courses. The remainder was for her graduate work. The completion of her undergraduate degree would qualify her for an increase in salary, and an additional increase with a graduate degree.

Joe announced two special gifts for Neal: a new *World Book* encyclopedia as a reference source in her classroom, and a 16-mm film projector and screen so that she could show educational films to her students.

The Best Teacher contest continued for six years, to 1951. Lou concluded that the contest "may not have had much effect" on changing teachers' salaries, but Miles and *QK* were "at least trying" to help.[28]

A few weeks after Witty's announcement of the first Best Teacher contest in January 1946, Glenn Seaborg appeared on *QK* again, this time with three of his colleagues, Drs. Harold Urey, Maria Mayer, and Arthur Jaffey in a QK Versus broadcast. The instructions John Lewellen sent to all of them about the format and the lack of difficulty of the questions were like those that he had sent to B_2H_2. But this was not the usual Quiz Kids competing with their parents, college professors, or U.S. senators. The difference between this and Lewellen's instructions to other groups was that this letter, as well as the material on the program, had to be "cleared by military security." Lewellen explained that the clearance "was no problem because the science questions all concern fairly elementary things." He thought that NBC continuity was more of a problem because "the network is very old-maidish about subjects that could be controversial."

Another difference between the usual QK Versus format and this broadcast was that Joe Kelly was not to be the Chief Quizzer. Clifton Utley, the news commentator who had auditioned for *QK* in June 1940 just before Joe Kelly came in and won the job, was going to be the "master of ceremonies."[29]

Joe took a leave of absence for six weeks, starting after the January 27 broadcast until his return on March 10. Larry Wolters, the radio critic for the *Tribune*, reported that Joe's physician "has ordered him to take a month's rest."³⁰ Forrest Owen remembered that the reason Joe took a medical leave was more specific than a simple month-long sabbatical; Joe had suffered a heart attack. There was, of course, an immediate scramble to find a temporary replacement. Rather than using just one stand-in Chief Quizzer, Lewellen decided to use several people. First up, on February 3, was Victor Borge, the Danish comedian and pianist. Borge, in Owen's estimation, was "terrible with the Kids." He made jokes throughout the broadcast rather than acting as the avuncular mentor that Joe was. Two weeks later, Oliver Cappelle, an executive at Miles Laboratories, stood in for Joe, and Owen thought "he did a good job."³¹

Other guest quizzers during Joe's absence were veteran radio personalities: Tom Breneman, the emcee of *Breakfast in Hollywood*, and John W. Vandercook, prolific author of 14 books and, starting in 1940, an NBC correspondent and news analyst. Cappelle, Breneman, Vandercook, and Utley apparently were acceptable substitutes for Joe, although they probably didn't exhibit his easy-going rapport with the Kids. Not everyone could do Joe's job easily.

QK continued to attract celebrity guests after the war: Captain Eddie Rickenbacker, World War I fighter pilot ace who was president of Eastern Airlines; Fred Vinson, secretary of the treasury; Li'l Abner creator Al Capp; Random House publisher Bennett Cerf; ex-heavyweight boxing champion Jack Dempsey; actors Burgess Meredith, Dinah Shore, Miriam Hopkins, Ole Olsen of the comedy team Olsen and Johnson (*Hellzapoppin'*), singer Allan Jones (*A Night at the Opera*), Roy Rogers and Gabby Hayes, Virginia Mayo, and Neil Hamilton.

> ☞ *If you drop the first letter from the name of an article every one of you listeners possesses it becomes, in its plural form, the word for "goodbye" in another language. Now, what is the article?*

Of course, John reduced the *QK* travel schedule after the bond rallies ended at the beginning of 1946, when the Treasury Department's aggressive bond marketing of the past six years concluded. Still, *QK* continued to travel. Just as before the war, appearances at special events for civic, charitable, and cultural organizations were the main reasons for travel to these on-location performances. As well, they might be guests on another radio program, but these appearances were usually just focused on self-promotion.

After the war their appeal was just as great as it had been at bond rallies and appearances at military bases and hospitals. In 1946 at the height of their fame, large quantities of mail arrived each week from veterans' hospitals. Triggered by this overwhelming response, John produced a weekly broadcast that November in which all the questions that Joe asked the Kids were submitted by hospitalized veterans.³² No doubt this special program was just as heartwarming to the listening audience as the volume of mail had been encouraging to John. Although we could view John's programming idea as another effort at promoting the show, not every special program was intended to build an audience. *Quiz Kids* was at its peak after the war, and this special show as well as the trips to help charitable events reflected Lou's work with nonprofit organizations before the war, when he was more concerned with helping them than with making money.

Typically, local communities and hospitals in various cities invited the Kids to be present at fund-raising events. Or, when it was coincidental to a trip, *QK* would air its weekly broadcast in other cities when the Kids were present to help raise money for a local Red Cross, the March of Dimes Foundation (the National Foundation for Infantile Paralysis), or any of several other charitable organizations. The easing of many of the difficulties of wartime travel made it feasible for *QK* to take these trips far from Chicago and its environs. As before and during the war, sponsorship by local businesses continued to be the customary method of garnering financial support for travel expenses.

The broadcast of December 8, 1946, was from the Library of Congress. *QK* came to Washington to be the featured entertainment for a gathering sponsored by the Pan American Union. When listening to the broadcast, we hear that the script submits no reason for their invitation. It sounded as if *QK* was simply there offering an interesting and pleasant diversion for an audience of diplomats and government officials from several south-of-the-border countries and key representatives from a number of other countries. The announcer, Durward Kirby, substituting for Bob Murphy, made the customary opening remarks for the broadcast. Kirby, an accomplished announcer, had been one of the failed prospects for the Chief Quizzer's job in 1940. Before introducing Joe Kelly to the audience, Kirby announced that the program had been "short-waved in English, Spanish, and Portuguese to the nations of Latin America," thus helping to create an exciting aura surrounding the broadcast.

To be expected, Joe's questions for the Kids that day were focused on Latin America ("There are some 30 countries and possessions in Central and South America, and the Caribbean. A listener wants you name 20 of them." "Would it have been possible for Simon Bolivar to meet George Washington?") A guest on the program was the nine-year-old daughter of the Colombian ambassador to the United States, Inez Elvira Santa Maria, whom Joe had invited "to sit beside me and ask the questions." One of the Kids from Chicago was Danny Martin, who was born in Lima, Peru, and had lived in the United States for only the previous two years. A "question" asked the Kids to imitate famous radio comedians (Fred Allen, Fibber McGee, Red Skelton). They did, and Danny translated their mimicry into Spanish. It wasn't really a normal *QK* question, not a test of intelligence, reasoning, or recitation of facts. It was just entertainment, with the added boost of Danny's translation.

Usually there were more compelling reasons than just having a *QK* broadcast as entertainment for such a special audience, especially an appearance that required the expense of overnight travel. The customary reason of finding new Kids that was the cornerstone of the pre-war *QK* travel schedule could not have been the motive this time. There was no local contest winner on the panel. There was a full contingent of five Chicago Kids on this show. Even though it was in Washington, a bond rally could not have been a reason. A curious listener might wonder.

The political atmosphere during the war years offers us a clue. In fact, there had been a heightened interest in Latin America even before the war. The Roosevelt administration was concerned about the influence of Germany and Italy in South America at that time. In 1940 President Roosevelt appointed Nelson Rockefeller to lead the Office of Inter-American Affairs. Part of its role was to broadcast radio programs in, and to, Latin America to counter propaganda from those two Axis powers and to promote good will between the United States and its Central and South American neighbors. This strategy continued throughout the war. The producers of network radio programs in the United States embraced the concept; they seemed to like the idea of expanding to Latin America.[33]

Notwithstanding the fact that the war was over when *QK* broadcast from the library, Roosevelt's plan, launched six years earlier to foster good will, was attractive to Lou and John. It was still a good reason for *QK* to accept the invitation for this Washington broadcast. Joe Kelly's script hinted at another reason, more subtle, almost imperceptibly woven into the fabric of that day's broadcast. We have to listen carefully to hear it.

Joe made an apparently spontaneous and innocuous remark on-air, couched in the diplomatic language of good will: "Someday we hope there will be *Quiz Kids* programs in all the Pan American countries, not just in the United States." Listening critically to Joe's buoyant statement we might hear the real reason that *QK* was in Washington for that Sunday afternoon broadcast.[34]

On the surface Joe's comment sounded infinitely optimistic, with unfathomable delight about international cooperation. But he could have been referring to other opportunities. As well as the noble effort of fostering good will among nations, American radio networks and the sponsors of their programs envisioned expanding into more markets in which to sell their products and services. Now that the war was over, international expansion once again came to mind. *Billboard* concluded that "technically, financially, and artistically," radio "south of the Rio Grande" in the past "four or five years zoomed to where it's a good carbon [copy] of U.S. radio." *Billboard* stated clearly that "south of the border was ripe for a boom."[35]

It may have been the goal of the Pan American Union to have *QK* provide brilliant entertainment, but it would have been equally beneficial for John Lewellen to open tangible possibilities for international expansion for the program. It was something that the staff had speculated about before the war.[36]

At the same time that *QK* broadcasts were on local stations during the 18 months before the Pearl Harbor attack, helping to push *QK* to national awareness, there was heady speculation among the staff, probably nothing more than a few brief conversations in the office, about international expansion. Of course, the escalation of the war in Europe before the attack on Pearl Harbor and indisputably after December 7 had precluded acting on any such notions. The Library of Congress broadcast sounded like a return to those optimistic, pre-war ambitions among the *QK* staff, and among other broadcasters, too. Coca-Cola, Philco Radio, Eversharp, and Pepsi Cola were significant advertisers in Mexico after the war.[37]

There was no reason to be coy about it. Joe's remark was polite and hopeful, but the message was clear. *QK* was prominent enough in broadcasting by 1946 that Lewellen, via Joe's script, could take to the public any ideas of expansion with no embarrassment. Through most of 1946 *QK* maintained a Hooper rating of between 7.4 and 8.4. There was no comparison with the double-digit ratings of the leading quiz shows of that period—*People Are Funny, Take It or Leave It, Can You Top This?*—but its ratings were strong enough to put the program on the list of the 15–20 leading quiz programs.[38] In 1946 *QK* was a desirable vehicle for many advertisers, north or south of the border.

A more solemn note overshadowed the excitement of the broadcast that afternoon. The featured guest speaker was to have been Dr. Leo S. Rowe, the director-general of the Pan American Union. It was appropriate to have him speak to the audience. The original plan was to broadcast from the Hall of the Americas in the Pan American Union building, a space large enough for all the assembled representatives. But Rowe had died three days earlier. At 6:25 P.M. December 5, 1946, while he was crossing Massachusetts Avenue in front of the Bolivian Embassy, a car hit him. Twenty-five minutes later Emergency Hospital in Washington pronounced him dead.[39] Roberto Aguilar of El Salvador, Rowe's long-time friend and colleague, took his place as the guest speaker on the broadcast.[40]

The broadcast had another famous guest. Senator Carl A. Hatch, who had appeared on *QK* as part of B_2H_2, was a guest judge. After explaining the reason for Rowe's absence, Joe thanked the library, "which made its facilities available as a courtesy to the Pan American Union" while describing Rowe as "a friend to all of us who believe in friendship among nations."

For reasons that we don't know, Rowe's death meant that the broadcast would not be in the Hall of Americas. To find another place and make the arrangements in less than three days was a challenge for the *QK* production staff. Joe's understated comment of gratitude to the library for offering its facilities may have been accurate and quite unembellished, but the effort to make these arrangements in just three days was far from simple. For the staff to make the change in that day's broadcast undoubtedly resulted in a round of unusually feverish activity, even if they were accustomed to the difficulties of spur-of-the moment alterations to their normal schedules.

This speeded-up pace of changing the site for the broadcast most likely involved an intense flurry of phone calls, telegrams, and messenger services, the only methods to communicate quickly at that time. The *QK* and library staffs completed this extreme change in venue in less than 68 hours. Fortunately the Library of Congress had adequate facilities and a spacious auditorium in their building available. The library's administration cooperated far beyond simple courtesy; the *QK* program was always on Sunday and the library was not open. Undoubtedly they had to bring in support personnel who would normally have the day off. Some supervisory and management people had to be present before and after the broadcast.

In making his sobering comments about the fate of Leo Rowe, Joe's delivery exhibited the appropriate deep-toned level of respect. It was factual and serious, unadorned by any maudlin or dramatic embellishments. John eliminated the usual *QK* sign-off of having the Kids say "Goodnight, Mr. Kelly." Instead, Joe simply stated, "This is Joe Kelly dismissing the Quiz Kids class until the same time next week." It was a tasteful, low-key ending, well-executed by Joe, the consummate radio professional. There was no end-of-show commercial from Durwood Kirby, just a suitable pause after Joe's final comment, followed by the NBC chimes.

There were other memorable broadcasts in the years immediately following the war. One happened seven weeks later in Miami in January 1947. The *QK* broadcast for January 26 was from the Orange Bowl where the program was the feature of a benefit for the local March of Dimes fund raising campaign. It was the first time the program had aired from Miami, and the local newspaper reported practically every move the Kids made to help build excitement for the Sunday broadcast. It was nearly a week of publicity coverage similar to the pre-war hoopla surrounding the Kids on their travels, including a demanding schedule reminiscent of their intense agendas in the few days before and during their appearances at the war bond rallies.

The Kids arrived in Miami Tuesday evening, January 21. The local newspaper and radio station were so excited about the arrival of the "famed Quiz Kids" that they couldn't wait. Even before their train pulled in, Louise Leyden, the *Miami Daily News* radio editor, boarded the train in West Palm Beach, about 70 miles north of Miami, along with representatives from Miami radio station WIOD and two railroad executives. Their plan was to interview Joe Kelly and the Kids from the train. While the radio personnel were busy setting up their equipment on the rear platform of the club car, Leyden began talking with the Kids. She asked them how they felt about being in Miami for the first time. As usual, the Kids turned the session around and interviewed her, hurling a barrage of questions and waiting eagerly for her answers: they wanted to know how far it was to the Keys, if you could see Cuba from the tip end of the state, and what Leyden would do if there were two governors in Florida ("Flip a coin to see which one you would keep?"), among other questions.

They had seen the set-up procedure dozens of times, but the Kids still were curious about the radio technicians who were getting their equipment ready. A Miami station broadcast their arrival and interview ten minutes before they chugged in to Miami. This broadcast was the first from a train since before the war. The Kids were excited. When they arrived, an equally excited entourage met the Kids at the platform. Representatives of the mayors of Miami, Miami Beach, and Coral Gables, the chairman of the Dade county chapter of the March of Dimes foundation, local Quiz Kid contest winner Paul Nay, and a group of others were on the platform. They took the Kids on Miami's largest hook-and-ladder fire truck to their hotel, the elegant Roney Plaza in Miami Beach.

Early the next morning they visited the studios of WIOD, where a reporter interviewed their mothers. The Kids were delighted to watch their mothers "face the microphone in place of their mothers watching them." Following the broadcast the party toured Miami Beach and other points of interest arriving at Hialeah racetrack in time for lunch. They had to leave before the start of the races because racing officials would not allow minors at the track once the races started.[41]

Thursday morning the Kids and their mothers visited local tourist attractions: two bird parks and a monkey "jungle." They must have been delighted to shed their heavy Chicago winter clothes for something more appropriate to the tropical weather of Miami in January. After the monkey jungle, they were interviewed twice. The first time was on the local *Man on the Street* radio program, and it featured Joe Kelly and Naomi Cooks, who, at eight years old, was the youngest of the Kids on this trip. The second interview was on a different radio station. The station's sports announcer interviewed Lon Lunde and Joel Kupperman, who were avid sports fans.[42]

Friday morning all the Kids went on an all-day fishing trip on Biscayne

Bay, accompanied by the *Miami Daily News* fishing editor, their mothers, and other members of the Chicago group. Conspicuously absent was Joe Kelly. Joe made an ironic excuse when he declined to join them, saying that he "couldn't go because he wasn't supposed to lift anything heavy," even though he had taken a five-week vacation less than a year earlier in Florida where ostensibly he went fishing, one of his favorite pastimes.[43] Irony, like schools of fish, ran swift and deep from Joe that morning. Included in the fishing trip for the Kids and their mothers was more sightseeing. The group visited a lighthouse on Key Biscayne, just six ocean miles from Miami Beach. They observed other settings on the island where MGM filmed scenes for their 1945 movie, *They Were Expendable*.[44]

There was no let-up in their schedule; it continued to be full. On Saturday from 9:30 to 10:00 the four Kids from Chicago — Naomi Cooks, Joel Kupperman, Lon Lunde, and Jack Rooney — appeared on *Crusader Kids*, a radio quiz program on Miami's WIOD-FM. It was another QK Versus program; the Kids competed with four grand-prize winners from the Miami area. After the broadcast there was some relief; the Kids had the remainder of the day to themselves.[45]

There were no tickets sold for the broadcast at the Orange Bowl the following day. The March of Dimes provided coin cards with pockets for 20 dimes that became the admission ticket. If anyone wanted to enter and didn't have a coin card, there were receptacles at the gates where they could drop a donation.[46] The agenda preceding the broadcast began at 2:45 P.M. with an invocation by the minister of the Central Baptist Church. A performance by four Miami area high school bands in full uniform paraded "in a colorful array down the field led by agile drum majorettes and baton twirlers." It was a performance that exhibited much of the fanfare usually associated with the annual New Year's Day football game at the Bowl.[47] Next, 100 children who had been cured of polio romped across the field to demonstrate "what can be accomplished with donations to the March of Dimes drive." After a brief address by the chairman of the local fund drive, the Kids, including Paul Nay, emerged from the south entrance of the stadium in their blue caps and gowns. Briefly, they played catch with a football, and then settled at their desks on a platform at the center of the field on the 30-yard line. Joe began the customary pre-broadcast warm-up session. Two former Quiz Kids, Inez Fox and Emily Israel, took part in the warm-up. Both, originally from Chicago, were students at the University of Miami. On air at 4:00, NBC broadcast *QK* on 142 stations nationwide.[48]

Frequently when *QK* broadcasts occurred on or near holidays, or at special events, questions were about those special days. This show offered no exception; questions on the broadcast mostly were about Florida.

JOE: If you wanted to fly to the nearest capital from Miami, where would you go?

Once again, we heard John's creativity at taking questions about a range of subjects and flavoring them to a specific event. Naturally, they had a Florida theme that day as Joe introduced the next question with a somewhat ironic tang by suggesting that the beachgoers of Miami were not human. "We've seen some interesting creatures since we've been here: an alligator, flamingos, people on the beach, and now, Laura Friel of Rochester, New York, has a rhyming question about some other creatures."

JOE: Supply the missing word with the name of an animal. Here's the first one. Listen closely. This one [animal] has colors to match a serape. He has only two toes and his name is _____."

Paul Nay had the correct answer in a few seconds. Joe continued.

JOE: Who was the ruler of Spain when Florida was discovered by Ponce de Leon?

Jack Rooney was quick with the answer along with some additional information. There were other topics for the Kids: music, language (an opportunity for the Kids to make puns), and a math question related to the revenue generated by this benefit performance.[49] Shortly after the Sunday broadcast the Chicago Kids and their entourage boarded a train to return home.

It had been a busy five days in Miami. Even so, their schedule included enough time for sightseeing and leisure time activities. Unlike their bond tours, when the appearances and performances left little time for pleasure, their required duties before the Sunday broadcast only amounted to one 30-minute radio performance on Saturday and a couple of brief interview sessions spread over the previous three days. The *Daily News* planned the rest of their activities as if they were simply tourists, except that they reported all their extra-curricular activities prominently in the newspaper. It was a Hollywood-style promotion: A blitz of stories to encourage attendance at the Orange Bowl were evident in the headlines every day. Starting with the interview and the broadcast from their train ten minutes before it arrived early in the week, and even covering Joe's declining to go on the fishing trip, the newspaper designed reports to the public to encourage interest in the Kids and the March of Dimes campaign. Sunday at the Orange Bowl an estimated 7,000 people "opened their pocketbooks to aid the drive against polio, and their umbrellas to protect themselves against inclement weather, which struck the only discordant note of the afternoon."[50] The Orange Bowl had a seating capacity for 30,000, but a slow drizzle that wet the stadium's seats and threatened to turn into a hard shower kept thousands of people away.

If you wanted to make light of it, you could have called it Chicago Week in the *Daily News*. Interest in the Chicago Kids that week was as great as interest in another, however infamous, former resident of Chicago. On Saturday, January 25, the night before the March of Dimes benefit, Al Capone died of a stroke and cardiac arrest at his home on Palm Island in Biscayne Bay between Miami and Miami Beach. The *Daily News* had been following his rapid decline in newspaper stories for the past week, just as they had the arrival of the Kids and their performance coming up at week's end. On Sunday, at the peak of their respective stories, the Kids and Capone shared the front page of the *Daily News* and actually dominated the local news that day. On that same front page was a less prominent announcement by Republic Pictures that Gene Autry's horse, Champion, had died at the age of 17 on the same day as Capone.

After their return home, *QK* continued its normal schedule of broadcasts and extracurricular activities. Two months after the Kids returned from Miami the subject of international expansion came up again. *QK* announced that international programming had already started. Willhelm Morgenstierne, the ambassador to the United States from Norway, was the guest speaker on a broadcast in March 1947. He spoke about a Norwegian *Quiz Kids* radio show, broadcast from Oslo, and patterned after the American program. He analyzed this Scandinavian version as "an experiment in world cooperation among children." He said that he hoped to work out an exchange appearance on their respective radio programs between an American Quiz Kid and a Norwegian Quiz Kid.[51] He concluded by saying that *Quiz Kids* programs in the two countries were "a fine thing for world democracy, in keeping with the spirit of the United Nations."[52] The Norwegian show debuted in November 1946. There was a version underway in Australia, so heartily received that it was the third most popular feature on that continent.[53]

The war was over; peace had arrived. If you agreed with Joe's confident thinking, when he planned to venture into sandwich shops, that there would be a full return to normal after the war you might predict a rosy future for *QK*. But that wasn't in the crystal ball.

ANSWERS

The answer is mho. *Spelled the other way it is* ohm, *after the German physicist Georg Ohm. Lord Kelvin named the mho. The difference between them is that the ohm is a unit of resistance and the mho is a unit of conductivity.*

The true weight would be 20 pounds. The error on one side would be inversely proportional to the error on the other. The relationship of the false light weight to the true weight would be the same as the relationship of the true weight to the false heavy weight. Let x equal the true weight, and you have the algebraic equation 10 is to x as x is to 40. So x equals 20.

The first signer of the Constitution was George Washington.

Radio. If you drop the R (the first letter), the word becomes adio and its plural is adios, which means "goodbye" in Spanish.

Nassau, Bahamas, is the closest capital, just 184 air miles from Miami. Jack Rooney knew the answer. The other Kids answered incorrectly with Havana (237 miles), and Tallahassee (405 miles).

The animal whose name rhymes with serape is an okapi. The okapi is an animal similar to a giraffe, found in Africa. It is about the size of an American elk.

Ponce de Leon first discovered Florida in 1513 under King Ferdinand. But he continued his exploration for eight more years until 1521. During the last two years of deLeon's exploration, Spain's monarch was Charles V.

14

Kids Will Be Kids

☞ *William Akers of Fry's Springs, Virginia, would like to know the answers to questions about our Quiz Kids program. It's a three-part question; you Quiz Kids just have to answer two of them correctly. Here they are: What's the reason that Quiz Kids was on the air? Why should we care? What does it all mean?*

It's an imaginary three-part question. Joe Kelly never asked it. If he had, Lou Cowan would have known the answer, his answer, to the first part. Actually, he could have had two answers. Why was *QK* on the air? Lou thought the program was "good radio." He wanted to show that bright children from ordinary families existed in the real world, and they were normal kids. They didn't attend elite, private schools. They weren't eggheads. And they weren't geeks. Certainly they were not sallow bookworms, sheltered from the sun, their skin pallid, their only nourishment coming from a steady incandescent stream of lamplight beaming down as they pored over encyclopedias during every waking hour.

Lou's other answer would have been less altruistic, more personal, and more in keeping with his career goals. He wanted to develop a successful radio property. But those could have been Lou's answers.

For the rest of us it's difficult. It's like solving a complex algebraic problem. We should start by combining the three segments of Joe's query into one question: What does it all mean; what is the significance of the program? To answer this question we should place *QK* in the context of some of the cultural changes that occurred at around the same time the program was born.

After the fears of the Depression started to subside in 1940, families started to change how they brought up their children. Behavioral psychologist Dr. John B. Watson's edicts about strict time schedules for feeding and toilet training were starting to erode. Instead, Benjamin Spock, after years of observing the effects of such rigidity, began to urge parents to be more relaxed and permissive, to accept their children's individuality, and to use common sense. His book *Child Care* became the handbook for the next couple of generations of parents and their children. By 1947, Spock's book had sold 47,000,000 copies worldwide. It became the bible for many young American couples.

But there were even more drastic changes starting to encroach on childhood and families, a direct result of the war. (During the war years, audiences listened to *QK* because they thought it was informative. But it was also reassuring and entertaining, a simple weekly escape from thinking about the war.)

If the kids of *Quiz Kids* exerted a gentle influence on the landscape of popular culture and its vocabulary during the 1940s, World War II gave birth to a profound difference in how many Americans lived on the home front during the war and after, including how they raised their children.

Adding to the familial tensions of the Depression, the war tore families apart. Conscripted fathers had to serve and live at U.S. military bases far from home in the United States or even farther when they served overseas. Many fathers who were not in the military and who worked in well-paid war industry jobs, out of necessity had to live far from home in the cities where they worked. Adding to these difficulties were serious housing shortages in the larger cities.[1] For these men the concept of family life was different than it had been before the war. Increasingly, mothers were away from home too, especially those whose husbands were in the military and had to work full time.

They needed to earn a living to supplement the reduction of family income, so housewives and mothers took jobs that were now available that had been traditionally exclusive to men. They worked on the production line in factories making equipment and materiel for the war. Working long hours, even though they may not have had to move elsewhere, they were away from their homes and children for the greater part of each day.

Often entire families moved to cities where the jobs were, sometimes from one coast to the other. Robert Griswold characterized this time as having several social factors causing serious alarm, many of them stemming from "migration, changing work patterns, hasty marriages, housing shortages, sexual promiscuity, unwanted pregnancies, and rising rates of juvenile delinquency."[2] The culmination of these factors alone was enough to bring about an alteration in the rearing of children.

Absent fathers and nearly absent mothers meant that their youngsters were often at home alone with no adult supervision.[3] With so much unsupervised care, juvenile delinquency became a social ill that was the cause of increasing concern, and perhaps a dire prediction of a future society defined as having no regard for law augmented by a pattern of violent behavior. In New York City, juvenile delinquency arrests in 1943 rocketed to 43 percent over the year before.[4] In other large metropolitan areas the results were similar. Analyzing reports from 318 of the nation's largest cities, J. Edgar Hoover commented on the seriousness of juvenile delinquency. He explained that

23 percent of all persons arrested in those largest cities were under the age of 21.[5] Senator Burton Wheeler was just as fearful as Hoover, predicting that the rise in juvenile delinquency would continue, and with it would come a disintegration of "morale and morals of the boys and girls of this country."[6]

After the war, the housing shortage continued. Six million families were sharing housing by 1947. Family counselors warned of an epidemic of marital crises caused by conflicts between generations living together.[7] Juvenile delinquency worried experts on children. It became a national issue, prompting a congressional investigation during the war at the end of 1943 and carrying over to early 1944.[8]

The consternation about juvenile delinquency and its effect on families and American life continued for years, in newspapers, periodicals, and in discussions on radio. The concern was once the featured point of discussion in a *QK* broadcast. Charles S. Wehrer, superintendent of schools in Wood Lake, Nebraska, was a special guest on the July 11, 1948, broadcast. After Joe Kelly introduced him he spoke about his recent trip to Washington where he had met with U.S. Attorney General Tom C. Clark to talk about ways to combat juvenile delinquency. During his guest appearance on *QK* he asked the Kids how they would cut down on this problem. As well as respecting their intelligence, Wehrer probably asked them because he thought that they represented an ideal childhood, far distanced from the ugliness of juvenile delinquency. Many people viewed the Kids in the same way. Hearing them week after week, or seeing them at their appearances in other cities throughout the United States, reinforced their conclusions that they represented a childhood that was slowly giving way to one that had moved from an idealized, innocent tradition to a street-wise, hardened delinquency.

After 1950 daily life for children didn't appear to be as simple as it had been before the war. The line of demarcation between adults and children was beginning to fade like the end-of-broadcast music cue written into a radio script. Neil Postman concluded that traditional childhood was disappearing at an alarming rate.

He thought that 1950 was the turning point, that childhood was actually obsolete.[9] It had disappeared in its traditional form. He pointed to the growth of television as the reason. Slowly the need for books was disappearing; there was less need to read in order to gather information. Anyone, a 3-year-old or a 63-year-old, could get the same information on television without having to read. Reading and understanding the text at its various levels of complexity had always created a boundary line between children and adults. Television eradicated the line separating childhood from adulthood.[10] For both, it was easier to watch a screen; neither had to think about abstract ideas.

Even with the stimulus of television to prompt the erasing of this invisible line between children and adults, children were asking to step into adolescence and adulthood long before television prompted them. In 1944 Catherine MacKenzie, a noted authority on child rearing, recognized that the perception of children was soon to change. As children started to become older adolescents, she wrote, they wanted "to be independent — to be thought of as grown ups and not treated as children."[11] But John Lewellen, Rachel Stevenson, and Roby Hickok often referred to all of the Quiz Kids as children, no matter what their ages.[12]

Countless articles in the mass media in the 1940s counseled about many of the facets of raising children to become responsible, independent adults. May Reynolds Sherwin saw the danger in not recognizing that their children need to grow into independence, otherwise, they would have grown-up children who were totally dependent on them to make their decisions for them.[13]

Simultaneously, part of the need for feeling grown-up was to savor the "joys of consumerism" and the satisfaction of buying products or services that would enhance their lives.[14] This was perhaps the real reason for how the perception of children changed after the war. At least it was how marketers perceived them.

During the Depression, most children had no money of their own for discretionary spending, even if it was for something that cost a few cents. As finances within families improved during the economic boom of the Forties, parents often gave their children a weekly allowance "ranging from five cents to three dollars." Some got a regular allowance but never knew how much it would be. Others had no such fixed allowance; they got money when they asked for it.[15]

After 1950, as Postman predicted, childhood changed because of the influence of commercial television. The marketers of products for children jumped on this opportunity with a range of products, starting with baby food and diapers, clothing, books, pediatric medicine, and all the while as children grew, toys.

Television programming for children was so powerful and influential that that it changed the toy industry. The allure of television seemed to be greater than radio had been. Manufacturers could aim their products at specific audiences within that growing market. Toys fit into two major categories: toys for boys and girls that were subtle guides for planning for the future, and educational toys for the increasingly child-centered culture that allowed adults to add to the skills that their children were learning in school. Historian Joseph Illick suggests that these categories "essentially turned child's play into work."[16] The field was huge. By the late 1950s the market for toys was $1.25 billion, 15 times the $83 million that consumers spent in 1940.[17]

In these affluent postwar years, as children matured they had more control of money. A combination of increased allowances from their parents and part-time jobs gave them discretionary funds to buy goods and services. Recorded music sold well, especially that aimed at the youth market, and advertisers on radio programs prospered because young people had the money to buy their products. Technological change lowered the cost of record players and radios, taking them out of the realm of being affordable only with adult incomes. In the 1940s only parents could afford to buy radios and phonographs. In the decade after the war the cost of radios and phonographs suddenly became within reach of their children. Elliott West argues that "young America was seizing control of part of the broadcasting and recording market and those industries quickly began to give them what they wanted."[18]

The overall effect of young people becoming consumers led to a dramatic change in popular culture. The postwar abundances led to youthful independence. The values championed by the older generation were becoming less important. Joseph Illick offers this as the reason for "widespread misbehavior and delinquency." Young people composed an "army" that was eager to "seek one another's opinions." They were a group that "challenged the influence of the family." They were a huge market for rock 'n' roll concerts, and of course for the recordings of the musicians who played to them.[19]

We can answer Joe Kelly's unasked question simply. What does it all mean? What's the significance of the program? As we listen to the broadcasts, we can assume any of several arguments on the debating platform about the concept and significance of *Quiz Kids*.

Was the program solely a way to enhance the value of education? There are many examples attested by the show's guests. But these may have been enhanced by John Lewellen's abilities as a persuasive speechwriter if he helped any of them with their on-air speeches about how the Kids represented the "best in the American educational system." Or, were these oral testimonials a way to overcome the disbelief by the show's professional and lay critics about the legitimacy of *QK*?

Perhaps we should define *Quiz Kids* as an argument for achievement of knowledge. Robert Hutchins, president of the University of Chicago, didn't think that the achievements of the Quiz Kids represented real knowledge. He was emphatic when he declared that "unrelated, miscellaneous facts, however odd, quant, or amazing, are not knowledge, in spite of any impression to the contrary given by the Quiz Kids or *Information Please*."[20]

Maybe we should agree with the adult Joel Kupperman's conclusion. He thought that *QK* was a superficial attempt to praise education while exploiting children.[21]

From the 1940s to the 1950s we see the last time that children were "children" (by traditional definition) in the United States. At that time children had little or no opportunity to make economic or social choices. Their parents selected and bought their clothing, provided their meals, and purchased their toys and games. Generally, children did what their parents told them to do, or they followed the social habits of their families.

After 1950 and the emergence of television throughout America, the innocent three-year-olds of the 1940s were on the cusp of being an audience for a vast cornucopia of products. As these tots grew they moved into childhood, preadolescence, and the teenage years with an increasing economic power of their own. In the eyes of energetic marketers, the last time they recognized children in the traditional sense was before television became the dominant in-home medium. After that watershed year, these marketers saw children as a targeted demographic. But when we listen to *Quiz Kids* we don't think of them as a marketer's demographic. We hear an unbridled, pristine innocence; despite their intelligence and command of information, the Kids were still kids. They represented the last time that children were allowed to be children. They still do.

15

Goodbye, Mr. Kelly

☞ *If you could have presented Christopher Columbus with a dog, what kind would have been most appropriate?*

By 1949 when *QK* began its fall season, the end of the radio program was imminent, although none of the ordinary production staff at 8 South Michigan realized it. If they had any apprehension, it was not spoken aloud nor was it widespread.[1] Apparently John and Lou anticipated it when Miles Laboratories withdrew their sponsorship for the summer months. This was the first time that Alka-Seltzer didn't sponsor *QK* during the summer. These two executives would have realized that this was a significant change, something for them to contemplate. The agreement with Miles must have included this annoying breach as a temporary contractual term; it seemed innocent enough, and not unusual. After all, for radio programs to have a 13-week summer "vacation" was an established precedent throughout the broadcasting industry. Still, there were other elements added to this new twist in the relationship with Miles that would have prompted Lou and John's concern.

The Hooper ratings, that closely watched thermometer of broadcasting health, were always near the base of any decision making by sponsors, whether admitted or not. When questioned, sponsors generally attributed any interruption of established sponsorships to a change in product sales or other directions in marketing. Nonetheless, ratings did exert an influence on decision making. By their tenuous nature, ratings were only an indication of interest. It was expected that ratings might move a fraction up or a fraction down each week. In the 1946–47 broadcasting season Hooper listed *QK* as the seventh-highest-rated show among daytime quiz shows broadcast on Saturday or Sunday. It had an 8.3 rating.[2] The following season, 1947–48, was better, more encouraging. *QK* recorded a 9.8 Hooper, making it the fifth highest in its category. But in the 1948–49 season, the Hooper was 6.8, a decline of 31 percent.[3] Evidently Lou and John had no doubts that such a shocking downdraft meant that *QK* was losing its audience.

15. Goodbye, Mr. Kelly

They tried a solution, an aggressive effort to find new Kids, hoping that having new Quiz Kids would be enough to make the show appealing to its audience once again.

The first step was easy. Immediately John arranged for many appearances by the Kids at schools in the Chicago area to try to find new candidates. There was no fanfare or publicity drive announcing this move. It was completely low-key. But as understated as it was, some of the Kids noticed this recruiting drive for what it was. Quiz Kid Patrick Conlon, age 12, did. Fifty-five years later he remembered, "John Lewellen made a distinct effort to visit schools to recruit new Quiz Kids. We put on shows in school auditoriums with the same format as our weekly radio shows." Of course the younger Kids were usually unaware of the business aspect of producing the program. Even the older Kids for the most part did not grasp anything about *QK* other than their own roles as panelists.[4]

The appearances at high schools were a minimal attempt at recruiting. There was a larger plan on the drawing boards. It was the second step, clearly more complicated, in the campaign to win back an audience, and thus to improve the Hooper. Larry Wolters, the radio columnist for the *Chicago Daily Tribune*, broke the story. He thought that *QK* was "branching out," and that Joe Kelly was "converting the program into a road show. He will journey to various cities where bright youngsters will have been selected in advance." What Wolters did not say was that the selection process was not a new idea; it was familiar. George Kamen had started the ball rolling nine years earlier.

There were some palpable differences this time. The current plan had local hopefuls from regional schools competing in contests using the *QK* broadcast format. A final panel was composed of five high scorers who would be on a *QK* network broadcast from their hometown, with Joe Kelly traveling from Chicago to be the Chief Quizzer. Wolters was polite in his spin on the change. He speculated that this new initiative gave the Chicago Kids a chance to "catch up on their studies." The *QK* announcer delivered the commercials on a pickup from Chicago.

At the same time, Wolters announced another chilling little blip to his readers. It was a simple announcement of a corporate decision by Miles. There would be fewer broadcasts with the Chicago Kids. Still, all was not lost. NBC would continue to broadcast *QK* from the Merchandise Mart, but not every week; only at various intervals throughout the season. John and Lou recognized that these little changes could be the foreshadowing of a downslide. It may have been obvious to them, but the warning flags simply weren't visible to the rest of the staff.

The fall season in 1949 began on September 11. The broadcast sounded reasonably familiar, completely self-assured. The format was the same as it had been for the previous 10 years of broadcasting. But there was about to be a notable change. Wolters reported it the next day in his column and it came true almost immediately. On the next broadcast, six days after Wolters described the change, the panel was to be composed of winners from four local contests in four different cities: Elkhart, Indiana; Flint, Michigan; Laurel, Mississippi; and Rochester, Minnesota.[5] There were none of the Chicago Kids on the panel. On this show, broadcast from Chicago, and on any of the shows when Kids from other cities made up the entire panel, there were no scores kept; there was no competition between the Kids to be among the leading three and thus to return the following week. Each participant received a $100 savings bond, just as the regular Chicago Kids did each week on the competitive show.[6] Most likely the reason the out-of-town Kids didn't have to compete in the established format when they came to Chicago was that they had already qualified as winners in their local contests. They had earned their stripes.

There was another variation of this process for the selection of local kids from other cities. Local contests using the *QK* format took place in five different cities in the United States at the same time. The winner from each city traveled to Chicago to appear on a customary network *QK* broadcast from the NBC studios at the Merchandise Mart, with Joe Kelly as the Chief Quizzer. Once more, there were none of the Chicago Kids on the panel.

Wolters was incorrect when he announced that this new travel initiative was Joe's idea. In reality this take-the-show-on-the-road concept was an extended variation of what *QK* had been doing before the war in its efforts to find new Kids, an adaptation of what they did during the war years when they traveled to appear at bond rallies, and a reworking of their continuing travel for appearances at fund-raising benefits after the war was over. Even the premise of finding new Kids from other cities, and thus perhaps expanding the show to be broadcast regionally, had been discussed in 1940.

We can see another underlying goal for this renewed travel schedule. John wanted to search for younger Kids because of the growth of television as the medium of choice in American households. This would explain his search of Chicago schools. It was a quick and handy (and inexpensive) way to find new and younger Kids. Starting in 1949, *QK* was now offered twice a week: once on radio, then, later in the week, on television, with a panel that was not exactly the same as the radio Kids. Some of the Kids were on both, but the television version opened the door to having younger Kids on. (What didn't change was that Joe Kelly was the Chief Quizzer on the television show, too.) Having a television panel composed of a majority of 14- and 15-year-old Quiz Kids was jolting to the widespread perception that they were all precocious little kids. Naturally when they reached their teenage years the Kids were on the verge of adulthood; their bodies had physically matured. The girls developed physically and the boys had deeper voices. Children were reaching puberty younger than ever before due to improved nutrition and health.[7] For the television audience these adolescents bordering on adulthood created a visual disbelief in the name *Quiz Kids*. They almost looked like and sounded like young adults.

The erroneous perception among *QK* listeners, practically from the debut broadcast, was that all the Kids were between five and ten years old. When the Kids traveled during the war, it became apparent to live audiences that some of these charming kids were beyond short pants and pinafores. But it didn't matter during those years. The Kids were still enough of a novelty that audiences ignored the fact that Richard Williams and Harve Fischman were teenagers. It was still exciting for people to be in the audience to witness the performance of these smart Kids. The basic traveling Kids during the war were fairly young. Between December 1943 and January 1946 when the bond drives formally ended, the core travel panel was Ruth Duskin (ages 9–11), Richard Williams (13–15), Joel Kupperman (7–9), and Harve Fischman (13–15). Even though it was an even split between the young Kids and the teenagers, audiences didn't seem to notice.

Comparing the radio shows in the years after 1949 with those of the early 1940s you would probably notice that it appears to be stale, the questions sounded repetitive, and Joe was more lenient with accepting answers. On the April 17, 1949, program some of the questions weren't questions: Joe asked the Kids to perform—to sing or to play musical instruments—quite a difference from Lou's concept for the program in 1940. It's true that from the beginnings of the program Joe would occasionally ask one of the Kids to sing, usually if there had been the name of a song that was the answer to a listener's question. "Can you sing a little of it?" Joe would ask. And sometimes there would be a brief rendition, often off key, sometimes hesitant, but charming nonetheless. But in the 1949 fall season, Joe seemed to ask the Kids to perform musically without any association with a question.

In general, the questions didn't seem to have the sparkle or the difficulty that they had had in the early years.[8] Throughout the years there were sometimes broadcasts when the Kids just weren't answering as many questions as they usually did. The show had a lot of dead air. It started to be boring for listeners; at least that's what the production staff feared. To solve this problem, one of the staff, a "judge," would take away Joe Kelly's question cards and replace them with cards with slightly easier questions for the Kids.[9]

Now, the opposite seemed to be true. The questions were not stimulating. When a program dragged, the staff could always hand a new question card to Joe so that he could add a difficult math question for Joel. Invariably, Joel's solution would rescue a show from mediocrity. Often the audience would be flabbergasted at the math question from Joe Kelly; it would sound almost impossible to understand, as was Kupperman's answer. We hear it on the April 10, 1949, broadcast:

> JOE: A man went into a bank to cash a check. The teller made a mistake and transposed the amount: giving him in dollars what the check called for in cents, and in cents what the check called for in dollars. After spending $3.50 he still had left [remaining] twice the original amount of the check. How much was the check made out for?
>
> JOEL: In the original check, let D [stand for] dollars, and C for the cents. So now you have two equations. The first is 2C + 50 = D. But you know C is more than D, so you borrow 100 and you get C + 50 = D + 100 or D = 2C-50. The other equation is 2D + 3 would equal 2C. But [actually] C-1 because you borrowed. And 2 D's = C-4 and D = 2C-50, so you're getting both equations for 2D. And 2D = 4C-100 and C-4. So 4C-100 = C-4. 3C = 96, and C = 32. Since 2D = C-4, D is one-half of 28, or 14. So the original check is $14.32.

Joel arrived at the answer in 1 minute, 9 seconds.

In the summer of 1949 *QK* was a sustaining program. As far as Alka-Seltzer was concerned, *QK* was on vacation, or in the language of broadcasting, on hiatus. That season's schedule was planned around the standard 39-week season, followed by a 13-week summer pause. Before that summer, *QK* had been on continuously with Alka-Seltzer since 1940. Miles did not sponsor the 13 weeks between the end of May and the beginning of September 1949. Lou ran the show anyway; his company paid all the expenses. The same summer schedule was true in 1950. As might be expected, the theme of the June 25, 1950, broadcast was the tenth anniversary of *QK*. Joe's first question set the tone:

> JOE: Why would the Woodman in *The Wizard of Oz* be an appropriate guest on this particular program today?
>
> SALLY ANN WILHELM: Because the Woodman was the Tin Man and tin is the gift a husband gives his wife on their tenth [wedding] anniversary.

It didn't matter that the program had changed. The Kids hadn't. They were still ebullient and upbeat, funny and wise, serious and knowledgeable. As if to recount their accomplishments in a verbal résumé on that tenth anniversary broadcast, John, conceivably with Lou's input, had prepared Joe's script carefully. It was a recitation of some of the interesting statistics about the program since its debut broadcast. Joe announced with great pride that since June 28, 1940, there had been 372 different Quiz Kids. The Chief Quizzer had asked the Kids 6,108 questions from listeners; they answered 5,437 correctly. Proudly, Joe defined what that meant. The Kids had answered correctly 89 percent of the questions, maintaining the percentage of correct answers that Joe had reported in 1941. Even more startling, the program had received 3,417,600 letters from its premiere in 1940 to its tenth anniversary in June 1950.[10] This recounting of statistics was perhaps a plea for Miles to continue their sponsorship. Perhaps it was a blatant attempt at attracting other sponsors to jump in with offers to support the show. Still, the Hooper continued to drop. For the 1949–50 season it was 6.5, not as great a drop as the previous year's 31 percent drop, but still heading downward.[11]

Once again the catch-penny expansion came to mind, but with no objections from NBC, as there were in 1941 when Jules Herbuveaux complained to Sidney Strotz. This time Joe Kelly stated the concept loud and clear as a positive force for change, as he promoted the idea. On the January 23, 1949, broadcast he cited several local sponsors who had *QK*-style programs on their hometown stations "just like our big nationwide *Quiz Kids* program."

He named five such programs: on WRAA in Williamsport, Pennsylvania, sponsored by Lundy's Paint and Wallpaper store; WTAP, Flint, Michigan, sponsored by Merchants and Mechanic Bank; WJBO, Baton Rouge, Louisiana, sponsored by Jack's Cookie Company; WTRC, Elkhart, Indiana, sponsored by the local First National Bank; and KOA, Denver, sustaining. Joe made a pitch to get more of them to join the campaign. He announced, "More and more of these local programs are getting underway" at NBC stations all across the country. He outlined the format and the sponsorship. At the same time he announced that the local weekly programs "are broadcast with competition among children selected from the schools in their own city in cooperation with school officials and teachers." The local programs would have their own Chief Quizzer. He said that the programs already being broadcast "tell us that their communities and school systems are wholeheartedly in support of this idea and fully appreciate the splendid contribution these local Quiz Kids programs make to education." Making a direct call for action, Joe concluded by telling listeners that if they wanted further information about how to sponsor a local Quiz Kids program, they should contact their local NBC station.[12]

To the home audience there appeared to be no difference in the program during the summer hiatus in 1949 when *QK* was a "sustainer," aside from no mention of Alka-Seltzer. But there was a clue. True to form, Joe identified the names of listeners who had submitted questions. One of them he identified as "Eliza Merrill of Denver, Colorado." This appears to be a fake name; Eliza Merrill Hickok was Roby![13] (Roby had left the staff two years earlier. She moved back to Cedar Rapids, where she married and lived for the rest of her life.) If John fabricated the name Eliza Merrill, then perhaps he created other names, too, and he and his staff wrote the questions they "submitted."

The program now seemed to be foundering. Perhaps no one on the production staff, including John, grasped another ancillary but significant change. Parker Brothers discontinued the "Quiz Kids Own Game Box" because of the decline in sales of the game. At the end of March 1951, once again Miles Laboratories dropped its sponsorship until after the summer. John did not attempt to keep the show on continuously. *QK* was off the air for nearly two months. It returned May 13, 1951, as a sustaining program.

One major difference between this iteration of the program starting in May and the sponsored programs of the previous months was that there were no requests for listeners to submit questions, and of course, no Zenith radios awarded for questions used or missed as before.[14] Now there was no identification of the listeners who submitted questions, suggesting that the staff had indeed created the questions or perhaps had they pulled them from the files of unused questions from the previous ten years. On sustaining broadcasts, at least for that summer, the Kids still received the usual $100 bond as they did during sponsored shows.

A major change occurred when Joe Kelly went on sick leave; he had suffered another heart attack. His replacement was Fran Allison, an experienced radio and television personality who played "Aunt Fanny" on Don McNeil's always popular morning show, *Breakfast Club*. She was also the "Fran" of the famous television program for children, *Kukla, Fran, and Ollie*. She was the Chief Quizzer until the broadcast of June 24, except for May 27 and June 3, when Oliver Capelle, promotions manager at Miles Laboratories, substituted for her. Capelle took over as Chief Quizzer from July 1 though August 19. Joe Kelly returned for the August 26 broadcast to assume once again his originating role of Chief Quizzer.

Even with the attempts to bump up ratings, the Hooper dropped once again, sinking to 4.0, down another 38 percent from 1949 to 1950.[15] The handwriting was on the wall.

By September 1951, Miles decided to drop its sponsorship. Usually a poor rating was the superficial reason given for a program to go off the air, and thereafter pundits debated the causes for audience disinterest. There is nothing certain about why an audience defects and sponsors usually don't spend time or money to find the answer. Social scientists might argue that changing tastes in the marketplace are the cause: the need for a "faster" social environment compared with its prewar tempo, or the more sophisticated viewpoint of returning war veterans, resulting from their exposure to other cultures. (*Quiz Kids* seemed old fashioned.) Perhaps the change in music is a clue. The faster tempos of bebop rather than the more sedate rhythms of prewar big band swing fit in more with the preferences of young adults living in an up-tempo social environment. Or it could be as simple as the emergence of quiz programs that offered larger monetary prizes. The audience of young adults was desired by advertisers, no matter what products or services they were promoting on the air.

But the reason given for this decision by Miles to drop its sponsorship was astounding, naïve, and unusual. It was as if *Quiz Kids* with its low Hooper was giving Alka-Seltzer a headache, and the public explanation for canceling was an attempt to mask the pain. "Strangely enough," reported Larry Wolters, "the sponsor is dropping them because their selling job was so successful." Rachel Stevenson saw it differently. It sounded incredible, but she said that the reason the program was going off the air was because "the sponsor felt that people were so familiar with Alka-Seltzer they [Miles Laboratories] didn't need to advertise it anymore."[16]

Miles claimed that they had saturated the *QK* audience with its products and that the only way they could expand sales via radio or television was with a new program. September 23, 1951, was to be the last broadcast for the *QK* radio program. Miles decided to switch its sponsorship to a television program, *One Man's Family*. That program would be on NBC's television network on alternate weeks.[17]

If the reason offered by Miles sounded superficial, there was some precedence for it. In 1946, five years earlier, C.E. Hooper, head of the Hooper ratings agency, identified a change in how stations viewed ratings and thus how advertisers chose to buy the programs they wanted to sponsor. He concluded that stations "have learned that time is no longer being bought and sold. Today it is audiences."[18]

Suddenly, without public explanation, Miles gave *QK* a two-week extension, until October 6. It had been a long run with Alka-Seltzer; 11 years and 4 months.

☞ *You already know that the battle of Bunker Hill was fought in the American Revolution. Do you know who won the battle?*

Notwithstanding the departure of Alka-Seltzer as their sponsor, *Quiz Kids* had already become part of contemporary American English as well as the language of popular culture, either by reference or as a metaphor for intelligent children. The term "quiz kid" meant anyone who "had all the answers."[19] Lou had designed some publicity early on to increase awareness of the program and to keep the ball rolling. When the Kids were in Los Angeles for their appearances on the Jack Benny program in the spring of 1941, Lou was able to get a favorable mention about *QK* written into the scripts for at least five feature films.[20]

But there is no list of the five films, and no systematic way to find those with Lou's plugs. A fortuitous viewing of one of them reveals that the mention — the "plug" — was not at all subtle. In the Gene Autry film *Heart of the*

Rio Grande, released on March 11, 1942, Autry is the manager of the fictional Smoke River Ranch, a dude ranch. Smiley Burnette is his sidekick, in his usual role offering comic relief to Autry's no-nonsense demeanor. A group of schoolgirls from an elite boarding school in a large metropolitan city, probably meant to be Chicago, comes to the ranch for their summer vacation. Autry asks Burnette to take the girls on a tour of the ranch. The following scene takes place in a barn, a Hollywood version of a barn, a crude outbuilding that the film's art director decorated with a few bales of straw and the obligatory tackle hanging from hooks and nails on 4 × 4 beams. Smiley shows them various pieces of farm equipment. "Over here," he observes in his trademark squeaky voice, "is a harvester. Does anyone know what a harvester is?" One of the girls says, "It was invented by Cyrus McCormack in 1841." "Are you sure you aren't one of those Quiz Kids?" the incredulous Burnette asks.[21] This plug was probably an easy placement for Lou, with help from Joe Kelly's influence with both stars. Before Lou created *QK*, the *National Barn Dance* with Joe Kelly featured Autry and Burnette frequently in the late 1930s.

An advertisement for Liggett's in Boston in September 1941 sold several back-to-school items: fountain pens for 49 cents, pen points, 12 for 10 cents, erasers for 5 cents, a 10-inch slide rule for 25 cents, and a pencil sharpener for 49 cents. The ad featured a small ad within the ad. It was a *Webster's Dictionary* for 98 cents with a copywriter's terse admonition suggesting the need for school children to be organized. "An apple for the teacher?" the ad asked and cautioned, "Better be like the Quiz Kids, prepared with information."[22]

One newspaper columnist, "staggered" by the new income tax forms, wondered if it would not be wise "to hire a quiz kid to fill them out."[23] In general, people applied the label Quiz Kid(s) to adults who had detailed knowledge of a variety of subjects.

The *Chicago Tribune* announced that *The Human Adventure*, a radio program broadcast with the cooperation of the University of Chicago, would have as its theme the growth of a baby on one weekly broadcast. The program would be in a dramatic format, based on research by Dr. Arnold Gesell, a psychologist and pediatrician who specialized in child development. The article said that because radio studios "don't ordinarily admit children under 6 (unless they are Quiz Kids)" one of the actors, Nannette Sargent, would "gurgle, laugh, cry and otherwise speak for the baby."[24]

With an outcry for academic reform, a newspaper column written in a comic deadpan suggested that the faculty of lexicographers at the University of Chicago prepare a shortened English language dictionary, no larger than a pocket volume of a detective story, and handy for use by "prodigies seeking the bachelor's degree at the age of 16." This would be part of the restructuring of the university to eliminate anything that was antiquated — the Phi Beta

Kappa key from professors' watch chains, the Gothic ornaments on buildings, the scrub oak trees on the campus — in short, "let them establish a brave new world with nothing older in it than a high school quiz kid."[25]

Reference to the Kids emerged on the front lines during the war. The army's 394th Regiment's Intelligence and Reconnaissance platoon was sprinkled with men from college programs who were assigned to replenish the badly depleted ranks in Europe during the winter of 1944. During their training at Camp Maxey, Texas, in the sweltering heat of July, these well educated men were disdainfully called Quiz Kids. But in fact, they were as "physically adept as they were academically proficient."[26] In December the platoon was sent to the village of Lanzerath, Belgium. The platoon was just 18 men. On December 16, the first day of the huge counter-offense — the now-famous Battle of the Bulge — they confronted 500 German troops advancing through Lanzerath. The Americans held them off but finally ran out of ammunition and had to surrender. Only one American was killed; 14 were wounded. There were 92 German casualties.[27] The captured "Quiz Kids" platoon was split up and the soldiers sent to various POW camps. Recognizing their heroism and perhaps their value as public relations, General Eisenhower sent six of the "Quiz Kids" home on June 17, 1945. Usually returning troops traveled by ship. This special group flew along with Eisenhower, his plane escorted by 100 bombers and fighter planes. Upon arrival in Washington, D.C., they were greeted in a "triumphant welcome," including 20 marching bands and throngs of government workers who were given a partial holiday to line the parade route from National Airport into the city.[28]

By the mid–1940s, dating among high school students was a widely accepted aspect of social life. American social and cultural habits had changed after the war, and social critics recognized that teenage dating was a relevant step toward fostering mature habits in young adults. Newspaper columnist Sheila John Daly referred to the Kids in one of her articles about dating written for teenage girls. She emphasized the importance of cleanliness — hair, fingernails, teeth, skin — to give the attractive, healthy appearance of a fashion model, because "even though a gal may have the brains of a Quiz Kid," it took good grooming to make her charm complete.[29]

Writing about George Sand, the 19th-century French author, newspaper columnist Vincent Starrett described one outstanding incident in her passionate life. She cut off her long hair and sent it to Alfred de Musset, a poet with whom she had an affair, in an attempt to heal a breach in their relationship. Starrett observed that the dramatic incident of the shorn locks has appeared frequently in life and in literature, and that "any quiz kid could name two further variations on the theme."[30]

In 1949, Gerald Taft of Northville, Michigan, bought a stallion for breeding from the Morgan Horse Farm near the University of Vermont. It was a tall horse, named Quizkid. Did the farm name it because it was smarter than any of the others in the stable? Could it solve complex math problems by tapping its hoof the requisite number of times? Could it recite all of the Kentucky Derby winners since 1875? No, the farm used its traditional method, based on the alphabet, to name the horse. Marin J. Melchior, a Morgan Farm staff member, reported that each year the farm selected a different letter in alphabetic sequence to name each horse born at the farm during the 12 months of any calendar year, and "once they used it, they could not repeat it." The year Quizkid was born was a "Q" year. Because there are not many proper names beginning with that letter, someone on the staff probably decided on Quizkid because of the popularity of *Quiz Kids*. Quizkid has remained on the chronological list of the names they used for horses in past years. To this day, the farm has not used that name again.[31]

J.D. Salinger used the Quiz Kids as the inspiration for creating the siblings of the Glass family in *Franny and Zooey*. The Glass siblings had all appeared on "*It's a Wise Child*," Salinger's fictional *QK* radio program.

In another literary reference, Russell Maloney, writing in the *New York Times* about American humor, thought that were only three noteworthy humorists at that time: Mark Twain, James Thurber, and S.J. Perelman. In his opinion "from a distance of fifty years, the only recognizable figure" was that of Twain. Maloney believed that "in the immediate foreground the biggest figures seem to be those of James Thurber and S.J. Perelman." He thought Thurber was a profound pessimist and a meticulous stylist, "as much a creature of his period in history as are the Quiz Kids."[32]

A contrarian reference came from *It Pays to Be Ignorant*, another network radio program in the Forties that was an anti-intellectual send-up of the esteemed *Quiz Kids* (and *Information Please*). This satirical show featured "a board of experts who are dumber than you are and can prove it." The show gave the panelists, three well-seasoned veterans of vaudeville, comedy film shorts, Broadway musical comedies and revues, an opportunity to make outrageous jokes ("Do married men live longer than single men? No, it only seems longer."). The panel also responded to questions with obvious answers ("How long does it take a ship to make a five-day journey?"). They invariably gave the wrong answer, providing another opportunity for them to offer more funny comments when they gave hilarious rationales for their replies.[33]

Woody Allen's film *Radio Days* offers a clear reference to *QK* in one brief scene. Woody Allen's voiceover narration sets the scene by saying that the only radio celebrity the family had ever met was "a 14-year-old mathematical genius of a quiz show my father loved, called 'The Whiz Kids.'" As Allen wrote the scene, one day he and his parents were visiting the zoo and his father noticed a family standing next to them, just as they were, a man and wife and their son. But he also noticed that the boy was a radio personality, a "Whiz Kid."[34] Clearly the Kid serves as an allusion to Joel Kupperman, one of the two *QK* math experts. (The other was Richard Williams.) It is more of a depiction of the importance of radio in those times than a documentary portrait of Kupperman or Williams. There is no doubt that Allen's most enduring memory of *QK* is Kupperman. The first thing many people remember about the program is Kupperman.[35] Allen's Kid is patronizing and condescending. But these were not traits acceptable to John Lewellen or Lou Cowan, nor were they generally characteristic of the real Quiz Kids.

More than just part of the language of popular culture in its time, *QK* has remained a lexicographer's reference. *Webster's New Collegiate Dictionary* defines the words "whiz kid" as a person who is unusually intelligent, clever, or successful especially at an early age. But it clearly states that the words and their definition are an "alteration of *Quiz Kid*, a member of a former popular quiz show."[36] It is a unique definition in American popular culture. No other standard general dictionary cites a radio program or performer in the etymology of a word.

Even now, decades after *QK* has gone off the air, its format continues to have an easy appeal. In 1961, Sophie Altman, a Washington-based mother of four, produced *It's Academic*, a weekly television quiz program that was a near-duplication of *QK*, with a panel of students from Washington-area high schools. Altman is now deceased, but the program is still on the air with contemporary producers and quizmasters. It is the longest-running television quiz show on air. *It's Academic* emanates from Washington, D.C., to the region surrounding it. There is a program in Charlottesville, no doubt influenced by the proximity to the University of Virginia, with the same name. Similar adaptations are in several cities in secondary markets, sometimes under different names, but all with the format of the Washington show.[37]

More recent was an attempt to create a television quiz show in January 2010 that almost sounds as if it came from Lou Cowan's fertile mind: *Our Little Genius*. The *New York Times* announced its debut on Fox a week before its scheduled debut. The producers, Mark Burnett and Mike Darnell, thought that children have a "remarkable ability to obsess about the most detailed subjects: train timetables, species of dinosaurs, the names of 18 different dolls and their imaginary occupations." Burnett and Darnell conceived the program to give "children 6 to 12 a chance 'to put their incredible knowledge to the test.'" Explaining in detail, Burnett said, "So much light is shined on gymnasts, football players, singers and actors. It's not often that you get a light shined on academics." The comparison with Lou's original concept and *QK* ended there because the prizes were so different. *Our Little Genius* was offering thousands of dollars to the contestants with the correct answers. The show's questions increased in difficulty over ten levels. The lowest and easiest level was worth $1,000, the highest was $500,000. Inevitably, the issue of whether $500,000 would put an unhealthy amount of pressure on these preteens bothered some clinical psychologists and behavioral experts.[38]

The Federal Communications Commission had other concerns. One of the parents of a child who was recruited for the program sent a letter to the commission alleging that a few days before a planned taping, a member of the *Our Little Genius* production staff reviewed a list of potential topics and "gave the answers to at least four questions that the child either did not know or about which he was unsure." Fox withdrew the program six days before its debut. It was the same issue that was behind the quiz show scandals of the late 1950s. The producers of those 1950s quiz programs simply ignored Section 508 of the Communications Act of 1934 which "makes it illegal for anyone to give, with the intent to deceive the viewing or listening public, assistance that will affect the outcome of a 'purportedly bona fide contest of intellectual knowledge or intellectual skill.'"[39]

With the exception of the amount of the prizes offered to the children, the reasoning and format of *Our Little Genius* were almost identical to Lou's reasoning in 1940 that gifted children could display the evidence of their precocity using their extraordinary intelligence rather than singing or tap dancing or playing a musical instrument.

☞ *Four of the mountain ranges making up the Appalachian Mountains have the name of a color. Can you name them?*

In October 1951 when Miles Labs withdrew their support, Lou believed that he would find a new sponsor. He reported that other networks were bidding for the program, and that there was little likelihood that the radio or television programs would be off the air for long, if at all. But Lou was too optimistic. *QK* radio went off the air for nearly a year. In September 1952 it was back on CBS as a sustaining program, but only for five weeks. It was back on air in November 1952 as a sustaining program until March 1, 1953. The program went off the air again on that date, but came back on the last day of May 1953, still sustaining, and as a weekly broadcast as usual. Evidently Lou remained convinced that he could sell it. But no prospective sponsor was interested enough to sign a contract.

The July 5, 1953, broadcast was the 598th, 13 years and one week since the debut on June 28, 1940. After the customary eight bars of "School Days," Joe most likely opened the program with, "Hello, everyone. This is your old Chief Quizzer himself, Joe Kelly, presenting America's famous Quiz Kids." There is no recording of that broadcast available, but on other sustaining broadcasts, Joe had taken on the announcer's job. If the questions that he asked the Kids that day were true to the established format, John had written them to reflect the Independence Day holiday: the Founding Fathers, the Revolution, and the Declaration of Independence, usually topics in which the Kids would excel. No doubt this was a bouncy, upbeat show as the 597 previous broadcasts had been. The Kids would be boisterous, still vocal and excited about sharing their knowledge, proving to America that they knew the answers.

Aside from all of that, this broadcast was different. At the end of the program, after the Kids voiced the final "Goodbye, Mr. Kelly," *Quiz Kids* was off the air; this was the last broadcast. After 20 months of on again and off again, the death was quick and clean, a perfect cut from an executioner's axe. There were no post-mortems about the end of the program by media analysts after this broadcast. None of the Chicago newspapers, national news magazines, show business periodicals, trade papers, or entertainment columnists covered it, commented on it, or discussed it. Simply, it was over. The smartest kids in America were silent.

ANSWERS

A Newfoundland. (Richard Weixler, age 7, answered this. It is an example of his love of language and puns, even at that age. Joe Kelly, on hearing his answer, explained the pun to the audience: "A new-found land! That's right! Good boy, Richard.")

The British won, but not until the Americans had run out of ammunition. The British casualties were 1,054 out of 3,500 men engaged. The American loss was 441.

The Blue Ridge, Green, White, and Black Mountains.

Appendix A:
Questions and Answers

These questions were asked on *Quiz Kids*. Some of them I heard on the digitized broadcasts; others come from shows that are not available to hear but were reported in magazines and newspaper columns in articles about the Kids. When you add these questions to those used in the chapters, there is a total of 100.

The questions used on the program were diverse, testing the Kids in mathematics, algebra, geometry, history, current political and cultural events, music, literature, fine arts, performing arts, mythology, economics, logic and reasoning. The answers are at the end of this section.

QUESTIONS

1. Identify the Iron Chancellor and the Iron Duke.
2. In what light opera, filmed as a movie, is a monarch concerned with "making the punishment fit the crime?"
3. What birds are used as symbols of (a) a curse; (b) vanity; (c) self-delusion?
4. Certain emotions are associated with colors. For example, we say "purple with rage." Now suppose you mixed the color of cowardice with the color of unhappiness, what color and what emotion would result?
5. Name the well-known choruses that are sung in the following operas: (a) *Faust*, by Gounod; (b) *Tannhäuser*, by Wagner; (c) Il *Trovatore*, by Verdi.
6. Who won the battle of Valley Forge in the winter of 1777-78?
7. What is an anatomical juxtaposition of two orbicular muscles in the state of contraction?
8. Which star in the flag of the United States of America represents the state of New York?
9. Three prisoners were before the bar: (a) the first was acquitted; (b) the second was absolved; (c) the third was exonerated. What happened to each?

10. The state of Virginia was named in honor of Elizabeth, the "virgin queen." What two states were named after kings?
11. Though you know nothing else about the occupation, you should know that when a shoemaker is about to make a boot, the first thing he uses is the _____.
12. The Gadsden Purchase was: (a) Ratified in what year? (b) Now a part of what state? (c) Purchased from whom?
13. If you were very thirsty, how many glasses of water could you drink on an entirely empty stomach?
14. Which of the many instruments in a symphony orchestra is used to give the pitch?
15. When burying a bone, why does a dog dig the earth with his paws, but replace it with his nose?
16. The name of what kind of postage stamp, pronounced in reverse, suggests what thing that England has not had since the coronation of its last king?
17. Bought is the past participle of buy; of what is the word "wrought" the past participle?
18. Why is a small pocket knife called a penknife?
19. Name the poem and the author of the poem from which the following first lines are taken: (a) "The curfew tolls the knell of parting day"; (b) "Sunset and evening star, and one clear call for me."
20. Define the following: (a) heliometer; (b) galvanometer; (c) anemometer.
21. United States senators are designated as "senior" and "junior" but are not fathers and sons. On what basis are they so designated?
22. You know the tongue twister about how much wood would a woodpecker peck if a woodpecker would peck wood. Can you give two reasons why the woodpecker pecks on wood?
23. The combined ages of Mary and Ann are 44 years. Mary is twice as old as Ann was when Mary was half as old as Ann will be when Ann is three times as old as Mary was when Mary was three times as old as Ann. How old are Mary and Ann?
24. A pun is supposed to be the lowest form of wit. Can you define a pundit?
25. If a document is signed John Doe et ux, and another signed John Doe et al., what is meant?
26. Would you be apt to have a copy of *Adam Bede* by Mary Ann Evans on your library shelf?
27. "Faint heart ne'er won fair lady" is a saying that might easily be associated with St. Valentine's Day. Can you think of the special days of celebration that might be associated with the following quotations: (a) Boys will be boys; (b) Where there is smoke there is always fire; (c) A bird in the hand is worth two in the bush.
28. Men of many countries have enlisted in World War II on the side of the allies. Name a Pole, a German, and a Prussian who fought for the colonists during the American Revolution.
29. A pilot flying an airplane that can fly around the world in 24 hours leaves New York at noon. What time is it when he flies over China?
30. If you had a stepsister and a half-sister, how would each be related to you?
31. A man living close to the northern border of the panhandle of Texas wishes to take his family to see the state capital. But on examining his map, he finds that he is closer to six other state capitals than his own. Can you name four of them?
32. If you were to take a space ship to the planet Pluto, what other planets might you wave to as you passed? Try to name them in the order in which you passed them, if possible.
33. What two members of the president's cabinet do not have titles beginning with "secretary of?"
34. Characters who go under an alias are generally regarded with suspicion, but these three are famous characters of fiction. Can you give their proper names?

35. If you are the pilot of an airplane cruising at 120 miles per hour for a period of three hours and the copilot is 24, how old is the pilot?
36. What reptile might be preferred by (a) a bookkeeper; (b) a baby; (c) an Indian?
37. A four-letter word meaning a small particle can be revised and defined as: (a) a separate piece of news; (b) to send forth; (c) a definite portion of duration. What is the word?
38. Here's a mathematical fact you might like to try on one of your friends, even though you might not know it now: What digit can be multiplied by any number up to ten, and the sum, added, will always be itself?
39. Residents of the state capital of Nebraska helped immortalize the name Lincoln when they named their city. Name the other three state capitals named after other United States presidents.
40. Identify the Shakespearean play in which you find each of these quotations about rain: (a) "It droppeth as the gentle rain from heaven"; (b) "When shall we three meet again, in thunder, lightning, or in rain?"; (c) "Is there not rain enough in the sweet heavens to wash it white as snow?"
41. Suppose there are five glasses of water and a plate of stuffed olives sitting in front of you. You eat one olive after drinking the first glass of water, two more olives after the second glass, etc., doubling the number of olives after each glass. When you've had five drinks and five helpings of olives, how many olive pits do you have?
42. If a chain is 20 feet long and each of its 80 links will hold 8½ pounds, how many pounds will the whole chain hold?
43. At one point in his travels described in *The Tramp Abroad*, why did Mark Twain boil a thermometer?
44. Before you stands a glass of water filled to the brim. Floating in it are two cubes of ice protruding above the rim of the glass. Will the water run over when the ice melts?
45. Would a steel ball fall faster through water at 20 degrees temperature, or water at 60 degrees temperature?
46. To become president of the United States, you must fulfill four requirements: you must be a native-born U.S. citizen, must be at least 35 years old, and must have lived in this country for at least 14 years. What is the fourth requirement?
47. What is the only four-letter word in the English language ending in "-eny"? (Answer within five seconds.)
48. When did the American flag have the largest number of stripes?
49. In what kind of store would you expect to find, as part of the regular stock, an adjutant, a rail, and a long-legged secretary?
50. If a salesman offered to sell you a houseboat on the River Styx, why would you call the prosecuting attorney?
51. Why didn't these pairs of famous operatic lovers ever marry? (a) Mario Cavaradossi and Floria Tosca; (b) Don José and Carmen; (c) Tannhäuser and Elisabeth.
52. What mileage would your odometer show if you drove from Fort Nassau to Fort Orange to Albany, N.Y.?
53. If you were traveling from the direction of the Boreas winds and wished to face into the Zephyr breezes, would you make a right or left turn?
54. Suppose you are an organist and wish to play a melody describing an ocean voyage. Would you play it: (a) sforzando, (b) tremolo, (c) unda maris?
55. If you flew directly south from Chicago to the Equator, would you land on the Pacific Ocean, South America, or Panama?
56. At least five of Shakespeare's plays have a character named "Antonio." Name three of them.
57. You may be penny-wise but can you define pennyroyal and pennywort?

APPENDIX A

ANSWERS

1. The Iron Chancellor was Otto von Bismarck, a German statesman. The Iron Duke was the Duke of Wellington, commander of the British forces at the Battle of Waterloo.
2. *The Mikado*, by Gilbert and Sullivan.
3. (a) Albatross; (b) peacock; (c) ostrich.
4. Yellow mixed with blue makes green. We say, "Green with envy."
5. (a) "Soldiers' Chorus; (b) "Pilgrims' Chorus; (c) "Anvil Chorus.
6. There was no actual battle. Washington's half-starved, freezing army was trying to keep itself alive, while the British luxuriated in Philadelphia in complete inactivity.
7. A kiss.
8. No star represents any particular state in the Union.
9. (a) Discharged because of inability to establish his guilt; (b) forgiven; (c) discharged as his innocence was proved.
10. Georgia was so called in honor of King George II of England. Louisiana was so called in honor of King Louis XIV of France.
11. The first thing he uses is the last.
12. (a) 1854; (b) Arizona; (c) Mexico.
13. Only one—after one has been drunk, the stomach is no longer empty.
14. The oboe—a flute-like wind instrument.
15. His paws operate only one way, he can't make them push the earth back.
16. The answer is "air mail," which in reverse makes "male heir." (When Joe Kelly asked this question on the November 21, 1948, *QK* broadcast, this answer was correct. It would not be today. George VI, whose reign began in 1936, only had two daughters, Elizabeth and Margaret. There was no male heir until 1952, when Elizabeth II acceded to the crown and her son, Charles, age three, became heir apparent.)
17. Wrought is the past participle of "work."
18. Its original use was for sharpening quill pens.
19. (a) "Elegy Written in a Country Churchyard," by Thomas Gray; (b) "Crossing the Bar," by Alfred, Lord Tennyson.
20. (a) A heliometer is an instrument for measuring small angles in the heavens; (b) a galvanometer is an instrument for detecting the presence of and ascertaining the force and direction of an electric current; (c) an anemometer is an instrument for measuring the wind's velocity.
21. Senior United States senator refers to the one elected first in each state, junior to the one elected last.
22. (a) To get his food, which is the larva of moths and beetles found in the wood; (b) To make his nest. Woodpeckers make a deep hole in a decaying tree or post.
23. Mary is 27½; Ann is 16½. (This question was submitted to Joel Kupperman by a staff member at *Encyclopedia Britannica*. *Britannica* employees and several engineers could not solve the problem and eventually gave up after long periods of trying to solve it. Joel answered it correctly in ten minutes.)
24. A pundit is very different from a pun; it is a term used to describe a very learned man.
25. John Doe et ux means John Doe and wife, John Doe et al. means John Doe and others.
26. No. Mary Ann Evans signed all her works as George Eliot.
27. (a) Halloween; (b) Fourth of July (Independence Day); (c) Thanksgiving Day.

28. Tadeusz Kosciuszko — Polish; Baron de Kalb — German; Baron Von Steuben — Prussian.
29. It would be noon, for the pilot would travel westward with the hour.
30. The stepsister would not be related to you, but would be your stepmother or stepfather's child by another marriage. Your half-sister would be related to you through either your father or mother, being one of their children by the present marriage.
31. His own state capital is in Austin, Texas (500 miles away). Closer to him are Oklahoma City, Oklahoma (225 miles); Santa Fe, New Mexico (250 miles); Denver, Colorado (300 miles); Cheyenne, Wyoming (385 miles); Topeka, Kansas (385 miles); and Denver, Colorado (400 miles).
32. Mars and Jupiter, Saturn, Uranus, and Neptune.
33. Attorney general and postmaster general.
34. (a) Edmund Dantes, (b) Phillip Noland, (c) Quasimodo.
35. Tell us your age and you'll have the answer.
36. (a) Adder; (b) rattlesnake; (c) moccasin.
37. The word is mite: (a) item; (b) emit; (c) time.
38. The number is 9. Example: Nine times 2 equals 18. One and 8 equals 9.
39. Jefferson City, Missouri; Madison, Wisconsin; Jackson, Mississippi.
40. (a) *The Merchant of Venice*; (b) *Macbeth*; (c) *Hamlet*.
41. None. The olives were stuffed.
42. The chain will hold 8½ pounds. (A chain is as strong as its weakest link, remember?)
43. He wanted to know the altitude. The boiling point of water goes down 2 degrees with every 1,100 feet of rise in altitude.
44. No. Water expands when frozen into ice and ice contracts when melting into water. (The Kids missed this.)
45. 60 degrees. Water at 20 degrees would be ice.
46. You must be elected.
47. Deny. (This question was also asked of 100 college students and 150 salesmen, who between them yielded only one correct answer. But a Quiz Kid got it at once.)
48. The flag had 15 stripes from 1795 to 1818, when the number was reduced to 13 by an act of Congress.
49. In a pet store. All three are birds, the last one being the snake-eating secretary bird.
50. The salesman would be a swindler, because the Styx is a mythical stream across which Charon ferried the souls of the dead.
51. (a) Mario Cavaradossi was arrested and shot as an enemy of the government, and Tosca committed suicide. Opera: *Tosca*, by Giacomo Puccini.
    (b) Don José was arrested for helping Carmen escape. By the time he was out of jail, fickle Carmen was in love with a toreador. José killed Carmen in the arena. Opera: *Carmen*, by George Bizet.
    (c) Tannhäuser was banned by the pope for living in Venus-Hill. He sought mercy in Rome, but the pope refused him absolution and Elisabeth died of a broken heart. Opera: *Tannhäuser*, by Richard Wagner.
52. None. Fort Nassau and Fort Orange are former names for Albany, N.Y.
53. A right turn. (Coming from the north winds and turning west into the west winds.)
54. Unda maris. (An organ stop meaning "wave of the sea.")
55. The Pacific Ocean.
56. *The Tempest, The Two Gentlemen of Verona, Much Ado About Nothing, The Merchant of Venice, Twelfth Night.*
57. Pennyroyal is a fragrant herb of the mint family. Pennywort is a plant of marsh herbs of the parsley family.

Appendix B:
The Quiz Kids,
Programs and Guests

Demo. 6/12/40. *Kids:* Joan Bishop, Cynthia Cline, Gerard Darrow, Van Dyke Tiers. *Notable Guest/Notes:* **Clifton Utley** audition, not broadcast

1. 6/28/40. *Kids:* Mary Ann Anderson, Joan Bishop, Gerard Darrow, Charles Schwartz, Van Dyke Tiers. *Notable Guest/Notes:* Dr. Harold Swenson, University of Chicago

2. 7/5/40. *Kids:* Mary Ann Anderson, Lois Ashbeck, George Coklas, Gerard Darrow, Van Dyke Tiers

3. 7/12/40. *Kids:* Joan Alizier, Lois Ashbeck, Cynthia Cline, Gerard Darrow, Van Dyke Tiers. *Notable Guest/Notes:* John Richards, headmaster, Lake Forest Academy

4. 7/19/40. *Kids:* Virginia Booze, Cynthia Cline, Gerard Darrow, Richard Kosterlitz, Van Dyke Tiers. *Notable Guest/Notes:* **Grant Wood**, American artist

5. 7/26/40. *Kids:* Cynthia Cline, Gerard Darrow, Van Dyke Tiers, Linda Wells, Lloyd Wells. *Notable Guest/Notes:* George Axtell, Northwestern University

6. 8/2/40. *Kids:* Cynthia Cline, Gerard Darrow, Mary Clare McHugh, Van Dyke Tiers, Marvin Zenkere. *Notable Guest/Notes:* Dr. Joseph Schwab, University of Chicago

7. 8/9/40. *Kids:* Cynthia Cline, Gerard Darrow, Clem Lane, Jr., Mary Clare McHugh, Van Dyke Tiers. *Notable Guest/Notes:* Henry Hillikin, Economics Dept., Kansas City University

8. 8/16/40. *Kids:* Cynthia Cline, Gerard Darrow, Emily Israel, Van Dyke Tiers, Robert Walls. *Notable Guest/Notes:* Myron Morrill, Department of Religion, Hamline University

9. 8/23/40. *Kids:* Jack Beckman, Cynthia Cline, Gerard Darrow, Van Dyke Tiers, Davida Wolfson. *Notable Guest/Notes:* Stewart McMullen, economics professor, Northwestern University

10. 8/30/40. *Kids:* Jack Beckman, Cynthia Cline, Gerard Darrow, Emily Israel, Van Dyke Tiers, Robert Walls. *Notable Guest/Notes:* Martin Grant, biology professor, Iowa State Teachers College

11. 9/4/40. *Kids:* Jack Beckman, Cynthia Cline, Emily Israel, Edith Lee James, Richard Williams. *Notable Guest/Notes:* Parker Wheatley

12. 9/11/40. *Kids:* Jack Beckman, Cynthia Cline, Geraldine Hamburg, Edith Lee James, Jack Lucal. *Notable Guest/Notes:* Curtis Mitchell, editor, *Movie and Radio Guide*

13. 9/18/40. *Kids:* Jack Beckman, Cynthia Cline, Geraldine Hamburg, Paul Kirk, Jack Lucal. *Notable Guest/Notes:* Hugh Matheson, Modern Language Dept., Lake Forest Academy

14. 9/25/40. *Kids:* Cynthia Cline, Gerard Darrow, Geraldine Hamburg, Jack Lucal, Van Dyke Tiers. *Notable Guest/Notes:* John Henry, mathematics professor, University of Minnesota
15. 10/2/40. *Kids:* Cynthia Cline, Gerard Darrow, Geraldine Hamburg, Jack Lucal, Van Dyke Tiers. *Notable Guest/Notes:* Katherine Waller, librarian, Evanston, Illinois, public schools
16. 10/9/40. *Kids:* Gerard Darrow, Muriel Deutsch, Geraldine Hamburg, Jack Lucal, Tim Osato. *Notable Guest/Notes:* Paul Hutchinson, editor, *Christian Century Magazine*
17. 10/1/406. *Kids:* Gerard Darrow, Lucille Kevill, Jack Lucal, Tim Osato, Elizabeth Wirth. *Notable Guest/Notes:* Bernard Geis, editor, *Coronet Magazine*
18. 10/23/40. *Kids:* Gerard Darrow, Barbara Hutchinson, Jack Lucal, Richard Williams, Elizabeth Wirth. *Notable Guest/Notes:* William Slaughter, college professor
19. 10/30/40. *Kids:* Jack Beckman, Barbara Hutchinson, **Gloria Jean** (child movie star), Jack Lucal, Richard Williams. *Notable Guest/Notes:* William McVeigh, college professor
20. 11/6/40. *Kids:* Jack Beckman, Cynthia Cline, Barbara Hutchinson, Jack Lucal, Richard Williams. *Notable Guest/Notes:* George Utley, librarian, Newberry Library, Chicago
21. 11/13/40. *Kids:* Cynthia Cline, Jack French, Gloria Hunt, Jack Lucal, Richard Williams. *Notable Guest/Notes:* Rear Admiral John Downes, U.S. Navy
022. 11/20/40. *Kids:* Jack Beckman, Arthur Haelig, Geraldine Hamburg, Jack Lucal, Richard Williams. *Notable Guest/Notes:* Homer Buckley, National Tuberculosis Association
23. 11/27/40. *Kids:* Jack Beckman, Cynthia Cline, Richard Frisbie, Jack Lucal, Richard Williams. *Notable Guest/Notes:* Daniel Rich, director, Art Institute of Chicago
24. 12/4/40. *Kids:* Jack Beckman, Cynthia Cline, Gerard Darrow, Jack Lucal, Frank Mangin. *Notable Guest/Notes:* **The Rev. E. J. Flanagan,** founder and head of Boys Town
25. 12/11/40. *Kids:* Jack Beckman, Cynthia Cline, Gerard Darrow, Jack Lucal, William Wegener. *Notable Guest/Notes:* Paul Gilbert, author, juvenile fiction
26. 12/18/40. *Kids:* Unknown. *Notable Guest/Notes:* George Utley
27. 12/25/40. *Kids:* Jack Beckman, Claude Brenner, Gerard Darrow, Lois Karpf, Van Dyke Tiers. *Notable Guest/Notes:* Charlotte Carr, director, Hull House, Chicago
28. 1/1/41. *Kids:* Claude Brenner, Sheilah Brenner, Pat Chandler, Gerard Darrow, Van Dyke Tiers. *Notable Guest/Notes:* Judith Waller, director, Public Service, NBC
29. 1/8/41. *Kids:* Joan Bishop, Cynthia Cline, Gerard Darrow, Van Dyke Tiers, Richard Williams. *Notable Guest/Notes:* **Dr. Allan Dafoe,** pediatrician who delivered Dionne quintuplets
30. 1/15/41. *Kids:* Sally Bogolub, Claude Brenner, Gerard Darrow, Corinne Shapira, Richard Williams. *Notable Guest/Notes:* Helen Herman, writer, *Liberty Magazine*
31. 1/22/41. *Kids:* Claude Brenner, Gerard Darrow, Corinne Shapira, Van Dyke Tiers, Richard Williams. *Notable Guest/Notes:* Dr. W. E. Shaw, president, Illinois Wesleyan University
32. 1/29/41. *Kids:* Claude Brenner, Nancy Bush, Joan McCullough, Van Dyke Tiers, Richard Williams. *Notable Guest/Notes:* Harry Miller, editor, *Youth Today Magazine*
33. 2/5/41. *Kids:* Unknown. *Notable Guest/Notes:* Ann Marsters, feature writer, *Chicago Herald American*
34. 2/12/41. *Kids:* Nancy Bush, Lois Hesse, Joan McCullough, Van Dyke Tiers, Richard Williams. *Notable Guest/Notes:* M. D. Potter, superintendent of schools, Milwaukee
35. 2/19/41. *Kids:* Nancy Bush, Nanni Kahn, Jack Lucal, Joan McCullough, Richard Williams. *Notable Guest/Notes:* Wilma McFarland, editor, *Child Life Magazine*
36. 2/26/41. *Kids:* Joan Bishop, Gerard

Darrow, Jack Lucal, Joan McCullough, Richard Williams. *Notable Guest/Notes:* **Rear Admiral Richard E. Byrd,** polar explorer
37. 3/5/41. *Kids:* Nancy Bush, Nancy Coggeshall, Nanni Kahn, Jack Lucal, Richard Williams. *Notable Guest/Notes:* Dorothy Lewis, Radio Council on Children's Programs
38. 3/12/41. *Kids:* Kenneth Bennett, Nancy Bush, Inez Fox, Jack Lucal, Richard Williams. *Notable Guest/Notes:* Dr. Preston Bradley, lecturer
39. 3/19/41. *Kids:* Claude Brenner, Inez Fox, Jack Lucal, Lois Piske, Richard Williams
40. 3/26/41. *Kids:* Claude Brenner, Jack Lucal, Patricia Muckian, Betty Swanson, Richard Williams
41. 4/2/41. *Kids:* Claude Brenner, Jack Lucal, Patricia Muckian, Betty Swanson, Richard Williams
42. 4/9/41. *Kids:* Joan Bishop, Claude Brenner, Cynthia Cline, Gerard Darrow, Richard Williams. *Notable Guest/Notes:* **Walt Disney**
43. 4/16/41. *Kids:* Joan Bishop, Claude Brenner, Cynthia Cline, Gerard Darrow, Richard Williams. *Notable Guest/Notes:* **Jack Benny**
44. 4/23/41. *Kids:* Joan Bishop, Claude Brenner, Gerard Darrow, Jack Lucal, Richard Williams. *Notable Guest/Notes:* Harold Gloyd, director, Museum of Natural History, Chicago
45. 4/30/41. *Kids:* Joan Bishop, Gerard Darrow, Edna Heenan, Jack Lucal, Richard Williams. *Notable Guest/Notes:* Gordon Swarthout, managing editor, *Movie and Radio Guide*
46. 5/7/41. *Kids:* Joan Bishop, Gerard Darrow, Jack Lucal, Corinne Shapira, Richard Williams
47. 5/14/41. *Kids:* Joan Bishop, Gerard Darrow, Jack Lucal, Betty Swanson, Richard Williams. *Notable Guest/Notes:* Bishop Bernard Sheil, founder, Catholic Youth Organization
48. 5/21/41. *Kids:* Unknown. *Notable Guest/Notes:* Major Lenox Lohr, former president of NBC
49. 5/28/41. *Kids:* Harve Fischman, Jack Lucal, Paul Sigmond, Betty Swanson, Richard Williams. *Notable Guest/Notes:* Army General J. L. Homer. QK was broadcast from Fort Sheridan, Illinois.
50. 6/4/41. *Kids:* Harve Fischman, Virginia Hajek, Jack Lucal, Betty Swanson, Richard Williams. *Notable Guest/Notes:* Joseph Binns, general manager, Stevens Hotel
51. 6/11/41. *Kids:* Harve Fischman, Jack Lucal, Dennis Shanahan, Betty Swanson, Richard Williams. *Notable Guest/Notes:* Harold Stassen, governor of Minnesota
52. 6/18/41. *Kids:* Margaret Dougherty, Jack Lucal, David Smothers, Betty Swanson, Richard Williams. *Notable Guest/Notes:* **Elinor Morgenthau,** wife of U.S. Secretary of the Treasury
53. 6/25/41. *Kids:* Joan Bishop, Claude Brenner, Cynthia Cline, Gerard Darrow, Jack Lucal, Van Dyke Tiers, Richard Williams. *Notable Guest/Notes:* Harold Swenson, Stevens College
54. 7/2/41. *Kids:* Margaret Dougherty, Jack Lucal, Melvin Silver, Betty Swanson, Richard Williams. *Notable Guest/Notes:* Ernest Pugmire, commander, Salvation Army
55. 7/9/41. *Kids:* Maurice Culhane, Margaret Dougherty, Jack Lucal, Joanna Tyrny, Richard Williams
56. 7/16/41. *Kids:* Claude Brenner, Margaret Dougherty, Jack Lucal, Harry Mauer, Richard Williams
57. 7/23/41. *Kids:* Claude Brenner, Gerard Darrow, Margaret Dougherty, Jack Lucal, Richard Williams
58. 7/30/41. *Kids:* Claude Brenner, Gerard Darrow, Margaret Dougherty, Jack Lucal, Tommy McFarland
59. 8/6/41. *Kids:* Cynthia Cline, Gerard Darrow, Jack Lucal, Van Dyke Tiers, and Richard Williams vs. one of their parents
60. 8/13/41. *Kids:* Claude Brenner, Cynthia Cline, Gerard Darrow, Margaret Dougherty, Jack Lucal
61. 8/20/41. *Kids:* Claude Brenner, Gerard Darrow, Jack Lucal, Betty Swanson, Richard Williams. *Notable Guest/Notes:* **Fiorello LaGuardia,** mayor of New York

62. 8/27/41. *Kids:* Gerard Darrow, Edna Heenan, Jack Lucal, Melvin Silver, Richard Williams. *Notable Guest/Notes:* General James Ulio, U.S. Army
63. 9/3/41. *Kids:* Joan Bishop, Cynthia Cline, Gerard Darrow, Van Dyke Tiers, Richard Williams
64. 9/10/41. *Kids:* Claude Brenner, Cynthia Cline, Gerard Darrow, Edna Heenan, Van Dyke Tiers
65. 9/17/41. *Kids:* Cynthia Cline, Emily Israel
66. 9/24/41. *Kids:* Claude Brenner, Gerard Darrow, Marie Gleason, Emily Israel, Van Dyke Tiers
67. 10/1/41. *Kids:* Gerard Darrow, Emily Israel, Julia Marwick, Jesse Miller, Van Dyke Tiers. *Notable Guest/Notes:* **Chester Lauck and Norris Goff (Lum 'n' Abner)**
68. 10/8/41. *Kids:* Robert Blauner, Gerard Darrow, Ruth Fisher, Emily Israel, Van Dyke Tiers
69. 10/15/41. *Kids:* Harve Fischman, Ruth Fisher, Virginia Hajek, Emily Israel, Van Dyke Tiers
70. 10/22/41. *Kids:* Harve Fischman, Ruth Fisher, Julia Marwick, George Morrison, Van Dyke Tiers
71. 10/29/41. *Kids:* Harve Fischman, Ruth Fisher, Julia Marwick, Mary Clare McHugh, Van Dyke Tiers
72. 11/5/41. *Kids:* Harve Fischman, Ruth Fisher, David Jenkins, Julia Marwick, Jeanne Zemek
73. 11/12/41. *Kids:* Harve Fischman, Ruth Fisher, David Jenkins, Julia Marwick, Gellert Seel
74. 11/19/41. *Kids:* Richard Banister, Ruth Duskin, Harve Fischman, David Jenkins, Julia Marwick
75. 11/26/41. *Kids:* Richard Banister, Ruth Duskin, Julia Marwick, Joe Teitz, Richard Williams
76. 12/3/41. *Kids:* Richard Banister, Ruth Duskin, Mary Markham, Ben Rasmusen, Richard Williams
77. 12/10/41. *Kids:* John Ashbery, Richard Banister, Joan Bishop, Ruth Duskin, Richard Williams
78. 12/17/41. *Kids:* Richard Banister, Joan Bishop, Claude Brenner, David Jenkins, Richard Williams. *Notable Guest/Notes:* Rear Admiral John Downes, from U.S. Naval Station, Great Lakes
79. 12/24/41. *Kids:* All past and present Quiz Kids at Christmas Party
80. 12/3/411. *Kids:* Joan Bishop, Claude Brenner, Jack Lucal, Mary Clare McHugh, Richard Williams
81. 1/7/42. *Kids:* Joan Bishop, Claude Brenner, Ruth Duskin, Jack Lucal, Richard Williams
82. 1/14/42. *Kids:* Ruth Duskin, Lawrence Friedman, Jack Lucal, Jean MacMahon, Richard Williams
83. 1/21/42. *Kids:* Ruth Duskin, Lawrence Friedman, Jack Lucal, Jean MacMahon, Richard Williams
84. 1/28/42. *Kids:* Claude Brenner, Gerard Darrow, Ruth Duskin, Harve Fischman, Richard Freeman, Richard Williams
85. 2/4/42. *Kids:* Ruth Duskin, Jack Lucal, Martin Ludwin, Jean McMahon, Richard Williams
86. 2/11/42. *Kids:* Gerard Darrow, Jack Lucal, Jean McMahon, Rosalie Pooler, Richard Williams
87. 2/18/42. *Kids:* Gerard Darrow, Jack Lucal, Jean McMahon, Billy Seaman, Richard Williams
88. 2/25/42. *Kids:* Gerard Darrow, Jay Dewing (contest), Jack Lucal, Jean McMahon, Richard Williams
89. 3/4/42. *Kids:* Gerard Darrow, Joel Fleck, Jean McMahon, Joan Moy, Richard Williams
90. 3/11/42. *Kids:* Gerard Darrow, Harve Fischman, Jean McMahon, Adrian Ostfeld, Richard Williams
91. 3/18/42. *Kids:* Gerard Darrow, Harvey Fischman, Jean McMahon, Richard Williams. *Notable Guest/Notes:* Margery Krueger, honor scholar
92. 3/25/42. *Kids:* Gerard Darrow, Harvey Fischman, Joel Fleck, Richard Williams. *Notable Guest/Notes:* **Mei Mei Lin**, Lin Yutang's daughter
93. 4/1/42. *Kids:* Gerard Darrow, Ruth Duskin, Harve Fischman, Joel Fleck, Richard Williams. *Notable Guest/Notes:* **Fred Allen**
94. 4/8/42. *Kids:* Gerard Darrow, Harve

Fischman, Jonathan Jackson, Juanita Rende, Richard Williams
95. 4/15/42. *Kids:* Gerard Darrow, Jack Donnelly, Harve Fischman, Rita Lauzon, Richard Williams
96. 4/22/42. *Kids:* Harve Fischman, Edwin Goldberger, Rita Lauzon, David Sher, Richard Williams
97. 4/29/42. *Kids:* Harve Fischman, Edwin Goldberger, Maxine Klein, Joel Kupperman, Richard Williams
98. 5/6/42. *Kids:* Ruth Duskin, Harve Fischman, Edwin Goldberger, Harker Rhodes, Richard Williams
99. 5/13/42. *Kids:* Ruth Duskin, Harve Fischman, Edwin Goldberger, Harker Rhodes, Richard Williams
100. 5/20/42. *Kids:* Reyna Cooper, Ruth Duskin, Harve Fischman, Jack Lucal, Richard Williams. *Notable Guest/Notes:* Father Flanagan, Boys Town
101. 5/27/42. *Kids:* Garth Drewry, Ruth Duskin, Dorothy Freeman, Jack Lucal, Richard Williams. *Notable Guest/Notes:* Dr. Leon Smith, dean, University College, University of Chicago
102. 6/3/42. *Kids:* Ruth Duskin, Virginia Hajeck, Hubert Jantscher, Jack Lucal, Richard Williams
103. 6/10/42. *Kids:* Ruth Duskin, Virginia Hajeck, Jack Lucal, Elinor Smith, Richard Williams
104. 6/17/42. *Kids:* Ann and John Bokman (twins), Jack Lucal, Elinor Smith, Richard Williams
105. 6/24/42. *Kids:* Joan Bishop, Claude Brenner, Cynthia Cline, Gerard Darrow, Jack Lucal, Van Dyke Tiers, Richard Williams
106. 7/1/42. *Kids:* Ann and John Bokman, Jack Lucal, Margaret Merrick, Richard Williams
107. 7/8/42. *Kids:* Tom Franklin, Jack Lucal, Margaret Merrick, Beverly Simpson, Richard Williams
108. 7/12/42. *Kids:* Unknown. *Notable Guest/Notes:* Richard Earnhart, national spelling champion
109. 7/19/42. *Kids:* Gerard Darrow, Richard Earnhart, Jack Lucal, Margaret Merrick
110. 7/26/42. *Kids:* Ruth Duskin, Harve Fischman, Jack Lucal, Van Dyke Tiers, Richard Williams
111. 8/2/42. *Kids:* Joan Bishop, Ruth Duskin, Harve Fischman, Margaret Merrick, Richard Williams
112. 8/9/42. *Kids:* Joan Bishop, Harve Fischman, Margaret Merrick, Van Dyke Tiers, Richard Williams
113. 8/16/42. *Kids:* Joan Bishop, Ruth Duskin, Margaret Merrick, Van Dyke Tiers, Richard Williams
114. 8/23/42. *Kids:* Joan Bishop, Ruth Duskin, Margaret Merrick, Van Dyke Tiers, Richard Williams
115. 8/30/42. *Kids:* Robert Bloch, Ruth Duskin, Margaret Merrick, William Nesbit, Richard Williams
116. 9/6/42. *Kids:* Margaret Merrick, William Nesbit, Richard Porter, Betty Swanson, Richard Williams
117. 9/13/42. *Kids:* Claude Brenner, Jack Lucal, William Nesbit, Van Dyke Tiers, Richard Williams
118. 9/20/42. *Kids:* Margaret Merrick, Richard Porter, Arthur Reinwald, Betty Swanson, Richard Williams
119. 9/27/42. *Kids:* Claude Brenner, Bill McNeill, Richard Porter, Betty Swanson, Richard Williams
120. 10/4/42. *Kids:* Claude Brenner, Gerard Darrow, Tommy Franklin, Bill McNeill, Richard Williams
121. 10/11/42. *Kids:* Joan Alizier, Claude Brenner, Gerard Darrow, Tommy Franklin, Joel Kupperman
122. 10/18/42. *Kids:* Claude Brenner, Gerard Darrow, Tommy Franklin, Joel Kupperman, Margaret Merrick. *Notable Guest/Notes:* **Chico Marx**
123. 10/25/42. *Kids:* Claude Brenner, Gerard Darrow, Joel Kupperman, Margaret Merrick, Ted Schultz. *Notable Guest/Notes:* Admiral John Downes
124. 11/1/42. *Kids:* Claude Brenner, Joel Kupperman, Jack Lucal, Margaret Merrick, Ted Schultz, James Watson
125. 11/8/42. *Kids:* Claude Brenner, Jack Lucal, Margaret Merrick, Rudy Vergara, James Watson. *Notable Guest/Notes:* J. M. Elizade, resident commissioner of the Philippines

126. 11/15/42. *Kids:* Claude Brenner, Ruth Duskin, Jack Lucal, Margaret Merrick, James Watson
127. 11/22/42. *Kids:* Gerard Darrow, Ruth Duskin, Harve Fischman, Margaret Merrick, Richard Williams
128. 11/29/42. *Kids:* Joan Bishop, Ruth Duskin, Jack Lucal, Margaret Merrick, Harry Pillman
129. 12/6/42. *Kids:* Joan Bishop, Ruth Duskin, Joel Kupperman, Margaret Merrick, Harry Pillman
130. 12/13/42. *Kids:* Ralph Adler, Stephen Adler, Joan Bishop, Joel Kupperman, Margaret Merrick
131. 12/20/42. *Kids:* Stephen Adler, Joan Bishop, Harve Fischman, Joel Kupperman, Margaret Merrick
132. 12/27/42. *Kids:* Stephen Adler, Harve Fischman, Joel Kupperman, Margaret Merrick, Donald Sevetson
133. 1/3/43. *Kids:* Stephen Adler, Harve Fischman, Joel Kupperman, Margaret Merrick, Van Dyke Tiers
134. 1/10/43. *Kids:* Ruth Duskin, Harve Fischman, Van Dyke Tiers, Richard Williams. *Notable Guest/Notes:* **Governor Harold Stassen, Alex Dreier,** NBC foreign correspondent
135. 1/17/43. *Kids:* Gerard Darrow, Harve Fischman, Margaret Merrick, Van Dyke Tiers, Richard Williams
136. 1/24/43. *Kids:* Smylla Brind (**Vanessa Brown**), Gerard Darrow, Harve Fischman, Joel Kupperman, Margaret Merrick. *Notable Guest/Notes:* **Sister Elizabeth Kenny**
137. 1/31/43. *Kids:* Claude Brenner, Harve Fischman, Joel Kupperman, Margaret Merrick, Richard Porter
138. 2/7/43. *Kids:* Claude Brenner, Harve Fischman, Joel Kupperman, Margaret Merrick, Davis Sher
139. 2/14/43. *Kids:* Harve Fischman, Donald Hastings, Joel Kupperman, Margaret Merrick, David Sher
140. 2/21/43. *Kids:* Ruth Duskin, Harve Fischman, Joel Kupperman, Margaret Merrick, Richard Williams. *Notable Guest/Notes:* **Jack Benny**
141. 2/28/43. *Kids:* Ruth Duskin, Harve Fischman, Joel Kupperman, Margaret Merrick, Richard Williams
142. 3/7/43. *Kids:* Ruth Duskin, Harve Fischman, Joel Kupperman, Van Dyke Tiers, Richard Williams
143. 3/14/43. *Kids:* Ruth Duskin, Harve Fischman, Joel Kupperman, Richard Williams
144. 3/21/43. *Kids:* Gerard Darrow, Ruth Duskin, Harve Fischman, Joel Kupperman, Richard Williams
145. 3/28/43. *Kids:* Gerard Darrow, Ruth Duskin, Harve Fischman, Joel Kupperman, Richard Williams. *Notable Guest/Notes:* **Fred Allen**
146. 4/4/43. *Kids:* Gerard Darrow, Ruth Duskin, Joel Kupperman, Paul Huebner, Richard Williams. *Notable Guest/Notes:* From Hammond, Indiana; war bond broadcast.
147. 4/11/43. *Kids:* Gerard Darrow, Ruth Duskin, Joel Kupperman, Paul Huebner, Richard Williams
148. 4/18/43. *Kids:* Gerard Darrow, Ruth Duskin, Joel Kupperman, Paul Huebner, Richard Williams
149. 4/25/43. *Kids:* Gerard Darrow, Ruth Duskin, Thomas Franklin, Joel Kupperman, Richard Williams
150. 5/2/43. *Kids:* Gerard Darrow, Ruth Duskin, Thomas Franklin, Harriet Kupperman, Richard Williams
151. 5/9/43. *Kids:* Robert Anver, Claude Brenner, Gerard Darrow, Ruth Duskin, Richard Williams
152. 5/16/43. *Kids:* Robert Anver, Claude Brenner, Gerard Darrow, Ruth Duskin, Richard Williams. *Notable Guest/Notes:* **Bing Crosby**
153. 5/23/43. *Kids:* Gerard Darrow, Ruth Duskin, Ann Llewellyn, William Nesbit, Richard Williams
154. 5/30/43. *Kids:* Gerard Darrow, Virginia Hajek, Joel Kupperman, William Nesbit, Richard Williams
155. 6/6/43. *Kids:* Gerard Darrow, Hugh Gallagher, Joel Kupperman, Barbara Scott, Richard Williams
156. 6/13/43. *Kids:* Claude Brenner, Gerard Darrow, Joel Kupperman, Richard Williams

157. 6/20/43. *Kids:* Claude Brenner, Gerard Darrow, Joel Kupperman, Barbara Scott, Richard Williams
158. 6/27/43. *Kids:* Claude Brenner, Gerard Darrow, Joel Kupperman, Sydelle Landfield, Richard Williams. *Notable Guest/Notes:* Jack Lucal, former Quiz Kid, returns as guest Chief Quizzer. Other guests: Cynthia Cline, Ruel Fischman, age 3. Third birthday broadcast
159. 7/4/43. *Kids:* Claude Brenner, Jerry Hamovit, Joel Kupperman, Margaret Merrick, Richard Williams
160. 7/11/43. *Kids:* Claude Brenner, Joel Kupperman, Margaret Merrick, Burton Ravins, Richard Williams
161. 7/18/43. *Kids:* Claude Brenner, Joel Kupperman, Ruth Mann, Margaret Merrick, Richard Williams
162. 7/25/43. *Kids:* Claude Brenner, Joel Kupperman, Margaret Merrick, Peter Reich, Richard Williams
163. 8/1/43. *Kids:* Anneka De Bruyn, Claude Brenner, Harve Fischman, Joel Kupperman, Richard Williams
164. 8/8/43. *Kids:* Anneka De Bruyn, Claude Brenner, Harve Fischman, Joel Kupperman, Richard Williams
165. 8/15/43. *Kids:* Claude Brenner, Harve Fischman, Joel Kupperman, Sydelle Landfield, Richard Williams
166. 8/22/43. *Kids:* Claude Brenner, Harve Fischman, Joel Kupperman, Sydelle Landfield, Richard Williams
167. 8/29/43. *Kids:* Claude Brenner, Smylla Brind, Hermine Duskin, Harve Fischman, Richard Williams
168. 9/5/43. *Kids:* Claude Brenner, Smylla Brind, Harve Fischman, William Nesbit, Richard Williams
169. 9/12/43. *Kids:* Claude Brenner, Patrick Conlon, Gerard Darrow, Harve Fischman, Richard Williams
170. 9/19/43. *Kids:* Gerard Darrow, Harve Fischman, Margaret Merrick, Richard Williams
171. 9/26/43. *Kids:* Gerard Darrow, Harve Fischman, Margaret Merrick, Richard Williams. *Notable Guest/Notes:* Richmond, Va.; war bond broadcast.
172. 10/3/43. *Kids:* Gerard Darrow, Harve Fischman, Joel Kupperman, Margaret Merrick, Richard Williams
173. 10/10/43. *Kids:* Ruth Duskin, Harve Fischman, Joel Kupperman, Richard Williams. *Notable Guest/Notes:* Detroit; war bond broadcast.
174. 10/17/43. *Kids:* Richard Allin, Gerard Darrow, Harve Fischman, Margaret Merrick, Richard Williams
175. 10/24/43. *Kids:* Hermine Duskin, Harve Fischman, Thomas Franklin, Margaret Merrick, Richard Williams
176. 10/31/43. *Kids:* Claude Brenner, Hermine Duskin, Harve Fischman, Margaret Merrick, Richard Williams
177. 11/7/43. *Kids:* Harve Fischman, Joel Kupperman, Ruth Mann, Margaret Merrick, Richard Williams
178. 11/14/43. *Kids:* James Alexander, **Joan Shepard,** plus regular Quiz Kids
179. 11/21/43. *Kids:* Gerard Darrow, Ruth Duskin, Harve Fischman, Joel Kupperman, Richard Williams. *Notable Guest/Notes:* **Eddie Cantor**
180. 11/28/43. *Kids:* Gerard Darrow, Ruth Duskin, Harve Fischman, Donald Griley, Joel Kupperman, Richard Williams
181. 12/5/43. *Kids:* Gerard Darrow, Ruth Duskin, Harve Fischman, Joel Kupperman, Richard Williams
182. 12/12/43. *Kids:* Gerard Darrow, Ruth Duskin, Harve Fischman, Joel Kupperman, James Shields, Richard Williams
183. 12/19/43. *Kids:* Claude Brenner, Patrick Conlon, Harve Fischman, Sydelle Landfield, Richard Williams
184. 12/26/43. *Kids:* Claude Brenner, Harve Fischman, Joel Kupperman, Sydelle Landfield, Richard Williams
185. 1/2/44. *Kids:* Patrick Conlon, Harve Fischman, Sydelle Landfield, Joan Shepard, Richard Williams
186. 1/9/44. *Kids:* Ruth Duskin, Harve Fischman, Joel Kupperman, James Phillips (local QK), Richard Williams. *Notable Guest/Notes:* From Pittsburgh, Pa.; war bond broadcast.
187. 1/16/44. *Kids:* Marion Brown, Harve Fischman, Cora Pattarson, Joan Shepard, Richard Williams
188. 1/23/44. *Kids:* Marion Brown, Harve

Fischman, Cora Pattarson, Joan Shepard, Richard Williams
189. 1/30/44. *Kids:* Marion Brown, Patrick Conlon, Harve Fischman, Cora Pattarson, Richard Williams
190. 2/6/44. *Kids:* Virginia Bangs, Patrick Conlon, Harve Fischman, Maxine Klein, Richard Williams
191. 2/13/44. *Kids:* Patrick Conlon, Harve Fischman, Thomas Franklin, Joan Shepard, Richard Williams
192. 2/20/44. *Kids:* Ruth Duskin, Harve Fischman, Joel Kupperman, Donald Mork, Richard Williams
193. 2/27/44. *Kids:* Ruth Duskin, Harve Fischman, Leonard Fox (local QK), Joel Kupperman, Richard Williams. *Notable Guest/Notes:* **Fred Allen**. From New York City; war bond broadcast.
194. 3/5/44. *Kids:* Ruth Duskin, Harve Fischman, Joel Kupperman, Joan Shepard, Richard Williams
195. 3/12/44. *Kids:* Ruth Duskin, Bernard Griesel, Margaret Merrick, Joan Shepard, Richard Williams
196. 3/19/44. *Kids:* Patrick Conlon, Bernard Griesel, Margaret Merrick, Barbara Scott, Richard Williams
197. 3/26/44. *Kids:* Patrick Conlon, Hermine Duskin, Ruel Fischman, Harriet Kupperman, Joel Kupperman. *Notable Guest/Notes:* "Young" Quiz Kids compete with "alumni" panel: Jack Beckman, Joan Bishop, Cynthia Cline, Jack Lucal, Van Dyke Tiers
198. 4/2/44. *Kids:* Claude Brenner, Patrick Conlon, Harriet Leavitt, Margaret Merrick, Richard Williams
199. 4/9/44. *Kids:* Claude Brenner, Sonia Comacho, Patrick Conlon, Margaret Merrick, Richard Williams
200. 4/16/44. *Kids:* Claude Brenner, Patrick Conlon, Ruth Duskin, Richard Lieb, Richard Williams
201. 4/23/44. *Kids:* Claude Brenner, Ruth Duskin, Richard Lieb, Betty Swanson, Richard Williams. *Notable Guest/Notes:* **Larry Adler,** famous harmonica musician
202. 4/30/44. *Kids:* Claude Brenner, Ruth Duskin, Joel Kupperman, Joan Shepard, Betty Swanson. *Notable Guest/Notes:* **Paul Draper,** famous tap dancer, who tapped the rhythm of three songs for the Kids to identify
203. 5/7/44. *Kids:* Claude Brenner, Richard Freeman, Joel Kupperman, Richard Porter, Betty Swanson. *Notable Guest/Notes:* **Brace Beemer (The Lone Ranger)**
204. 5/14/44. *Kids:* Ruth Duskin, Harve Fischman, Robert Haller (local QK), Joel Kupperman, Richard Williams. *Notable Guest/Notes:* From Fort Wayne, Indiana; war bond broadcast.
205. 5/21/44. *Kids:* Claude Brenner, Richard Freeman, Richard Porter, **Jane Powell,** Betty Swanson
206. 5/28/44. *Kids:* Claude Brenner, Harve Fischman, Richard Freeman, Richard Porter, Betty Swanson
207. 6/4/44. *Kids:* Joel Kupperman, Harve Fischman, Richard Freeman, Richard Porter, Betty Swanson
208. 6/11/44. *Kids:* Ruth Duskin, Harve Fischman, Joel Kupperman, Shirley Bersadsky, Richard Williams. *Notable Guest/Notes:* From New Orleans; war bond broadcast.
209. 6/18/44. *Kids:* Ruth Duskin, Harve Fischman, Joel Kupperman, Martha Lowe (local Quiz Kid), Richard Williams. *Notable Guest/Notes:* From Memphis; war bond broadcast.
210. 6/25/44. *Kids:* Claude Brenner, Harve Fischman, Ruel Fischman, Richard Freeman, Joel Kupperman
211. 7/2/44. *Kids:* Claude Brenner, Harve Fischman, Ruel Fischman, Richard Freeman, Joel Kupperman
212. 7/9/44. *Kids:* Harve Fischman, Ruel Fischman, Richard Freeman, Joel Kupperman, Ann Lee
213. 7/16/44. *Kids:* Ruth Duskin, Harve Fischman, Joel Kupperman, Verne Vance (local Quiz Kid), Richard Williams. *Notable Guest/Notes:* From Omaha, Nebraska; war bond broadcast.
214. 7/23/44. *Kids:* David Davis, Harve Fischman, Richard Freeman, Joel Kupperman, Ann Lee
215. 7/30/44. *Kids:* Marjorie Bruce, John Cook, David Davis, Harve Fischman, Joel Kupperman

216. 8/6/44. *Kids:* Marjorie Bruce, David Davis, Harve Fischman, Floyd Gardner, Joel Kupperman
217. 8/13/44. *Kids:* Marian Brown, David Davis, Harve Fischman, Floyd Gardner, Joel Kupperman
218. 8/20/44. *Kids:* Patrick Conlon, David Davis, Harve Fischman, Joel Kupperman, Ruth Mann. *Notable Guest/Notes:* David, Harve, and Joel take turns as Chief Quizzer in place of Joe Kelly, who is on vacation
219. 8/27/44. *Kids:* Patrick Conlon, David Davis, Harve Fischman, Joel Kupperman, Ruth Mann
220. 9/3/44. *Kids:* Patrick Conlon, Harve Fischman, Joel Kupperman, Ruth Mann, Philip Marcus
221. 9/10/44. *Kids:* Ruth Duskin, Harve Fischman, Joel Kupperman, Jerome Malone (local QK), Richard Williams. *Notable Guest/Notes:* From Seattle; war bond broadcast.
222. 9/17/44. *Kids:* Ruth Duskin, Harve Fischman, Joel Kupperman, Richard Williams. *Notable Guest/Notes:* From Portland, Oregon; war bond broadcast.
223. 9/24/44. *Kids:* Patrick Conlon, David Davis, Shelley Davis, Harve Fischman, Philip Marcus. *Notable Guest/Notes:* **Victor Borge** substitutes for Joe Kelly.
224. 10/1/44. *Kids:* Patrick Conlon, Laurie Darling, David Davis, Harve Fischman, Lonny Lunde
225. 10/8/44. *Kids:* Patrick Conlon, Ruth Duskin, Harve Fischman, Lonny Lunde, Ronald Youngblood
226. 10/15/44. *Kids:* Ruth Duskin, Harve Fischman, Ruel Fischman, Thomas Franklin, Ronald Youngblood
227. 10/22/44. *Kids:* Joanne Berg, Ruth Duskin, Harve Fischman, Thomas Franklin, Richard Williams. *Notable Guest/Notes:* **Desiré Defauw,** conductor of the Chicago Symphony orchestra
228. 10/29/44. *Kids:* Maurguerite Bangert, Kenneth Childers, Harve Fischman, Thomas Franklin, Richard Williams
229. 11/5/44. *Kids:* Maureen Buckley, Patrick Conlon, Harve Fischman, Thomas Franklin, Richard Williams. *Notable Guest/Notes:* **Inge Manski,** soprano of the Chicago Civic Opera company
230. 11/12/44. *Kids:* Maureen Buckley, Patrick Conlon, Harve Fischman, Joel Kupperman, Richard Williams
231. 11/19/44. *Kids:* Maureen Buckley, Harve Fischman, Joel Kupperman, Richard Williams. *Notable Guest/Notes:* **Bob Hope**
232. 11/26/44. *Kids:* Ruth Duskin, Harve Fischman, Joel Kupperman, Gene Latimer (local Quiz Kid). *Notable Guest/Notes:* From Salt Lake City; war bond broadcast.
233. 12/3/44. *Kids:* Maureen Buckley, Patrick Conlon, Harve Fischman, Joel Kupperman, Richard Williams. *Notable Guest/Notes:* From Navy Pier, Chicago, where navy's Sixth War Loan Exhibit was being held.
234. 12/10/44. *Kids:* Harve Fischman, Joel Kupperman, Lonny Lunde, Virginia Rhoads, Richard Williams
235. 12/17/44. *Kids:* Maurgerite Bangert, Joanne Berg, Harve Fischman, Lonny Lunde, Richard Williams
236. 12/24/44. *Kids:* Maurgerite Bangert, Patrick Conlon, David Davis, Harve Fischman, Richard Williams
237. 12/31/44. *Kids:* Maurgerite Bangert, Patrick Conlon, David Davis, Harve Fischman, Richard Williams
238. 1/7/45. *Kids:* Maurgerite Bangert, Patrick Conlon, Harve Fischman, Fern Turnley, Richard Williams
239. 1/14/45. *Kids:* Andre Aerne, Maurgerite Bangert, Harve Fischman, Gunther Hollander, Richard Williams. *Notable Guest/Notes:* New feature for QK called "Spotlight Question," submitted by a nationally known celebrity. First question by **Jack Benny.**
240. 1/21/45. *Kids:* Maurgerite Bangert, Harve Fischman, Gunther Hollander, Joel Kupperman, Richard Williams
241. 1/28/45. *Kids:* Ann Farrell, Harve Fischman, Gunther Hollander, Joel Kupperman, Richard Williams
242. 2/4/45. *Kids:* Ann Farrell, Harve Fischman, Joel Kupperman, Jack Mendelsohn, Richard Williams. *Notable*

Guest/Notes: "Spotlight Question" by First Lady **Eleanor Roosevelt**.

243. 2/11/45. *Kids:* Patrick Conlon, Ann Farrell, Harve Fischman, Kent McPherron, Richard Williams

244. 2/18/45. *Kids:* Patrick Conlon, Ruth Duskin, Harve Fischman, Joel Kupperman, Richard Williams. *Notable Guest/Notes:* "Spotlight Question" by **Father Flanagan** of Boys Town.

245. 2/25/45. *Kids:* Ruth Duskin, Anne Farrell, Harve Fischman, Gunther Hollander, Richard Williams

246. 3/4/45. *Kids:* Patrick Conlon, Harve Fischman, Joel Kupperman, Richard Williams. *Notable Guest/Notes:* **Ralph Edwards** (*Truth or Consequences*), "Spotlight Question" by Admiral **Frederick Horne**, vice-chief Naval Operations.

247. 3/11/45. *Kids:* Patrick Conlon, Harve Fischman, Joel Kupperman, Richard Willams. *Notable Guest/Notes:* **Gertrude Lawrence**, actress, makes appeal for radios for servicemen. "Spotlight Question" by **Henry Wallace**, U.S. Secretary of Commerce.

248. 3/18/45. *Kids:* Patrick Conlon, Harve Fischman, Joel Kupperman, Richard Williams. *Notable Guest/Notes:* U.S. senators **Harold H. Burton, Joseph Ball, Thomas G. Hart,** and **Carl A. Hatch**.

249. 3/25/45. *Kids:* Ann Farrell, Harve Fischman, Lonny Lunde, Richard Williams. *Notable Guest/Notes:* Secretary of Agriculture **Claude Wickard** spoke from Washington. "Spotlight Question" by **Jack Dempsey**.

250. 4/1/45. *Kids:* Warren Cavior (contest winner), Ruth Duskin, Ann Farrell, Harve Fischman, Richard Williams. *Notable Guest/Notes:* "Spotlight Question" by **Dr. Harry Emerson Fosdick** of Riverside Church, New York.

251. 4/8/45. *Kids:* Dean Barry, Ruth Duskin, Harve Fischman, Joel Kupperman, Richard Williams. *Notable Guest/Notes:* "Spotlight Question" by **J. Edgar Hoover**.

252. 4/15/45. *Kids:* Ruth Duskin, Harve Fischman, Joel Kupperman, Alan Stamm, Richard Williams. *Notable Guest/Notes:* "Spotlight Question" by **Henry J. Kaiser**.

253. 4/22/45. *Kids:* Ruth Duskin, Harve Fischman, Lorene Heath, Joel Kupperman, Richard Williams. *Notable Guest/Notes:* "Spotlight Question" by **John Steurat Curry**.

254. 4/29/45. *Kids:* Patrick Conlon, Ruth Duskin, Harve Fischman, Jim Strock, Richard Williams

255. 5/6/45. *Kids:* Dean Barry, Lorene Heath, Philip Marcus, Kent McPherron, Alan Stamm

256. 5/13/45. *Kids:* Patrick Conlon, Ruth Duskin, Harve Fischman, Alan Stamm, Richard Williams. *Notable Guest/Notes:* Mother's Day program. Panel versus their mothers.

257. 5/20/45. *Kids:* Patrick Conlon, Ruth Duskin, Harve Fischman, Alan Stamm, Richard Williams

258. 5/27/45. *Kids:* Patrick Conlon, Harve Fischman, David B. Knight, Joel Kupperman, Richard Williams. *Notable Guest/Notes:* From Dallas; war bond rally. U.S. Senator **Thomas Connally** spoke from San Francisco.

259. 6/3/45. *Kids:* Ruth Duskin, Harve Fischman, Joel Kupperman, Iris Wilcox (local QK), Richard Williams. *Notable Guest/Notes:* From Buffalo; war bond rally.

260. 6/10/45. *Kids:* Ruth Duskin, Harve Fischman, Judy Graham, Garland Russell, Richard Williams

261. 6/17/45. *Kids:* Richard Adams (local QK), Ruth Duskin, Harve Fischman, Joel Kupperman, Richard Williams. *Notable Guest/Notes:* From Des Moines; war bond rally.

262. 6/24/45. *Kids:* Ruth Duskin, Harve Fischman, Judy Graham, Philip Marcus, Richard Williams

263. 7/1/45. *Kids:* Patrick Conlon, Sheila Conlon, Hermine Duskin, Ruel Fischman, Joel Kupperman. *Notable Guest/Notes:* Former Quiz Kids: Joan Bishop, Cynthia Cline, Richard Frisbie, Jack Lucal, Van Dyke Tiers

264. 7/8/45. *Kids:* Harve Fischman, Judy Graham, Lorene Heath, Richard Williams, Nancy Wong

265. 7/15/45. *Kids:* David Davis, Harve

Fischman, Judy Graham, Kent McPherron, Richard Williams
266. 7/22/45. *Kids:* David Davis, Harve Fischman, Judy Graham, Kent McPherron, Richard Williams
267. 7/29/45. *Kids:* Robert Easton Burke, Harve Fischman, Judy Graham, Kent McPherron, Richard Williams
268. 8/5/45. *Kids:* Robert Burke, Harve Fischman, Judy Graham, Harry Sebel, Richard Williams
269. 8/12/45. *Kids:* Dean Barry, Harve Fischman, Judy Graham, Harry Sebel, Richard Williams
270. 8/19/45. *Kids:* Dean Barry, Harve Fischman, Judy Graham, Harry Sebel, Richard Williams. *Notable Guest/Notes:* Secretary of the Treasury **Frederick Vinson**
271. 8/26/45. *Kids:* Robert Burke, Patrick Conlon, Judy Graham, Harry Sebel, Richard Williams
272. 9/2/45. *Kids:* Robert Burke, Patrick Conlon, Harve Fischman, Harry Sebel, Richard Williams
273. 9/9/45. *Kids:* Robert Burke, Ruth Duskin, Harve Fischman, Thomas Howe, Richard Williams
274. 9/16/45. *Kids:* Robert Burke, Harve Fischman, Joel Kupperman, Stella Lyman, Richard Williams
275. 9/23/45. *Kids:* Robert Burke, Harve Fischman, Joel Kupperman, Stella Lyman, Richard Williams
276. 9/30/45. *Kids:* Robert Burke, Harve Fischman, Judy Graham, Thomas Howe, Richard Williams. *Notable Guest/Notes:* Captain **Eddie Rickenbacker**
277. 10/7/45. *Kids:* Harve Fischman, Judy Graham, Joel Kupperman, Richard Williams. *Notable Guest/Notes:* Broadcast from Cleveland.
278. 10/14/45. *Kids:* Unknown
279. 10/21/45. *Kids:* Robert Burke, Sydel Finfer, Harve Fischman, Joel Kupperman, Richard Williams
Broadcast cancelled for *A Lady Takes a Walk*. 10/28/45. *Kids:* Live and West Coast repeat broadcast cancelled.
280. 11/4/45. *Kids:* Naomi Bernards, Robert Burke, Harve Fischman, Joel Kupperman, Richard Williams. *Notable Guest/Notes:* **Kay Kyser**
281. 11/11/45. *Kids:* Robert Burke, Patrick Conlon, Sheila Conlon, Harve Fischman, Richard Williams. *Notable Guest/Notes:* **Glenn T. Seaborg**
282. 11/18/45. *Kids:* Robert Burke, Judy Graham, Joel Kupperman, Richard Williams
283. 11/25/45. *Kids:* Robert Burke, Patrick Conlon, Harve Fischman, Joan Shepard, Richard Williams
284. 12/2/45. *Kids:* Robert Burke, Harve Fischman, Joel Kupperman, Richard Williams. *Notable Guest/Notes:* U.S. senators **Joseph Ball, Abe Murdock, William Stanfill, Glen Taylor. Senator Kenneth McKellar** is guest judge.
285. 12/9/45. *Kids:* Robert Burke, Ruth Duskin, Harve Fischman, Joel Kupperman, Richard Williams. *Notable Guest/Notes:* **Fred Allen**
286. 12/16/45. *Kids:* Judith Benjamin, Patrick Conlon, Harve Fischman, Joan Shepard, Richard Williams
287. 12/23/45. *Kids:* Harve Fischman, Judy Graham, Joel Kupperman, Joan Shepard, Richard Williams
288. 12/30/45. *Kids:* Unknown
289. 1/6/46. *Kids:* Harve Fischman, Judy Graham, Thomas Howe, Joel Kupperman, Ronald Weintraub
290. 1/13/46. *Kids:* Harve Fischman, Judy Graham, Thomas Howe, George Roemer, Richard Weixler. *Notable Guest/Notes:* **Dinah Shore**
291. 1/20/46. *Kids:* Ruth Duskin, Harve Fischman, Judy Graham, George Roemer, Richard Weixler
292. 1/27/46. *Kids:* Ruth Duskin, Harve Fischman, Richard Goddard. Judy Graham, John Pollock. *Notable Guest/Notes:* **Victor Borge**
293. 2/3/46. *Kids:* Ruth Duskin, Harve Fischman, Judy Graham, Joel Kupperman, John Pollock. *Notable Guest/Notes:* **Victor Borge** substitutes for Joe Kelly.
294. 2/10/46. *Kids:* Harve Fischman, Judy Graham, Joel Kupperman, John Pollock, Richard Weixler. *Notable Guest/Notes:* **Tom Breneman,** emcee of *Breakfast in Hollywood,* guest Chief Quizzer

295. 2/17/46. *Kids:* Patrick Conlon, Harve Fischman, Judy Graham, John Pollock, Richard Weixler. *Notable Guest/Notes:* Oliver Capelle, an executive at Miles Laboratories, guest Chief Quizzer
296. 2/24/46. *Kids:* Ruth Duskin, Harve Fischman, Judy Graham, Joel Kupperman. *Notable Guest/Notes:* Kids compete with four famous atomic scientists: **Arthur H. Jaffey, Maria Mayer, Glenn T. Seaborg, Harold C. Urey.** Clifton Utley substitutes for Joe Kelly.
297. 3/3/46. *Kids:* Naomi Bernards, Harve Fischman, Judy Graham, Joel Kupperman, Richard Weixler. *Notable Guest/Notes:* **John W. Vandercook,** news commentator, substitutes for Joe Kelly.
298. 3/10/46. *Kids:* Naomi Bernards, Harve Fischman, Judy Graham, Joel Kupperman, DiAnne Mathre. *Notable Guest/Notes:* **Carol Stone.** Joe Kelly returns from vacation.
299. 3/17/46. *Kids:* Harve Fischman, Ronald Garber, Judy Graham, Joel Kupperman, DiAnne Mathre. *Notable Guest/Notes:* **Ole Olsen** of the comedy team **Olsen and Johnson**
300. 3/24/46. *Kids:* Maureen Buckley, Harve Fischman, Judy Graham, Joel Kupperman, Richard Weixler
301. 3/31/46. *Kids:* Nomi Bernards, Maureen Buckley, Ruth Duskin, Judy Graham, Rochelle Liebling
302. 4/7/46. *Kids:* Maureen Buckley, Harve Fischman, Joel Kupperman, Henry Tobinski, Richard Weixler. *Notable Guest/Notes:* **Jack Dempsey**
303. 4/14/46. *Kids:* Maureen Buckley, Harve Fischman, Joel Kupperman, Rochelle Liebling, Henry Tobinski
304. 4/21/46. *Kids:* Harve Fischman, Joel Kupperman, Helen Jasper, Rochelle Liebling, Richard Weixler
305. 4/28/46. *Kids:* Harve Fischman, Joel Kupperman, Helen Jasper, Rochelle Liebling, Richard Weixler
306. 5/5/46. *Kids:* Ruth Duskin, Harve Fischman, Joel Kupperman, Rochelle Liebling, Richard Weixler. *Notable Guest/Notes:* **Artur Rodzinski,** conductor, New York Philharmonic
307. 5/12/46. *Kids:* Ruth Duskin, Harve Fischman, Joel Kupperman, Rochelle Liebling, Richard Weixler. *Notable Guest/Notes:* Mother's Day program with their mothers
308. 5/19/46. *Kids:* Ruth Duskin, Harve Fischman, Richard Goddard, Joel Kupperman, Rochelle Liebling
309. 5/26/46. *Kids:* James DeZutter, Ruth Duskin, Harve Fischman, Joel Kupperman, Richard Weixler. *Notable Guest/Notes:* First winner of Best Teacher Awards announced.
310. 6/2/46. *Kids:* Ruth Duskin, Harve Fischman, Joel Kupperman, Rochelle Liebling, Richard Weixler. *Notable Guest/Notes:* From Detroit; appearance at event celebrating the 50th anniversary of the automotive industry.
311. 6/9/46. *Kids:* Ruth Duskin, Harve Fischman, Joel Kupperman, Rochelle Liebling, Richard Weixler. *Notable Guest/Notes:* **Jack Benny**
312. 6/16/46. *Kids:* Patrick Conlon, Ruth Duskin, Harve Fischman, Joel Kupperman, Richard Weixler. *Notable Guest/Notes:* Father's Day program, with their fathers. 6:30 national network broadcast cancelled for U.S. Open Golf championship broadcast. Regularly scheduled Pacific repeat broadcast only.
313. 6/23/46. *Kids:* Patrick Conlon, Ruth Duskin, Harve Fischman, Arthur Fogel, Joel Kupperman. *Notable Guest/Notes:* **Dr. Wilfred J. Funk,** eminent lexicographer, and famous actor **Otto Kruger**
314. 6/30/46. *Kids:* Patrick Conlon, Naomi Cooks, Harve Fischman, Joel Kupperman, John Pollock
315. 7/7/46. *Kids:* Patrick Conlon, Naomi Cooks, Roger Goebel (contest winner), Joel Kupperman, John Pollock
316. 7/14/46. *Kids:* Patrick Conlon, Naomi Cooks, Joel Kupperman, John Pollock, Alan Sankstone. *Notable Guest/Notes:* Cut in from Los Angeles with Harve Fischman.
317. 7/21/46. *Kids:* Patrick Conlon, Naomi Cooks, Ruth Duskin, Joel Kupperman, Alan Sankstone. *Notable Guest/Notes:* Cut in from Los Angeles with Harve Fisch-

man interviewing former Quiz Kid **Vanessa Brown,** now a movie star.

318. 7/28/46. *Kids:* Naomi Bernards, Ruth Duskin, Joel Kupperman, Alan Sankstone, Bryan Woods
319. 8/4/46. *Kids:* Naomi Bernards, Ruth Duskin, Harve Fischman, Joel Kupperman, DiAnne Mathre
320. 8/11/46. *Kids:* Naomi Bernards, Dean Barry, Harve Fischman, Lonny Lunde, Jack Rooney
321. 8/18/46. *Kids:* Naomi Bernards, Dean Barry, Lonny Lundy, Jack Rooney, Richard Weixler
322. 8/25/46. *Kids:* Naomi Bernards, Dean Barry, Lonny Lundy, Jack Rooney, Richard Weixler
323. 9/1/46. *Kids:* Naomi Bernards, Naomi Cooks, Lonny Lunde, Norman Miller, Jack Rooney
324. 9/8/46. *Kids:* Naomi Bernards, Naomi Cooks, Lonny Lunde, Norman Miller, Jack Rooney
325. 9/15/46. *Kids:* Ruth Duskin, George Hust, Lonny Lunde, David Nasatir, Jack Rooney
326. 9/22/46. *Kids:* Lee Abrams, Naomi Bernards, Ruth Duskin, Lonny Lunde, Norman Miller, Gurrie Rhoads, Jack Rooney
327. 9/29/46. *Kids:* Naomi Cooks, Ruth Duskin, Joel Kupperman, Jack Rooney, Richard Weixler. *Notable Guest/Notes:* First broadcast under a new contract with Miles Labs, on a new station (WMAQ), and a new time (Sundays, 3 P.M. [Central]). Edith Binker, winner of 1946 Best Teacher contest.
328. 10/6/46. *Kids:* Patrick Conlon, Naomi Cooks, Ruth Duskin, Joel Kupperman, Jack Rooney. *Notable Guest/Notes:* **Allan Jones**, actor and singer, father of Jack Jones
329. 10/13/46. *Kids:* Broadcast cancelled for *The Parade of Stars* program. *Notable Guest/Notes: The Parade of Stars* was a preview of new and old programs returning for the fall season. The broadcast featured at least 31 radio personalities and their shows, including *QK*.
330. 10/20/46. *Kids:* Naomi Cooks, Ruth Duskin, Joel Kupperman, Lonny Lunde, Jack Rooney. *Notable Guest/Notes:* Secretary of Treasury **John Snyder** announces that the U.S. Treasury silver medal for distinguished service is awarded to the program for its part in the war, victory, and savings bond drives.
331. 10/27/46. *Kids:* Naomi Cooks, Ruth Duskin, Joel Kupperman, Lonny Lunde, Jack Rooney. *Notable Guest/Notes:* **Roy Rogers** and **Gabby Hayes**
332. 11/3/46. *Kids:* Robert Burns, Judy Graham, Joel Kupperman, Lonny Lunde, Jack Rooney. *Notable Guest/Notes:* **Bennett Cerf,** president, Random House publishing
333. 11/10/46. *Kids:* Ruel Fischman, Judy Graham, Joel Kupperman, Lonny Lunde, Jack Rooney. *Notable Guest/Notes:* Movie actress **Virginia Mayo**
334. 11/17/46. *Kids:* Ruel Fischman, Judy Graham, Joel Kupperman, Lonny Lunde, Richard Sedlack
335. 11/24/46. *Kids:* Naomi Cooks, Joel Kupperman, Lonny Lunde, Daniel Martin, Richard Sedlack. *Notable Guest/Notes:* Actor **Neil Hamilton**
336. 12/1/46. *Kids:* Naomi Cooks, Joel Kupperman, Lonny Lunde, DiAnne Mathre, Richard Sedlack. *Notable Guest/Notes:* Program honors National 4-H Club members who are attending their national conference in Chicago. U.S. Secretary of Agriculture **Clinton P. Anderson** speaks from Washington.
337. 12/8/46. *Kids:* Naomi Cooks, Joel Kupperman, Lonny Lunde, Daniel Martin, Jack Rooney. *Notable Guest/Notes:* Broadcast from the Library of Congress. The Kids are guests of the Pan American Union.
338. 12/15/46. *Kids:* Patrick Conlon, Joel Kupperman, Lonny Lunde, DiAnne Mathre, Richard Weixler. *Notable Guest/Notes:* Famous Shakespearean actor **Maurice Evans**
339. 12/22/46. *Kids:* Patrick Conlon, Naomi Cooks, Joel Kupperman, Lonny Lunde, DiAnne Mathre, Richard Weixler. *Notable Guest/Notes:* Actress **Gertrude Lawrence**
340. 12/29/46. *Kids:* Patrick Conlon, Naomi

Cooks, Joel Kupperman, Lonny Lunde, Richard Weixler. *Notable Guest/Notes:* More than 50 former Quiz Kids are guests, interviewed by Joe Kelly. Among them are Claude Brenner, Cynthia Cline, Jack Lucal, Betty Swanson, Richard Williams.
341. 1/5/47. *Kids:* Patrick Conlon, Naomi Cooks, Joel Kupperman, Lonny Lunde, Richard Weixler.
342. 1/12/47. *Kids:* Patrick Conlon, Joel Kupperman, Lonny Lunde, David Prochaska, Corinne Templeton
343. 1/19/47. *Kids:* Dean Barry, Patrick Conlon, Joel Kupperman, Michael Mullin, Corinne Templeton
344. 1/26/47. *Kids:* Naomi Cooks, Joel Kupperman, Lon Lunde, Paul Nay (contest), Jack Rooney. *Notable Guest/Notes:* From Miami. Broadcast is from Orange Bowl appearance at fund-raiser for March of Dimes.
345. 2/2/47. *Kids:* Dean Barry, Patrick Conlon, Ruth Duskin, Lonny Lunde, Michael Mullin. *Notable Guest/Notes:* **Dr. Paul Witty** announces kickoff for Outstanding Teacher of 1947 contest.
346. 2/9/47. *Kids:* Dean Barry, Patrick Conlon, Ruth Duskin, Bernard Griesel, Michael Mullin. *Notable Guest/Notes:* **Edith Binker,** winner of Outstanding Teacher of 1946, and former Quiz Kid, Andre Aerne
347. 2/16/47. *Kids:* Robert Burns, Ruth Duskin, Bernard Griesel, Michael Mullin, David Prochaska. *Notable Guest/Notes:* Guest is Marcia Cook, the "Drugstore Queen" of Southern California.
348. 2/23/47. *Kids:* Naomi Cooks, Joel Kupperman, Lonny Lunde, Jack Rooney. *Notable Guest/Notes:* Broadcast from Baltimore for official opening of national 1947 Red Cross drive with local Baltimore drive. Guests: U.S. representatives **Margaret Chase Smith, W. J. Bryan Dorn** and U.S. senators **Homer E. Capehart** and **Carl A. Hatch.**
349. 3/2/47. *Kids:* Naomi Cooks, Joel Kupperman, Lonny Lunde, Jack Rooney. *Notable Guest/Notes:* Broadcast from NBC studios in New York. **Fred Allen.**
350. 3/9/47. *Kids:* Robert Burns, Naomi Cooks, Bernard Griesel, Joel Kupperman, David Prochaska. *Notable Guest/Notes:* **Wilhelm Morgenstierne,** ambassador to the United States from Norway, talks about a Norwegian Quiz Kids program.
351. 3/16/47. *Kids:* Patrick Conlon, Bernard Griesel, Joel Kupperman, Michael Mullin, David Prochaska. *Notable Guest/Notes:* St. Patrick's Day broadcast, with QK Lonny Lunde as a guest, playing a song he wrote and dedicated to Joe Kelly.
352. 3/23/47. *Kids:* Patrick Conlon, Naomi Cooks, Ruth Duskin, Bernard Griesel, Joel Kupperman. *Notable Guest/Notes:* **William Benton,** assistant secretary of state for Public Affairs, speaks about UNESCO from Washington. The next day he makes keynote speech at the national conference of UNESCO.
353. 3/30/47. *Kids:* Dean Barry, Patrick Conlon, Ruth Duskin, Joel Kupperman, Richard Weixler. *Notable Guest/Notes:* **Caleb F. Gates,** chancellor of the University of Denver, speaking from Denver. Gates reports a recent poll with questions about citizenship shows that the Kids made almost perfect scores.
354. 4/6/47. *Kids:* Patrick Conlon, Ruth Duskin, Joel Kupperman, Lonny Lunde, Richard Weixler. *Notable Guest/Notes:* **Joe E. Brown,** famous comic actor
355. 4/13/47. *Kids:* Patrick Conlon, Naomi Cooks, Ruth Duskin, Joel Kupperman, Lonny Lunde. *Notable Guest/Notes:* **Dr. Wendell Stanley,** who shared the 1946 Nobel Prize in chemistry, speaking from NBC New York studios, compliments *QK* on encouraging interest in chemistry and other sciences. **Ted Lyons,** manager of the Chicago White Sox, from the dugout at Wrigley Field. The kids ask him questions.
356. 4/20/47. *Kids:* Patrick Conlon, Joel Kupperman, Lonny Lunde, Mark Mullin
357. 4/27/47. *Kids:* Patrick Conlon, Joel Kupperman, Mark Mullin, David Prochaska, Corrine Templeton. *Notable Guest/Notes:* The voice of a woman is heard as "Mrs. Hush Hush," a gimmick used on

the NBC radio program *Truth or Consequences*.

358. 5/4/47. *Kids:* Patrick Conlon, Naomi Cooks, Joel Kupperman, Mark Mullin, Corrine Templeton. *Notable Guest/Notes:* **Ralph Edwards,** creator and emcee of *Truth or Consequences*

359. 5/11/47. *Kids:* Patrick Conlon, Naomi Cooks, Joel Kupperman, Mark Mullin, Corrine Templeton. *Notable Guest/Notes:* Mother's Day program. Mothers of today's panel are guests. From New York, Mrs. Frederick Murray, American Mother of the Year 1947.

360. 5/18/47. *Kids:* Patrick Conlon, Naomi Cooks, Paul Hannon (local Quiz Kid), Joel Kupperman, Mark Mullin. *Notable Guest/Notes:* Broadcast from Denver. Kids are in Denver, invited by the Denver Committee of the American Aid to France, to help raise money for a health center for destitute children of Brest, France.

361. 5/25/47. *Kids:* Patrick Conlon, Naomi Cooks, Joel Kupperman, Mark Mullin, Corrine Templeton. *Notable Guest/Notes:* Today's program honors the youngest and oldest of the 245 Kids who have been on the program to date, with the oldest, Lois Ashbeck, age 22, and the youngest, Richard Goddard, age 4.

362. 6/1/47. *Kids:* Joel Kupperman, Lonny Lunde, Mark Mullin, Michael Mullin, Corrine Templeton. *Notable Guest/Notes:* Broadcast from the Stevens Hotel in Chicago. 5,500 members of the National Association of Music Merchants attend the broadcast. **Dr. Paul Witty** announces winner of Best Teacher of 1947 contest.

363. 6/8/47. *Kids:* Sydney Coleman (contest), Patrick Conlon, Joel Kupperman, Lonny Lunde, Michael Mullin. *Notable Guest/Notes:* **Aline Neal,** winner of 1947 Best Teacher contest. **Charles Beardsley,** chairman of the board, Miles Laboratories, presents her with the award.

364. 6/15/47. *Kids:* Sydney Coleman, Patrick Conlon, Joel Kupperman, Lonny Lunde, Michael Mullin. *Notable Guest/Notes:* Father's Day program. Fathers of today's panel are guests. Joining the parents who are quizzed today is Bob Murphy, usual announcer for *QK,* who is a substitute "father" for Sydney Coleman.

365. 6/22/47. *Kids:* David Prochaska. Remainder of panel is unknown. *Notable Guest/Notes:* One of the questions for the Kids is about the chinchilla. David Prochaska answers all the parts of the question correctly and is surprised with a gift of a real, live chinchilla, worth $1,650.

366. 6/29/47. *Kids:* Robert Burns, Sheila Conlon, Ruel Fischman, Richard Weixler, Gary (last name uinknown). *Notable Guest/Notes:* Seventh anniversary program. Five ex–Quiz Kids (Cynthia Cline, Harve Fischman, Jack Lucal, Betty Swanson, and Richard Williams) are guests.

367. 7/6/47. *Kids:* Sydney Coleman, Naomi Cooks, Joel Kupperman, Lonny Lunde, David Prochaska

368. 7/13/47. *Kids:* Robert Burns, Naomi Cooks, Lonny Lunde, David Prochaska

369. 7/20/47. *Kids:* Robert Burns, Ruel Fischman, Joel Kupperman, Lonny Lunde, Corinne Templeton. *Notable Guest/Notes:* Joe Kelly's last program before he leaves for vacation.

370. 7/27/47. *Kids:* Dean Barry, Ruel Fischman, Lonny Lunde, Corinne Templeton, Joan (last name unknown). *Notable Guest/Notes:* Everett Mitchell emcee of the *National Farm and Home Hour,* substitutes for Joe Kelly, who is on vacation.

371. 8/3/47. *Kids:* Dean Barry, Joel Kupperman, Lonny Lunde, Virginia Rodes, Corinne Templeton. *Notable Guest/Notes:* **Bob Murphy,** usually the announcer for *QK,* substitutes for Joe Kelly.

372. 8/10/47. *Kids:* Robert Burns, Patrick Conlon, Joel Kupperman, Lonny Lunde, Corinne Templeton. *Notable Guest/Notes:* **Emmett Kelly,** famous hobo clown of Ringling Brothers and Barnum & Bailey Circus. This is the first time Emmett Kelly has ever spoken in a public appearance. **Bill Odom,** famous pilot, speaks from Chicago airport, where he has just returned from a solo around-the-world flight. Joe Kelly returns.

373. 8/17/47. *Kids:* Patrick Conlon, Joel

Kupperman, Lonny Lunde, Corinne Templeton, Richard Weixler. *Notable Guest/Notes:* Henry MacCracken, president emeritus of Vassar College, who speaks about the importance of education for young people.

374. 8/24/47. *Kids:* Patrick Conlon, Naomi Cooks, Lonny Lunde, Corinne Templeton. *Notable Guest/Notes:* Mrs. Charles Sewell, administrative director of the Associated Women of the American Farm Bureau Federation, representing over 1,500,000 farm women.

375. 8/31/47. *Kids:* Robert Burns, Patrick Conlon, Ruth Duskin, Lonny Lunde, John Pollack. *Notable Guest/Notes:* Former Quiz Kid Cynthia Cline. Cynthia sings several songs. She announced this week that she's engaged to be married. Kelly wishes her a happy married life and mentions that she is the seventh of Quiz Kids graduates who is married or about to be married.

376. 9/7/47. *Kids:* Sandra Bagus, Patrick Conlon, Lonny Lunde, Michael Mullin, John Pollack. *Notable Guest/Notes:* Paul Witty, speaking from New York, says that one of the things he learned from reading entries to Best Teacher contest is that some of the letters told why those students did not like certain teachers.

377. 9/14/47. *Kids:* Naomi Cooks, Joel Kupperman, Mark Mullin, David Prochaska, Marilyn (last name unknown [contest winner]). *Notable Guest/Notes:* Broadcast from Syracuse, New York. Featured today is the release of a homing pigeon bound for Chicago. Kelly scribbles a message for the pigeon and promises to read it on air whenever the pigeon arrives. Pigeon is shown to studio audience, then taken outside and released. As a joke, Kelly asks the *Kids:* "If you were sending a message from Syracuse to Chicago by homing pigeon, at what speed do you think it would be delivered?" Joel says that he'll wait until the pigeon reaches Chicago for the answer.

378. 9/21/47. *Kids:* Patrick Conlon, Joel Kupperman, Lonny Lunde, Michael Mullin, Donald (last name unknown). *Notable Guest/Notes:* Joe Kelly reports that there has been no report from the homing pigeon released in Syracuse.

379. 9/28/47. *Kids:* Sandra Bagus, Patrick Conlon, Joel Kupperman, Lonny Lunde, Michael Mullin. *Notable Guest/Notes:* **Garry Moore**, emcee of *Take It or Leave It* (the famous "$64 question" program). Joe reports that the homing pigeon is still lost.

380. 10/5/47. *Kids:* Robert Burns, Patrick Conlon, Joel Kupperman, Lonny Lunde, Corinne Templeton. *Notable Guest/Notes:* Guests: **Jack Benny and Fred Allen**, from Los Angeles and New York. Benny and Allen are plugging their own broadcasts, returning that evening for the new season. The customary "feud" between them begins again.

381. 10/12/47. *Kids:* Naomi Cooks, Joel Kupperman, Lonny Lunde, Darice Richman, Corinne Temnpleton. *Notable Guest/Notes:* Famous actor **Jimmy Stewart**, who acts as Chief Quizzer for part of the broadcast.

382. 10/19/47. *Kids:* Patrick Conlon, Joel Kupperman, Lonny Lunde, John Pollack, Richard Weixler. *Notable Guest/Notes:* Paul Witty, who announces a new essay contest for high school seniors in cooperation with the American Heritage Foundation. Contest is open to every high school senior in the United States. The subject of the essay is "What America Means to Me."

383. 10/26/47. *Kids:* Patrick Conlon, Naomi Cooks, David Cross, Joel Kupperman, Richard Weixler. *Notable Guest/Notes:* Broadcast from the Kent Theatre in Chicago. The Kids are guests of the Lions International. The occasion is the launching of Child Health Week.

384. 11/2/47. *Kids:* Maureen Buckley, Patrick Conlon, Joel Kupperman, Robert Ochoa (contest winner), David Prochaska. *Notable Guest/Notes:* **John K. M. McCaffery**, moderator of the radio program *Author Meets the Critics*

385. 11/9/47. *Kids:* Patrick Conlon, Ruth Duskin, Joel Kupperman, Mark Mullin, David Prochaska. *Notable Guest/Notes:*

Paul Witty talks about essay contest. Former Quiz Kid Harve Fischman gives high school senior's viewpoint about the essay contest.

386. 11/16/47. *Kids:* Robert Buirns, Patrick Conlon, Ruth Duskin, John Pollock, David Prochaska. *Notable Guest/Notes:* Quiz Kid Darice Richman is a special guest, playing the piano for some of the musical questions.

387. 11/23/47. *Kids:* Patrick Conlon, Ruth Duskin, Lonny Lunde, John Pollack, Darice Richman. *Notable Guest/Notes:* Actor **John Garfield,** Herold C. Hunt, president of the American Association of School Administrators and general superintendent of the Chicago school system

388. 11/30/47. *Kids:* Bill Brubaker (contest), Naomi Cooks, Joel Kupperman, Lonny Lunde, Mark Mullin. *Notable Guest/Notes:* Broadcast from Montgomery, Alabama. Invited by local Lions Club to a benefit for their Blind Club. Guests: actress Elise Mayfield, **Aline Neal,** winner of 1947 Best Teacher contest.

389. 12/7/47. *Kids:* Ruth Duskin, Joel Kupperman, Lonny Lunde, Mark Mullin, John Pollack. *Notable Guest/Notes:* **Dr. Lewis M. Terman**, noted educator and child psychologist from Stanford University and author of a book about gifted children

390. 12/14/47. *Kids:* Sandra Bagus, Robert Burns, Ruth Duskin, Joel Kupperman, Lonny Lunde. *Notable Guest/Notes:* **Emery Walker, Jr.**, dean of admissions, Brown University

391. 12/21/47. *Kids:* Patrick Conlon, Ruth Duskin, Joel Kupperman, Lonny Lunde, Darice Richman. *Notable Guest/Notes:* Annual Quiz Kids Christmas party. Guests are 125 children and their mothers. These are children whose fathers were lost in World War II.

392. 12/28/47. *Kids:* Patrick Conlon, Ruth Duskin, Joel Kupperman, Lonny Lunde, Darice Richman. *Notable Guest/Notes:* Announcement of winners in high school essay contest

393. 1/4/48. *Kids:* Patrick Conlon, Ruth Duskin, Joel Kupperman, Lonny Lunde, Richard Weixler

394. 1/11/48. *Kids:* Patrick Conlon, Ruth Duskin, Joel Kupperman, Lonny Lunde, Janice Metios (contest winner). *Notable Guest/Notes:* Janice is winner of the *Chicago Daily News* "Quizdown Contest."

395. 1/18/48. *Kids:* Patrick Conlon, Ruth Duskin, Rochelle Liebling, Lonny Lunde, Corinne Templeton. *Notable Guest/Notes:* Tie-in from New York with Norwegian Quiz Kid Hildur (last name incomplete), visiting with group of 20 high school students from Scandanavian countries. Hildur says that the Norwegian QK program is a link between the young people of the two countries.

396. 1/25/48. *Kids:* Naomi Cooks, Joel Kupperman, Lonny Lunde, Michael Mullin, Richard Weixler. *Notable Guest/Notes:* Actress **Peggy Ann Garner.** Broadcast from Louisville, KY, where Kids are appearing on behalf of the 1948 March of Dimes fund-raising campaign.

397. 2/1/48. *Kids:* Robert Burns, Naomi Cooks, Joel Kupperman, Lonny Lunde, Michael Mullin

398. 2/8/48. *Kids:* Patrick Conlon, Rochelle Liebling, Lonny Lunde, Virgina Rose, Corinne Templeton. *Notable Guest/Notes:* **Dr. George F. Zook**, president of the American Council on Education, speaks from Washington, D.C.

399. 2/15/48. *Kids:* Patrick Conlon, Rochelle Liebling, Lonny Lunde, David Prochaska, Corinne Templeton

400. 2/22/48. *Kids:* Patrick Conlon, David Freifelder, Greta Lorge, Lonny Lunde, Corinne Templeton

401. 2/29/48. *Kids:* Patrick Conlon, David Freifelder, Juliann (last name unknown), Lonny Lunde, Corinne Templeton

402. 3/7/48. *Kids:* Patrick Conlon, Richard Craven, David Freifelder, Joel Kupperman, Lonny Lunde,. *Notable Guest/Notes:* **Dave Garroway**, who presents Joe Kelly with the Radio Best magazine Silver Mike Award in recognition of his outstanding success as a radio performer.

403. 3/14/48. *Kids:* Patrick Conlon, Joel Kupperman, Lonny Lunde, Mark Mullin. *Notable Guest/Notes:* Broadcast from University of Chicago. QK entertaining at the midwinter alumni reunion. Kids vs. male alumni, including Richard Craven's father and Lonny Lunde's father.

404. 3/21/48. *Kids:* Patrick Conlon, Richard Craven, David Freifelder, Joel Kupperman. *Notable Guest/Notes:* **Martin H. Kennelly,** mayor of Chicago, who presents Joe Kelly with the Radio Miror magazine award for "favorite quizmaster" in a recent listener poll.

405. 3/28/48. *Kids:* Patrick Conlon, Richard Craven, David Freifelder, Joel Kupperman, Lonny Lunde

406. 4/4/48. *Kids:* Patrick Conlon, Richard Craven, James Koch, Joel Kupperman, Lonny Lunde

407. 4/11/48. *Kids:* Robert Burns, Patrick Conlon, Joel Kupperman, Lonny Lunde, Corinne Templeton. *Notable Guest/Notes:* Broadcast from Detroit for fund-raising benefit for Dearborn Boys' Club

408. 4/18/48. *Kids:* Patrick Conlon, Richard Craven, Joel Kupperman, Lonny Lunde, Jck Rooney

409. 4/25/48. *Kids:* Joel Kupperman, Lonny Lunde, Nancy McCreery, David Prochaska, Jack Rooney. *Notable Guest/Notes:* Joel Kupperman competes with an adding machine expert and an abacus expert. They are given three sets of 8 two-digit numbets to add. Joel answers first with the right answer each time. He answers within 1.1 seconds each time.

410. 5/2/48. *Kids:* Naomi Cooks, David Greenstein, Joel Kupperman, Lonny Lunde, David Prochaska

411. 5/9/48. *Kids:* Patrick Conlon, Naomi Cooks, Joel Kupperman, Michael Mullin. *Notable Guest/Notes:* Mother's Day program. Broadcast features the Kids and their mothers, brothers, and sisters. First half of show the Kids compete with their mothers. On the second half the Kids compete with their brothers and sisters: Sheila Conlon, George Cooks, Harriet Kupperman, Mark Mullin.

412. 5/16/48. *Kids:* Naomi Cooks, Whit Humphries, Joel Kupperman, Lonny Lunde, Noreen Novick

413. 5/23/48. *Kids:* Joel Kupperman, Rochelle Liebling, Lonny Lunde, Noreen Novick. *Notable Guest/Notes:* Oscar Ewing, of the federal Office of Education, who congratulates QK for sponsoring the annual Best Teacher contest.

414. 5/30/48. *Kids:* Unknown. *Notable Guest/Notes:* **Dr. Paul Witty** announces winner of 1948 Best Teacher contest.

415. 6/6/48. *Kids:* David Freifelder, Helen Jasper, Joel Kupperman, Lonny Lunde, Mark Mullin. *Notable Guest/Notes:* **Charles S. Beardsley** presents Best Teacher award to Roy Fisher. Joe Kelly presents Beardsley with the Melvin Joes Award from the Lions association for outsanding service to youth through the QK program and the Best Teacher contests.

416. 6/13/48. *Kids:* David Freifelder, John Galinas, Joel Kupperman, Lonny Lunde, Mark Mullin. *Notable Guest/Notes:* Roger Kvam, winner of the World Affairs essay contest for high school students by the *Minneapolis Star*

417. 6/20/48. *Kids:* Patrick Conlon, Naomi Cooks, Joel Kupperman, Mark Mullin. *Notable Guest/Notes:* Father's Day broadcast with Kids competing with their fathers. Special guest is Joe Kelly, Jr., who is Joe Kelly's son. Joe Jr. is the Chief Quizzer for part of the program while Joe Sr. joins the panel of fathers.

418. 6/27/48. *Kids:* John Galinas, Joel Kupperman, Lonny Lunde, Mark Mullin, Corinne Templeton. *Notable Guest/Notes:* Eighth anniversary broadcast. Pickup from Los Angeles where former Quiz Kid Harve Fischman, now a student at UCLA, reports on the activities of other ex–Quiz Kids.

419. 7/4/48. *Kids:* Nanette Hector, Joel Kupperman, Lonny Lunde, Nancy McCreery, Corinne Templeton. *Notable Guest/Notes:* Fourth of July theme for questions.

420. 7/11/48. *Kids:* Sheila Conlon, Gary Griswold, Joel Kupperman, Lonny Lunde, Corinne Templeton. *Notable Guest/Notes:* Charles S. Wehrer, superintendent of schools, Wood Lake, Nebraska

421. 7/18/48. *Kids:* Gary Griswold, Joel

Kupperman, Lonny Lunde, Corinne Templeton

422. 7/25/48. *Kids:* Joel Kupperman, Lonny Lunde, Michael Mullin, Corinne Templeton, Robert (last name unknown)

423. 8/1/48. *Kids:* Joel Kupperman, Lonny Lunde, Melvin Miles, Michael Mullin, Corinne Templeton

424. 8/8/48. *Kids:* Joel Kupperman, Douglas Maurer, Melvin Miles, Mark Mullin, Corinne Templeton

425. 8/15/48. *Kids:* Harriet Fry, Joel Kupperman, Ira Lee, Michael Mullin, Corinne Templeton

426. 8/22/48. *Kids:* Patrick Conlon, Harriet Fry, Joel Kupperman, Ira Lee, Melvin Miles. *Notable Guest/Notes:* Guests: Harmonica team Bob and Agnes Ballentine

427. 8/29/48. *Kids:* Patrick Conlon, George Cooks, Joel Kupperman, Melvin Miles, Kathleen Rhodes

428. 9/5/48. *Kids:* Patrick Conlon, George Cooks, Joel Kupperman, Melvin Miles, Darice Richman. *Notable Guest/Notes:* **Gene Autry**

429. 9/12/48. *Kids:* Patrick Conlon, George Cooks, Joel Kupperman, Melvin Miles, Darice Richman. *Notable Guest/Notes:* Major Lenox Lohr, president of the Chicago Museum of Science and Industry, and former president of NBC. Lenox talks about the railroad fair in progress in Chicago.

430. 9/19/48. *Kids:* Patrick Conlon, Joel Kupperman, Melvin Miles, David Prochaska, Darice Richman. *Notable Guest/Notes:* A salute to the American Heritage Foundation and its Freedom Train. Pickup from NBC studios in New York as Edward Shugrue, national director of the foundation, speaks about the contribution by *QK* when the program sponsored the essay contest for high school seniors. The subject of the essay was "What America Means to Me." The essay of one of the entrants was inspired by the Freedom Train tour.

431. 9/26/48. *Kids:* Patrick Conlon, David Freifelder, Joel Kupperman, Lonny Lunde, Melvin Miles

432. 10/3/48. *Kids:* Patrick Conlon, Sheila Conlon, Joel Kupperman, Lonny Lunde, David Prochaska

433. 10/10/48. *Kids:* Patrick Conlon, Jerry King, Joel Kupperman, Lonny Lunde, Corinne Templeton. *Notable Guest/Notes:* John Cory, executive director, American Library Association

434. 10/17/48. *Kids:* Patrick Conlon, Jerry King, Joel Kupperman, Rochelle Liebling, Lonny Lunde. *Notable Guest/Notes:* Broadcast from St. Louis at benefit for Malcolm Bliss Hospital.

435. 10/24/48. *Kids:* Hermine Duskin, Joel Kupperman, Lonny Lunde, Melvin Miles, Michael Mullin

436. 10/31/48. *Kids:* Joel Kupperman, Lonny Lunde, Melvin Miles, Eden Unterman. *Notable Guest/Notes:* Robert Preston, president, Junior Achievement, Inc.

437. 11/7/48. *Kids:* Miriam Anver, Patrick Conlon, Donald Freifelder, Joel Kupperman, Lonny Lunde. *Notable Guest/Notes:* Mabel Studebaker, president, National Education Association

438. 11/14/48. *Kids:* David Freifelder, Joel Kupperman, Lonny Lunde, Nancy McCreery, Richard Weixler. *Notable Guest/Notes:* **Dr. Paul Witty,** who outlines the details of the Best Teacher contest

439. 11/21/48. *Kids:* Ruth Duskin, Joel Kupperman, Lonny Lunde, Brant Ross, Riochard Weixler. *Notable Guest/Notes:* Thanksgiving broadcast

440. 11/28/48. *Kids:* Patrick Conlon, Ruth Duskin, Joel Kupperman, Lonny Lunde, Richard Weixler. *Notable Guest/Notes:* Lawrence Allen of Bend, Oregon, representative of the 4-H Club. Dr. Phillip Moore, dean of the graduate school at the University of Notre Dame, reports on the educational system in Australia. Pickup from Sydney, Australia.

441. 12/5/48. *Kids:* Patrick Conlon, Ruth Duskin, Joel Kupperman, Lonny Lunde, Melvin Miles.

442. 12/12/48. *Kids:* Patrick Conlon, Ruth Duskin, Joel Kupperman, Lonny Lunde, Melvin Miles. *Notable Guest/Notes:* Dr. Willard C. Olson, director of research in child development, University of Michigan

443. 12/19/48. *Kids:* Patrick Conlon, Ruth Duskin, Joel Kupperman, Lonny Lunde, Melvin Miles. *Notable Guest/Notes:* Christmas program

444. 12/26/48. *Kids:* Patrick Conlon, Ruth Duskin, Joel Kupperman, Lonny Lunde, Melvin Miles.

445. 1/2/49. *Kids:* Patrick Conlon, Naomi Cooks, Ruth Duskin, Joel Kupperman, Mark Mullin

446. 1/9/49. *Kids:* Patrick Conlon, Naomi Cooks, Ruth Duskin, Joel Kupperman, Mark Mullin

447. 1/16/49. *Kids:* Naomi Cooks, Joel Kupperman, Lonny Lunde, Melvin Miles, Darice Richman. *Notable Guest/Notes:* Broadcast from Charlotte, North Carolina. *QK* in Charlotte to help benefit for local March of Dimes drive. Herbert H. Baxter, mayor of Charlotte, speaks.

448. 1/23/49. *Kids:* Clifford Hart, George Herget, Jr., Allen Hitchins, Paul Hornon, Ross Poland Clifford Hart (contest), George Herget, Jr. (contest), Allen Hitchins (contest), Paul Hornon (contest), Ross Poland (contest). *Notable Guest/Notes:* Today the *QK* panel is composed of five winners of contests from five cities across the nation.

449. 1/30/49. *Kids:* Patrick Conlon, Ruth Duskin, Joel Kupperman, Brenda Liebling, Michael McLane. *Notable Guest/Notes:* Movie star **Smiley Burnette**

450. 2/6/49. *Kids:* Michael Burton, Patrick Conlon, Ruth Duskin, Joel Kupperman, Brenda Liebling

451. 2/13/49. *Kids:* Patrick Conlon, Ruth Duskin, Joel Kupperman, Brenda Liebling, David Prochaska

452. 2/20/49. *Kids:* Patrick Conlon, Ruth Duskin, Joel Kupperman, Michael Leburkien, Brenda Liebling

453. 2/27/49. *Kids:* Patrick Conlon, Donald Hall, Joel Kupperman, Brenda Liebling, Corinne Templeton

454. 3/6/49. *Kids:* Patrick Conlon, Joel Kupperman, Ira Lee, Brenda Liebling, Melvin Miles

455. 3/13/49. *Kids:* Patrick Conlon, Joel Kupperman, Greta Lee, Melvin Miles, John Pollack. *Notable Guest/Notes:* Helen Bolstad, editor, *Radio Mirror* magazine. She presents "Best Quizmaster on the Air" award to Joe Kelly for the second consecutive year. **Al Capp,** cartoonist, creator of L'il Abner, speaks from New York.

456. 3/20/49. *Kids:* Patrick Conlon, Julienne Hector, Joel Kupperman, Noreen Novick, John Pollack

457. 3/27/49. *Kids:* Patrick Conlon, Naomi Cooks, Joel Kupperman, Noreen Novick, Arnold Stoper. *Notable Guest/Notes:* Attorney General **Tom C. Clark** speaks from Washington.

458. 4/3/49. *Kids:* Patrick Conlon, Naomi Cooks, David Freifelder, Joel Kupperman, Richard Weixler. *Notable Guest/Notes:* Pickup from NBC studios in New York: **Dr. Paul Witty** announces the winner of the Best Teacher contest.

459. 4/10/49. *Kids:* Patrick Conlon, David Drummond (contest winner), David Freifelder, Joel Kupperman, Richard Weixler. *Notable Guest/Notes:* Phylis Haag, winner of 1949 Best Teacher contest. Charles Beardsley, chairman of Miles Laboratories, presents her with the award.

460. 4/17/49. *Kids:* Patrick Conlon, David Freifelder, Joel Kupperman, Melvin Miles

461. 4/24/49. *Kids:* Jeanne Boudreaux, Rae Hillman, Jane Philips, George Temple, William Trussell. *Notable Guest/Notes:* Today, the Quiz Kids are five winners of contests in five different cities. No score is kept. Actor **Clifton Webb** pickup from NBC in New York, asking Kids questions as he assumes his role of Mr. Belvedere, from his movie of the same name.

462. 5/1/49. *Kids:* Margery Carlson, Patrick Conlon, Lonny Lunde, Melvin Miles, Corinne Templeton. *Notable Guest/Notes:* **Tauno Hannikainen**, associate conductor, Chicago Symphony Orchestra

463. 5/8/49. *Kids:* Patrick Conlon, Lonny Lunde, Melvin Miles, David Prochaska, Corinne Templeton. *Notable Guest/Notes:* Mother's Day broadcast with mothers of the five Kids as special guests

464. 5/15/49. *Kids:* Patrick Conlon, Lonny Lunde, Melvin Miles, David Prochaska, Corinne Templeton. *Notable Guest/Notes:*

Ernestine Carey, author, *Cheaper by the Dozen*

465. 5/22/49. *Kids:* Patrick Conlon, Lonny Lunde, Melvin Miles, Vance Norum, Gurrie Rhoads

466. 5/29/49. *Kids:* Patrick Conlon, Brenda Liebling, Lonny Lunde, Vance Norum, Noreen Novick

467. 6/5/49. *Kids:* Patrick Conlon, Joel Kupperman, Brenda Liebling, Lonny Lunde, Noreen Novick

468. 6/12/49. *Kids:* Thomas Banshoff, Lawrence Gingold, Charles Reeder, Ellen Ross, Edwin Sapinsley. *Notable Guest/Notes:* Today's panel consisted of the five contest winners from five different cities.

469. 6/19/4. *Kids:* Patrick Conlon, Joel Kupperman, Lonny Lunde, Melvin Miles. *Notable Guest/Notes:* Father's Day broadcast with fathers of the panel of Kids as special guests. Last show until September.

470. 9/11/49. *Kids:* Patrick Conlon, Ruth Duskin, Joel Kupperman, Lonny Lunde, Melvin Miles. *Notable Guest/Notes:* First broadcast of new season.

471. 9/18/49. *Kids:* Rae Hillman, Marilyn Peterson, Jo Ann Phillips, Max (last name unknown). *Notable Guest/Notes:* Today's panel consisted of the four contest winners from four different cities.

472. 9/25/49. *Kids:* Dennis, Dianne, Joanne, Tom (last names unknown). *Notable Guest/Notes:* Broadcast from Cincinnati. Panel is four local wiinners from public and parochial schools of Cincinnati. Albert E. Cash, mayor of Cincinnati.

473. 10/2/49. *Kids:* Suellen Bowden, Howard Burdett, Donald Henke, James Phelps, William Thomas. *Notable Guest/Notes:* Broadcast from Cincinnati. The five Quiz Kids are winners of Cincinnati school contests.

474. 10/9/49. *Kids:* Patrick Conlon, Ruth Duskin, Joel Kupperman, Lonny Lunde, Melvin Miles. *Notable Guest/Notes:* Actor **Thomas Mitchell**, Clara Littledale, editor, *Parents Magazine,* who presents an award to *QK* in recognition of its accomplishments.

475. 10/16/49. *Kids:* Patrick Conlon, Joel Kupperman, Brenda Liebling, Lonny Lunde, Gurrie Rhoads. *Notable Guest/Notes:* Ex-Quiz Kid Joan Bishop

476. 10/23/49. *Kids:* Neil Aaron, Adrienne Baptiste, Malcolm Mitchell, Judy Ann Oberfelder, Norman Schaeffer. *Notable Guest/Notes:* Broadcast from New York. The five Quiz Kids for today are contest winners from public and parochial schools in New York.

477. 10/30/49. *Kids:* Victoria Helbok, Malcolm Mitchell, Ellen Papier, Norman Schaeffer, Leon (last name unknown). *Notable Guest/Notes:* Broadcast from New York. Joe Kelly and his "Assistant Quizzer" Melvin Miles visit from Chicago. The five Quiz Kids for today are contest winners from public and parochial schools in New York.

478. 11/6/49. *Kids:* Malcolm Mitchell, Norman Schaeffer, Alan, James, and Richard, whose last names are unknown. *Notable Guest/Notes:* Dr. Andrew D. Holt, president, National Education Association, who announces the Best Teacher contest.

479. 11/13/49. *Kids:* Patrick Conlon, Joel Kupperman, Brenda Liebling, Lonny Lunde, William McCue

480. 11/20/49. *Kids:* Patrick Conlon, Naomi Cooks, Joel Kupperman, Lonny Lunde, Melvin Miles. *Notable Guest/Notes:* Broadcast from Duluth

481. 11/27/49. *Kids:* Patrick Conlon, Joel Kupperman, Lonny Lunde, Corinne Templeton

482. 12/4/49. *Kids:* Barbara, Bert, Carl, Leland, William (last names unknown). *Notable Guest/Notes:* Broadcast from Washington, D.C. The five Kids today are contest winners from D.C. region schools.

483. 12/11/49. *Kids:* Barbara, Margaret, Marthus, Michael, Teddy (last names unknown). *Notable Guest/Notes:* Broadcast from Washington, D.C. The five Kids today are more contest winners from D.C. region schools. Dr. R. I. Grigsby, U.S. Department of Education.

484. 12/18/49. *Kids:* Patrick Conlon, Lonny Lunde, John McClory, Darice Richman, Corinne Templeton

485. 12/25/49. *Kids:* Patrick Conlon, Joel Kupperman, Brenda Liebling, Rochelle Liebling, Melvin Miles. *Notable Guest/Notes:* Christmas program

486. 1/1/50. *Kids:* Patrick Conlon, Ruth Duskin, Lonny Lunde, Melvin Miles, Corinne Templeton

487. 1/8/50. *Kids:* Patrick Conlon, Joel Kupperman, Brenda Liebling, Lonny Lunde. *Notable Guest/Notes:* Broadcast from Ann Arbor. Kids compete with four University of Michigan professors.

488. 1/15/50. *Kids:* Clifton Hill, Edward Hines, Norman Lane, Mary Montgomery, Hannah (last name unknown). *Notable Guest/Notes:* The five Kids today are from five cities, and have been invited to Chicago for the broadcast.

489. 1/22/50. *Kids:* Ruth Duskin, Lonny Lunde, Corinne Templeton, Harvey Templeton, Fred (last name unknown)

490. 1/29/50. *Kids:* Patrick Conlon, Naomi Cooks, Joel Kupperman, Melvin Miles. *Notable Guest/Notes:* Broadcast on tape from New York. Kids compete with five professors from four colleges in New York.

491. 2/5/50. *Kids:* Patrick Conlon, Ruth Duskin, Harvey Dytch, Lonny Lunde, Harvey Templeton

492. 2/12/50. *Kids:* Ruth Duskin, Harvey Dytch, Lonny Lunde, Jack Owen. *Notable Guest/Notes:* Actor and comedian **Billy DeWolfe**

493. 2/19/50. *Kids:* Fred Blackwell, Alfred Ferris, David McLaughlin, Virginia Miller, Jerry Torm. *Notable Guest/Notes:* Five panelists are local winners of *QK* contests in five cities throughout the United States.

494. 2/26/50. *Kids:* Ruth Duskin, Harvey Dytch, Lonny Lunde, Sally Ann Wilhelm, Joyce (last name unknown). *Notable Guest/Notes:* Dr. Philip M. Houaser, acting director, U.S. Bureau of Census

495. 3/5/50. *Kids:* Ruth Duskin, Harvey Dytch, Caroline Jaffee, Fred Klaus, Lonny Lunde.

496. 3/12/50. *Kids:* Ruth Duskin, Harvey Dytch, Chester Hermanski, Lonny Lunde, Albert Rice

497. 3/19/50. *Kids:* Harvey Dytch, Rosita Lightbourn, Lonny Lunde, Albert Rice. *Notable Guest/Notes:* Special Guest Quiz Kid is Ted Meyers, recent Iowa state contest winner conducted by the National Society for Crippled Children and Adults in connection with the annual Easter Seals campaign

498. 3/26/50. *Kids:* Naomi Cooks, Harvey Dytch, Joel Kupperman, Rosita Lightbourn, Lonny Lunde. *Notable Guest/Notes:* **Victor Borge**

499. 4/2/50. *Kids:* Patrick Conlon, Harvey Dytch, Joel Kupperman, Brenda Liebling, Lonny Lunde. *Notable Guest/Notes:* Broadcast from Evanston, Illinois. Kids compete agains five university professors from Northwestern University.

500. 4/9/50. *Kids:* Harvey Dytch, Brenda Liebling, Milton Meyers, Robert Senescu, Wendy Stocking. *Notable Guest/Notes:* Anniversary program. This is the 500th *Quiz Kids* broadcast. The panel today features "baby Quiz Kids," with an average age of 5 1/2 years.

501. 4/16/50. *Kids:* Richard Barber, Patricia Ann Bowen, Michael Lanzarone, Herbert Rule, Alan Stemm. *Notable Guest/Notes:* The five Kids today are from five cities. They have been invited to Chicago for the broadcast.

502. 4/23/50. *Kids:* Naomi Cooks, Harvey Dytch, Joel Kupperman, Lonny Lunde, Sally Ann Wilhelm. *Notable Guest/Notes:* Dr. Paul Witty announces Best Teacher contest winner, Pauline Powers, Youngstown, Ohio.

503. 4/30/50. *Kids:* Naomi Cooks, Harvey Dytch, Joel Kupperman, Lonny Lunde, Sally Ann Wilhelm. *Notable Guest/Notes:* Charles Beardsley, chairman of Miles Laboratories, presents awards to winner of 1950 Best Teacher contest.

504. 5/7/50. *Kids:* Naomi Cooks, Harvey Dytch, Joel Kupperman, Lonny Lunde, Sally Ann Wilhelm

505. 5/14/50. *Kids:* Ruth Duskin, Harvey Dytch, Joel Kupperman, Lonny Lunde, Melvin Miles. *Notable Guest/Notes:* Mother's Day Broadcast. The mothers take part in answering questions with the Kids.

506. 5/21/50. *Kids:* Ruth Duskin, Harvey Dytch, Joel Kupperman, Lonny Lunde, Melvin Miles. *Notable Guest/Notes:* Carolyn Walker, 14-year-old high school student from Wichita, winner of two awards for unusual heroism.

507. 5/28/50. *Kids:* Ruth Duskin, Harvey Dytch, Joel Kupperman, Melvin Miles, Vicki Vala. *Notable Guest/Notes:* **Dorothy Shay**, the Park Avenue Hillbilly singing star

508. 6/4/50. *Kids:* Harvey Dytch, Brenda Liebling. *Notable Guest/Notes:* Broadcast from Mooseheart, Illinois. This program honors the children of Mooseheart, an institution for orphaned children maintained by the Moose Lodge. Added to the panel of the two regular Kids are three "citizens" of Mooseheart: David, Genevieve, and Pat (last names are not available).

509. 6/11/50. *Kids:* Richard Daly, Jeanne Dell, Judith Gore, Harry Smith, Sherrill Smith, Janet Winslow. *Notable Guest/Notes:* Kids are winners of local contests in five other cities.

510. 6/18/50. *Kids:* Patrick Conlon, Ruth Duskin, Joel Kupperman, Melvin Miles, Mark Mullin. *Notable Guest/Notes:* Father's Day broadcast. Fathers of Kids answer questions along with them.

511. 6/25/50. *Kids:* Unknown. *Notable Guest/Notes:* Beginning with this broadcast, *QK* will be sustaining until September. Start of today's broadcast delayed because of the beginning of the Korean war.

512. 7/2/50. *Kids:* Patrick Conlon, Joel Kupperman, Melvin Miles, Mark Mullin, Marlene Richman

513. 7/9/50. *Kids:* Patrick Conlon, Joel Kupperman, Mark Mullin, Marlene Richman, William (last name unavailable). *Notable Guest/Notes:* **Tom Coriven**, famous impersonator, better known as Uncle Tom Coriven

514. 7/16/50. *Kids:* Patrick Conlon, Harvey Dytch, Joel Kupperman, Melvin Miles, Mark Mullin, Marlene Richman. *Notable Guest/Notes:* The Kids run the program. All of the adult staff members are at home, listening. Six Kids are the "cast"; each takes a turn as the Chief Quizzer while the other five answer questions. Patrick is the first "Joe Kelly," followed by Mark, Joel, Melvin, Marlene, Harvey. Lonny Lunde is the organist and scorekeeper. Harvey is the anouncer.

515. 7/23/50. *Kids:* Patrick Conlon, Jonathan Glogower (contest winner), Joel Kupperman, Marlene Richman, Frank VanderPloeg. *Notable Guest/Notes:* **Felix Adler**, famous circus clown with Ringling Brothers and Barnum and Bailey, and actor **Edmund O'Brien**

516. 7/30/50. *Kids:* Patrick Conlon, Joel Kupperman, Brenda Liebling, Lonny Lunde, Frank VanderPloeg. *Notable Guest/Notes:* U.S. Secretary of Treasury John W. Snyder, speaking from Washington, congratulates the Kids for how their bonds are used to further their education.

517. 8/6/50. *Kids:* Patrick Conlon, Harvey Dytch, Joel Kupperman, Lonny Lunde, Frank VanderPloeg. *Notable Guest/Notes:* Eddie Anderson, Holy Cross football coach. He talks about how players are selected for the All-Star game.

518. 8/13/50. *Kids:* Patrick Conlon, Harvey Dytch, Joel Kupperman, Lonny Lunde, Frank VanderPloeg. *Notable Guest/Notes:* Guests are five distinguished visitors from five countries, in Chicago for the First Internaional Trade Fair.

519. 8/20/50. *Kids:* Patrick Conlon, Harvey Dytch, Joel Kupperman, Lonny Lunde, Frank VanderPloeg. *Notable Guest/Notes:* Ex-Quiz Kid Shelley Davis, 14 years old, who has returned to Chicago from his studies in New York to play a concert.

520. 8/27/50. *Kids:* Patrick Conlon, Harvey Dytch, Joel Kupperman, Lonny Lunde, Angos Perez-Macias. *Notable Guest/Notes:* **Evelyn Knight**, vocalist, and ex–Quiz Kid Diane Mathre, newly elected Secretary of the Advisory Council on Youth Participation.

521. 9/3/50. *Kids:* Panel unknown, script unavailable. *Notable Guest/Notes:* Maxine Cothern, Miss Alaska, who will be her state's representative at the Miss America contest in Atlantic City.

522. 9/10/50. *Kids:* Patrick Conlon, Harvey

Dytch, Joel Kupperman, Brenda Liebling, Lonny Lunde. *Notable Guest/Notes:* First program of new season, sponsored by Miles Laboratories.

523. 9/17/50. *Kids:* Patrick Conlon, Joel Kupperman, Brenda Liebling, Lonny Lunde, Melvin Miles. *Notable Guest/Notes:* Kids compete with a panel of representatives from the Chicago Kiwanis Club

524. 9/24/50. *Kids:* Patrick Conlon, Allan Goldman (contest winner), Joel Kupperman, Brenda Liebling, Lonny Lunde. *Notable Guest/Notes:* **Tito Guizar**, folk singer, known as the "singing idol of the Americas"

525. 10/1/50. *Kids:* Patrick Conlon, Joel Kupperman, Millea Levin, Lonny Lunde, Michael Mullin. *Notable Guest/Notes:* **Frankie Laine**, pop singer

526. 10/8/50. *Kids:* Patrick Conlon, Joel Kupperman, Lonny Lunde, Michael Mullin, Benita Perlman (contest winner). *Notable Guest/Notes:* William F. Waugh, judge of the Probate Court, Cook County, who is the Chief Quizzer, while Joe Kelly has the day off.

527. 10/15/50. *Kids:* Patrick Conlon, Naomi Cooks, Joel Kupperman, Melvin Miles, Michael Mullin. *Notable Guest/Notes:* Fraternal Order of the Eagles are guests in the live audience. Kids compete with five Eagles in the quiz session. The Eagles win the contest scoring 159 points to 157 for the Kids.

528. 10/22/50. *Kids:* Patrick Conlon, Naomi Cooks, Joel Kupperman, Melvin Miles, Michael Mullin. *Notable Guest/Notes:* This program has a travel theme. Frank Higgins, a lecturer for the Fitzpatrick Travel Bureau.

529. 10/29/50. *Kids:* Naomi Cooks, Joel Kupperman, Millea Levin, Melvin Miles, Michael Mullin. *Notable Guest/Notes:* Dr. Corma Mowrey, president, National Education Association

530. 11/5/50. *Kids:* Naomi Cooks, Joel Kupperman, Millea Levin, Michael Mullin, Sally Ann Wilhelm. *Notable Guest/Notes:* Five members of the American Legion compete with the Kids. Guests: **Vanessa Brown**, Erle Cocke, Jr., national commander, American Legion.

531. 11/12/50. *Kids:* Patrick Conlon, Howard Klein, Joel Kupperman, Frank VanderPloeg, Sally Ann Wilhelm. *Notable Guest/Notes:* Guests are famous athletes: Hamilton Richardson, national Junior Tennis champion, **Andy Pafko,** center fielder for the Chicago Cubs, Clint Frank, former All-American football player for Yale University, Clem Pavilonis, star center of the DePaul University basketball team.

532. 11/19/50. *Kids:* Parick Conlon, Harvey Dytch, Joel Kupperman, Lonny Lunde, Bette Sartinoff. *Notable Guest/Notes:* Kids compete with five members of Rotary International. Program includes a Thanksgiving tribute.

533. 11/26/50. *Kids:* Harvey Dytch, Melvin Miles. *Notable Guest/Notes:* Studio audience is composed of 4-H Club members. Five specially selected club members join the two regular Kids to make the panel. Gerard Ungaro, president of the National Society for Crippled Children and Adults, presents *QK* and its sponsor an award in appreciation for stimulating interest in support of crippled children

534. 12/3/50. *Kids:* Naomi Cooks, Harvey Dytch, Lonny Lunde, Wendy Stocking, Sally Ann Wilhelm. *Notable Guest/Notes:* Five members of the Lions International compete with the Kids. Quiz Kid Patrick Conlon is the Chief Quizzer because Joe Kelly is one of the panelists for the Lions.

535. 12/10/50. *Kids:* Penny Bergstrom, Hermine Duskin, Brenda Liebling, Lonny Lunde, Frank VanderPloeg. *Notable Guest/Notes:* **George Schick**, assistant conductor, Chicago Symphony Orchestra. Lonny Lunde presents a preview of his concert debut in nine days at a Chicago Symphony young people's concert.

536. 12/17/50. *Kids:* Patrick Conlon, Harvey Dytch, Lonny Lunde, Melvin Miles, Sally Ann Wilhelm. *Notable Guest/Notes:* **Rex Allen**, popular cowboy movie star and singer. Kids compete with a panel of five members of the Elks charitable organization.

537. 12/24/50. *Kids:* Patrick Conlon, Lonny Lunde, Melvin Miles, Wendy Stocking, Sally Ann Wilhelm. *Notable Guest/Notes:* Program is taped and is a fantasy visit to the home of Santa Claus at the North Pole.
538. 12/31/50. *Kids:* Unknown. *Notable Guest/Notes:* Program taped, no script
539. 1/7/51. *Kids:* Naomi Cooks, Harvey Dytch, Joel Kupperman, Lonny Lunde, Christopher Stevens. *Notable Guest/Notes:* Dr. Paul Witty announces the start of the 1951 Best Teacher contest.
540. 1/14/51. *Kids:* Patrick Conlon, Hermine Duskin, Harvey Dytch, Joel Kupperman, Robert Genowith (contest winner). *Notable Guest/Notes:* Dr. James Arnold, Institute of Nuclear Studies at the University of Chicago
541. 1/21/51. *Kids:* Patrick Conlon, Lonny Lunde, Frank VanderPloeg, Sally Ann Wilhelm, Susan Winer. *Notable Guest/Notes:* **Studs Terkel**
542. 1/28/51. *Kids:* Penny Bergstrom, Pat Conlon, Harvey Dytch, Joel Kupperman, Marlene Richman. *Notable Guest/Notes:* **Maureen Stapleton**
543. 2/4/51. *Kids:* Patrick Conlon, Naomi Cooks, Harvey Dytch, Joel Kupperman, guest Quiz Kid, name not available (contest winner). *Notable Guest/Notes:* This program honors the observance of Children's Dental Health day. Five dentists compete with Quiz Kids.
544. 2/11/51. *Kids:* Leonard Isaacs (contest winner), Joel Kupperman, Lonny Lunde, Frank VanderPloeg, Sally Ann Wilhelm. *Notable Guest/Notes:* **George Schick**, assistant conductor, Chicago Symphony Orchestra
545. 2/18/51. *Kids:* Penny Bergstrom, Patrick Conlon, Joel Kupperman, Corinne Templeton, Frank VanderPloeg
546. 2/25/51. *Kids:* John Conteiguglia, Richard Conteiguglia (contest winners), Harvey Dytch, Joel Kupperman, Mark Mullin, Sally Ann Wilhelm
547. 3/4/51. *Kids:* Harvey Dytch, Joel Kupperman, Lonny Lunde, Sally Ann Wilhelm, Karen (last name unknown). *Notable Guest/Notes:* Theme of this program is unusual occupations.
548. 3/11/51. *Kids:* Patrick Conlon, Harvey Dytch, Michael Mullin, Frank (last name not available, contest winner), Robert (last name not available, contest winner). *Notable Guest/Notes:* St. Patrick's Day program
549. 3/18/51. *Kids:* Patrick Conlon, Harvey Dytch, Jay Katzel (contest winner), Joel Kupperman, Lonny Lunde. *Notable Guest/Notes:* Program in cooperation with members of the American Legion Women's Auxiliary. Five Legion women compete with Kids.
550. 3/25/51. *Kids:* Harvey Dytch, others unknown. *Notable Guest/Notes:* Broadcast from Houston. Harvey receives a live pony, a gift from Montie Ritchie of the J. A. Ranch.
551. 5/13/51. *Kids:* Patrick Conlon, Lonny Lunde, Michael Mullin, Frank VanderPloeg, Sally Ann Wilhelm. *Notable Guest/Notes:* Program resumes today. Beginning with this broadcast QK will be sustaining until fall season. Fran Allison replaces Joe Kelly as Chief Quizzer; Joe is on sick leave.
552. 5/20/51. *Kids:* Patrick Conlon, Stuart Holnick, Lonny Lunde, Melvin Miles, Michael Mullin
553. 5/27/51. *Kids:* Patrick Conlon, Lonny Lunde, Melvin Miles, Michael Mullin, Betty Saphron. *Notable Guest/Notes:* Oliver Capelle, sales promotion manager at Miles Laboratories, is Chief Quizzer today
554. 6/3/51. *Kids:* Patrick Conlon, Naomi Cooks, Lonny Lunde, Michael Mullin, Wendy Stocking.
555. 6/10/51. *Kids:* Patrick Conlon, Naomi Cooks, Harvey Dytch, Lonny Lunde, Michael Mullin. *Notable Guest/Notes:* Dr. Paul Witty announces winners of Best Teacher contest. Fran Allison is Chief Quizzer.
556. 6/17/51. *Kids:* Patrick Conlon, Naomi Cooks, Joel Kupperman, Lonny Lunde, Frank VanderPloeg. *Notable Guest/Notes:* Father's Day broadcast. The fathers of today's Kids compete with them. Fran Allison is Chief Quizzer.
557. 6/24/51. *Kids:* Patrick Conlon, Joel Kupperman, Lonny Lunde, Frank Van-

derPloeg, Sally Ann Wilhelm. *Notable Guest/Notes:* Eleventh anniversary celebration for *QK* program. Last program for Fran Allison.
558. 7/1/51. *Kids:* Patrick Conlon, Joel Kupperman, Lonny Lunde, Frank VanderPloeg, Sally Ann Wilhelm. *Notable Guest/Notes:* July 4th broadcast. Oliver Capelle is chief Quizzer until further notice.
559. 7/8/51. *Kids:* Patrick Conlon, Lonny Lunde, Melvin Miles, Mark Mullin, Sally Ann Wilhelm. *Notable Guest/Notes:* Featured on the broadcast is a 14-minute taped excursion with the Kids in a blimp.
560. 7/15/51. *Kids:* Patrick Conlon, Rochelle Liebman, Lonny Lunde, Frank VanderPloeg, Sally Ann Wilhelm. *Notable Guest/Notes:* **Rosemary Clooney**
561. 7/22/51. *Kids:* Patrick Conlon, Harvey Dytch, Ruth Kanaster, Lonny Lunde, Sally Ann Wilhelm. *Notable Guest/Notes:* J. Y. Henderson, veterinarian, Ringling Brothers and Barnum and Bailey Circus
7/29/51. Broadcast cancelled today for special program, *Pilgrimage to Plymouth*
562. 8/5/51. *Kids:* Patrick Conlon, Joel Kupperman, Lonny Lunde, Melvin Miles, Sally Ann Wilhelm. *Notable Guest/Notes:* **Art Tatum**, famous jazz pianist
563. 8/12/51. *Kids:* Patrick Conlon, Joel Kupperman, Lonny Lunde, Frank VanderPloeg, Sally Ann Wilhelm
564. 8/19/51. *Kids:* Patrick Conlon, Harvey Dytch, Joel Kupperman, Lonny Lunde, Sally Ann Wilhelm. *Notable Guest/Notes:* Last broadcast for Oliver Capelle
565. 8/26/51. *Kids:* Patrick Conlon, Joseph Darweesh (contest winner), Lonny Lunde, Melvin Miles, Sally Ann Wilhelm. *Notable Guest/Notes:* Joe Kelly returns as Chief Quizzer.
566. 9/2/51. *Kids:* Patrick Conlon, Lonny Lunde, William McCue, Frank VanderPloeg, Sally Ann Wilhelm. *Notable Guest/Notes:* **Ella Fitzgerald**, famous jazz singer. Former Qiuz Kid Claude Brenner visits.
567. 9/9/51. *Kids:* Naomi Cooks, Harvey Dytch, Lonny Lunde, Sally Ann Wilhelm
568. 9/16/51. *Kids:* Patrick Conlon, Naomi Cooks, Lonny Lunde, Melvin Miles, Sally Ann Wilhelm. *Notable Guest/Notes:* Actress **Maggie McNamara**
569. 9/23/51. *Kids:* Patrick Conlon, Mary Ann Halberdeen, Lonny Lunde, Frank VanderPloeg, Sally Ann Wilhelm
570. 9/29/51. *Kids:* Patrick Conlon, Harvey Dytch, Joel Kupperman, Lonny Lunde, Sally Ann Wilhelm. *Notable Guest/Notes:* Everett Mitchell, emcee, National Farm and Home Hour. Starting with this broadcast, and hereafter, QK will be aired Saturday 1:30–2:00 P.M.
571. 10/6/51. *Kids:* Patrick Conlon, Naomi Cooks, Joel Kupperman, Lonny Lunde, Melvin Miles. *Notable Guest/Notes:* This is the last sponsored radio broadcast of *Quiz Kids*.

Appendix C: *Quiz Kids* Program Chronology

Dates	Network	Day	Central Time
June 28, 1940–August 30, 1940	NBC Red	Friday	9:30 P.M.
September 4, 1940–July 8, 1942	NBC Blue	Wednesday	7:00 P.M.
July 12, 1942–September 22, 1946	NBC Blue	Sunday	6:30 P.M.
September 29, 1946–June 19, 1949	NBC	Sunday	3:00 P.M.
September 11, 1949–March 25, 1951	NBC	Sunday	2:30 P.M.
May 13, 1951–September 23, 1951	NBC	Sunday	6:00 P.M.
September 29, 1951–October 6, 1951	NBC	Saturday	12:30 P.M.
September 14, 1952–October 12, 1952	NBC	Sunday	3:00 P.M.
November 16, 1952–March 1, 1953	NBC	Sunday	3:30 P.M.
May 31, 1953–July 5, 1953	NBC	Sunday	5:00 P.M.

Chapter Notes

Chapter 1

1. Gerald Nachman, *Raised on Radio* (New York: Pantheon, 1998), 327.
2. Paul Cowan, "My Father's Children," *Village Voice*, March 29, 1983, 15.
3. Nachman, *Raised on Radio,* 327.
4. Louis Cowan, "The Reminiscences of Mr. Louis Cowan" (New York: Oral History Research Office, Columbia University, 1978), 26.
5. Cowan, "My Father's Children," 15.
6. Beth Twiggar, "Quiz Kids Come to Town to Make a Film," *New York Herald Tribune*, February 2, 1941, VI, 4.
7. Don Moore, "The Quiz Kids," *Movie and Radio Guide*, August 31–September 6, 1940, 39.
8. "Quiz Kids Information Please in Short Pants," *Spotlite Magazine*, January 1941, 26.
9. Cowan, "My Father's Children," 34.
10. Cowan, "Reminiscences," 164.
11. Cowan, "Reminiscences," 26.
12. Eliza "Roby" (Hickok) Kesler, interview by author, Cedar Rapids, Iowa, April 9–10, 2004.
13. Eliza Merrill Hickok, *The Quiz Kids* (Boston: Houghton Mifflin, 1947), 196.
14. Cowan, "Reminiscences," 26.
15. Hickok, *The Quiz Kids,* 196.
16. Ann Marsters, "'Quiz Kids' Originator Tells Woes of Founding Program," *Chicago Herald-American*, January 6, 1941, 13.
17. LuAnn Lewellen, telephone interview by author, June 10, 2004.
18. Roby (Hickok) Kesler, telephone interview by author, December 17, 2004.
19. "The Quiz Kids and How They Grew," n.p., 1948, Ruth Duskin Feldman collection, 1.
20. Walter Selden, "Louis Cowan Interview on the Quiz Kids," March 30, 1941, 2, Feldman collection.
21. Pence James, "Boy, 4, Identifies 365 Birds from Pictures, Tells Habits," *Chicago Daily News*, April 23, 1937, 44.
22. Sidney James, "Prodigy's Progress: Gerard Darrow," *Life*, September 29, 1941, 54.
23. James, "Prodigy's Progress," 49.
24. Selden, "Louis Cowan Interview," 2.
25. Marsters, "Quiz Kids' Originator," 13.
26. Frank A. Randall, *History of the Development of Building Construction in Chicago*, 2d ed., revised and expanded by John H. Randall (Urbana: University of Illinois Press, 1999), 143.
27. Randall, *History of the Development,* 202.
28. Joan (Bishop) Barber, telephone interview by author, July 13, 2004.
29. Weldon Melick, "Have You a Quiz Kid in Your Home?" *Coronet*, March 1942, 4.
30. Marsters, "Quiz Kids' Originator," 25.
31. Marsters, "Quiz Kids' Originator," 13.
32. Hickok, *The Quiz Kids,* 199.
33. "Academy Awards USA: Awards for 1940," www.imdb.com, accessed February 1, 2012.
34. Cowan, "Reminiscences," 29.
35. Marsters, "Quiz Kids' Originator," 25.
36. Hickok, *The Quiz Kids,* 198.
37. Cowan, "Reminiscences," 26.
38. Nachman, *Raised on Radio,* 328.
39. Selden, "Louis Cowan Interview," 2.
40. Paul Cowan and Rachel Cowan, *Mixed Blessings: Marriage Between Jews and Christians* (New York: Doubleday, 1987), 10.
41. J. P. McEvoy, "Quiz Kids," *Cue*, September 7, 1940, 18.

42. Cowan, "Reminiscences," 27.
43. "Milestones in Elkhart," http://www.entrepreneur.com/tradejournals/article/print/12926667.html, accessed March 4, 2011.
44. Edgar A. Thompson, "Little Mental Giants," *The Milwaukee Journal*, July 14, 1940, 10.
45. Selden, "Louis Cowan Interview," 3.
46. Cowan, "Reminiscences," 27.
47. John Lewellen, letter to Joan Bishop, June 19, 1940 (private collection).
48. "Low Air Dough in Chicago," *The Billboard*, November 9, 1940, 6.
49. Harry C. Kopf, "Chi Radio Production Thrives Without 'Names,'" *Variety*, January 8, 1941, 87.
50. Herb Sanford, "Looking Ahead," *The Billboard*, April 12, 1941, 12.
51. Ralph Edwards, "The Quiz Program Operates as a Modern Business Organization," *Variety*, January 8, 1941, 103.
52. John Lewellen, letter to H.W. Tiers, May 27, 1940, George Van Dyke Tiers collection.
53. John Lewellen to Joan Bishop, May 17, 1940 (private collection).
54. "Five Little Thinkers," *Time*, July 15, 1940, 46.
55. Marsters, "Quiz Kids' Originator," 25.
56. John Lewellen to H.W. Tiers, May 27, 1940, Tiers collection.
57. Hickok, *The Quiz Kids*, 2.
58. Marsters, "Quiz Kids' Originator," 25.
59. *Quiz Kids* program (audition, not broadcast), June 12, 1940, NBC-MOB Radio Collection, Library of Congress.
60. Garrick Utley, email to author, September 1, 2009.
61. Michael Kosser, *How Nashville Became Music City USA* (Milwaukee: Hal Leonard, 2006), 1–2.
62. Cowan, "Reminiscences," 28.
63. Hickok, *The Quiz Kids*, 2–3.
64. "Rachel Stevenson Oral History" (Chicago: Museum of Broadcast Communications, recorded June 23, 1995).
65. John Lear, "The Magnificent Ignoramus," *The Saturday Evening Post*, July 8, 1944, 76.
66. Marsters, "Quiz Kids' Originator," 25.
67. Hickok, *The Quiz Kids*, 7.
68. "Rachel Stevenson Oral History."
69. John Lewellen to Joan Bishop, June 19, 1940.
70. Marsters, "Quiz Kids' Originator," 25.
71. *Broadcasting Yearbook* (Washington: Broadcasting Publications, 1941), 132.
72. Cowan, "Reminiscences," 29.
73. Cynthia (Cline) Newgarden, telephone interview by author, January 21, 2009.
74. Cowan, "Reminiscences," 29.
75. Marsters, "Quiz Kids' Originator," 25.
76. Hickok, *The Quiz Kids*, 8.
77. Forrest Owen, telephone interview by author, August 26, 2004.
78. Hickok, *The Quiz Kids*, 8.
79. John Lewellen to Joan Bishop, June 19, 1940.
80. Cynthia (Cline) Newgarden, interview by author, Plattsburgh, New York, July 9, 2009.
81. Norman Modell, "Chicago," in "Radio Talent" column, *The Billboard*, July 20, 1940, 7.
82. "Agreement between Quiz Kids, Inc. and H.W. and Ruth B. Tiers," June 1940, 1–3 Tiers collection.
83. Hickok, *The Quiz Kids*, 9.
84. "Rachel Stevenson Oral History."
85. Lear, "Magnificent Ignoramus," 13.
86. Lear, "Magnificent Ignoramus," 76.
87. Hickok, *The Quiz Kids*, 12.
88. Lear, "Magnificent Ignoramus," 76.
89. "Quiz Kids," script for broadcast of September 11, 1940, Wade Radio Continuity, Cynthia (Cline) Newgarden collection.

Chapter 2

1. Holly Cowan Shulman, interview by author, Charlottesville, Va., February 24, 2005.
2. Cowan, "Reminiscences," 7.
3. Selden, "Louis Cowan Interview," 15.
4. Museum of Public Relations, "1915: I was positively uninterested in the dance," http://www.prmuseum.com/bernays/bernays_1915.html, accessed May 7, 2009.
5. Alix Spiegel, "Freud's Nephew and the Origins of Public Relations," NPR online newsletter, www.prmuseum.com, accessed May 7, 2009.
6. Selden, "Louis Cowan Interview," 16–21.
7. Walter Selden, "Quiz Kid No. One," n.p., n.d., 2–4 (private collection).
8. Lawrence Grossman, interview by author, New York, N.Y., March 24, 2005.
9. Roby (Hickok) Kesler, interview by author, April 9, 2004.
10. Ibid.
11. Hickok, *The Quiz Kids*, 38.
12. *Quiz Kids* broadcast, March 25, 1951,

NBC-MOB Radio Collection, Library of Congress.
13. Lear, "Magnificent Ignoramus," 13.
14. Anna Rothe, ed., *Current Biography 1945* (New York: H.W. Wilson, 1946), 319.
15. Ibid.
16. Willford I. King, Oswald W. Knauth, and Frederick R. Macaulay, *Income in the United States: Its Amount and Distribution 1909–1919*, vol. 2, ed. Wesley C. Mitchell (New York: National Bureau of Economic Research, 1922), Table 17D, 206.
17. Rothe, *Current Biography 1945*, 320.
18. Lear, "Magnificent Ignoramus," 74.
19. Cynthia (Cline) Newgarden, telephone interview by author, September 21, 2009.
20. Thompson, "Little Mental Giants," 10 (see chap. 1, n. 43).
21. Cynthia (Cline) Newgarden, interview by author, July 9, 2009.
22. Norman Modell, "Chicago," in "Radio Talent" column, *The Billboard,* July 20, 1940, 7.
23. "Quizmaster Kills Burglar," *Chicago Tribune,* April 22, 1947, 1.
24. "Hunt Surviving Burglar in Case of Quizmaster," *Chicago Tribune,* April 23, 1947, 4.
25. Lucy R. Milligan, letter to Margaret Cuthbert, February 25, 1941, NBC Collection, Wisconsin Historical Society, Box 85, Folder 27.
26. Sidney Strotz, memorandum to Margaret Cuthbert, February 27, 1941, NBC Collection, Wisconsin Historical Society, Box 85, Folder 27.
27. Hickok, *The Quiz Kids*, 21.
28. Hickok, *The Quiz Kids*, 35, 39.
29. Observed by the author, during a visit with Roby (Hickok) Kesler, in Cedar Rapids, April 2004.
30. Hickok, *The Quiz Kids*, 17.
31. Hickok, *The Quiz Kids*, 19.
32. Robert VanGiezen and Albert E. Schwenk, "Compensation from Before World War I Through the Great Depression," U.S. Department of Labor, www.bls.gov, posted January 30, 2003, accessed February 3, 2012.
33. Hickok, letter to Joseph Bailey, September 27, 1940, 1–2, Eliza (Hickok) Kesler collection.
34. Joseph Bailey, note to Louis Cowan, September 28, 1940, attached to Eliza Merrill Hickok's *curriculum vitae*, Kesler collection.
35. Roby (Hickok) Kesler, interview by author, April 9, 2004.

36. Roby (Hickok) Kesler, telephone interview by author, December 17, 2004.
37. Eliza Merrill Hickok, "Chapter 11: The Kiwi Stamps His Foot," in *Eliza in Wonderland* (unpublished manuscript, undated, n.p.). This was the first draft and proposal for her book that eventually became *The Quiz Kids.*
38. Hickok, *The Quiz Kids*, 17.
39. Mildred O'Neill, "Women in Radio," *Radio Daily, New York City*, March 28, 1945, 4.
40. Nachman, *Raised on Radio,* 329.
41. Joel Kupperman, letter to Mary Ann Kucera, November 29, 2005.
42. Chris Miller, "Interview with Rachel Stevenson" (Washington, D.C.: Broadcast Pioneers Library Oral History Program, May 1978).
43. "Rachel Stevenson Oral History."
44. Ibid.
45. Miller, "Interview with Rachel Stevenson."
46. Forrest Owen, telephone interview by author, August 10, 2004.
47. Dan Haefele, "Confessions of a Radio Agency Man," SPERDVAC Radiogram, September, 1994, 8.
48. George Kamen, letter to Van Dyke Tiers, January 31, 1941 Tiers collection.
49. Van Dyke Tiers, interview by author, St. Paul, Minn., December 8, 2004.
50. Claude Brenner, interview by author, Lexington, Mass., December 18, 2004.
51. "Legends Bio: Kay Kamen," Disney Legends, http://legends.disney.go.com, accessed June 12, 2009, n.p.
52. Samuel Eliot Morison and Henry Steele Commager, *The Growth of the American Republic,* vol. 2, 3rd ed. rev. (New York: Oxford University Press, 1942), 554.

Chapter 3

1. Val Adams, "Youth," in "News of Television and Radio" column, *New York Times,* January 22, 1956, 103.
2. Hickok, *The Quiz Kids*, 24.
3. Wendell Johnson, "The Quiz Kids and What It Takes to Become One," review of *The Quiz Kids* by Eliza Merrill Hickok, *Chicago Sun Book Week,* April 27, 1947, 3.
4. Ruth (Fisher) Henoch, interview by author, Potomac, Maryland, October 14, 2009.
5. Helen Gilmore-Herman, "Do These

Kids Know All the Answers?" *Liberty*, January 25, 1941, 19.

6. Richard Williams, emails to author, August 21 and 27, 2012.

7. Clark Rodenbach, "Brains Pay? Ask Quiz Kid," n.p., February 19, 1945, Tiers collection.

8. Alton Cook, "Guest Columnist Writes on Behavior of the Quiz Kids," in Paul Kennedy column, *Cincinnati Ohio Post*, April 2, 1942, n.p.

9. Richard Williams, email to author, August 21, 2012.

10. Cook, "Guest Columnist."

11. Richard Williams, telephone interview by author, August 23, 2012.

12. Hickok, *The Quiz Kids*, 25.

13. Hickok, *The Quiz Kids*, 41–42.

14. Weldon Melick, "Have You a Quiz Kid?" 4.

15. Hickok, *The Quiz Kids*, 31.

16. John Dunning, *On the Air* (New York: Oxford University Press, 1998), 562.

17. Marian McBride, "Radio's Brightest Young People," *The Milwaukee Journal*, April 7, 1947, n.p.

18. "Rachel Stevenson Oral History."

19. Richard Williams, email to author, August 21, 2012.

20. Hickok, *The Quiz Kids*, 26.

21. Melick, "Have You a Quiz Kid?" 4–5.

Chapter 4

1. Robert S. Stephan, "G.O.P. Antics Provide Signpost of Democracy," *The Cleveland Plain Dealer*, June 29, 1940, 13, and "Gale Page to Devote All Her Time to Radio," *The Cleveland Plain Dealer*, July 5, 1940, 11.

2. Robert S. Stephan, "Pearce Makes Star of Old Pal 'Elmer Blurt,'" *The Cleveland Plain Dealer*, July 6, 1940, 11.

3. "Young America Is Getting Its Chance," *Daily Boston Globe*, July 14, 1940, C8.

4. Modell, "Quiz Kids," *The Billboard*, July 13, 1940, 8.

5. "Five Little Thinkers," 46.

6. Norman Siegel, "'Quizz Kids' Eclipse Elders on Radio's Newest Brain Buster," *The Cleveland Press*, July 5, 1940, 23.

7. Frank Niessen, "Kids in Clover," *Chicago Herald-American*, Saturday Home Magazine, October 5, 1940, 2.

8. Norman Siegel, "Local Girl Musician Thrilled by Success of Friend's Outstanding Tune Hit," *The Cleveland Press*, August 17, 1940, 16.

9. Rita Danforth, "'Quiz Kid's' Slip," letter to editor, *Movie and Radio Guide*, n.d., n.p., Newgarden collection.

10. "Rehearsals Short," *Chicago Herald-American*, Quiz Kids Special Section, September 3, 1941, 1.

11. Niessen, "Kids in Clover," 11.

12. Roby (Hickok) Kesler, interview by author, April 10, 2004.

13. Siegel, "Watches 'Quiz Kids' Answer Difficult Questions Correctly on Unrehearsed Program," *The Cleveland Press*, August 26, 1940, 8.

14. Gilmore-Herman, "Do These Kids Know All the Answers?" 18.

15. Niessen, "Kids in Clover," 2.

16. Newspaper clipping, n.d., n.p., Claude Brenner collection.

17. *Quiz Kids* program (audition, not broadcast), June 12, 1940, NBC-MOB Radio Collection, Library of Congress.

18. Hickok, *The Quiz Kids*, 15.

19. Selden, "Louis Cowan Interview," 5–6.

20. Forrest Owen, telephone interview by author, November 5, 2012.

21. "Radio's Highest Rated Programs During Radio's Golden Age," http://web.archive.org/web, accessed June 15, 2009.

22. "*Quiz Kids* press release," April 30, 1944, Kesler collection.

23. "Sponsors Still Love Mail," *The Billboard*, August 7, 1943, 10.

24. Clinton B. Allsopp, vice president, Postal Telegraph-Cable Co., telegram to Charles S. Beardsley, August 31, 1940, Cynthia (Cline) Newgarden collection.

25. QK broadcast, September 18, 1940, NBC-MOB radio collection, Library of Congress.

26. Mary Ann Kucera, telephone interview by author, March 27, 2009.

27. Selden, "Louis Cowan Interview," 8.

28. "Radio's Production Costs," *The Billboard*, November 16, 1940, 8.

29. Selden, "Louis Cowan Interview," 7.

30. "Dolton Boy Prodigy on N.B.C. Air Show," August 8, 1940, n.p., Newgarden collection.

31. Stephan, "G.O.P. Antics," 13.

32. Norman Modell, "Chicago," in "Radio Talent" column, *The Billboard*, October 26, 1940, 8.

33. "Quiz Kids," in "Program Reviews" column, *Radio Daily*, September 5, 1940, 6.

34. "The Weather," *Chicago Tribune*, June 22–28, 1940, 1.
35. Siegel, "Watches 'Quiz Kids,'" 8.
36. Phil Orbanes, telephone interview by author, May 6, 2009. Orbanes is the author of *The Game Makers: The Story of Parker Brothers* (Cambridge: Harvard Business School, 2004).
37. "'Quiz Kids' Now Wards of State," *The Billboard*, September 28, 1940, 7.
38. Pence James, "Now We Know How Cold It Is at Twice Zero," *Chicago Daily News*, November 14, 1940, 1.
39. "Chicago," *Radio Daily*, November 19, 1940, 4.
40. "Chapter XXVII: The Milwaukee Auditorium," *History of Milwaukee*, www.hellomilwaukee.com, accessed May 8, 2010, 423.
41. "Thrills, Beauty at Aqua Show," *The Milwaukee Journal*, Sports and Markets and Classified Section, November 18, 1940, 1.
42. "Audience Forms Brilliant Setting for Manikins at Style Show at Auditorium," *The Milwaukee Journal*, November 18, 1940, 14.
43. Advertisement for Aqua Star and Style Show, *The Milwaukee Journal*, November 10, 1940, Section II, 5.
44. "Quiz Kids Do Their Stuff at Aqua Star and Style Show," *The Milwaukee Journal*, Sports and Markets and Classified Section, November 19, 1940, 1.
45. Jerome Cornfield, telephone interview by author, December 17, 2010.
46. Edgar A. Thompson, "'Quiz Kid' Expert Unimpressed by His Earnings," in "Riding the Airwaves" column, *The Milwaukee Journal*, Green Sheet section, November 19, 1940, 2.
47. Cornfield, interview by author, December 8, 2010.
48. Advertisement for Boston Store, *The Milwaukee Journal*, November 19, 1940, 16.
49. Edgar A. Thompson, "Milwaukee Youngster to Broadcast with Quiz Kids," in "Riding the Airwaves" column, *The Milwaukee Journal*, Green Sheet section, November 18, 1940, 2.
50. "Lou Cowan Works Out an Elaborate Dept. Store Tie for 'Quiz Kid' Program," *Variety*, December 18, 1940, 23.

Chapter 5

1. Louis Cowan to Van Dyke Tiers, January 17, 1941 Tiers collection.
2. Norman Modell, "Chicago," in "Radio Talent" column, *The Billboard*, December 28, 1940, 19.
3. Cynthia (Cline) Newgarden, telephone interview by author, March 4, 2009.
4. "20th Century Limited," www.wikipedia.com, accessed January 11, 2011.
5. Joan (Bishop) Barber, telephone interview by author, July 14, 2004.
6. Script for Kaynee Quiz Kids boys' clothing, n.p., n.d., Newgarden collection.
7. Mark Murphy, "6 Precocious Scholars from Chicago," *New York Post*, January 4, 1941, 9.
8. Twiggar, "Quiz Kids," 4.
9. Roby Hickok to parents, January 12, 1941 Kesler collection.
10. Murphy, "6 Precocious Scholars," 9.
11. Richard Williams, telephone interview by author, August 3, 2009.
12. Beaux Arts Apartment Hotel Dining Room Menu, Wednesday, January 8, 1941, Tiers collection.
13. Hickok, *The Quiz Kids,* 70.
14. Norman Modell, "Chicago," in "Radio Talent" column, *The Billboard*, January 18, 1941, 8.
15. Murphy, "6 Precocious Scholars," 9.
16. Henry R. Lieberman, "That 'Quiz Kid' Gerard Darrow," *PM,* January 6, 1941, 15.
17. Paul Healy, "What's a Whelk? Gerard Knows Right Answer," *Chicago Tribune*, November 17, 1940, part 3, 6.
18. "Beat the Quiz Kids," *Chicago Herald-American*, n.d. [1941], n.p., Brenner collection.
19. "City Children to Test Brains of 'Quiz Kids,'" *New York Journal and American*, January 5, 1941, 8-B.
20. George Kamen to Cynthia Cline, January 5, 1941, Newgarden collection.
21. "Leslie M. Roush," http://www.imdb.com/name/nm0745890/, accessed August 20, 2009.
22. The American Widescreen Museum, "Cinecolor," http://www.widescreenmuseum.com/oldcolor/cinecolor2.htm, accessed August 18, 2009.
23. Roby Hickok to parents, January 12, 1941.
24. Eileen Creelman, "The Quiz Kids, Five of Them, Make Their First Movie Short in Astoria," in "Picture Plays and Players" column, *New York Sun*, January 8, 1941, 26.
25. Roby Hickok to parents, January 12, 1941.
26. "Lucky Smarties," in column "Stand

By: Radio News and Notes," *Scholastic*, January 27, 1941, 34.

27. "1st Lady Stumps 'Expert,'" *New York Journal-American*, January 10, 1941, section 2, 24.

28. Roby Hickok to parents, January 12, 1941.

29. Cynthia (Cline) Newgarden, interview by author, July 9, 2009.

30. Hickok, *The Quiz Kids*, 141.

31. "1st Lady Stumps 'Expert,'" 1.

32. Ibid., 24.

33. "Quiz Kids ASK Questions, Too; Turn Tables on Their In-quiz-itor," *New York Journal and American*, January 11, 1941, 4.

34. Roby Hickok to parents, January 12, 1941.

35. "1st Lady Stumps 'Expert,'" 1.

36. Roby Hickok to parents, January 12, 1941.

37. "Parents of Quiz Kids Shine over Air in Final Show," *Chicago Herald-American*, February 22, 1941, 24.

38. "Cowan Agency, Fizdale Take Awards," *The Billboard*, April 26, 1941, 6.

Chapter 6

1. "Chicago," *Radio Daily*, January 28, 1941, 4.

2. James, "Prodigy's Progress," 49 (see chap. 1, n. 22).

3. Norman Modell, "Chicago," in "Radio Talent" column, *The Billboard*, January 18, 1941, 8.

4. Selden, "Louis Cowan Interview," 11–12.

5. Roby (Hickok) Kesler, interview by author, April 10, 2004.

6. Walter Wade, letter to Niles Trammell, October 28, 1941, Box 483, Folder 3, NBC Collection, Wisconsin Historical Society.

7. Selden, "Louis Cowan Interview," 9.

8. Selden, "Quiz Kid No. One," 6.

9. Selden, "Louis Cowan Interview," 9.

10. Roby (Hickok) Kesler, interview by author, April 9, 2004.

11. Selden, "Quiz Kid No. One," 6.

12. Forrest Owen, telephone interview by author, November 5, 2012.

13. "Vox Pop: The Show that Traveled America," Library of American Broadcasting, www.lib.umd.edu, accessed February 6, 2011.

14. "Dr. I.Q.," www.wikipedia.com, accessed March 8, 2011.

15. Jack French, "WLS: The Voice of the Prairie," www.otrsite.com, accessed May 5, 2004.

16. Forrest Owen, telephone interview by author, November 5, 2012.

17. "'Quiz Kids' Get Disney," reported February 1, 1941, in *The Billboard*, February 8, 1941, 7.

18. Selden, "Louis Cowan Interview," 13.

19. Roby Hickok to parents, January 12, 1941.

20. "Cowan Agency, Fizdale Take Awards," 6.

21. Joseph Bailey to Van Dyke Tiers, January 28, 1941, Tiers collection.

22. "Precocious Gang Prepares to Level Things at Home," *Chicago Herald-American*, February 17, 1941, n. p.

23. "Parents Outsmart Quiz Kids. Elders Demonstrate They Know a Great Deal, Too," *Chicago Herald-American*, February 22, 1941, 5.

24. Louis Cowan, letter to H.W. Tiers, February 22, 1941, Tiers collection.

25. Forrest Owen, telephone interview by author, August 26, 2004.

26. Advertisement for Pennsylvania Railroad, *Life*, February 10, 1941, 84.

27. "U.S. Must Fight if Nazis Win, Educators Hear," *The Atlantic City Press*, February 25, 1941, 2.

28. "Many Brilliant Speakers for Teachers' Rally," *The Atlantic City Press*, February 2, 1941, 16.

29. Selden, "Louis Cowan Interview," 13.

30. Seventeenth Annual Program Associated Exhibitors, National Education Association, February 25, 1941, n. p., Tiers collection.

31. Joseph Bailey to Van Dyke Tiers, February 21, 1941, Tiers collection.

32. Roby Hickok to family, March 7, 1941.

33. John K. Hutchens, "Child Wonders," *New York Times*, February 27, 1944, X7.

34. Roby Hickok to family, March 18, 1941.

35. "Challenger (train)," www.wikipedia.com, accessed January 22, 2010.

36. "Big Radio Show for Brit. Children Fund," and "To George Burns and Gracie Allen," advertisement by Canadian War Finance Radio Committee, *Variety*, February 19, 1941, 26, 30.

37. "Stars Do Their Share — Add $35,000 to Greek Aid Fund," *Chicago Herald-American*, April 3, 1941, 8.

38. Newgarden, interview by author, July 9, 2009.

39. "Greek Benefit Raises $50,000 for War Relief," *Chicago Tribune*, April 3, 1941, 2; "Stars Do Their Share."

Chapter 7

1. Kate Reed, "Meet the Quiz Kids," *Child Life*, April 1941, 157.
2. Roby Hickok to family, n.d., probably April 1, 1941, or shortly before.
3. *The Official Guide of the Railways* (New York: National Railway Publications, April, 1941), 808.
4. Selden, "Louis Cowan Interview," 12.
5. Roby Hickok to family, March 18, 1941.
6. Hickok, *The Quiz Kids*, 120.
7. Roby Hickok to family, March 7, 1941.
8. "Arthur L. Beardsley, President Alka-Seltzer," *Hollywood Knickerbocker Hotel Topics* (newsletter), April 8, 1941, 1; "Walter Wades Are Here with Quiz Kids," *Topics*, April 12, 1941, 1.
9. Cynthia (Cline) Newgarden, telephone interview by author, March 6, 2011.
10. *The Jell-O Program*, broadcast April 6, 1941, International Jack Benny Fan Club collection. It was customary at that time to name programs after the product advertised on the broadcasts. Eventually the program's name was changed to *The Jack Benny Program*.
11. Hickok, "If I Had a Rocking Chair," *Eliza in Wonderland* (preliminary manuscript for *The Quiz Kids*), n.d., 8–9, Kesler collection.
12. "Rachel Stevenson Oral History."
13. *Jack Benny Program*, April 6, 1941.
14. Hickok, *The Quiz Kids*, 118–22.
15. Roby Hickok, letter to Bernice Cranston, April 10, 1941. Bernice Cranston worked at Louis Cowan Company in Chicago.
16. "Benny and Masterminds," n.p., n.d. [1941], Brenner collection.
17. Roby Hickok to Bernice Cranston, April 10, 1941.
18. Meyer Zolotareff, "Filmland Tour Glorious, Say Quiz Kids," n.p., n.d. [1941], Brenner collection.
19. "Children's Hour," n.d. [1941], 30, Brenner collection.
20. Roby Hickok to Bernice Cranston, April 10, 1941.
21. Roby Hickok to family, n.d., probably Saturday, March 29, 1941.
22. Roby Hickok to family, April 11, 1941.
23. Jane Withers was one of the most popular child film stars of the 1930s and '40s, appearing with Shirley Temple in the film *Bright Eyes*.
24. Sylvia Kahn, "We Asked the Quiz Kids," *Modern Screen*, July, 1941, 44–5, 73.
25. Roby Hickok to Bernice Cranston, April 10, 1941.
26. Ibid.
27. Gay's Lion Farm promotional brochure, n.d., Newgarden collection.
28. "Gay's Lion Farm," www.wikipedia.org, accessed March 24, 2011.
29. "Up to 419," *Topics*, April 13, 1941, 4.
30. Roby Hickok to Bernice Cranston, April 10, 1941.
31. "Quiz Kids in Movieland," April 1941, n.p., Brenner collection.
32. *Jack Benny Program*, April 13, 1941.
33. Los Angeles Breakfast Club promotional mailing for April 16, 1941, Newgarden collection.
34. Roby Hickok to family, March 18, 1941.
35. Hickok, *The Quiz Kids*, 122.
36. Old Time Radio Collection, *Quiz Kids* broadcast, April 16, 1941.
37. Frederick C. Othman, "Quiz Kids Even Know Answer to Hollywood," *New York Morning Telegraph*, April 22, 1941, 2.
38. Othman, "Quiz Kids in Movies," April 23, 1941, n.p., Brenner collection.
39. Roby Hickok to Bernice Cranston, April 10, 1941.
40. Roby Hickok to family, April 11, 1941; Roby Hickok to Bernice Cranston, April 13, 1941.
41. Hickok, *The Quiz Kids*, 88.
42. Roby Hickok to Bernice Cranston, April 12, 1941.
43. "Quiz Kids," Wade Radio Continuity script for program 12, September 11, 1940, 2, Newgarden collection.
44. Hickok, *The Quiz Kids*, 88.
45. Roby Hickok to Bernice Cranston, April 12, 1941.
46. Roby Hickok to Bernice Cranston, April 13, 1941.
47. Roby Hickok to family, April 12, 1941.
48. Newgarden collection. Her autograph book shows a date of April 11, 1941 written by Eleanor Powell on the day she entered her autograph. This was the date when the Kids visited MGM, where they went to the sound stage to see Powell doing a scene with John Carroll for their film *Lady Be Good*.
49. *Jack Benny Program*, April 20, 1941.
50. Newgarden collection.

51. Wade to Trammel, October 28, 1941 (see chap. 6, n. 9).
52. Roby Hickok to family, April 19, 1941.
53. "Rachel Stevenson Oral History."

Chapter 8

1. Nat Green, "Chicago," in "Radio Talent" column, *The Billboard*, April 12, 1941, 12.
2. "Precocious One-Year-Old," *Newsweek*, July 7, 1941, 46.
3. "Blue Network First Place Winners of the Movie-Radio Guide Poll," in "'Breakfast Club' Cops Program Tops!" National Broadcasting Company advertisement, *Variety*, April 16, 1941, 29.
4. "Winners of The Billboard's Radio Publicity and Exploitation Survey," *The Billboard*, May 3, 1941, 10.
5. Advertisement for Louis G. Cowan Company, *The Billboard*, May 3, 1941, 8.
6. "More Station P.A. Shows," *The Billboard*, May 3, 1941, 8.
7. Tom Gorman, "Exploitation, Good and Bad," *Variety*, January 8, 1941, 6.
8. *Colgate-Palmolive-Peet Company Bill Stern Sports Newsreel of the Air* script, April 27, 1941, Newgarden collection.
9. "Advertisers, Agencies, Stations," *The Billboard*, September 30, 1941, 6.
10. "Renew Quiz Kids," *Variety*, September 17, 1941, 30.
11. "Radio's Production Costs," *The Billboard*, October 11, 1941, 6.
12. Laurence M. Olney, *The War Bond Story* (Washington: U.S. Savings Bond Division, 1971), 26.
13. "'Quiz Kids' to Aid Defense," *The Billboard*, May 31, 1941, 7.
14. Quiz Kids NBC Program Notes, May 28, 1941, Library of Congress Recorded Sound Division.
15. "Five U. of C. Savants to Match Wits with Youthful Quintet," *Chicago Tribune*, June 1, 1941, S1.
16. "Midway Alumni Give $455,098 to Aid Fund Drive," *Chicago Daily News*, June 7, 1941, 4.
17. "Quiz Kids Meet Profs—Who Won? Tsk, Tsk," *Chicago Herald-American*, June 8, 1941, 1.
18. "Quiz Kids Outquiz Professors," *Des Moines Sunday Register*, June 15, 1941, 3.
19. "'Quiz Kids' Birthday," *Chicago Herald-American*, June 24, 1941, 8.

20. "Statistics, 1941," *Variety*, January 7, 1942, 147.
21. "Precocious One-Year-Old," *Newsweek*, July 7, 1941, 46.
22. "Radio Quiz Kids Stop at Dayton on Way to Chautauqua Program," *Dayton (Ohio) Daily News*, June 29, 1941, 9.
23. "Quiz Kids Stop Off in Dayton," *Dayton Sunday Journal-Herald*, June 29, 1941, 10.
24. June Provines, "Quiz Kid's Pet," in "Front Views and Profiles" column, *Chicago Tribune*, July 31, 1941, 11.
25. "Quiz Kid Slips; Asks 'Who's Hitler?'" *Chicago Herald-American*, July 26, 1941, 3.
26. Joseph Bailey to Van Dyke Tiers, July 25, 1941, Tiers collection.
27. "Listen! With Glynn," *Washington Post*, August 27, 1941, 26.
28. Ben Kaplan, "For the Love of Mike," *Providence (Rhode Island) Evening Bulletin*, August 1941, n.p., Brenner collection.
29. "Quiz Kids Enjoy Day at Meade," on or about August 27, 1941, n.p., Brenner collection.
30. "Quiz Kids Guests at Meade," *Baltimore Post*, August 27, 1941, n.p., Brenner collection.
31. "Quiz Kids Enjoy Day at Meade."
32. "What's Going On and Where," *Washington Post*, August 27, 1941, 15.
33. "In Chicago," in "From the Production Centres" column, *Variety*, December 10, 1941, 28.
34. "Jordan's Starts Contest to Find Boston 'Quiz Kid,'" *Boston Globe*, October 2, 1941, 26.
35. "'Quiz Kids' Short Gets Heavy Plugging in Hub," *Variety*, October 22, 1941, 15.
36. Advertisement for Hovey's, *Boston Globe*, September 25, 1941, 7.
37. "Quiz Kids' Premiere!" *Chicago Herald-American*, September 3, 1941, Quiz Kids Special Section, 1.
38. Nat Green, "Quiz Kids Short in Chi Theater Debut," *The Billboard*, September 13, 1941, 7.
39. Program from the American Legion Auxiliary States Dinner, September 17, 1941 (private collection).
40. Program Notes, September 17, 1941.
41. Program Notes, August 6, 1941,
42. Joseph Bailey to Van Dyke Tiers, September 30, 1941, Tiers collection.
43. "It's Their Turn Now: A Quiz by the Quiz Kids," *Liberty*, February 14, 1942, 25, 53.
44. Joseph Bailey to Cynthia Cline, October 2, 1941, Newgarden collection.

45. Ruth Duskin Feldman, *Whatever Happened to the Quiz Kids?* (Chicago: Chicago Review Press, 1982), 36.
46. Joseph Bailey to Van Dyke Tiers, November 4, 1941, Tiers collection.
47. Ben Bodec, "3-Hour Marathon of Entertainment Forms NBC's 15th Birthday Party," *Variety*, November 19, 1941, 41.
48. Joseph Bailey to Van Dyke Tiers, November 10, 1941, Tiers collection.
49. "Inside Stuff—Radio," *Variety*, October 29, 1941, 35.
50. Christopher H. Sterling and John M. Kittross, *Stay Tuned* (Belmont, California: Wadsworth, 1978), 511.
51. Corey Deitz, "How Many Radio Stations Are There in the United States?" http://www.about.com, accessed June 22, 2011.
52. "53d Show Staged by Triangle Club," *New York Times*, November 22, 1941, 10.
53. "Quiz Kids Kidded at Triangle Show," *New York Times*, December 20, 1941, 25.
54. Joseph Bailey to Van Dyke Tiers, November 18, 1941, Tiers collection.
55. Joseph Bailey to Van Dyke Tiers, November 28, 1941.
56. "Pull Up a Chair — It's *Quiz Kid* Time," *Tractor Works Attractor* (company newsletter), November 1941, 8, Tiers collection.
57. Joseph Bailey to Van Dyke Tiers, December 2, 1941.
58. Joseph Bailey to Van Dyke Tiers, December 8, 1941.
59. Hickok, *The Quiz Kids*, 33–39.
60. Roby Hickok to family, November 14, 1942.

Chapter 9

1. *Quiz Kids* program (audition, not broadcast), June 12, 1940, NBC-MOB Radio Collection, Library of Congress.
2. Newgarden collection.
3. Ruth Fisher Henoch, letter to author, September 27, 2009.
4. Cynthia (Cline) Newgarden, interview by author, July 9, 2009.
5. Rodenbach, "Brains Pay?" (see chap. 3, n. 5).
6. Jo Ranson, "'Quiz Kids' to Air Wisdom from N.Y.," in "Jo Ranson's Radio Dial Log" column, *Brooklyn Eagle*, January 8, 1941, 20.
7. Hickok, *The Quiz Kids*, 79.
8. Arthur Inman, letter to Cynthia Cline, September 5, 1940, Newgarden collection.
9. Dewey L. Suit to Cynthia Cline, November 26, 1941.
10. Charles E. Pecker to Cynthia Cline, September 11–November 27, 1940.
11. Charles W. Bullock to Cynthia Cline, August 21, 1940.
12. Martha Ann Dieffenbacher to Cynthia Cline, August 26, 1940.
13. Johnny Mandel to Cynthia Cline, May 19, 1942.
14. Mrs. William Pfeiffer to Cynthia Cline, October 8, 1941.
15. John Lewellen to Cynthia Cline, July 16, 1941.
16. Mrs. Helen DeVeaux Baker to the "Quiz Kids," March 13, 1941.
17. Joseph Bailey to Cynthia Cline, November 14, 1941.
18. Bernice Cranston to Cynthia Cline, September 6, 1941.

Chapter 10

1. "Ask the Kids" in "New Program Ideas" column, *Radio Daily*, October 16, 1940, 6.
2. "Recess Time" in "Radio Reviews" column, *Variety*, December 18, 1940, 38.
3. "Kid Wizards," *Variety*, January 22, 1941, 46.
4. "WHN's Kid Wizards Attract a Sponsor," *Variety*, February 26, 1941, 33.
5. "More Clever Kids," *Variety*, April 23, 1941, 34.
6. "NBC Refuses 'Kids of the Week' as Too Much Like 'Quiz Kids,'" *Variety*, May 7, 1941, 31.
7. Joseph Bailey, letter to Bob McKee (NBC), May 6, 1941, Box 483, Folder 3, 1–2, NBC Collection, Wisconsin Historical Society.
8. Jules Herbuveaux, memo to Sidney Strotz, May 9, 1941, Box 483, Folder 3, NBC Collection, Wisconsin Historical Society.
9. Strotz to Herbuveaux, May 13, 1941, Box 483, Folder 3, NBC Collection, Wisconsin Historical Society.
10. Strotz, memo to William S. Hedges, May 13, 1941, Box 483, Folder 3, NBC Collection, Wisconsin Historical Society.
11. "Smartie Kids on WSNY," *Variety*, July 29, 1942, 32.
12. "Schoolteachers Tied In on I.Q. Junior Quiz," *Variety*, June 11, 1941, 28.
13. "Dr. I.Q.," www.wikipedia.com, accessed March 8, 2011.
14. "4 Professors to become 'Quiz Kids,'"

Atlanta Constitution, January 25, 1943, 15; "Book Week Play Given in Acworth," *Atlanta Constitution*, November 14, 1943, C 16. These are just two examples from one city in one year. A search in newspapers, nationally, would show this same pattern repeated frequently.
  15. "'Old Quiz Kids' to Battle with Cradle Crew," *Chicago Tribune*, March 26, 1944, N4.

Chapter 11

  1. Sam Honigsberg, "Chicago," in "Radio Talent" column, *The Billboard*, February 21, 1942, 7.
  2. Joe Kelly, "Just Ask the Quiz Kids" (New York: Famous Music Corp., 1942), author's collection.
  3. "Chi Sun Adds WLS to Large Schedule," *The Billboard*, April 11, 1942, 6.
  4. Selden, "Louis Cowan Interview," 10.
  5. "Louis G. Cowan Citation on Outstanding Single Program Exploitation," *The Billboard*, May 9, 1942, 9.
  6. "Statistics: 1941," *Variety*, January 7, 1942, 147.
  7. "Various Items About the Wireless," *New York Times*, January 11, 1942, X12.
  8. "Inside Stuff—Radio," *Variety*, April 15, 1942, 35.
  9. Gail Compton, "Six Inquisitive Quiz Kids Lap Up Farm Lore," *Chicago Tribune*, October 24, 1942, 15.
  10. "You Can't Milk a Heifer, 6 Quiz Kids'll Discover," *Chicago Tribune*, October 23, 1942, 12.
  11. Compton, "Six Inquisitive Quiz Kids," 15.
  12. "Quiz Kids Pass Army Air Tests with Flying Colors!" *Chicago Herald-American*, August 26, 1942, n.p., Brenner collection.
  13. "Quiz Kids Quizzed by Army; Find Aviation Cadet Test Easy," *Chicago Daily News*, August 26, 1942, n.p., Brenner collection.
  14. Roby Hickok to family, October 24, 1942.
  15. Ibid.
  16. Roby Hickok to family, November 2, 1942.
  17. "Army Takeover Forces 'WLS Barn Dance' to Move to Smaller Chi House," *Variety*, September 9, 1942, 27.
  18. "'Quiz Kids' Give War Bonds," *The Billboard*, July 3, 1943, 8.
  19. Loretta Britten and Paul Mathless, eds., *Decade of Triumph: The 40s* (New York: Time-Life, 1999), 62.
  20. Allan M. Winkler, *Homefront U.S.A.: America During World War II* (Arlington Heights, Ill: Harlan Davidson, 1986), 24.
  21. Cabell Phillips, *The 1940s: Decade of Triumph and Trouble* (New York: Macmillan, 1975), 72.
  22. Richard B. Lingeman, *Don't You Know There's a War On?* (New York: G.P. Putnam's Sons, 1970), 29.
  23. Cowan, "Reminiscences," 27.
  24. Gerd Horten, *Radio Goes to War* (Regents of the University of California, 2002), 41.
  25. Cowan, "Reminiscences," 27.
  26. Roby (Hickok) Kesler, interview by author, April 9, 2004.
  27. "Lou Cowan, Owner of 'Quiz Kids,' Is Newcomer to Army's Radio Section," *Variety*, January 21, 1942, 22.
  28. "Lou Cowan Temporarily Heads OWI's New York Office," *Variety*, September 2, 1942, 38.
  29. Forrest Owen telephone interview by author, November 5, 2012.
  30. "May Defer Key Radio Men," *Variety*, February 25, 1942, 29.
  31. "Quiz Kids Back Too Soon, Will Miss Benny Party," in "Radio Parade" column, *Chicago Herald-American*, April 23, 1941, 31.
  32. Roby Hickok to family, October 24, 1942.
  33. Jarvis M. Morse, "*Paying for a World War: The United States Financing of World War II*" (unpublished manuscript, private collection), 1. Morse was a participant in the planning and execution of the bond program from its inception to its eventual conversion to peacetime activities in 1947. His text was written shortly after the end of the war while the events of the program were still fresh in the minds of other department personnel whom he interviewed for his history.
  34. Morse, "Paying for a World War," 281.
  35. Lingeman, *Don't You Know*, 296.
  36. "Buy Bonds—and Sell Them," *The Billboard*, May 16, 1942, 3.
  37. Hickok, *The Quiz Kids*, 50–2.
  38. Morse, "Paying for a World War," 270.
  39. "The Quiz Kids to Sell Bonds Here Sept. 19," *The Washington Post*, n. d., September 1943, n. p., private collection.
  40. Morse, "Paying for a World War," 213.
  41. "'Quiz Kids' on Bond Selling Tour," *The Billboard*, September 18, 1943, 7.

42. Congressional Record, Vol. 89, Part 6, September 21, 1943, 7697.
43. "Casadeus [sic] to Be on Air Today; Will Play Here Next Month," *The Atlanta Constitution*, September 19, 1943, 7D.
44. "Jack Benny Back Tonight with Full Cast," *The Atlanta Constitution*, October 10, 1943, 10C.
45. "Chicago Woman's Club to Hear Two Guest Speakers," *Chicago Tribune*, August 22, 1943, F6.
46. Feldman, *Whatever Happened*, 91.
47. *Six Kids and the War...*, promotional brochure, The Blue Network, American Broadcasting Company, n.d., 1–8.
48. Dale Banks, "What's New from Coast to Coast," *Radio Mirror*, July 1944, 6.
49. Program Notes, October 20, 1946.
50. Program Notes, passim.
51. Morse, "Paying for a World War," 216.
52. "'Any Bonds Today' 100% Free," *Variety*, June 11, 1941, 25.
53. "Stars to Arrive on Wednesday," *The Washington Post*, September, 1943, n. p.
54. Morse, "Paying for a World War," 214–15.
55. "3 Baseball Clubs Set for Contest," *New York Times*, June 25, 1944, S3.
56. "This Date in Baseball," *New York Times*, June 26, 2004, D5.
57. "3-Cornered Baseball Game Yields $56,500,000 in Fifth Bond Drive," *New York Times*, June 27, 1944, 1.
58. Ray Corio, "Question Box," *New York Times*, January 28, 1985, C9.
59. Forrest Owen, telephone interview by author, November 5, 2012.

Chapter 12

1. Cynthia (Cline) Newgarden, interview by author, July 9, 2009.
2. *Quiz Kids* broadcast, September 5, 1948.
3. "Dixon Woman's Club Hears 'Inside Story' about 'Quiz Kids,'" newspaper clipping, April 3, 1943, n.p., Kesler collection.
4. "Gasoline Rationing on the Home Front During World War II," www.prewarbuick.com, accessed September 27, 2006.
5. Roby Hickok to family, August 19, 1943.
6. Roby Hickok to family, June 12, 1943.
7. Lingeman, *Don't You Know*, 241.
8. John Lewellen, letter to Senator Harold H. Burton, January 9, 1945, Harold H. Burton Papers, Box 42, *Quiz Kids*, 1945, Library of Congress.
9. John Lewellen to Burton, February 21, 1945.
10. John Lewellen to Burton, January 9, 1945.
11. Jerry N. Hess, "Oral History Interview with Dr. Walter H. Judd," April 13, 1970, Washington, D.C. Harry S. Truman Library and Museum, Independence, Mo.
12. Wilson D. Miscamble, *From Roosevelt to Truman: Potsdam, Hiroshima, and the Cold War* (New York: Cambridge University Press, 2007), 22.
13. John Lewellen to Burton, January 9, 1945, Harold H. Burton Papers, Box 42, *Quiz Kids*, 1945, Library of Congress.
14. Program Notes, March 14, 1948.
15. John Lewellen to Burton, et al., "Notes for the Senators on Quiz Kids Program March 18," 1–2.
16. Lewellen to Burton, March 21, 1945.
17. Burton to Lewellen, March 26, 1945.
18. Roby Hickok to family, October 24, 1942.
19. *Quiz Kids* press release, September 20, 1943, Kesler collection.
20. Larry Wolters, "The Quiz Kids' Five Years — An American Story," *Chicago Tribune*, July 1, 1945, SW4.
21. Feldman, *Whatever Happened*, 91.
22. *Quiz Kids* press release, October 25, 1943.
23. *Quiz Kids* press release, September 20, 1943.
24. Roby Hickok to family, August 19, 1943.
25. Roby Hickok to family, July 27, 1943.
26. Roby Hickok to family, August 19, 1943.
27. Roby Hickok to family, August 14, 1943.
28. "'Quiz Kid' Can Accept $2,000-a-Week Job," *The Atlanta Constitution*, August 12, 1943, 8.
29. Hickok, *The Quiz Kids*, 127.
30. "Mischa Elman, Jennie Tourel on WGST," *The Atlanta Constitution*, August 15, 1943, 6D, and Program Notes, August 15, 1943.
31. Roby Hickok to family, August 19, 1943.
32. Roby Hickok to family, August 30, 1943.
33. Roby Hickok to family, August 28, 1943.
34. Roby Hickok to Louis Cowan, John Lewellen, and Fred Ashman, August 28, 1943, Kesler collection.
35. Hedda Hopper, "Looking at Hollywood," *Chicago Tribune*, September 8, 1943, 26.

36. Geoffrey Perrett, *Days of Sadness, Years of Triumph* (New York: Coward, McCann, Geoghegan, 1973), 362.
37. Feldman, *Whatever Happened*, 37–8.
38. Cowan, "My Father's Children," 15.

Chapter 13

1. Hedda Hopper, "Looking at Hollywood" column, *Chicago Tribune*, March 24, 1945, 16.
2. Larry Wolters, "Farmer Quiz Show Opens on Thursday," *Chicago Tribune*, November 30, 1947, NH.
3. Paul S. Boyer, *By the Bomb's Early Light: American Thought and Culture at the Dawn of the Atomic Age* (New York: Pantheon, 1985), 12.
4. John Lewellen, letter to Seaborg, June 12, 1946; "Atom Bomb #2," 4, The Papers of Glenn Theodore Seaborg, Box 571, Folder 5, "Quiz Kids," Library of Congress. This was a script prepared by John Lewellen for a series of recordings of a dramatization to explain the atomic bomb.
5. Eleanor Roosevelt, "October 25, 1946," in *My Day* column, United Feature Syndicate, Inc., 1946, n. p.
6. Boyer, *Bomb's Early Light*, 5.
7. Richard Williams, email to author, March 10, 2012.
8. *QK* broadcast, November 11, 1945.
9. Joseph Illick, *American Childhoods* (Philadelphia: University of Pennsylvania Press, 2002), 27.
10. Williams, email to author, March 10, 2012.
11. Raymond Gram Swing, ABC radio newscast, April 26, 1946; A.J. Muste, *Not by Might: Christianity, the Way to Human Decency (New York, 1947)*, both quoted in Boyer, *Bomb's Early Light*, 191–92.
12. *QK* broadcast, November 11, 1945.
13. "Quiz Kids Scoop World on Two New Elements," *Chicago Tribune*, November 20, 1945, 18.
14. Arthur G. Levy, letter to Glenn Seaborg, November 23 1945, Glenn T. Seaborg Papers, Library of Congress.
15. Glenn T. Seaborg, letter to Arthur G. Levy, November 28, 1945, Seaborg Papers.
16. Levy to Seaborg.
17. Gladys A. Reichard, letter to Glenn Seaborg, November 21, 1945, Seaborg Papers.
18. "The Quiz Kids: 50 Years Ago, a Bunch of Educated Upstarts Became Radio's Smash Hit," *Chicago Tribune*, December 2, 1990, 28. This article was adapted from a story originally commissioned for *Memories* magazine, which had suspended publication.
19. McEvoy, "Quiz Kids," 17 (see chap. 1, n. 41).
20. Claude Brenner, interview by author, December 18, 2004.
21. Patrick Conlon, interview by author, New York, New York, November 5, 2004.
22. *QK* broadcast, October 31, 1948.
23. Lon Lunde, interview by author, Des Plaines, Illinois, December 9, 2004.
24. Conlon, interview by author, November 5, 2004.
25. Cowan, "Reminiscences," 30.
26. "Quiz Kids Plan Contest to Pick Best Teacher," *Chicago Tribune*, January 26, 1946, 19.
27. "Mississippi School Teacher Wins $2,500 Quiz Kids' Award," *Chicago Tribune*, June 1, 1947, N12.
28. Cowan, "Reminiscences," 30.
29. Lewellen to Seaborg, February 21, 1946, Seaborg Papers.
30. Larry Wolters, "Anne McKnight Makes Bow in 'Boheme' Today," *Chicago Tribune*, February 3, 1946, N8.
31. Forrest Owen, telephone interview by author, September 10, 2004.
32. "Use Veterans' Posers as Quiz Kid Session," *Chicago Tribune*, November 17, 1946, S10.
33. "South American Goodwill Series Via CBS Clicks," *Variety*, September 18, 1940, 23; "'Vox Pop' May Visit Latin Lands," *Variety*, January 29, 1941, 25; "South America a Columbus Theme;" "Lutherans into Latin Republics on Transcriptions," *Variety*, April 23, 1941, 31; "Byington Brazilians 'Renew' with Royal," *Variety*, April 23, 1941, 31; "Musicians Union Kills NBC Idea to Shortwave Dance Bands on the Cuff," *Variety*, April 23, 1941, 31.
34. *QK* broadcast, December 8, 1946.
35. "Mex., Cuban Facsimile of U.S. Air," *The Billboard*, March 2, 1946, 10.
36. Roby (Hickok) Kesler, interview by author, April 10, 2004.
37. "Mex, Cuban," *The Billboard*, March 2, 1946.
38. "Editors Crown Radio's Best: Favorite Quiz and Contest Programs," *The Billboard*, March 9, 1946, 8–9; "Drug Talent Cost Index," *The Billboard*, March 16, 1946, 8; "Quiz Talent Cost Index," *The Billboard*,

March 30, 1946, 11; "Nighttime Talent Cost Index," *The Billboard*, November 9, 1946, 11.

39. "Dr. Leo S. Rowe Killed by Auto; Head of Pan American Union," *Washington Post*, December 6, 1946, 1.

40. There appears to be an inconsistency about the name of the delegate to the UNRRA from El Salvador whose appearance was as a substitute for Leo Rowe. On the broadcast, Joe Kelly gives his full name as Roberto Aguilar. NBC notes his name as Roberto Aguilar Drisgueros. The difference between the two names is cultural. Aguilar was the last name of Roberto's father, the traditional method of assigning a family name to children in the United States. But in El Salvador, it is customary to use a family name that includes the last name of the father followed by the maiden name of the mother. Thus, NBC's use of the full name Roberto Aguilar Drisgueros is the more conventional form in El Salvador.

41. Louise Leyden, "Quiz Kids Arrive Here to Spur March of Dimes Toward Goal," *Miami Daily News*, January 22, 1947, 1-B.

42. "Jungle Birds Make Friends with Visiting Quiz Kids," *Daily News*, January 23, 1947, 1-B.

43. Program Notes, February 3–March 10, 1946.

44. Leyden, "Quiz Kids Hook Big Ones on Biscayne Bay 'Voyage,'" *Daily News*, January 25, 1947, 1.

45. Ibid., and in *Radio Highlights* column, *Daily News*, January 24, 1947, 14-B.

46. Leyden, "Broadcast by Quiz Kids to Fill Stadium Today," *Daily News*, January 26, 1947, 16-A.

47. Leyden, "Quiz Kid Bowl Broadcast Enriches March of Dimes," *Daily News*, January 27, 1947, 2-A.

48. Leyden, "Broadcast by Quiz Kids," *Daily News*, January 26, 1947, 1-A.

49. QK broadcast, January 26, 1947.

50. Leyden, "Quiz Kid Bowl."

51. Program Notes, March 9, 1947.

52. QK broadcast, March 23, 1947.

53. Larry Wolters, "Two New Shows Have Debuts on WGN Tonight," *Chicago Tribune*, March 7, 1947, 36.

Chapter 14

1. Stephanie Coontz, *The Way We Never Were: American Families and the Nostalgia Trap* (New York: Basic, 1992), 26.

2. Robert L. Griswold, *Fatherhood in America* (New York: Basic, 1993), 167.

3. William M. Tuttle, Jr., "Daddy's Gone to War": The Second World War in the Lives of America's Children (New York: Oxford University Press, 1993), 110.

4. "Felonies up 10.4% in City in Last Year," *New York Times*, April 4, 1945, 23.

5. "Auto Thefts Higher; Youth Chief Culprit," *New York Times*, September 10, 1944, 32.

6. Griswold, *Fatherhood in America*, 169, citing the U.S. Congress, Senate, Subcommittee on Military Affairs, *Hearings on Married Men Exemption: Drafting of Fathers*, 78 Cong. 1st sess., 1943, 4–5.

7. Coontz, *Way We Never Were*, 26.

8. Griswold, *Fatherhood in America*, 167, citing several sources, among them: U.S. Congress, Senate, Subcommittee of the Committee on Education and Labor, *Hearings on Wartime Health and Education: Juvenile Delinquency*, Parts 1, 4, 78th Congress, 1944.

9. Neil Postman, *The Disappearance of Childhood* (New York: Delacorte, 1982), 75.

10. Postman, passim.

11. Catherine MacKenzie, "Wanting to Grow Up," *New York Times Magazine*, June 11, 1944, 33.

12. John Lewellen to Seaborg, February 21, 1946; Chris Miller, "Interview with Rachel Stevenson," *American Women in Radio and Television*, May 1978; Roby Hickok to family, October 24, 1942.

13. May Reynolds Sherwin, "Let Your Children Grow Up," *Parents Magazine*, June 1944, 23.

14. Postman, *Disappearance of Childhood*, 96–97.

15. Ruth Hildreth Abild, "Money in His Pocket," *Parents Magazine*, May 1944, 91.

16. Joseph E. Illick, *American Childhoods* (Philadelphia: University of Pennsylvania Press, 2002), 120.

17. Elliott West, *Growing Up in Twentieth Century America* (Westport: Greenwood, 1996), 197.

18. West, *Growing Up*, 204.

19. Illick, *American Childhoods*, 121.

20. Edward Barry, "Field Museum at 50th Year, Changes Name," *Chicago Tribune*, September 16, 1943, 24.

21. Feldman, *Whatever Happened*, 254.

Chapter 15

1. Marjorie (Beach) Hoffman, telephone interview by author, May 17, 2012.

2. Harrison B. Summers, *A Thirty-Year History of Programs Carried on National Radio Networks in the United States: 1926–1956* (Columbus: Ohio State University, Department of Speech, 1958), 142.
3. Summers, *Thirty-Year History,* 151, 159.
4. Patrick Conlon, interview by author, November 5, 2004.
5. Larry Wolters, "Quiz Kids Going on Road Soon in Talent Search," *Chicago Tribune,* September 12, 1949, B8.
6. Program Notes, September 18, 1949, October 2, 1949.
7. Illick, *American Childhoods,* 121.
8. *QK* broadcast, April 17, 1949.
9. "Rachel Stevenson Oral History."
10. *QK* broadcast, June 25, 1950.
11. Summers, *Thirty-Year History,* 167.
12. *QK* broadcast, January 23, 1949.
13. *QK* broadcast, May 15, 1949.
14. Program Notes, May 13, 1951.
15. Summers, *Thirty-Year History,* 176.
16. "Rachel Stevenson Oral History."
17. Larry Wolters, "Reprieve Keeps Quiz Kids on Air 2 More Weeks," *Chicago Tribune,* September 24, 1951, C4.
18. "Hooper Says 'Uprising' a Question of Low Ratings," *The Billboard,* March 23, 1946, 19.
19. Author unknown, "*The Quiz Kids and How They Grew,*" 2, Feldman collection.
20. Selden, "Louis Cowan Interview," 9.
21. *Heart of the Rio Grande,* Republic Pictures, 1942.
22. Advertisement for Liggett's, *Boston Globe,* September 5, 1941, 16.
23. Charles Collins, "Mr. Pepys Starts It Right," in "A Line o' Type or Two" column, *Chicago Tribune,* January 8, 1944, 12.
24. "Radio Program Will Dramatize Baby's Growth," *Chicago Tribune,* February 17, 1944, 23.

25. Charles Collins, "Aut Caesar Aut Nullus," in "A Line o' Type or Two" column, *Chicago Tribune,* February 24, 1944, 12.
26. Victorino Matus, "When a Puzzled Enemy Met the 'Quiz Kids,'" review of *The Longest Winter* by Alex Kershaw, *The Wall Street Journal,* December 7, 2004, D11.
27. "Battle of Lanzerath Ridge," www.wikipedia.com, accessed September 7, 2012.
28. "Ike Flies 6 GI Quiz Kids Home," *Chicago Tribune,* June 17, 1945, 1.
29. Sheila John Daly, "Here Comes the Grooming," *Chicago Tribune,* February 11, 1945, C8.
30. Vincent Starrett, "Books Alive" column, *Chicago Tribune,* May 13, 1945, E8.
31. Marin J. Melchior, telephone interview by author, May 31, 2012.
32. Russell Maloney, "American Humor Has Yielded a Rich and Varied Harvest," *New York Times,* October 6, 1946, BR5.
33. "It Pays to Be Ignorant," www.wikipedia.org, accessed February 8, 2012.
34. *Radio Days,* Orion Pictures Corporation, 1987.
35. I asked Roby about the fact that when I mentioned *QK* to people who remembered the program, the first thing that they would say was often, "Quiz Kids. Ah yes, Joel Kupperman."
36. *Webster's New Collegiate Dictionary* (Springfield, Mass.: G. and C. Merriam, 1981), 1,328.
37. Douglas Martin, "Sophie B. Altman, Who Started Quiz Show in 1961, Dies at 95," *New York Times,* May 29, 2008, C11.
38. Edward Wyatt, "Oh, Just Answer the Question, Honey," *New York Times,* January 6, 2010, C1, 6.
39. Edward Wyatt, "F.C.C. Opens an Inquiry for a Game Show on Fox," *New York Times,* February 20, 2010, B1, 4.

Bibliography

Abild, Ruth Hildreth. "Money in His Pocket." *Parents Magazine*, May 1944.
"Academy Awards USA: Awards for 1940." www.imdb.com. Accessed February 1, 2012.
Adams, Val. "Youth." In "News of Television and Radio" column, *The New York Times*, January 22, 1956, 103.
"Advertisers, Agencies, Stations." *The Billboard*, September 30, 1941, 6.
"Agreement between Quiz Kids, Inc. and H.W. and Ruth B. Tiers." June 1940. George Van Dyke Tiers collection.
"'Any Bonds Today' 100% Free." *Variety*, June 11, 1941, 25.
Aqua Star and Style Show advertisement. *The Milwaukee Journal*, November 10, 1940, Section II, 5.
"Army Takeover Forces 'WLS Barn Dance' to Move to Smaller Chi House." *Variety*, September 9, 1942, 27.
"Arthur L. Beardsley, President Alka-Seltzer." *Hollywood Knickerbocker Hotel Topics* (newsletter), April 8, 1941, 1.
"Ask the Kids." In "New Program Ideas" column. *Radio Daily*, October 16, 1940, 6.
"Audience Forms Brilliant Setting for Manikins at Style Show at Auditorium." *The Milwaukee Journal*, November 18, 1940, 14.
"Auto Thefts Higher; Youth Chief Culprit." *The New York Times*, September 10, 1944, 32.
Banks, Dale. "What's New from Coast to Coast." *Radio Mirror*, July 1944, 6.
"Battle of Lanzerath Ridge." www.wikipedia.com. Accessed September 7, 2012.
Beaux Arts Apartment Hotel Dining Room Menu. Wednesday, January 8, 1941. Tiers collection.
"Bernays Reflects on His Career and the Public Relations Profession." Link to "1915. Diaghilev's Ballet Russes American Tour." www.prmuseum.com. Accessed May 7, 2009.
"Big Radio Show for Brit. Children Fund," and "To George Burns and Gracie Allen." Advertisement by Canadian War Finance Radio Committee. *Variety*, February 19, 1941, 26, 30.
"Blue Network First Place Winners of the Movie-Radio Guide Poll." In "'Breakfast Club' Cops Program Tops!" National Broadcasting Company advertisement. *Variety*, April 16, 1941, 29.
"Book Week Play Given in Acworth." *Atlanta Constitution*, November 14, 1943, C16.
Boston Store advertisement. *The Milwaukee Journal*, November 19, 1940, 16.
Boyer, Paul S. *By the Bomb's Early Light*. New York: Pantheon, 1985.
Britten, Loretta, and Paul Mathless, eds. *Decade of Triumph: The 40s*. New York: Time-Life, 1999.
Broadcasting Yearbook. Washington: Broadcasting Publications, 1941.
"Buy Bonds and Sell Them." *The Billboard*, May 16, 1942, 3.
"Casadeus [sic] to Be On Air Today; Will Play Here Next Month." *The Atlanta Constitution*, September 19, 1943, 7D.
"Challenger (train)." www.wikipedia.com. Accessed January 22, 2010.
"Chapter XXVII: The Milwaukee Auditorium." *History of Milwaukee*. www.hellomilwaukee.com. Accessed May 8, 2010.

"Chi Sun Adds WLS to Large Schedule." *The Billboard*, April 11, 1942, 6.
"Chicago Woman's Club to Hear Two Guest Speakers." *Chicago Tribune*, August 22, 1943, F6.
"Chicago." *Radio Daily*, November 19, 1940, 4, and January 28, 1941, 4.
"Children's Hour." Claude Brenner collection, unidentified source, n.d., 1941, n.p.
Chip Off the Old Block. Feature Film. Universal Pictures. Released February 1, 1944.
"Cinecolor." http://www.widescreenmuseum.com/oldcolor/cinecolor2.htm. Accessed August 18, 2009.
"City Children to Test Brains of 'Quiz Kids.'" *New York Journal and American*, January 5, 1941, 8-B.
Colgate-Palmolive-Peet Company Bill Stern Sports Newsreel of the Air. Script, April 27, 1941. Cynthia (Cline) Newgarden collection.
Collins, Charles. "Aut Caesar Aut Nullus." In "A Line o' Type or Two" column. *Chicago Tribune*, February 24, 1944, 12.
———. "Mr. Pepys Starts It Right." In "A Line o' Type or Two" column, *Chicago Tribune*, January 8, 1944, 12.
Compton, Gail. "Six Inquisitive Quiz Kids Lap Up Farm Lore." *Chicago Tribune*, October 24, 1942, 15.
Cook, Alton. "Guest Columnist Writes on Behavior of the Quiz Kids." In Paul Kennedy column, *Cincinnati Ohio Post*, April 2, 1942, n.p.
Coontz, Stephanie. *The Way We Never Were*. New York: Basic, 1992.
Corio, Ray. "Question Box." *The New York Times*, January 28, 1985, C9.
"Cowan Agency, Fizdale Take Awards." *The Billboard*, April 26, 1941, 6.
Cowan, Louis. "The Reminiscences of Mr. Louis Cowan." New York: Oral History Research Office, Columbia University, 1978.
Cowan, Paul, and Rachel Cowan. *Mixed Blessings: Marriage Between Jews and Christians*. New York: Doubleday, 1987.
———. "My Father's Children." *Village Voice*, March 29, 1983, 13–15, 34.
Creelman, Eileen. "The Quiz Kids, Five of Them, Make Their First Movie Short in Astoria." In "Picture Plays and Players" column. *New York Sun*, January 8, 1941, 26.
Daly, Sheila John. "Here Comes the Grooming." *Chicago Tribune*, February 11, 1945, C8.
Danforth, Rita. "'Quiz Kid' Slip." Letter to editor, *Movie and Radio Guide*, n.d., n.p., Newgarden collection.
Deitz, Corey. "How Many Radio Stations Are There in the United States?" http://www.about.com. Accessed June 22, 2011.
"Dixon Woman's Club Hears 'Inside Story' About 'Quiz Kids.'" April 3, 1943, n.p., Eliza (Hickok) Kesler collection.
"Dr. I.Q." www.wikipedia.com. Accessed March 8, 2011.
"Dr. Leo S. Rowe Killed by Auto; Head of Pan American Union." *The Washington Post*, December 6, 1946, 1.
"Dolton Boy Prodigy on N.B.C. Air Show." Newspaper clipping, unidentified source, August 8, 1940, n.p., Newgarden collection.
"Drug Talent Cost Index." *The Billboard*, March 16, 1946, 8.
Dunning, John. *On the Air*. New York: Oxford University Press, 1998.
"Editors Crown Radio's Best: Favorite Quiz and Contest Programs." *The Billboard*, March 9, 1946, 8–9.
Edwards, Ralph. "The Quiz Program Operates as a Modern Business Organization." *Variety*, January 8, 1941, 103.
Feldman, Ruth Duskin. *Whatever Happened to the Quiz Kids?* Chicago: Chicago Review Press, 1983.
"Felonies up 10.4% in City in Last Year." *The New York Times*, April 4, 1945, 23.
"53d Show Staged by Triangle Club." *The New York Times*, November 22, 1941, 10.
"1st Lady Stumps 'Expert.'" *New York Journal-American*, January 10, 1941, section 2, p. 10.
"Five Little Thinkers." *Time*, July 15, 1940, 46.
"Five U. of C. Savants to Match Wits with Youthful Quintet." *Chicago Tribune*, June 1, 1941, S1.
"Fly Denounces N.A.B. Leaders, Chain Directors." *St. Louis Post-Dispatch*, May 15, 1941, 1, 8, 9.
"4 Professors to Become 'Quiz Kids.'" *Atlanta Constitution*, January 25, 1943, 15.

French, Jack. "WLS: The Voice of the Prairie." www.otrsite.com. Accessed May 5, 2004.
"Gasoline Rationing on the Home Front During World War II." www.prewarbuick.com. Accessed September 27, 2006.
"Gay's Lion Farm." www.wikipedia.org. Accessed March 24, 2011.
Gay's Lion Farm promotional brochure. N.d., Newgarden collection.
Gilmore-Herman, Helen. "Do These Kids Know All the Answers?" *Liberty*, January 25, 1941, 19.
Gorman, Tom. "Exploitation, Good and Bad." *Variety*, January 8, 1941, 6.
"Greek Benefit Raises $50,000 for War Relief." *Chicago Tribune*, April 3, 1941, 2.
Green, Nat. "Chicago." In "Radio Talent" column, *The Billboard*, April 12, 1941, 12
———. "Quiz Kids Short in Chi Theater Debut." *The Billboard*, September 13, 1941, 7.
Griswold, Robert L. *Fatherhood in America*. New York: Basic, 1993.
Haefele, Dan. "Confessions of a Radio Agency Man." *SPERDVAC Radiogram*, September 1994, 8.
Hardart, Marianne, and Lorraine B. Diehl. *The Automat: The History, Recipes, and Allure of H & H's Masterpiece*. New York: Clarkson Potter, 2002.
Healy, Paul. "What's a Whelk? Gerard Knows Right Answer." *Chicago Tribune*, November 17, 1940, part 3, 6.
Heart of the Rio Grande. Feature Film. Republic Pictures. Released March 11, 1942 (USA).
Heide, Robert, and John Gilman. "The Master of Marketing." http://scoop.diamondgalleries.com. Accessed September 1, 2004.
Hess, Jerry N. "Oral History Interview with Dr. Walter H. Judd." April 13, 1970. Washington, DC. Harry S. Truman Library and Museum, Independence, Mo.
Hickok, Eliza M. "Eliza in Wonderland." Preliminary manuscript for *The Quiz Kids*. N.d. Kesler collection.
Hickok, Eliza Merrill. *The Quiz Kids*. Boston: Little Brown, 1947.
Honigsberg, Sam. "Chicago." In "Radio Talent" column. *The Billboard*, February 21, 1942, 7.
"Hooper Says 'Uprising' a Question of Low Ratings." *The Billboard*, March 23, 1946, 19.
Hopper, Hedda. "Looking at Hollywood." *Chicago Tribune*, March 24, 1945, 16.
———. "Looking at Hollywood." *Chicago Tribune*, September 8, 1943, 26.
Horten, Gerd. *Radio Goes to War*. Berkeley, CA: University of California Press, 2002.
Hovey's advertisement. *Daily Boston Globe*, September 25, 1941, 7.
"Hunt Surviving Burglar in Case of Quizmaster." *Chicago Tribune*, April 23, 1947, 4.
Hutchens, John K. "Child Wonders." *The New York Times*, February 27, 1944, X7.
Illick, Joseph E. *American Childhoods*. Philadelphia: University of Pennsylvania Press, 2002.
"In Chicago." In "From the Production Centres" column. *Variety*, December 10, 1941, 28.
"Inside Stuff—Radio." *Variety*, April 15, 1942, 35.
"Inside Stuff—Radio." *Variety*, October 29, 1941, 35.
"It Pays to Be Ignorant." www.wikipedia.org. Accessed February 8, 2012.
"It's Their Turn Now: A Quiz by the Quiz Kids," *Liberty*, February 14, 1942, 25, 53.
"Jack Benny Back Tonight with Full Cast." *The Atlanta Constitution*, October 10, 1943, 10C.
James, Pence. "Boy, 4, Identifies 365 Birds from Pictures, Tells Habits." *Chicago Daily News*, April 23, 1937, 44.
———. "Now We Know How Cold It Is at Twice Zero." *Chicago Daily News*, November 14, 1940, 1.
James, Sidney. "Prodigy's Progress: Gerard Darrow." *Life*, September 29, 1941, 49, 52, 54, 56, 59.
Johnson, Wendell. "The Quiz Kids and What It Takes to Become One." Review of *The Quiz Kids*, by Eliza Merrill Hickok. *Chicago Sun Book Week*, April 27, 1947, 3.
"Jordan's Starts Contest to Find Boston 'Quiz Kid.'" *Daily Boston Globe*, October 2, 1941, 26.
"Jungle Birds Make Friends with Visiting Quiz Kids." *Miami Daily News*, January 23, 1947, 1-B.
Kahn, Sylvia. "We Asked the Quiz Kids." *Modern Screen*, July 1941, 44–5, 73.
Kaplan, Ben. "For the Love of Mike." *Providence (Rhode Island) Evening Bulletin*, August 1941, n.p., Brenner collection.
Kelly, Joe. "Just Ask the Quiz Kids." Sheet Music. New York: Famous Music Corp., 1942.
"Kid Wizards." *Variety*, January 22, 1941, 46.

King, Willford I., Oswald W. Knauth, and Frederick R. Macaulay. *Income in the United States: Its Amount and Distribution 1909–1919*. Vol. I. Wesley C. Mitchell, ed. New York: National Bureau of Economic Research, 1922.
Kopf, Harry C. "Chi Radio Production Thrives Without 'Names.'" *Variety*, January 8, 1941, 87.
Kosser, Michael. *How Nashville Became Music City USA*. Milwaukee: Hal Leonard, 2006.
Lear, John. "The Magnificent Ignoramous." *The Saturday Evening Post*, July 8, 1944, 76.
"Legends Bio: Kay Kamen." Disney Legends. http://legends.disney.go.com. Accessed June 12, 2009.
"Leslie M. Roush." http://www.imdb.com/name/nm0745890/. Accessed August 20, 2009.
Leyden, Louise. "Broadcast by Quiz Kids to Fill Stadium Today." *Miami Daily News*, January 26, 1947, 16-A.
———. "Quiz Kids Arrive Here to Spur March of Dimes Toward Goal." *Miami Daily News*, January 22, 1947, 1-B
———. "Quiz Kid Bowl Broadcast Enriches March of Dimes." *Miami Daily News*, January 27, 1947, 2-A.
———. "Quiz Kids Hook Big Ones on Biscayne Bay 'Voyage.'" *Miami Daily News*, January 25, 1947, 1.
Lieberman, Henry R. "That 'Quiz Kid' Gerard Darrow." *PM*, January 6, 1941, 15.
Liggett's advertisement. *Boston Globe*, September 5, 1941, 16.
Lingeman, Richard. *Don't You Know There's a War On?* New York: G.P. Putnam's Sons, 1970.
"Listen! With Glynn." *The Washington Post*, August 27, 1941, 26.
Los Angeles Breakfast Club promotional mailing. Newgarden collection.
"Lou Cowan, Owner of 'Quiz Kids,' Is Newcomer to Army's Radio Section." *Variety*, January 21, 1942, 22.
"Lou Cowan Temporarily Heads OWI's New York Office." *Variety*, September 2, 1942, 38.
"Lou Cowan Works Out an Elaborate Dept. Store Tie for 'Quiz Kid' Program." *Variety*, December 18, 1940, 23.
"Louis G. Cowan Citation on Outstanding Single Program Exploitation." *The Billboard*, May 9, 1942, 9.
Louis G. Cowan Company advertisement. *The Billboard*, May 3, 1941, 6.
"Low Air Dough in Chicago." *The Billboard*, November 9, 1940, 6.
"Lucky Smarties." In column "Stand By: Radio News and Notes." *Scholastic*, January 27, 1941, 34.
MacKenzie, Catherine. "Wanting to Grow Up." *The New York Times Magazine*, June 11, 1944, 33.
Maloney, Russell. "American Humor Has Yielded a Rich and Varied Harvest." *The New York Times*, October 6, 1946, BR5
"Many Brilliant Speakers for Teachers' Rally." *The Atlantic City Press*, February 2, 1941, 16.
Marsters, Ann. "'Quiz Kids' Originator Tells Woes of Founding Program." *Chicago Herald-American*, January 6, 1941, 13, 25.
Martin, Douglas. "Sophie B. Altman, Who Started Quiz Show in 1961, Dies at 95." *New York Times*, May 29, 2008.
Matus, Victorino. "When a Puzzled Enemy Met the 'Quiz Kids.'" Review of *The Longest Winter*, by Alex Kershaw. *The Wall Street Journal*, December 7, 2004, D11.
"May Defer Key Radio Men." *Variety*, February 25, 1942, 29.
McEvoy, J. P. "Quiz Kids." *Cue*, September 7, 1940, 18.
Melick, Weldon. "Have You a Quiz Kid in Your Home?" *Coronet*, March 1942, 3–10.
"Mex., Cuban Facsimile of U.S. Air." *The Billboard*, March 2, 1946, 10.
"Midway Alumni Give $455,098 to Aid Fund Drive." *Chicago Daily News*, June 7, 1941, 4.
"Milestones in Elkhart," http://www.entrepreneur.com/tradejournals/article/print/12926667.html. Accessed March 4, 2011.
Miller, Chris. "Interview with Rachel Stevenson." Washington, DC: Broadcast Pioneers Library Oral History Program, May 1978.
Miscamble, Wilson D. *From Roosevelt to Truman: Potsdam, Hiroshima, and the Cold War*. New York: Cambridge University Press, 2007.
"Mischa Elman, Jennie Tourel on WGST." *The Atlanta Constitution*, August 15, 1943, 6D, and NBC Program Notes, August 15, 1943, n.p.

"Mississippi School Teacher Wins $2,500 Quiz Kids' Award." *Chicago Tribune*, June 1, 1947, N12.
Modell, Norman. "Chicago." In "Radio Talent" column. *The Billboard*, July 20, 1940, 7.
_____. "Chicago." In "Radio Talent" column. *The Billboard*, October 26, 1940, 8; December 28, 1940, 19; January 18, 1941, 8.
_____. "Quiz Kids." *The Billboard*, July 13, 1940, 8.
Moore, Don. "The Quiz Kids." *Movie and Radio Guide*, August 31–September 6, 1940, 39.
"More Clever Kids." *Variety*, April 23, 1941, 34.
"More Station P.A. Shows." *The Billboard*, May 3, 1941, 8.
Morison, Samuel Eliot, and Henry Steele Commager. *The Growth of the American Republic*. 3d ed., rev. 2 vols. New York: Oxford University Press, 1942.
Morse, Jarvis M. *Paying for a World War: The United States Financing of World War II*. Private collection.
Murphy, Mark. "6 Precocious Scholars from Chicago." *New York Post*, January 4, 1941, 9.
Nachman, Gerald. *Raised on Radio*. New York: Pantheon, 1998.
"Nazis Dig in for Air Raids; London Ladies of Night in Tin Hats." *Los Angeles Evening Herald and Express*, April 1, 1941, A9.
"NBC Refuses 'Kids of the Week' as Too Much Like 'Quiz Kids.'" *Variety*, May 7, 1941, 31.
Niessen, Frank. "Kids in Clover." *Chicago Herald-American*, Saturday Home Magazine, October 5, 1940, 2.
"Nighttime Talent Cost Index." *The Billboard*, November 9, 1946, 11.
The Official Guide of the Railways. New York: National Railway Publications, April 1941.
O'Neill, Mildred. "Women in Radio." *Radio Daily, New York City*, March 28, 1945, 4.
Olney, Laurence M. *The War Bond Story*. Washington: U.S. Savings Bond Division, 1971.
Othman, Frederick C. "Quiz Kids Even Know Answer to Hollywood." *New York Morning Telegraph*, April 22, 1941, 1, 2.
_____. "Quiz Kids in Movies." April 23, 1941. Brenner collection, unidentified source.
"Parents of Quiz Kids Shine Over Air in Final Show." *Chicago Herald-American*, February 22, 1941, 24.
"Parents Outsmart Quiz Kids. Elders Demonstrate They Know a Great Deal, Too." *Chicago Herald-American*, February 22, 1941, 5.
Pennsylvania Railroad advertisement. *Life*, February 10, 1941, 84.
Perrett, Geoffrey. *Days of Sadness, Years of Triumph*. New York: Coward, McCann, Geoghegan, 1973.
Phillips, Cabell. *The 1940s: Decade of Triumph and Trouble*. New York: Macmillan, 1975.
Postman, Neil. *The Disappearance of Childhood*. New York: Delacorte, 1982.
"Precocious Gang Prepares to Level Things at Home," *Chicago Herald-American*, February 17, 1941, n.p.
"Precocious One-Year-Old." *Newsweek*, July 7, 1941, 46.
Program from the American Legion Auxiliary States Dinner, September 17, 1941. Private collection.
Provines, June. "Quiz Kid's Pet." In "Front Views and Profiles" column. *Chicago Tribune*, July 31, 1941, 11.
"Pull Up a Chair — It's *Quiz Kid* Time." *Tractor Works Attractor* (company newsletter), November 1941. Tiers collection.
"'Quiz Kid' Can Accept $2,000-a-Week Job." *The Atlanta Constitution*, August 12, 1943, 8.
"Quiz Kid Slips; Asks 'Who's Hitler?'" *Chicago Herald-American*, July 26, 1941, 3
"Quiz Kids." In "Program Reviews" column. *Radio Daily*, September 5, 1940, 6.
"Quiz Kids." Script for Quiz Kids broadcast. Wade Radio Continuity, September 11, 1940. Newgarden collection.
"The Quiz Kids and How They Grew," author not identified. N.p., 1948. Ruth Duskin Feldman collection.
"Quiz Kids ASK Questions, Too; Turn Tables on Their In-quiz-itor." *New York Journal and American*, January 11, 1941, 4.
"Quiz Kids Back Too Soon, Will Miss Benny Party." In "Radio Parade" column. *Chicago Herald-American*, April 23, 1941, 31.
"'Quiz Kids' Birthday." *Chicago Herald-American*, June 24, 1941, 8.

"Quiz Kids Do Their Stuff at Aqua Star and Style Show." *The Milwaukee Journal*, Sports and Markets and Classified Section, November 19, 1940, 1.
"Quiz Kids Enjoy Day at Meade." On or about August 27, 1941. Brenner collection, unidentified source.
"The Quiz Kids: 50 Years Ago, a Bunch of Educated Upstarts Became Radio's Smash Hit." *Chicago Tribune*, December 2, 1990, 28.
"'Quiz Kids' Get Disney." *The Billboard*, February 8, 1941, 7.
"'Quiz Kids' Give War Bonds," *The Billboard*, July 3, 1943, 8.
"Quiz Kids Guests at Meade." *Baltimore Post*, August 27, 1941. Brenner collection.
"Quiz Kids in Movieland." April 1941, n.p. Brenner collection, unidentified source.
"Quiz Kids Information Please in Short Pants." *Spotlite Magazine*, January 1941, 26.
"Quiz Kids Kidded at Triangle Show." *The New York Times*, December 20, 1941, 25.
"Quiz Kids Meet Profs — Who Won? Tsk, Tsk." *Chicago Herald-American*, June 8, 1941, 1.
"'Quiz Kids' Now Wards of State." *The Billboard*, September 28, 1940, 7.
"'Quiz Kids' on Bond Selling Tour." *The Billboard*, September 18, 1943, 7.
"Quiz Kids Outquiz Professors." *Des Moines Sunday Register*, June 15, 1941, 3.
"Quiz Kids Pass Army Air Tests with Flying Colors!" *Chicago Herald-American*, August 26, 1942, n.p. Brenner collection.
"Quiz Kids Plan Contest to Pick Best Teacher." *Chicago Tribune*, January 26, 1946, 19.
"Quiz Kids' Premiere!" *Chicago Herald-American*, September 3, 1941, Quiz Kids Special Section, 1.
"Quiz Kids Quizzed by Army; Find Aviation Cadet Test Easy." *Chicago Daily News*, August 26, 1942, n.p. Brenner collection.
"Quiz Kids Scoop World on Two New Elements." *Chicago Tribune*, November 20, 1945, 18.
"'Quiz Kids' Short Gets Heavy Plugging in Hub." *Variety*, October 22, 1941, 15.
"Quiz Kids Stop Off in Dayton." *Dayton Sunday Journal-Herald*, June 29, 1941, 10.
"'Quiz Kids' to Aid Defense." *The Billboard*, May 31, 1941, 7.
"The Quiz Kids to Sell Bonds Here Sept. 19." *The Washington Post*, September 1943, n.d., n.p. Private collection.
"Quiz Talent Cost Index." *The Billboard*, March 30, 1946, 11.
"Quizmaster Kills Burglar." *Chicago Tribune*, April 22, 1947, 1.
Radio Days. Feature Film. Orion Pictures Corporation. Released January 30, 1987 (USA).
"Radio Program Will Dramatize Baby's Growth." *Chicago Tribune*, February 17, 1944, 23.
"Radio Quiz Kids Stop at Dayton on Way to Chautauqua Program." *Dayton Daily News*, June 29, 1941, 9.
"Radio's Highest Rated Programs During Radio's Golden Age." http://web.archive.org/web. Accessed June 15, 2009.
"Radio's Production Costs." *The Billboard*, November 16, 1940, 8; October 11, 1941, 6.
Randall, Frank A. *History of the Development of Building Construction in Chicago.* 2nd ed. Rev. and expanded by John D. Randall. Urbana: University of Illinois Press, 1999.
Ranson, Jo. "'Quiz Kids' to Air Wisdom from N.Y." In "Jo Ranson's Radio Dial Log" column. *Brooklyn Eagle*, January 8, 1941, 20.
"Recess Time." In "Radio Reviews" column. *Variety*, December 18, 1940, 38.
Reed, Kate. "Meet the Quiz Kids." *Child Life*, April 1941, 157.
"Rehearsals Short." *Chicago Herald-American*, Quiz Kids Special Section, September 3, 1941, 1.
"Renew Quiz Kids." *Variety*, September 17, 1941, 30.
Rodenbach, Clark. "Brains Pay? Ask Quiz Kid." Publication unidentified, February 19, 1945, n.p. Tiers collection.
Rolo, Charles J. *Radio Goes to War.* New York: G.P. Putnam's Sons, 1942.
Roosevelt, Eleanor. "October 25, 1946." In *My Day* column. United Feature Syndicate, Inc., n.p.
Rothe, Anna, ed. *Current Biography 1945.* New York: H.W. Wilson, 1946.
Sanford, Herb. "Looking Ahead." *The Billboard*, April 12, 1941, 12.
"Schoolteachers Tied In On I.Q. Junior Quiz." *Variety*, June 11, 1941, 28.
Script for Kaynee Quiz Kids boys' clothing, n.d. Newgarden collection.
Selden, Walter. "Louis Cowan Interview on The Quiz Kids." March 30, 1941. Feldman collection.

_____. "Quiz Kid No. One." Article based on "Louis Cowan Interview on the Quiz Kids." N.d. Feldman collectikon.
Seventeenth Annual Program Associated Exhibitors, National Education Association. February 25, 1941. Tiers collection.
Sherwin, May Reynolds. "Let Your Children Grow Up." *Parents Magazine*, June 1944, 23.
Siegel, Norman. "Local Girl Musician Thrilled by Success of Friend's Outstanding Tune Hit." *The Cleveland Press*, August 17, 1940, 16.
_____. "'Quizz' Kids Eclipse Elders on Radio's Newest Brain Buster." *The Cleveland Plain Dealer*, July 5, 1940, 23.
_____. "Watches 'Quiz Kids' Answer Difficult Questions Correctly on Unrehearsed Program." *The Cleveland Plain Dealer*, August 26, 1940, 8.
Six Kids and the War.... Promotional brochure, The Blue Network, American Broadcasting Company. Private collection.
"Smartie Kids on WSNY." *Variety*, July 29, 1942, 32.
Spiegel, Alix. "Freud's Nephew and the Origins of Public Relations," NPR online newsletter. www.prmuseum.com. Accessed May 7, 2009.
"Sponsors Still Love Mail." *The Billboard*, August 7, 1943, 10.
Starrett, Vincent. "Books Alive" column. *Chicago Tribune*, May 13, 1945, E8.
"Stars Do Their Share Add $35,000 to Greek Aid Fund." *Chicago Herald-American*, April 3, 1941, 8.
"Stars to Arrive on Wednesday." *The Washington Post*, September 1943, n.p.
"Statistics, 1941." *Variety*, January 7, 1942, 147.
Stephan, Robert S. "Gale Page to Devote All Her Time to Radio." *The Cleveland Plain Dealer*, July 5, 1940, 11.
_____. "G.O. Antics Provide Signpost of Democracy." *The Cleveland Plain Dealer*, June 29, 1940, 13.
_____. "Pearce Makes Star of Old Pal 'Elmer Blunt.'" *The Cleveland Plain Dealer*, July 6, 1940, 11.
Sterling, Christopher H., and John M. Kittross. *Stay Tuned*. Belmont, CA: Wadsworth, 1978.
Stevenson, Rachel. "Rachel Stevenson Oral History." Recorded June 23, 1995. Museum of Broadcast Communications, Chicago.
Summers, Harrison B. *A Thirty-Year History of Programs Carried on National Radio Networks in the United States: 1926–1956*. Columbus: Ohio State University, Department of Speech, 1958.
"This Date in Baseball." *The New York Times*, June 26, 2004, D5.
Thompson, Edgar A. "Little Mental Giants." *The Milwaukee Journal*, July 14, 1940, 10.
_____. "Milwaukee Youngster to Broadcast with Quiz Kids." In "Riding the Airwaves" column, *The Milwaukee Journal*, Green Sheet section, November 18, 1940, 2.
_____. "'Quiz Kid' Expert Unimpressed by His Earnings." In "Riding the Airwaves" column, *The Milwaukee Journal*, Green Sheet section, November 19, 1940, 2.
"3 Baseball Clubs Set for Contest." *The New York Times*, June 25, 1944, S3.
"3-Cornered Baseball Game Yields $56,500,000 in Fifth Bond Drive." *The New York Times*, June 27, 1944, 1.
"Thrills, Beauty at Aqua Show." *The Milwaukee Journal*, Sports and Markets and Classified Section, November 18, 1940, 1.
Tuttle, William M., Jr. *Daddy's Gone to War*. New York: Oxford University Press, 1993.
"20th Century Limited." www.wikipedia.com. Accessed January 11, 2011.
Twiggar, Beth. "Quiz Kids Come to Town to Make a Film." *New York Herald Tribune*, February 2, 1941, sec. 6, 4.
"U.S. Must Fight if Nazis Win, Educators Hear." *The Atlantic City Press*, February 25, 1941, 2.
"Up to 419." *Hollywood Knickerbocker Hotel Topics*, April 13, 1941, 4.
"Use Veterans' Posers as Quiz Kid Session." *Chicago Tribune*, November 17, 1946, S10.
VanGiezen, Robert, and Albert E. Schwenk. "Compensation from before World War II through the Great Depression." U.S. Department of Labor. www.bls.gov. Posted January 30, 2003. Accessed February 3, 2012.
"Various Items About the Wireless." *The New York Times*, January 11, 1942, X12.
"Vox Pop: The Show That Traveled America." Library of American Broadcasting. www.lib.umd.edu. Accessed February 6, 2011.

"Walter Wades Are Here with Quiz Kids." *Topics*, April 12, 1941, 1.
"The Weather." *Chicago Tribune*, June 22–28, 1940, 1.
Webster's New Collegiate Dictionary. Springfield, MA: G. and C. Merriam, 1981.
West, Elliott. *Growing Up in Twentieth Century America*. Westport, CT: Greenwood, 1996.
"What's Going On and Where." *The Washington Post*, August 27, 1941, 15.
"WHN's Kid Wizards Attract a Sponsor." *Variety*, February 26, 1941, 33.
Winkler, Allan M. *Home Front USA: America During World War II*. Arlington Heights, IL: Harlan Davidson, 1986.
"Winners of The Billboard's Radio Publicity and Exploitation Survey." *The Billboard*, May 3, 1941, 10.
Wolters, Larry. "Anne McKnight Makes Bow in 'Boheme' Today." *Chicago Tribune*, February 3, 1946, NS.
_____. "Farmer Quiz Show Opens on Thursday." *Chicago Tribune*, November 30, 1947, NH.
_____. "The Quiz Kids' Five Years—An American Story." *Chicago Tribune*, July 1, 1945, SW4
_____. "Quiz Kids Going on Road Soon in Talent Search." *Chicago Tribune*, September 12, 1949, B8.
_____. "Reprieve Keeps Quiz Kids on Air 2 More Weeks," *Chicago Tribune*, September 24, 1951, C4.
Wyatt, Edward. "F.C.C. Opens an Inquiry for a Game Show on Fox." *The New York Times*, February 20, 2010, B1, 4.
_____. "Oh, Just Answer the Question, Honey." *The New York Times*, January 6, 2010, C1, 6.
"You Can't Milk a Heifer, 6 Quiz Kids'll Discover." *Chicago Daily-Tribune*, October 23, 1942, 12.
"Young America Is Getting Its Chance." *Daily Boston Globe*, July 14, 1940, C8.
Zolotareff, Meyer. "Filmland Tour Glorious, Say Quiz Kids." Unidentified source, n.d., 1941, n.p. Brenner collection.

Collections

Claude Brenner collection.
Cynthia (Cline) Newgarden collection.
Eliza (Hickok) Kesler collection.
George Van Dyke Tiers collection.
International Jack Benny Fan Club collection.
Joan (Bishop) Barber collection.
Quiz Kids broadcasts. NBC-MOB radio collection. Library of Congress.
Quiz Kids NBC Program Notes. Library of Congress Recorded Sound Division.
Seaborg, The Papers of Glenn Theodore. Library of Congress.
Senator Harold H. Burton Papers. Library of Congress.
Wisconsin Historical Society. NBC collection.

Index

Numbers in **_bold italics_** indicate pages with photographs.

Academy Awards (Oscars) 15
acquisition by movie studios 97–98
Adams, Franklin P. 9
Alec Templeton Time 7, 18, 20
Allen, Fred 120, 136, ***198***, 209
Allen, Gracie 114
Allison, Fran 246
American society 2; labor relations, the Great Depression 2, 14, 18, 168
Anderson, Eddie (Rochester) 119; *see also* Rochester
Anderson, Mary Ann 27–28
anxiety of *Quiz Kids* (program) production staff 99
assumption of age of Kids 123–24, 242–43
Atlantic City 108
atom bomb 2, 213; fear of devastation 214, 215–16, 218, 219; federal government public relations campaign 214, 219–20; use of atomic energy 220; *see also* Seaborg, Glenn
audience-building 22, 63, 70, 100–3, 104, 106, 110, 118–19, 162–63, 179, 188, 196, 199; change in programming 198; Postal Telegraph Cable Company 64; special format 105, 107, 109; *see also* celebrity guests; mail from listeners; NEA (National Association of School Superintendents); Quiz Kids — Parents; Quiz Kids Versus
audience interest 98–99, 100
auditions for quizmaster 22–25
authenticity of program 56–60, 197–98; *see also* Siegel, Norman
Autry, Gene 199, 247–48
awards for *Quiz Kids* (program) 143–45

awareness of program 247; *see also* Autry, Gene; popular culture

Bailey, Joe 17, 21, 27, 42, 45, 49, 51, 53, 57, 103, 112, 130, 146, 156–57, 160–61, 162, 169, 172, 177, 186–87
Banister, Richard 52
Barrymore, Lionel 114
Beardsley, Charles 18, 28, 37, 64, 125, 132, 141, 165
Beaux Arts apartments 81, 83, ***86***, ***87***
Beckman, Jack 80
Beloin, Eddie 117–18, 120, 122, 125–26, 133, 140
Benny, Jack 6, 98, 103, 104, 113, 116, ***121***, 134–36, 158, ***201***; *see also* Jack Benny show
Benny, Joan 131
Bernays, Edward 31, 66, 93
Best Teacher contests 221–23
Bishop, Joan 12–13, 19, 23, 27, 50, 81, ***82***, ***85***–***87***, 117, 118, ***121***, 124, 125, ***130***, 131, 132, 133, 137, 150, 151, 153, 155
Blue Network 20
Borge, Victor 224
Brainard, Bertha 79, 98, 103, 110, 179
Brenner, Claude 80, 116, ***121***, 123, 124, ***130***, 133, 134, 137, 140, 150, 150, 155, 158, 182, ***203***, 220
B_2H_2 202–6
Burke, Robert ***217***
Burns, George 114

C.A.B. (Cooperative Analysis of Broadcasting) 60–61, 63
Cantor, Eddie 166, 198, ***204***
celebrity guests 198, 224
Challenger 113

INDEX

change in programming 198, 243–44, 245, 246
characteristics of Quiz Kids (children) 11, 52–53, 251
Chicago's Music Row 12; El 12
City of Los Angeles (train) 114, 116
Cline, Cynthia 14, 23, 27, 69, 73, 79, 80, 81, *82*, 84, *85–87*, 89, *90*, 91, 97, 107, 114, 117, *121*, 126, 127, 129, *130*, 133, 136, 137, 140, 146, 150, 153, 155, 156, 158; *see also* Newgarden, Cynthia (Cline)
coaching Quiz Kids (children) with answers 18, 55, 58–60
competitors 170–72; catch-penny promotion 173, 245; formats of competitors 174–75; on NBC network 170, 172, 174; reaction by Lou Cowan, Walter Wade, and Joe Bailey 172–74, 175;
Conlon, Patrick 220–21, 241
Conlon, Sheila *217*
contemporary imitators 251–52
contract with kids for program 27
Cornfield, Jerome 74–75
Cowan, Louis G. 7–9, 11–22, 24, 26, 28, 29, 51, 54, 57, 58, 63, 65, 66, 75, 79, 89, 90, 97, 102, 105, 107–8, 112, 117, 125, 140–41, 143, 162, 179, 185, 188, 207, 223, 252; background 30–33; control of program, attention to details 64, 113, 124, 157, 198, 240; demeanor 33; on education 8
Cowan, Paul 8–9
Cowan, Polly 15, 51, 79, 90
Crabbe, Buster 73
Crosby, Bing 114, *202*
Crosby, Bob 114
curiosity and manners of Quiz Kids (children) 91, 111–12, 138, 152–53; value to Treasury Department 195

Darrow, Gerard 11–12, 13, 23, 27, 56–*58*, 59, 69, 74, 80, 81, *82*, 83, *84–87*, 91, 96–97, 107, 111, 112, 114, 116, 118, 119, *121*, 122–23, 123, 124, *128–*29, *130*, 132, 133, 134, 136, 137, 140, *149*, 150, 151, 153, 155, 158, 159, 191–92, *202*, *203*, *204*, 220
Day, Dennis 119, 122, 124
Defense Bonds 147–48; *see also* War Bonds
demonstration recordings 11, 16, 20
determining size of radio audience 60–61, 62; staff tension 99; *see also* C.A.B. (Cooperative Analysis of Broadcasting); C.E. Hooper Company (Hooper ratings)
Dietrich, Marlene 114
Disney, Walt 103, 114, 118, 127, 129–30, 159
Durbin, Deanna 114, 133

Duskin, Ruth 53, 124, *163*, *192*, *202*, *203*, *204*; *see also* Feldman, Ruth (Duskin)

exploitation and publicity 130–33, 134, 136–37, 143–45, 154, 155–56, 179

Fadiman, Clifton 9
Feldman, Ruth (Duskin) 2, 4, 157, 207; *see also* Duskin, Ruth
Fields, W.C. 136
Fischman, Harvey 53, *58*, *149*, 151, 155, 158, 182, *192*, *203*, *204*, 207, 218
Fisher, Ruth 49, *58*, 166
fountain of ideas 11

Grand Central Terminal 81
Greek war relief benefit 113–14, 116

Hamburg, Geraldine 74
Harris, Phil 119, 120, 122, 123, 124
Hickok, Eliza Merrill 2–3, 4, 16, 22, 24, 28, 40; background 41–42; joins staff 42–44; *see also* Roby
Hollywood Knickerbocker Hotel 132–33
Hooper ratings 61, 63, 99, 240, 245, 246
Hope, Bob 15, *199*, *200*
Horn and Hardart Automats 82–83

impressions of New York City 79, 81
Information Please 7, 9, 55
interest by film production studios 97, 207; *see also* Universal Pictures
interest in Latin America 226
international expansion 227, 232

James, Pence 11, 12, 13, 14, 70
James, Sidney 12, 13, 16
The Jell-O Program (Jack Benny show) 62–63, 104, 110, 112, 118–20, 124, 141; April 6 program 120; April 13 program 133–34; April 20 program 139–40; writers 115, 116, 117–18, 122, 125–26, 133, 135; *see also* Beloin, Eddie; Greek war relief benefit; Morrow, Bill

Kamen, George 46–48, 54, 66, 71–72, 75, 79, 80, 82, 84–85, 90, 102, 160, 179, 188, 195
Kaynee Company 80
Kelly, Joe 7, 23–25, 26, 27–28, *38*, 39, 40, *41*, 56, 57, *58*, 60, *63*, 65–66, 79, 80, 89–90, 96, 111, 117, 124, 134–35, 151, 158, 177, *178*, 179, *200*, 207, 215, 225, 226, 227, 228, 252–53; background 34–37; heart attack 223–24, 246; job insecurity 28, 37, 40, 64–65, 213; kills burglar 39; search for new Kids 241; sense of humor 90, 91; *see also* temporary replacements

Kieran, John 9, 56
Kirby, Durwood 22
Kupperman, Joel 44, 52, *92*, 123, 181, *192*, *198–99*, *203*, *204*, 207, 208–9, 210, 221, 243–44
Kyser, Kay 32

LaGuardia, Fiorello 78, 84, *85*, 152
Levant, Oscar 9
Lewellen, John 10, 12, 13, 19, 20, 21, 25, 27, 29, 34, *41*, 50, 52, 59, 79, 90, 103, 105, 107, 108, 111, 112, 116, 117, 118, 125, 127, 130, 141, 146, 148, 151, 181–83, 188, *200*, 202, 215, 216, 224, 253; background 33; creating questions for program 33–34; personality 197
Lewellen, LuAnn 10–11
Livingstone, Mary 119, 124, 134
Louis G. Cowan Company 14, 15, 21, 68, 143, 179, 221; *see also* naming the program
Lucal, Jack 73, 80, 107, 117, *130*, 133, 138, *149*, 150, 155
Lunde, Lon 221

mail from listeners 61–62, 63, 163, 165–69
marketing the program 26, 69–70, 71–72, 113, 131, 154, 157–58, 159, 177, *178*; "Beat the Quiz Kids" column and contest 93–94, 106–7
Marwick, Julia *58*
Marx, Chico 138–39, *203*, 224
Marx, Groucho 138, 139
Marx Brothers 138–39
McHugh, Mary *58*, 81, *82*, *85*, *86*, 90
memory 36, 54
Merchandise Mart 26
merchandising for program 66, 69, *72*, 75, 102, 160, 179; paper cut-out dolls 66, *67*, 80, 156, 157; "Quiz Kids collection" 80, 102; Quiz Kids Dictionary 69; *see also* Kamen, George; Kaynee Company; Parker Brothers; Whitman Publishing
Merrick, Margaret 155, *203*
MGM 132, 137–38
Miles Laboratories (Alka-Seltzer) 3, 18, 22, 25, 63, 109, 118; change in contract 240, 244, 246; contract for show 19, 65, 99–100, 147, 169, 200, 246–47; sales increase 99; *see also* scheduling
military recruiting exams 181–83
Morrow, Bill 117–18, 120, 122, 125–26, 133, 140
musicians' union ban 188–89

naming the program 14–15; legality of name 25–26

NBC 18, 20, 26, 79, 104, 158, 170, 171; guidelines for *Quiz Kids* (program) 21
NEA (National Association of School Superintendents) 104–5, 106, 108–10; advancing value of education 110; *see also* Atlantic City
Newgarden, Cynthia (Cline) 36, 166; *see also* Cline, Cynthia
nitpicking 96, 123, 220–21

O'Connor, Donald 207
Orbanes, Phil 67
Owen, Forrest 45–46, 195, 224

Pan American Union 225–26; broadcast from the library of Congress 227–28; *see also* interest in Latin America
Paramount Pictures 78, 83, 86, 87–88, *89*, 97, 103, 137, 152, 153–54, 158, 207; *see also* interest by film production studios
Parker Brothers 67, *68*, 69, 75, 102, 246
Parks, Jimmy 17–18
personal appearances 73, 145–47, 148, *149*, 150–52, 155, 159, 160–61, 162, 179, 180–81, 188, 202, 206, 209, 224–25, 228–32; *see also* Bill Stern; military recruiting exams; Pan American Union; war loan rallies
popular culture 247; *Radio Days* 250–51
Princeton Triangle Club 31, 159
Prochaska, David *203*
production budgets 19, 147, 200

Quiz Kids (program) format 10, 21–22, 171; change in format 241–42
Quiz Kids — Parents 105, 155
Quiz Kids Versus 109, 110, 119, 149–50, 152, 153, 175, 202, 205, 209, 212; *see also* B_2H_2; personal appearances
quiz programs 1, 19–20

radio columnists 55
radio history 2, 14; advertising agencies 17; "idea shows" 19; *Quiz Kids* on tape 3; recordings (transcriptions) 3–4, 125
radio programs: family listening 1
raising children 234
Red Network 20
references to *Quiz Kids* (program) in language 248–51; *see also* popular culture
Reiner, Manny 75
remuneration for Kids 27, 65
Roby *41*–43, 50, 53, 57, 79, *84*, 88, 89–90, 91–92, 96, 99, 105–6, 110, 115–16, 117, 118, 120, 123, 125, 126, 127, 130–31, 137, 139, 141, 146, 161–62, 167, 181–83, 201–2, 208, 245

Rochester 119, 122, 134, 140
Rooney, Jack 231
Roosevelt, Eleanor 6, 83, 90, 91, 215–16
Roush, Leslie M. 86–88, 153

Saalfield Publishing 66, 69, 80, 156
scheduling 7, 65, 187
scholarly excellence 7–9, 53; *see also Information Please*
Seaborg, Glenn 4, 215–18, *217*, 223; discovery of two new elements 218; naming new elements 218–19
search for new Kids 17, 70, 73, 75–76; search for younger Kids 242; *see also* assumption of age of Kids
selection of prospective Quiz Kids (children) 13–14, 17, 49; attitude toward learning 54; audition 53; interview 51; letters to office 50, 52; personality 53; questionnaire 49, 51–52; *see also* characteristics
short films 69, 77–78, 86, 154–55, 158; *see also* LaGuardia, Fiorello; Paramount Pictures; Roush, Leslie M.
Siegel, Norman 55–58, 69
Sigmund, Paul *149*
Simmons, Ed 21, 22
size of staff 51, 61
societal changes 234; consumerism and perception of children 237–38; daily life for children 236–37; economic power of young people 239; juvenile delinquency 235–36
sophistication of Kids 96–97
Spiegel, Babette 14, 15, 25
Spiegel, John 221–22
Spiegel, Pauline (Polly) 10, 15, 51
sponsors 18; interest by other sponsors 65; local sponsors 245
statistics about Quiz Kids (children) 150, 179–80, 244–45
Stephan, Robert 55, 65
Stern, Bill 146–47
Stevenson, Rachel 25, 28, *41*, 44–45, 247
Super Chief 113, 141

Templeton, Alec 7, 18, 19
temporary replacements 223–24, 246
Tiers, George Van Dyke 14, 23, 27, 28, 36, *58*, 69, 70, 80, 81, *82*, 83, *85–87*, *90–*92, 97, 107, 150, 151, 153, 155, 158, 160, 182, 220
travel to other cities 72–73, 77, 79, 101–2, 103–4, 105–6, 111–12, 113, 140, 151, 162, 210; arrival in New York City (1941) 81, *82*; *The Jell-O Program*; Milwaukee Auditorium 73; pranks and practical jokes 92; sightseeing 81, 90, 137; visit to Congress 91; visit to White House 90–91; *see also* Beaux Arts Apartments; *Challenger*; *Super Chief*; *Twentieth Century Limited*; *Vox Pop*; war loan rallies; West Coast trip (1941)
Twentieth Century Limited 79

U.S. Treasury Department 147–48, 152, 187–88, 194, 195, 212; award to *Quiz Kids* 193
Universal Pictures 207–8, 209; *see also* Kupperman, Joel
Utley, Clifford 23, 59–60, 223, 224

visit to movie studios 137, 138
Vox Pop 101, 102

Wade, Jeff 18, 21, 57
Wade, Walter 21, 23–24, 28, 56, 118, 141, 172, 175
Wade Advertising Agency 18, 21, 63, 79, 175
Walt Disney Studios 103, 126–29, *130*
War Bonds 148, 187, 194–95
war loan rallies 188, 190–91, *192*, 193–95, 212; anti-Semitism 210
Weixler, Richard *201*
West, Mae 114
West Coast trip (1941) 112–13, 116–17, 120, *121*; anxiety about 115, 116, 118–19; promotion and publicity 130–33, 134, 136–37; Sanity Test 138–39, 146; visit to movie studios 138; *see also* anxiety of *Quiz Kids* production staff; City of Los Angeles (train); exploitation; Fields, W.C.; Marx, Chico; Marx Brothers
Whitman Publishing *68–69*
Wilhelm, Sally Ann 244
Williams, Richard 50–51, 53, 59, 80, 81–*82*, *85–87*, 90, 107, 116, *121*, 124, 126 127, *130*, 132, 136, 140, *149*, 150, 151, 153, 155, 166, *192*, *204*, 210, 218; *see also* Horn and Hardart Automats
Wilson, Don 119, 120, 158
Withers, Jane *130*–31
Wizard of Oz 15
WLS 7, 31
World War II 1, 2, 14, 87, 108, 114, 160, 162, 183, 208; "home front" 2, 168, 183–84, 200, 210–11; juvenile delinquency 2, 235–36; Lend Lease 2, 147; military conscription and volunteering 2, 184–87; mood 10, 158–59, 184, 213; travel difficulties 200–2, 209; *see also* atom bomb; societal changes

Zenith radio 62, 63, 184

www.ingramcontent.com/pod-product-compliance
Ingram Content Group UK Ltd.
Pitfield, Milton Keynes, MK11 3LW, UK
UKHW041924140426
5217IPUK00014B/311